THE SCIENCE OF SOCIAL REDEMPTION

McGill, the Chicago School, and the Origins of Social Research in Canada

In the 1920s, Canada's first department of sociology was established at McGill University; ten years later the department was engaged in a bitter philosophical struggle with its parent institution. Sociology's direction, increasingly political in the face of Depression-era social problems, was fundamentally at odds with the conservative principles of the business leaders who governed McGill. This conflict lies at the heart of Marlene Shore's remarkable work of intellectual history, a work that at once explores the issue of academic freedom, traces the growth of a discipline and the influences that shaped it, and evokes the texture of academic life in the early twentieth century.

Shore follows the development of sociology from a Christian doctrine of social concern to a discipline that venerated science and implicitly criticized active reform. She locates in Canadian intellectual traditions, particularly that of the Baptists, the basis for the strong links that were forged between McGill and the influential Chicago school of sociology under Robert Park. Her reading of the contributions of Canadians to the theories developed in that environment – especially Roderick McKenzie's work on the theory of human ecology and the metropolis-hinterland thesis of Carl Dawson – thus directly challenges the view that the discipline as it was practised at McGill was an 'import,' or marginal to Canadian intellectual life. In particular she demonstrates the political and intellectual importance and influence of the work done at McGill under Dawson's aegis – by such figures as S.D. Clark, Everett Hughes, and Leonard Marsh – and the debt owed by Canadian historical writing to the same traditions.

From this many-layered analysis comes a clear sense not only of an emerging discipline at McGill but also of its place in the development of social science in North America more generally. The story of sociology at McGill also reveals the shaky foundations of academic freedom and the key role played by academic politics in the interwar years. Most important, it rescues for contemporary readers and scholars the thought and work of many individuals whose shaping influence on Canadian intellectual life has been overlooked or forgotten.

MARLENE SHORE teaches history at Wilfrid Laurier University.

MARLENE SHORE

THE SCIENCE OF
SOCIAL REDEMPTION
McGill, the Chicago School, and the Origins of Social Research in Canada

UNIVERSITY OF TORONTO PRESS

Toronto Buffalo London

© University of Toronto Press 1987
Toronto Buffalo London
Printed in Canada
ISBN 0-8020-5733-0 (cloth)
ISBN 0-8020-6645-3 (paper)

Printed on acid-free paper

Canadian Cataloguing in Publication Data

Shore, Marlene Gay, 1953–
    The science of social redemption

    Includes bibliographical references.
    ISBN 0-8020-5733-0 (bound) ISBN 0-8020-6645-3 (pbk.)

    1. Sociology – Canada – History. 2. Canada –
    Intellectual life – History. 3. McGill University –
    History. 4. Chicago school of sociology – History.
    I. Title.

    HM22.C3S48 1987   301′.0971   C87-093462-7

COVER DESIGN BY AL FOTI

This book has been published with the help of a grant from the Social Science
Federation of Canada, using funds provided by the Social Sciences and
Humanities Research Council of Canada, and a grant from the Andrew W.
Mellon Foundation to University of Toronto Press.

For my parents

Contents

Acknowledgments

Throughout the research, writing, and production of this study I received generous assistance from many people. Archivists at the University of Toronto and McGill University – Noël Dupuis and Rob Michel, in particular – facilitated the task of sifting through administrative papers. Relatives in Montreal made my long research trips to that city pleasant; the research itself was made possible by scholarships from the Canada Council, the Social Sciences and Humanities Research Council of Canada, and the government of Ontario.

I owe incalculable debts to friends and colleagues with whom I discussed not only the substance of this work but the difficulties involved in writing it. In different ways they were all helpful, and to that extent Sela Cheifetz, Joel Shore, Helen Rodd, and Mitchell Shannon – all trained in disciplines vastly different from my own – directly contributed to the completion of this study. Mitch also endured, with stoic patience, my unpredictable moods. Dennis Magill, a member of the Sociology Department at the University of Toronto, kindly allowed me to use some of the material he collected for his own study on the history of Canadian sociology. Sharon Kingsland, a member of the Department of the History of Science at Johns Hopkins University, read the manuscript, offering both advice and the encouragement to publish it. I am also grateful in that regard to Professors John Beattie and William Berman of the History Department at the University of Toronto. At University of Toronto Press, Gerald Hallowell and Susan Kent provided sound editorial advice as well as support for the study. Although enormously busy with his own work, Al Foti took the time to design the cover for this book.

Ever since this study began as a doctoral dissertation I have been fortunate to have the backing of Arthur Silver and Carl Berger, members of the University of Toronto History Department. Arthur Silver took on the unpleasant task of building up my spirits every time I grew despondent over the progress of my work. Carl Berger contributed what was probably the most important factor to the end product: the certainty that a history of a social-science discipline was worth pursuing. I derived great encouragement from his enthusiastic reaction as the subject grew to be even more wide ranging than either of us initially had imagined.

A portion of chapter 3 has appeared as 'Carl Dawson and the Research Ideal: The Evolution of a Canadian Sociologist,' in the Canadian Historial Association *Annual Papers* (1985), pages 45 to 73.

Introduction

This study revolves around the development of sociology at McGill University during the interwar years. It is not, however, an educational or departmental history but an intellectual study that attempts a multi-tiered task. One of its objectives is to illustrate the manner in which an institution, by virtue of the measures it enforces as well as the strength of its traditions, shapes the character of a discipline. Another is to examine the evolution of that discipline in terms of its own intellectual roots and theoretical underpinnings, and from that vantage point to assess the way it interpreted and was modified by the social conditions it attempted to analyse. Very little work of this nature has been undertaken in Canadian historical writing, although in the United States the history of the behavioural sciences is a growing field, its importance manifested in the publication of such studies as *The Organization of Knowledge in Modern America, 1860–1920* (1979) by Johns Hopkins University Press. The emergence of sociology at McGill University and the successes and reverses it experienced cannot be understood in isolation from the major issues and problems that individuals faced within and outside the walls of academe in the early twentieth century. And in the attempt to explain the discipline's development within this broader context, the third and final aspect of this study grows. What better than an analysis of sociology – a discipline dealing with society and searching to find within it the forces that made for order and fragmentation – to present a social and intellectual history of a particular period?

In effect, history of the social sciences is intellectual history, and while each of the issues outlined above is important in itself, the overall objective here is to convey a sense of the texture of life in the early twentieth century, particularly the 1920s and 1930s. That being the case, the themes are not examined independently but are interwoven throughout the study to present one coherent story. What emerges is a picture of the interwar years that shows what happened to the social-gospel and social-reform movements of the late nineteenth century after the disillusioning experience of the First World War. In an era in which there was a tremendous faith in science, those reform impulses were channelled into institutional and scientific pursuits. This constituted part of a more general emphasis on economic productivity; a widespread conviction that such productivity would ensure national and international stability contributed to the belief that industrial efficiency would solve all social ills, and that notion, combined with fears of unrest stemming from the post-war economic depression, changed the shape of university education. Moreover, out of military necessity, the sciences had become extremely important during the war, and their continued strength in the years that followed forced a reassessment of the role of the arts in the university curriculum. Some academics felt that the traditional humanities had to become more attuned to 'common life'; others, agreeing, went a step further, couching their disciplines in scientific frameworks, adopting from the biological sciences theories that seemed most useful for analysing human society. They were impelled to do so for a number of reasons. Among them was a desire to eschew political and social activism; along with that went the necessity of competing with the sciences for research monies from the newly established philanthropic foundations; another more slowly developing aim was to prove to private and governmental agencies that social scientists could be called upon to provide advice in policy formulation. The eagerness of some social scientists to imitate the natural sciences in this manner, finally, also represented an acceptance and accommodation of Darwinian theories and a break with the traditions of British idealism.

On another plane, the particular research interests of McGill sociologists reveal much about the nature of Canadian society outside institutions of higher learning during this period. Their investigations of the city, specifically Montreal – its physical growth, industries, residential and occupational patterns, the extension of its economic influence through improvements in transportation – and of frontier settlement, immigration, race relations, and unemployment bespoke a society undergoing and attempting to adjust to rapid industrialization and urbanization. Sociology's quick fall into disrepute at McGill during the Depression years, moreover, the jealousy it aroused from professors of traditional disciplines, the impression it gave of being at the centre of intellectual ferment, and the battles over academic freedom in which its members became involved illustrate how undefined the university's role in society continued to be in the interwar years and how strong were the fears of social and political radicalism during the 1930s.

McGill took the lead among Canadian universities in offering courses in scientific sociology. An examination of why that was the case and how the discipline functioned in an atmosphere that was at first intellectually (though never financially) supportive and then turned hostile reveals much about the different intellectual traditions of Canadian universities and the institutional constraints that operated upon a variety of disciplines. Because of its status as a private institution supported by the anglophone economic elite of Montreal, McGill had been shaped by a strong utilitarian ethos since at least the 1850s and was noted nationally – and international-ly – for its scientific and medical achievements.

In the period during which this study opens, McGill already possessed an international reputation for its accomplishments in science and medicine; the work of Wilder Penfield in neurology and J.B. Collip in biochemistry added to its stature. The trend towards specialization that began in the late nineteenth century (largely attributable to progress in the sciences) and the lack of attention paid to their own disciplines gave many arts professors cause for complaint, but McGill's utilitarian philosophy acquired a new dimension in the aftermath of the First World War, one in which the arts also had a significant role to play. Like many North American universities McGill suffered financially and psychologically from the effects of the war – rooms and laboratories were turned over for military use, and enrolment declined as male students enlisted for war service. Nevertheless, a strong sense of service to the community emerged out of the war experience, and many educational spokespersons searched for ways to perpetuate that purposefulness in the post-war years. The argument that it was McGill's duty to make Canada a front-ranking industrial nation not only fulfilled that objective but helped to marshal the resources of all disciplines towards one specific end. It was partly out of a desire to create 'human efficiency,' for instance, that social work and then sociology grew at McGill. No less important a factor in the introduction of those courses were social and economic conditions in Montreal: the war had created severe economic problems in the city, resulting in widespread work stoppages in 1919, murmurings about Bolshevism, and fears of social upheaval. Those circumstances, in addition to charity expenditures that, to their minds, showed little in the way of immediate effectiveness, prompted the city's anglophone social-welfare leaders to push for the creation of a department of social service. They believed that it should serve as a training program for professional social workers as well as a co-ordinating centre for the city's social-welfare efforts. Partly at the request of the Joint Theological Board of the religious colleges affiliated with McGill (which were helping to fund the program), courses in sociology were offered in the school. When the director, John Howard Toynbee Falk, a man who before the war had worked with the major social-reform leaders of Canada, Britain, and the United States and afterwards became a staunch advocate of efficiency, resigned, the university hired a theoretical sociologist – Carl Dawson – who, in addition to directing the social-work program, was also responsible for teaching sociology courses in the Faculty of Arts.

On an institutional level the circumstances of Dawson's appointment reflected a general trend in the development of sociology in North America – its development as a separate subject out of theology and social work. But Dawson's background and education illuminate more about the intellectual evolution of sociology, and hence he provides an excellent focus for explaining how the discipline evolved from a Christian doctrine of social concern into a subject that venerated science and implicitly criticized active reform. Moreover, the factors that prompted him to choose a career in sociology illustrate that the specific branch of the discipline that he established at McGill – that of the Chicago school – had greater affinity with Canadian intellectual traditions than has been heretofore recognized. In that respect this study argues that it is incorrect to regard McGill sociology as an American import, by contrast with the sort of British sociology developed at Queen's and Toronto. The point made here is that it represented a different legacy – that of the Baptists of northern North America. Dawson was born and raised in the Maritimes, a region in which the Baptists had forged close ties with their American cousins; he received his BA from Acadia, a university recognized to be more American in character than any other Canadian institution of higher learning; he attended the University of Chicago's Divinity School, which by the time Dawson arrived in 1914 had already attracted many Canadians of the Baptist faith, some of whom went on to become influential faculty members. It was Dawson's encounter there – in a school that was in the vanguard of change in theological doctrine – with modernist ideas and with the influential social and psychological theories of John Dewey and other members of the Psychology Department, in addition to his wartime experience, that prompted him to leave the ministry for a career in social science. It was a rich and complex blend of ideas that nurtured this decision and one that is evident in his doctoral dissertation, 'The Social Nature of Knowledge,' done under Robert Park's supervision. Showing that all culture and knowledge, morals and ideals had social origins, Dawson concluded that even fact was not fixed truth but represented the decision of individuals to agree on certain points and issues. While never rejecting religion outright, he came to believe that it was simply the highest expression of group interests, that it should be analysed as such, and that research – a collection of facts that allowed one to see behind the values that particular societies hold dear at certain times – presented the best possibility for social improvement.

In his search for facts regarding human society, Dawson was guided by the theory that became the hallmark of Chicago sociology – human ecology. Dealing with the process of change in human communities, it derived from a scientific theory that gained popularity in the American midwest at the turn of the century, at a time when that region was being transformed by human settlement and Chicago was emerging as its dominant urban centre. An offshoot of biology concerned with plant and animal communities, scientific ecology dealt with the formation of individual organisms but also focused on the relation of each kind and individual to its environment, as well as on the ways in which plants and animals were distributed in their communities. It went beyond a simple description of those communities, however, to explain the processes that endowed them with their structures and promoted changes within them. Chicago sociologists found this branch of biology appealing because it provided suggestions for explaining – and describing – the flux and mobility that seemed to characterize human society in the interwar years and was evident in migratory movements and in the extension of transportation and communications networks. Furthermore, it stressed the complex relations prevailing between organisms and the environment, and this was very compatible with views of human nature put forward by the influential Chicago social psychologists. The sociologists relied upon a myriad of ecological studies, but the most influential work was Frederic Clements' *Plant Succession: An Analysis of the Growth of Vegetation*, published in 1916. His argument that plant formations were arranged in a succession of zones constituting stages of evolutionary growth, and that the higher life-forms succeeded the lower ones by pushing the existing population out of an area and forcing it to settle in a zone on the rim of its original habitat, was the concept they utilized to explain the growth of cities, regions, and their internal divisions.

Although it was Robert Park who first suggested that ecology should be the model that sociologists employed in their studies of human society, he was not the major formulator of the social theory. It is in the examination of the theory's major systematizers that this study once again shows the strong links that existed between Canadian social science and the University of Chicago. Dawson dabbled in ecological theory; his and Warner Gettys' textbook was the first major sociological work to use ecology for its basic framework. But the most important exponent of the theory was Roderick McKenzie. Born in a Manitoba prairie town, McKenzie was educated first at the University of Manitoba in Winnipeg, a city which on the eve of the First World War appeared to be emerging as the dominating metropolitan centre of the Canadian west. Once at Chicago he expanded upon human ecology to use it as a tool for explaining territorial organization, and the ideas he advanced in that regard about metropolitan dominance not only became an integral part of Chicago sociology but penetrated into Canadian historical writing. Although it was partly from Chicago sociology that Canadian historians derived their ideas about metropolitan dominance, the role played by McKenzie in laying the groundwork for those theories has not been well documented. The examinations here of his work, of Dawson's on population areas and physiographic regions in Canada, and of S.D. Clark's relatively unknown McGill master's thesis dealing with the ecological basis of Canadian nationalism, all illustrate that there are very strong parallels between Chicago-McGill sociology and the work of Harold Innis.

The adoption of the major tenets of Chicago social philosophy and ecology led Dawson to consider society to be an order that transcended its individual members and progressed in accordance with the principles of successional development. The significance of such ideas was that they emphasized the influence of the environment in shaping social structure, values, culture, mores, and institutions. In so doing, those who held and developed them rejected the idea that genetic predisposition or inherited traits could explain the character of nations and ethnic groups. Armed with these convictions, Dawson set out to investigate different parts of Canada and, within the framework of a theory that emphasized transition, strove to explain and describe the changes occurring in early twentieth-century Canada. Although he and his students first focused their attention on Montreal, the addition of another of Park's students – Everett Hughes – to the department in 1927 enabled them to expand their sphere of investigation. Because of his attraction to rural sociology, Dawson decided to examine regional development and the adaptation and adjustment of settlers in the Canadian west; because of his fascination with race relations and the effects of industrial change, Hughes chose French Canada. At the time that Hughes began teaching at McGill, much rhetoric had been expended on the changes taking place within French Canadian society, but no university had studied it in anything but a historical way.

The inception of the Canadian Frontiers of Settlement series enabled Dawson to apply his theories about metropolitanism – and regionalism, the other side of the coin – in a major study of the development of the Canadian west. He was not, however, the only social scientist for whom the project presented an opportunity to research a subject of long-held interest, and the present study deals with the broad range of interests that shaped the project. Conceived as part of a larger investigation of pioneer belts throughout the world, the project originated in the United States and reflected the preoccupations of American social scientists, particularly the interest they took during the 1920s in international migration and the battle they were waging with natural scientists over who had the right – and the expertise – to undertake migration research. Moreover, American social scientists recognized that the project would demonstrate to governments and policy-makers their usefulness as policy advisers. Canadian academics were quick to see the same advantage. They were aware of the circumstances that made the post-war years an opportune time to carry out such a study in western Canada: responsibility for control of natural resources, including ungranted lands, had passed from the federal government to the provinces of Manitoba, Alberta, and Saskatchewan. New settlement policies were anticipated, and it was expected that they would depart from the traditional policy of free land; with that, changes in the machinery directing and controlling immigration were inevitable. In short, recognizing that the prairie provinces would soon take a more direct interest in colonization and immigration, Canadian social scientists knew that there was no better time for them to offer their assistance. More pragmatically, involvement in the pioneer-belts project provided them with research funds that they had found difficult to obtain.

Financial support for the social sciences from private and public sources was practically non-existent in Canada during the interwar years. Aided by a grant from the Rockefeller Foundation to encourage the development of the social sciences in Canada, however, McGill sociology expanded during the 1930s. As part of an interdisciplinary Social Science Research Project dealing with unemployment and immigration in Montreal and other parts of Canada, its graduate students examined the problems Canada was experiencing as it became more urbanized and attempted to absorb a large and diverse population into its economic mainstream. In this and in a number of other ways the Social Science Research Project is an important story in the early years of Canadian social science. It illustrates that there was a small network of Canadian academics who had successfully cultivated ties with influential foundation representatives in order to win money for their disciplines; on another level it represents an attempt to reintegrate knowledge (after the decline of moral philosophy) by focusing on single issues from different perspectives. Finally, it reveals the precarious position the social sciences held at McGill. At first willingly endorsed by McGill's industrialist-laden Board of Governors, the Social Science Research Project came under the direction of Leonard Marsh, a young graduate of the London School of Economics, whose Fabian socialism and membership in the League for Social Reconstruction irritated the businessmen and was one of the factors in the project's demise. Although the Social Science Research Project became the object of the administration's attacks upon political radicalism in the 1930s, it nevertheless left an indelible mark upon Canadian life. Marsh's *Report on Social Security*, which was published in 1943 and became the basis of the Canadian social-welfare system, derived in large measure from the ten years of work he had done at McGill in connection with the Social Science Research Project.

This study, while focusing upon a specific time-span and subject, covers a broad range of ideas in institutional, social, and intellectual history. It delves into the atmosphere of the interwar years, the politics of academe, the development of ideas, and the impact of academic study; it demonstrates the broad links that existed between McGill sociology and the development of social science in North America more generally; it reveals the weak foundation of academic freedom and the great importance of academic politics in Canada during the interwar years. Finally, by examining a discipline that has been variously described as an import or marginal, it rescues from oblivion many individuals and traditions that have shaped Canadian intellectual life but have been forgotten or overlooked.

THE SCIENCE OF SOCIAL REDEMPTION

1

McGill University and the Tradition of Utility

The early history of McGill University – or McGill College, as it was known until 1885 – was closely connected with the development of Montreal as the commercial capital of Canada. McGill only began to flourish in the 1850s, when the anglophone merchant class of that city assumed its domination over the economic life of Quebec; during the first half of the nineteenth century it stagnated under the weight of problems that had their origins in the larger social conflicts then affecting the province. Because of the tensions between the English and French, the college did not open its doors until thirty years after provision was made for its construction. Even when that crisis was settled, rivalries between different anglophone groups created problems in its administration. It was only with the arrival of John William Dawson that the college began to progress. Dawson, a native of Pictou County, Nova Scotia, was selected as principal by the new members of the Royal Institution for the Advancement of Learning – McGill's governing body – because his educational philosophy seemed to accord with their own. As merchants and professionals they believed that the college should offer not a classical curriculum but courses in moral philosophy, political economy, agricultural chemistry, and law – subjects suited to the needs of a young, developing colony.[1]

I

J.W. Dawson's tenure as principal of McGill spanned five decades, during which time the university was transformed by economic and social change. When Dawson arrived in Montreal in 1855, McGill offered virtually no courses in science; by the time he retired in 1893, it offered courses in all scientific fields, including physics and chemistry. It had acquired an international reputation by serving as host to both the American and British Associations for the Advancement of Science and could boast of one of the finest faculties of medicine in North America, thanks to the work of Sir William Osler.[2] When Dawson reviewed the first twenty years of his principalship, he looked back with satisfaction at the progress the university had made up to that point, and particularly at his decision to preserve only a few of the classical subjects that had been taught prior to his arrival. While he did not deny that the classical curriculum was valuable, he did not think it was an appropriate form of education for a college situated in a young colony to offer. Canada was not Britain, he argued, and lacked the educated gentry who could have supported such an institution; if McGill had continued in the path laid out by his predecessor, John Bethune, he was certain that it would have acquired a reputation for being an impractical institution and never would have grown. Nevertheless, when Dawson retired in 1893, he lamented the fact that the Faculty of Arts had suffered during his principalship. J.G. Bourinot's presidential address to the Royal Society of Canada that year could only have been a painful reminder to him of the problem. In a review of Canadian arts and letters Bourinot attributed the lack of high culture in Canada to the emphasis upon material success that pervaded Canadian society.[3] He contended that Canada had contributed nothing to the spiritual elevation of mankind because its universities were too utilitarian and its intellectuals pursued political or scientific careers rather than literary endeavours. Although he did not object to scientific writing that was broad and liberated the mind from specialization, or to the pursuit of wealth when it served as a foundation for better things, he was critical of the fact that Canadians had not seen fit to support cultural or philanthropic ventures.[4]

In its emphasis upon science and professional training McGill in the second half of the nineteenth century followed a path of deveolopment not unlike that of many American institutions of higher learning. As Laurence Veysey has shown, the availability of surplus capital in the years after the Civil War was critical in determining the character of American higher education in that period.[5] Whereas earlier reforms of the classical curriculum had all failed because of an insufficiency of funds, in the second half of the nineteenth century the universities were pushed even further in the direction of utilitarianism by their dependency upon the upper middle class. Since university spokesmen identified higher education with material success in order to attract the support of the wealthy, they were compelled to implement the courses that gave substance to their claims. As the philanthropy of the Cornells, Hopkinses, and Rockefellers shaped the character of the American university, so the benefactions of the Molsons, Redpaths, and Strathconas nurtured McGill's growth. McGill's Board of Governors turned to the wealthy anglophone community of Montreal for assistance after failing to obtain any kind of permanent endowment for the university from a variety of different governments. From very early on, however, McGill's benefactors established a tradition of giving money for new ventures and to the scientific disciplines, leaving the university without adequate funds for everyday operations.[6] In order to circumvent that problem the university's officials tried to obtain assistance from the residents of other provinces by claiming that McGill was a national university and that its freedom from governmental interference made it an excellent place for graduate studies.[7]

However much McGill's survival depended upon the support of Montreal's merchants and professionals, Dawson's decision to build up the sciences stemmed from an additional concern. Like many educators of the period, he was confronted with the problem of having to respond to the public's interest in science and technology and at the same time ensure that the inherited social and religious traditions of British North America were not undermined by progress in those areas. Dawson and his contemporaries were not afraid of science in itself. In fact, Dawson saw it as 'liberalizing truth,' in contrast to the doctrine of ultramontanism, then popular among members of the French Canadian clerical hierarchy. What concerned them was the effect that excessive experimentation and speculation would have upon the religious beliefs of their students. By making natural theology and moral philosophy a major part of the curriculum, they taught their students to accommodate new scientific discoveries to religious principles and to relate the life of the mind to business and commerce. They found support for their objectives in Scottish Common Sense philosophy and in Baconian science, both of which were suspicious of scholasticism and did not require denying the existence of God: the major philosophers of the Scottish Common Sense school, Thomas Reid and William Hamilton, had rejected the philosophical scepticism of David Hume and argued that man had the capacity to arrive at moral truth through the principles of common sense;[8] Bacon had argued that man could come to know reality by observing nature empirically, and his popularizers – educators, journalists, and clergymen – turned his theorties into a philosophy that suggested that knowledge was founded upon experience and entailed nothing more than a classification of facts and phenomena.[9]

In addition to inculcating young British North Americans with religious and moral principles, moral philosophy and natural theology were integrative disciplines. Their dominance in the curriculum was intended to serve as a safeguard against specialization, which many educators feared was encouraged by the emphasis upon science and professional training. Although that tendency was held in check for a while, once moral philosophy and natural theology lost the force of their influence, there was no stopping the advance of specialization and vocational training in higher education. The process occurred more rapidly and at an earlier date in the United States than in Canada – there, the popularization of Darwin gave utilitarianism its greatest impetus. Influenced by Darwin's major publicists, Herbert Spencer and Thomas Huxley, who argued that the most important kinds of human activity were those that catered to self-preservation, the care of offspring, and good citizenship, a number of American academics contended that institutions of higher learning had an obligation to prepare students for life. The disciplines they considered to be the most suitable for that task were the natural and social sciences because they taught people how to manufacture, survive, and guard against disease.[10] There was one small group, nevertheless, the proponents of cosmopolitan culture, who carried on the traditions of moral philosophy in their admiration for mental discipline and in their distaste for practicality and minute investigation.[11] In Canada moral philosophy remained intact until the end of the nineteenth century, but it continued to affect the character of Canadian higher education for several decades thereafter. One of its most distinctive influences was the fact that the elective system never became as popular in Canada as in the United States.[12]

When Dawson left McGill, the sciences continued to progress, stimulated by the impetus that he had given them but lacking the more humanistic edge they possessed when moral philosophy and natural theology had constituted a major part of the curriculum. The Board of Governors heeded Dawson's words about the weakness of the Faculty of Arts and chose as his successor someone who they thought would be able to build up the arts without hindering the progress that had been made in the sciences. But under the principalship of Sir William Peterson, a classicist educated at Edinburgh, Oxford, and Göttingen, the arts continued to languish while advances in scientific training and research proceeded at a faster rate than ever. The most notable achievement of Peterson's administration was the research in physics undertaken by Ernest Rutherford and Frederick Soddy which led to a new theory of atomic structure.[13] The First World War and the creation of the National Research Council of Canada in 1916 served as further catalysts to the development of science, and during the principalship of Sir Arthur Currie, McGill continued to expand its scientific research and engineering programs. In that period its international reputation was also enhanced by the presence of such people as Wilder Penfield, who helped to establish the Montreal Neurological Institute, and J.B Collip, whose work in biochemistry attracted widespread attention.[14]

Although the scientific and medical faculties stole the limelight, McGill's humanities departments did not entirely stagnate during the 1920s. Enrolment in the Faculty of Arts climbed as returning veterans and an unprecedented number of women attended the university. With overcrowded classrooms, there was a need for additional teaching staff, and many professors began to complain about the neglect that their disciplines were suffering at the hands of the university's administrators. Though the Arts building had to accommodate nearly a thousand students more than when it first opened, the Board of Governors consistently refused to renovate it, claiming that the university lacked the funds for the expansion. They managed to find the resources to add a new wing to the Engineering building, however, but did nothing to improve the facilities of the Faculty of Arts until it was finally condemned as a hazard.[15] When he became dean of Arts in 1924, Ira Mackay, formerly a professor of constitutional law, pleaded with the Board of Governors to take more interest in the welfare of the non-scientific disciplines. He argued that by funding the sciences more generously than the other departments, they had not only created a hierarchy within the university but demonstrated an inability to run the university as anything other than a profit-bearing institution. He informed them that the university's endowment was not meant to be spent in such a way as to produce more dollars and commodities but to nurture 'an ultimate human entity called education, upon which no money value can possibly be placed.' Ironically, perhaps sensing the futility of his philosophical arguments, he finally appealed to them with a very practical argument: 'I know that the scientific departments usually claim larger appropriations than the pure arts departments on the grounds that they are carrying on research work. Nevertheless, there is the clear gloss to be put on this claim, and that is that the great claims of post-graduate research are by no means limited to scientific subjects. If a student of physiology may discover Insulin and save many lives, so may a student of Political Science or History become a Chatham or a Peel and save an empire or prevent a world-war.'[16]

II

Attacks upon the practical concerns of university administrators were not the monopoly of McGill professors. The reaction to utilitarianism became particularly acute in the aftermath of the First World War, when many academics regarded the lack of intellectual substance in higher education as a manifestation of the moral bankruptcy that had led Western society to war. Some pointed to the declining interest in the classics as a symptom of the malaise; others were disturbed about the high enrolment of men in the professional faculties at a time when women were beginning to dominate the traditional humanities courses. But whatever their particular griev-ance, most academics concurred that the universities were being strangled by the trend towards specialization and vocational training that had begun in the late nineteenth century. Proclamations such as Stephen Leacock's, that knowledge had become nothing more than a collection of scattered interests as a result of that phenomenon, were not unusual.[17] Arthur Eustace Morgan, the ill-fated principal of McGill, conveyed a similar sentiment when he remarked at his installation in 1935, 'Students are set to dig a narrow furrow, often also they dig so assiduously and so deeply that they lose sight of the man working similarly in the next furrow.'[18]

Intellectual histories of higher education have suggested that the interwar years constituted a difficult period in the development of most North American universities because the major educational philosophies of the nineteenth century had lost the force of their influence by that time and nothing had been found to replace them. In *The Emergence of the American University* Laurence Veysey has shown that no coherent philosophy infused American higher education after 1910. Despite the fact that academics pledged their allegiance to one of the three educational ideas – vocationalism, research, and culture – that had nurtured the university in the decades after the Civil War, the outlines of those philosophies had all been blurred, and no one really understood their significance.[19] In *A Disciplined Intelligence* A.B. McKillop has concluded that the uncertainty within Canadian society over whether the university should act as the guardian of traditional values or as an agent for social improvement made the first quarter of the twentieth century an unhappy time to be in Canadian academic life.[20] Although many academics advocated the reintegration of knowledge as the solution for the intellectual crisis of their time, there was little consensus among them on how that synthesis should be created; their views on that issue were shaped by different concerns and were dedicated to a variety of objectives.

Academics trained in the moral-philosophy tradition saw in the reinte-gration of knowledge a way to restore intellectual coherence and moral substance to higher education. They admired the way in which the nineteenth-century curriculum, dominated by moral philosophy and natural theology, had introduced the student to a wide range of subjects while providing him with a set of moral values. Apart from criticizing the elective system and demanding that three or four years in the arts be established as a prerequisite for entrance into the professional faculties, however, they had little else to suggest. Though trained in the moral-philosophy tradition himself, Ira Mackay, for instance, recognized that the economic and social changes of the early twentieth century had irrevocably altered the nature of higher education. The old colleges simply trained enough doctors, lawyers, and ministers to serve small, autonomous communities, he once explained. But science, commerce, and technology had destroyed the independence of those communities and in so doing had compelled the universities to respond to national and international demands. He was not surprised that they had found it difficult to maintain an intellectually coherent curriculum while training students for numerous professions, promoting scientific research, and preserving the traditional humanities.[21]

There was at least one educational spokesman who believed it was possible to recapture the intellectual ethos of the nineteenth-century college, despite the fact that its curriculum was too limited for the needs of the twentieth century. Alexander Meiklejohn, who was extremely influential in shaping American liberal education during the 1920s in his capacity as president of Amherst College, argued that the old colleges had provided students with an education that was appropriate for any profession they entered by training them to live in society. He contended that modern universities could accomplish the same ends by teaching their students about man's moral experience, common speech, social relations, political institutions, and the world of nature that surrounded them; he believed that such a course of study would also encourage them to think about knowledge as an integrated whole.[22]

Like many academics of his generation, Meiklejohn understood the way in which scientific discoveries had destroyed moral philosophy and natural history's ability to integrate all knowledge: the facts uncovered by scientific investigations not only shattered old beliefs and values but could not be assimilated within the traditional disciplines with their rigid boundary lines. Unlike his contemporaries, however, Meiklejohn did not consider this to be an irreparable problem. After all, he argued, men such as Leibnitz, Spinoza, Kant, and Hegel had succeeded in re-establishing the unity of knowledge after the findings of astronomers, physicists, and chemists called into question the ideas their generations held sacred. It was the duty of twentieth-century scholars, he insisted, and more particularly of the liberal colleges, to think through the significance of recent scientific discoveries and create a new synthesis of knowledge rather than to add undigested facts to a catalogue of information. [23]

In their concern with social relations and political institutions, the social sciences came close to fitting Meiklejohn's recommendations for liberal education. Having lost the common starting-points and interests they possessed when they were subsumed under moral philosophy, however, they were also beset by the problem of intellectual fragmentation. [24] One Philosophy professor at Smith College was upset that social scientists showed no awareness of the relationship between their disciplines and moral philosophy, and tried to explain the influence that the older subject had had upon the newer studies of society. Though its ultimate purpose had been to suggest improved ethical relations among men, Gladys Bryson argued, moral philosophy offered a comprehensive treatment of human relations and institutions through discussions of human nature, social forces, marriage and family relationships, and the history of institutions. When all those abstractions evolved into separate disciplines, they became more elaborate and less conscious of their relationship to each other than had once been the case; they nevertheless continued to reflect the influence of moral philosophy in their tendency to generalize about human nature. Bryson wondered whether social scientists recognized the irony in that, especially when they took such pains to make their studies 'scientific.' [25]

The emergence of numerous interdisciplinary projects for the scientific study of society was another manifestation of the impulse towards the integration of knowledge during the interwar years. According to the promotional literature on the subject, these projects were rooted in the desire of social scientists to restore intellectual unity to their disciplines after the years of specialization. Cetainly Stephen Leacock supported McGill's Social Science Research Project in the early years of its existence for that reason; unlike other Canadian universities, [26] McGill had followed the American example of compartmentalizing the social sciences, and the interdisciplinary project allowed them to be reintegrated, at least on a small scale. But most of the participants in that and similar projects were not interested in re-establishing the links that existed between their disciplines when they were part of moral philosophy. Some simply hoped that they might find solutions for social problems by working together with scholars trained in different fields; others were motivated by more pragmatic concerns. The founders of the earliest American projects expected the universities to suffer financially in the 1920s as the result of a post-war depression. Fearful of the effect that would have on their research efforts, they tried to make their work more palatable to outside agencies from which they might hope for support. They knew that the major American philanthropic foundations, recently organized along bureaucratic lines and dedicated to encouraging intellectual co-operation themselves, would finance large-scale studies of society that purported to be scientific.[27] McGill's principal and Board of Governors turned to those agencies for slightly different but equally practical reasons. Learning that the Rockefeller Foundation had earmarked grants for human-relations research, they submitted a proposal to organize a graduate program in that area. They were motivated less by their social concerns than by the fact that it was difficult for them to find any other resources to support the social sciences. They recognized that a grant from the foundation would enable them to offer graduate courses in the social sciences that would attract students from all across the country and serve as a counterpoise to the newly established social-studies program at the University of Montreal.

University administrators had as many reasons for advocating the reintegration of knowledge as did academics. They understood that its widespread appeal and imprecise meaning made it a handy device to invoke in order to win faculty support for their policies. Throughout the interwar years each of McGill's principals promised to work towards that goal, but the character of their pledges changed as the state of international affairs worsened. In the mid-1930s, A.E Morgan presented what was a more philosophical argument. He believed that the world was searching for a purpose in which it was the duty of the university to assist. He was afraid, however, that because institutions of higher learning had concentrated so much upon professional training, they were incapable of producing men and women endowed with the capacity to undertake that task. He contended that in order to allow their students to see the world in fuller perspective, the universities would have to provide the right conditions for the development of personality and flexibility. (Morgan's liberality in that regard contributed to the difficulties he experienced as principal of McGill.) F. Cyril James's appeals were more immediate and utilitarian, but when he was installed as principal on 12 January 1940, the Second World War had already begun.

Most principals use their inaugural addresses to impart their views on the purpose of higher education, but James argued at his installation that his remarks were more than oratorical. The great democratic nations, he proclaimed, were afflicted by political and social controversies arising from the fact that mankind had not adapted to the changes engendered by the Great War before another world war began. If under these circumstances the universities continued to confine themselves to studies that were far removed from social problems, they would cease to be a vital social force; mankind would have no recourse but to turn to the superficial solutions of demagogues, and Western society would collapse. 'Neither love of the humanities nor a deep interest in scientific research can make a man entirely happy in Shangri-la,' he argued, 'if civilization is disintegrating outside the walls of his refuge.' James accordingly announced that, unlike his predecessors, he would be instituting no new courses of study during his administration. Thanks to the work of former principals, he insisted, McGill already offered instruction in all major areas; it now had a duty to co-ordinate and integrate knowledge in such a way as to produce solutions for society's problems. 'Whether we like it or no,' he contended, 'we are faced with the task of adapting human society to the new environment that has been created by two centuries of progress and mechanical invention. That problem must be the central focus of research and education.'[28]

The turbulent events of the 1930s may have created the urgency in James's proposals, but there was nothing particularly original about any of them. From the earliest years of college education in North America, university spokesmen had argued that institutions of higher learning had an obligation to provide moral leadership to society; their ideas about what that entailed might have changed over the years, but the underlying philosophy had not. By the 1920s and 30s, moreover, many individual disciplines had a social orientation – the fields of health and social work were only the most obvious examples; the Social Science Research Project was devoted to the study of unemployment and immigrant adjustment in Montreal and other parts of Canada, as well as to intellectual co-operation. The originality of James's proposal lay in the scale of integration that it envisaged. While James conceded that the social sciences had made an important contribution to intellectual co-operation in the 1920s and 1930s through the agency of their interdisciplinary projects, he also suggested that they had not done enough. 'When the problem of society is conceived in its widest sense,' he contended, 'it is apparent that every field of knowledge must be called upon to make important contributions to the ultimate solution.' James recognized that his proposal would meet with considerable resistance from the faculty because of its single-minded, utilitarian nature. He therefore tried to assure his audience that academics would still be free to pursue their own research interests, 'as scholarship demanded.' Nevertheless, he insisted that the university was compelled to synthesize their independent findings and criticized anyone who objected for holding antiquated ideas about the purpose of higher education: 'Much of the present controversy regarding the functions of a university arises out of the fact that the Victorians were not curious enough. Those who insist that knowledge is significant for its own sake, and those who endeavour to organize instruction along the lines of professional training, both stem from the educational disputes of the nineteenth century. Huxley could find words of praise for the traditions of scholasticism as well as for scientific investigation but neither he nor his contempories [sic] made any attempt to determine the relationship between the two.'[29]

James believed that the structure of higher education had to be reformed to accord with the ideological convictions of the twentieth century. He made no apologies for the fact that a more closely co-ordinated curriculum might deprive faculty members of a certain amount of control over the development of their disciplines; he seemed to suggest that this was only in keeping with the dominant political attitudes of the age. The nineteenth-century curriculum, he explained, was designed by a generation who believed that the resources of the world were plentiful enough to allow each man to determine the course of his own life in education, business, or politics. But in recent years mankind had rejected laissez-faire as a political philosophy because of its inherent dangers. In medicine, James contended, a policy that allowed everyone to do as he pleased only threatened a population confronted with an epidemic; in business it encouraged the unwise exploitation of resources and 'extortion' by unfettered monopolies.[30]

If certain McGill faculty members were suspicious of the motives behind such arguments, they had good reason. James was not the first of the university's principals to advocate the integration of knowledge from a political perspective. In 1939 his predecessor, Lewis Williams Douglas, invited a number of eminent scholars to speak at McGill on the topic of 'The State in Society.' The purpose of the symposium, as Douglas explained, was to encourage intellectual co-operation in the social sciences. 'Isolationism in the curriculum,' he argued, had been as destructive to scholarship and teaching in those disciplines as economic nationalism had been to the state of international diplomacy.[31] Since the social sciences constituted one of the few areas where academics were not working in isolation at McGill, it was odd that they should have been the targets of such criticism. But in the nine years of its existence, the Social Science Research Project had evolved into something quite different from what the university's officials had envisaged, and it was partly his desire to counteract its influence that prompted Douglas to organize the special lecture series.

McGill's Social Science Research Project was conceived early in 1930, before the full effects of the Great Depression had manifested themselves in Montreal and other parts of Canada. Those involved in the initial planning thought the project should deal with the relationship among industry, community, and employment. In that way, they believed, the university would gain access to the facilities of Montreal's major industries, and the students involved in the project would learn how important those enterprises had been to the city's development. A number of industrialists on the Board of Governors were enthusiastic enough about that goal to agree to serve on the project's executive committee. Within a short period of time, however, they had reason to wash their hands of the entire scheme: Sir Arthur Currie, principal of McGill from 1920 to 1933, had appointed Leonard Marsh, a young graduate of the London School of Economics, as the project's director. Although Marsh was well qualified for the task because of his experience as assistant secretary on Sir William Beveridge's study of London life and labour, his political convictions and organizational techniques irritated the businessmen. They decided to resign from the project shortly after its inception, not so much because of Marsh's Fabian beliefs but because they had no patience for the long meetings and 'memo-harangues.' When they withdrew, the remaining members of the executive committee, Carl Dawson and Everett Hughes of the Department of Sociology, C. Kellogg of Psychology, and at one point Frank Scott of the Faculty of Law, selected students and topics as they pleased.

The Social Science Research Project continued to develop autonomously until the late 1930s, when the university's officials wondered why they had ever allowed it to have so much freedom:[32] it had churned out a number of studies that were not particularly complimentary to either government or industry; further, the criticism of Canadian immigration policy in Lloyd Reynold's book *The British Immigrant* (1935) annoyed the chancellor of the university, Sir Edward Beatty, who also happened to be president of the Canadian Pacific Railway. Although the Board of Governors attributed the critical nature of the project to the influence of the 'collectivists' on the executive committee, the truth of the matter was that the studies could not help but cast business and government in an unfavourable light: they dealt with employment, unemployment, and immigrant adjustment and were researched and written in the midst of an economic depression. The university's officials nevertheless feared that McGill was turning into a centre for socialist propaganda and in 1937 began to formulate a number of policies to combat the problem. The first was to hire a new principal; for two years they had watched the university's relationship with the business community of Montreal strained to the breaking-point because A.E.

Morgan was unable to communicate with the city's industrialists and refused to muzzle the more politically outspoken members of staff.[33] Sir Edward Beatty took it upon himself to find a more suitable candidate for the office, and decided that L.W. Douglas was eminently qualified for the job.

An American citizen whose grandfather had been a major McGill benefactor, Lewis Williams Douglas had served as director of the budget in Franklin Delano Roosevelt's New Deal administration between 1933 and 1934. He was also a trustee of the Rockefeller Foundation and a graduate of Amherst College. At Amherst, he once claimed, the ideas of Alexander Meiklejohn made an impression upon him 'which no vicissitudes of life could erase.' Certainly the influence was evident in Douglas's installation address, in which he pledged to work for the integration of knowledge.[34] In more recent reminiscences of his days at McGill he has also expressed his disappointment at not having been able to accomplish that goal while he was principal and attributed his failure to the attitudes of the faculty members. 'The accepted method of putting each category of learning into its cubbyhole was so deeply rooted in custom,' he remarked, 'that like Bagehot's "Cake of Custom," it was hard to crack.'[35] He neglected to mention, however, that he was partly reponsible for implementing the policies that deprived the social sciences of their 'unified sense of purpose,'[36] but given his own ideas regarding the integration of knowledge and his attitude towards collectivist theories, the oversight is understandable. In 1935 Douglas delivered a series of lectures at Harvard University on 'The Liberal Tradition.' In those addresses he condemned bureaucracy and government involvement in economic planning as 'tyranny of the state in disguise';[37] the men he invited to speak at McGill in 1939 – Robert Warren (professor of Economics at the Institute for Advanced Study at Princeton University), Leo Wolman (professor of Economics at Columbia University), and Henry Clay (economic adviser to the Bank of England, and formerly professor of Social Economics at the University of Manchester) – shared his views on liberalism, nationalism, and the limits of parliamentary government. There was a close connection between Douglas's political convictions and educational philosophy, one that was clearly revealed in the foreword he wrote for the published edition of the McGill lecture series. There he held up the work of Adam Smith as the best model for the integration of knowledge, arguing that Smith had been unjustly attacked as an apostle of laissez-faire when in reality he was a moral philosopher who had produced a comprehensive and integrated view of the social problems of his time by 'weaving strands of observable fact and interpretations of economic and social phenomena into a stout fabric' that had dominated

Western society until the 1930s.[38] In order to ensure the continuation of that tradition at McGill, Douglas not only invited a number of orthodox economic theorists to speak at the university; he also helped Beatty to strengthen the powers of the principal and Board of Governors in order to combat the intellectual ferment, centred in the social-science departments, that threatened to undermine it. At the beginning of the Second World War he decided to return to the United States, but not before entrusting F. Cyril James with the task of seeing that those policies were carried out.[39] To a large degree the proposals that James presented for the integration of knowledge on the day of his installation were extensions of Douglas's strategy.

III

By pleading for intellectual co-operation and strengthening their own powers, McGill's administrators hoped to quell the social unrest that plagued their university in the late 1930s. While their policies were formulated in response to the Depression, they also represented the culmination of a trend that had been developing over a much longer period of time. The increasing domination of institutions of higher learning by business executives and bureaucrats, men who brought new managerial techniques to the administration of the university, fundamentally altered the nature of academic life in the early twentieth century. F. Cyril James was one of this new breed of administrator; so, too, was L.W. Douglas, despite his denunciation of government bureaucracy. Both wanted to rationalize the university's curriculum and administrative structure, and their demands for the integration of knowledge were partly intended to achieve those objectives. Many faculty members recognized that and opposed their policies on those grounds. The conflicts that plagued McGill in the 1930s, then, revolved as much around administrative issues as they did ideological ones.

In the United States, rank and file professors began to be denied a voice in determining major institutional policy at the end of the nineteenth century. At that time business executives poured into university governing boards, and administrative positions, such as deanships and departmental chairmanships, multiplied. Within a decade there were dire predictions about the effects that such a division of power would have upon academia. Perhaps the most famous was Thorstein Veblen's. In *The Higher Learning in America* (1918) he warned that business trustees would ultimately destroy the university's most important purpose – the development of culture – because of their obsession with efficiency and their tendency to treat the academic staff as though they were employees.[40]

The governing boards of most Canadian universities did not consist of great numbers of businessmen until after the First World War, the period in which techniques of bureaucratic management also became popular in Canada. McGill, however, was an exception. It had a long history of drawing its Board of Governors from Montreal's business community, and the members of that body had always exerted a powerful influence over the university's development. In the 1920s, however, some McGill faculty members were displeased with the way in which such men as W.M. Birks (president of Henry Birks and Sons, and director of Sun Life Assurance), Sir Herbert Holt (president of the Royal Bank and Montreal Light, Heat, and Power Consolidated), J.W. Ross (director of Sun Life Assurance), Sir Charles B. Gordon (director of the Bank of Montreal), J.W. McConnell (president and managing director of the St Lawrence Sugar Refineries, director of the Bank of Montreal, and of Montreal Light, Heat, and Power), as well as Sir Edward Beatty (president of the CPR, and director of the Bank of Montreal)[41] managed the university's affairs. Echoing Veblen's sentiments, Ira Mackay contended that their policy of treating professors like employees and forcing them to compete for funds was detrimental to the well-being of the university. Stephen Leacock complained that such men were turning the university into a utilitarian institution by catering to practical needs.[42]

The pre-eminent role that the Board of Governors played in McGill's development was reflected in the university's administrative structure. As was the case with most North American institutions of higher learning, McGill's principal was responsible to the Board of Governors;[43] beginning in 1852, all holders of that office were appointed by the board and, with the exception of a short period in the 1930s, were ex officio members of that body. The Board of Governors also wielded enormous power within the Corporation, which, until 1935, was the highest academic authority at McGill. (Apart from the governors, the Corporation consisted only of the principal and Fellows of the university, and the latter were appointed from outside the institution by the Board of Governors.) By the 1930s the Corporation had grown to be so large and unwieldy, however, that its control over academic matters was only theoretical, and changes in the university's governing structure were imminent. After the death of Sir Arthur Currie in 1933, there was a two-year vacancy in the office of the principal, and a committee under the direction of the university registrar used that opportunity to redistribute the powers of the university's constituent bodies. They abolished the Corporation and established a senate, composed only of teaching and research staff, as the highest academic body in the university. They also gave a selection board the right to nominate any person to a full professorship and relegated the principal to an advisory position in the promotion of staff. Although he was to be included in the professorial selection boards and apprised of the deans' recommendations for junior staff, the new statutes curbed the principal's powers and gave rather more to the academic staff through their various departments and faculties. The new division of power was short lived. After some experience with the new statutes, L.W. Douglas and Sir Edward Beatty found them unsatisfactory and implemented a new set in 1939, simply explaining to the faculty that the principles upon which the 1935 statutes were based were wholly different from those that had inspired the university's statutes in the past.[44] Presumably they meant that the administration's powers had been weakened too much and that the status quo had to be restored. Indeed, under the new statutes the principal was once again named an ex officio member of the Board of Governors.

Many McGill faculty members were upset about the changes that Beatty and Douglas had implemented: some complained that with his new powers the principal could not be considered a colleague; the dean of Engineering regarded the amendments as a turning-back of the democratic clock.[45] On the day of James's installation the Faculty of Arts and Science met to discuss the whole issue. A number of them, upset that they had not been told about the amendments before they were enacted, decided to express their dissatisfaction to the senate of the university. Their resolution passed by only a small margin of votes and did not receive the backing of several departmental chairmen, but it was a strong condemnation of the administration none the less. It criticized the Board of Governors for failing to consult the faculty prior to the implementation of the statutes and suggested that machinery be set up to ensure faculty participation in the future. The fact that the Board of Governors discussed the proposed revisions with three faculty representatives – Otto Maass of the Department of Chemistry, Cyrus Macmillan of the Department of English, and J. Meakins of the Faculty of Medicine – and subsequently submitted drafts of the amendments to all the faculty deans does not seem to have assuaged the anger of the faculty. They regarded their exclusion from the early deliberations as an example of the division between academic and administrative judgment that had been occurring more frequently in recent years and was becoming harmful to the well-being of the university.[46] In an early draft of the resolution they suggested even more strongly that the Board of Governors did not understand the nature of academic life:

Resolved: That the Senate be informed that this Faculty deplores, and regards as disturbing to the espirit de corps of the University, the fact that its members were not provided with an opportunity either to render any professional advice based upon experience, or even to submit considered suggestions, in regard to the recent enactment of new university statutes, inasmuch as these statutes bear upon the professional work, the organization, the ideas, and the aims of this Faculty.

The members of this Faculty desire to assert their belief that the paramount assets of the staff of this University must be high scholarship, inspiring guidance, the presence of able students, and the material provision for existence and advance. It is regarded as essential that the operation of the University should be conducted primarily in such a manner as to enhance these assets, and in addition by consultation and application, to implement the experience of those who devote their lives to university work.[47]

One of James's first tasks as principal was to deal with the discontent that the new statutes had generated. On 29 January 1940 he met with the Faculty of Arts and Science in order to respond to their resolution to the senate. In a special address he implied that their ideas about academia were outdated. The Board of Governors had not asked for faculty approval of the statute revisions because that would have made the amendment procedure slow and impractical, he argued. The governors were under an obligation to run the university as efficiently as possible in order to make the faculty's work easier. That, too, was the rationale behind the new administrative structure that they had created. Under the new statutes, he explained, each faculty was reponsible for supervising the curriculum and regulating the courses and research activities in its own area. That was no small task, James contended, for it included most of the things upon which the reputation of the university rested. The senate was responsible for co-ordinating the activities of all the faculties and could propose amendments to the statutes, but the Board of Governors had final authority over the 'fabric' of the university, the administration of its funds, and the provision of an administrative structure 'which best enabled faculty members to carry out their work.' Such a division of power was not anti-democratic, he claimed, but one of separate responsibilities and specific powers, traditional throughout the British Empire and the United

States and typical of the governing structure of most large universities. 'In the nature of things,' he insisted, 'such division must exist.'[48]

James attempted to mollify the faculty's anger by assuring them that the statutes were only the 'dry bones' of the university and that it really could not function without the close co-operation and loyalty of the members of its 'family,' It was a concession that could not have appeased very many of them, especially since he asked them to withdraw the resolution from the senate and expunge it from their own records, reminding them that co-operation could not be achieved 'by the censorious criticism of men who were working for the good of the university within the framework of their legal powers.' Although the faculty agreed to withdraw the resolution from the senate, they asked James to act on it independently. With respect to the Faculty of Arts minutes, however, they considered it important that their clearly expressed opinions on the matter remain on record.[49]

James's speech did very little to defuse the discontent within the university. A year later the atmosphere was still bad enough to prompt him to seek advice from the former dean of Arts, Charles Hendel, then teaching at Yale, on how to handle the 'morale problem.' Hendel suggested to James that he cultivate friendly associations with the younger members of staff. The statutes had destroyed their feeling of allegiance to the university, he wrote, and the sense of hopelessness among them was strong.[50] McGill's younger faculty members were particularly upset about the new tenure policy that had been implemented in 1939. Although it gave life appointments to faculty who were associate professors at the time of its enactment, it limited all future appointments to that position to a period of five years. It also stipulated that assistant professors were only to be appointed for a period of three years, though it gave tenure to anyone who had then been on staff for ten years and was at least forty years of age, or who had been on staff for five years and was at least forty-five years of age.[51] In private communication L.W. Douglas explained the advantages of the new system to Sir Edward Beatty: 'it will allow us to calculate on a fairly rapid turn-over of the younger men, selecting here and there, as they pass through, those whom we think competent to carry on as the older men retire.'[52]

The new tenure policy was not implemented simply to weed out the academically incompetent. Throughout the 1930s the Board of Governors had subjected social-science professors, especially those connected with the League for Social Reconstruction, to close scrutiny. Although they took specific action only against King Gordon, by eliminating his chair of Christian Ethics in the United Theological College, they wondered what to do about the others. Under pressure from a number of businessmen, politicians, and even educators, they toyed with the idea of firing Eugene Forsey as far back as 1931. Sir Arthur Currie explained to Premier Taschereau that he had once suggested to Stephen Leacock that Forsey's contract not be renewed. 'But you know how all professors attach great importance to what they are pleased to call "academic freedom,"' he wrote. 'If we let Forsey go, it will be heralded from one end of Canada to the other that McGill dismisses its professors because of their political views, that we are a class university; one in which freedom of speech is not tolerated. He would have been dismissed long ago,' Currie continued, 'except that we hoped the years might bring wisdom to him and that we could avoid a "Forsey incident" at McGill.'[53] By redefining tenure below the rank of full professor, McGill's officials found a way to rid the university of its more troublesome members while circumventing the whole issue of academic freedom. In 1941 Forsey was fired on the grounds that he had never completed his PH D; in the same year Leonard Marsh was informed that his lectureship in the Department of Economics would terminate as soon as the Rockefeller Foundation grant for the Social Science Research Project expired.

Although McGill's principals were generally cautious about speaking out against academic freedom, Sir Edward Beatty was less restrained. He believed he had the right to make proclamations on the subject since it was his duty as chancellor to command public confidence in McGill. (He neglected to mention, however, that he was also protecting the interests of the Board of Governors, who were underwriting the university's deficits during the Depression.) Because Canadians were used to civility and looked to the universities for leadership during periods of social unrest, he argued, academics were under an obligation to choose their words carefully in public. It was one thing for them to express their opinions openly within the university – it was 'a democracy of intellect,' Beatty contended. But those who made 'wild and unguarded statements', based upon a misreading of history in public only undermined the cause of higher education in general. He insisted that the temptation to such errors was greater in some fields than others: 'The mathematician seldom attains the headlines of the daily press as the result of exaggeration of mathematical truth. The botanist is not likely to risk a libel suit in his description of the habits of plants.'[54]

More than fear of the bad publicity they might bring to the university explained Beatty's antipathy towards the social sciences; he saw no real purpose for them. He believed that the university's most important function was to assist in the development of the country's natural resources, a task that it could only achieve by teaching its students fact. 'We live in a world of fact,' he argued in 1937 in a speech on 'Freedom and the Universities.' 'We must recognize that fact exists. For this reason, I suggest that nothing can be more important in thought of any kind than [that] it should be based on accurate knowledge and presentation of fact.' Although Beatty conceded that ideas had been important in shaping human progress in the past, he insisted that there had been too much 'wandering' in the realm of metaphysics in more recent years, with the result that students were not prepared for employment. 'The young men and women who sit in your halls will have their lives shaped by what you tell them,' he admonished his audience. 'It is the experience of only too many employers in this country to have engaged in their services young men and women who, on the record of their academic distinction, and their share in the activities of university life, might be regarded as almost certain of immediate success, and then to find that the progress of these young people in business must be delayed a year or two while experience enables them to forget the erroneous statements of fact, and the intemperate descriptions of social phenomena to which they have been exposed during their education.'[55]

Beatty was not the only McGill official who criticized professors for their less than utilitarian philosophies of education. Speaking in his capacity as 'Official Visitor' to McGill at L.W. Douglas's installation as principal, the governor general of Canada criticized academics for forgetting that the university had an obligation to provide its students with the means to earn a livelihood. 'A smattering of general culture will be of little use to a young man if he is going to starve,' Lord Tweedsmuir argued. 'A university should be an employment bureau. There is a special opportunity for a university like McGill located in a great city like Montreal.' Although Tweedsmuir did not mean to suggest that the university should abandon its role as the trustee of humane learning, only that it should strive to find the right balance between the cultural and the technical, serious scholars must have found his argument difficult to accept when he held up as the perfect example of such equilibrium 'the excellent series of handbooks called the Foundation Library, which the great railway of which our Chancellor is head is issuing to its employees.'[56]

It could be argued that Beatty and Tweedsmuir were impelled by the economic problems of the 1930s to insist that McGill provide its students with a useful education. Since the university was dependent upon private benefactions for its survival, it literally could not afford to be regarded as an impractical, isolated institution. Still, however much their convictions may have been shaped by the exigencies of the time, the dominant role that similarly utilitarian philosophies had played in McGill's development cannot be overlooked. When F. Cyril James met with the Faculty of Arts on 29 January 1940, he ridiculed them for requesting more power within the university when they had not even exercised their own reponsibilities. The Arts division had not improved its courses for a quarter of a century, he charged. Some of the courses were so inferior that they were subjects of universal criticism and humour.[57] James's remarks were not entirely justified. The Arts division had instituted a number of new courses since the First World War – music and sociology were among them. They may not have attained the success of their scientific counterparts, but the blame was not to be placed entirely on the faculty. When J.B. Brebner undertook a survey of Canadian higher education for the Social Science Research Council of Canada in 1945, he arrived at some disturbing conclusions regarding the ability of Canadian universities to produce anything of intellectual significance. It seemed to him that the situation at McGill was an example of the kind of problem that militated against such a development. 'Up to the present, it seems fair to say, Canadian universities have been regarded by the public, and to some degree by themselves, as service institutions of a narrow utilitarian kind, with somewhat grudging tolerance for theoretical studies, normally in the Faculty of Arts. It must be argued, for instance, that some of the difficulties which have plagued McGill in the past generation have been able to persist because there was not a sufficiently intense conviction that the Faculty of Arts is the pulsing heart of a university.'[58]

McGill's status as a private institution in the commercial capital of Canada and the influence of the moral-philosophy tradition created an atmosphere at that university that was inimical to the development of theory and culture. Those factors not only contributed to the low regard in which the arts, and later the social sciences, were held at McGill but more specifically determined the pattern of their development. Lacking much in the way of financial and intellectual support from the university,[59] the social sciences were left to develop on their own, often as nothing more than marginal departments. They were compelled to turn to American sources for assistance, and not surprisingly undertook studies patterned on American examples. It was only in the 1930s, when their ideas seemed to challenge certain orthodoxies, that they received attention, and even then they were largely misunderstood.

2

Social Service and the Origins of Sociology

In the United States sociology evolved as a discipline out of theology and social work, emerging as a distinct subject in the 1880s. The first course in the field was taught at the University of Kansas in 1889, but by the end of 1892 at least nineteen other institutions offered instruction in the area. Prime among them was the University of Chicago, which, though newly opened itself, could boast of having the first department of sociology in the world. The swift development of sociology in the United States during the late nineteenth century owed much to the increasing popularity of utilitarian education, but its widespread acceptance was attributable to the social unrest that resulted from the rapid urban and industrial growth of the period. Sociology embraced discussions on the nature of society and its numerous social problems, Christian philanthropy and guidance.[1] To a generation who witnessed the labour disturbances of the 1890s with alarm and worried about the effect of industrialization and urbanization on the social order, it accordingly had great appeal.

Throughout the initial period of its existence sociology maintained strong ties with social work, a situation facilitated by the fact that many social workers, particularly those involved in the settlement movement, took university degrees and did work in sociology. Moreover, their teachers – the pioneer sociologists Albion Small of the University of Chicago, Franklin Giddings of Columbia, Charles Cooley of Michigan, and E.A. Ross of Stanford and Wisconsin – emphasized the relationship between social work and sociology. All of these stressed that while the two disciplines were distinct, both dealt with human beings and their social relationships: sociology was concerned with the laws and principles that governed those relationships; social work provided the data to formulate and test the theories. When the process of specialization and standards of research rose within the university in the early twentieth century, this alliance weakened. As sociologists began to criticize social workers for being too value-oriented and lacking in objectivity, social workers charged that sociologists were too concerned with theory and not sufficiently practical to deal with social problems.[2]

In Canada sociology also developed out of theology and social work in response to the problems created by urbanization and industrialization, but it did not gain status as an independent subject until a much later period – in some universities, not until the 1960s. The mistrust of specialization in most Canadian institutions of higher learning and the slower rate of urban and industrial growth did not give the discipline a fertile breeding-ground. If sociology were offered at all, it was taught in theological colleges or under the aegis of political-science departments. McGill, however, was an exception. There, a separate Department of Sociology was established in 1922. The university's strong utilitarian ethos gave the discipline the impetus to develop, but the economic problems and social conditions that came to light in Montreal, then Canada's largest urban centre, in the aftermath of the First World War were also major stimuli.

McGill's Department of Sociology evolved out of the Department of Social Study and Training, which the university established in 1918 in response to post-war economic conditions. Though primarily a social-work program, open to anyone who worked or intended to seek employment in social-welfare agencies, hospitals, prisons, and church ministries, that department offered courses in both theoretical and applied sociology. After three years of operation, however, for a number of academic and financial reasons to be discussed below, the university decided to restructure the program and separate sociology from social work. The director of the Department of Social Study and Training, a man with considerable experience as a social-work administrator, resigned in protest, and was replaced by a theoretical sociologist whose training, though it was from the University of Chicago, was actually in divinity.

As in the United States, modern sociology evolved at McGill out of theology and social work. Unlike the American model upon which it was patterned, however, it was not shaped by the social concerns of the 1890s but by the educational philosophy that developed at McGill in response to the First World War.

I

Like many North American universities, McGill suffered financially and psychologically from the effects of the Great War. The work of many of its departments was interrupted as classrooms, lecture halls, and laboratory equipment were turned over for military use, and two buildings were converted into barracks to house the university's own siege batteries. The university also sustained an enormous loss of revenue owing to the withdrawal of many of its students: from a figure of 2,123 in 1914, enrolment dropped to 1,303 in 1917–18.[3] A large part of that decline was attributable to enlistments: in the academic session of 1917–18 and at the beginning of the next year, the number of females in the Faculty of Arts exceeded the number of males, although the situation changed with the return of student soldiers after the armistice. If the impact of the war had not been debilitating enough, the university was compelled to shut its doors for six weeks in the fall of 1918. The Spanish influenza had reached epidemic proportions in Montreal by that point, and as the death rate in the city rose, schools, theatres, and law courts were all closed by civic order. Some thought was even given to closing and quarantining the port because of the overcrowding in the city's hospitals and sanitariums, but the idea was rejected as being too disruptive to trade and potentially dangerous during wartime.[4]

In the years immediately following the war McGill's problems continued apace. With its faculty weakened and facilities in a state of neglect and disrepair, classes were in some cases two or three times as large as those of the pre-war years. The hundreds of student soldiers who returned to continue their studies after two, three, or four years' absence helped to swell enrolment figures; so, too, did the veterans whom the university accepted into first year on a somewhat lower matriculation standard than was ordinarily expected. Although the federal government instituted a loans program in the fall of 1918 to assist disabled veterans wishing to pursue an interrupted course of study (and later extended the aid to all veterans), the universities were left to provide those students with whatever remedial classes were necessary. McGill offered these classes free of charge (but at a cost to itself of about ten thousand dollars, which later disturbed its officials).[5]

Despite these difficulties McGill officials were proud of the role that their university had played during the war. (It was a contribution that the Carnegie Foundation for the Advancement of Teaching awarded with the gift of one million dollars to the university in 1920.) More than 2,500 of its students and 90 faculty members had served in the armed forces. Out of that number, 522 were wounded and 341 were killed in action, and 382 received decorations or honours, 2 of which were the Victoria Cross.[6] The university had encouraged enlistment by granting credit for an entire academic year to anyone who volunteered for overseas service and by organizing its own battalion, which trained on the campus grounds under the direction of Sir Auckland Geddes, professor of Anatomy in the Faculty of Medicine. The sight of these men going through their daily paces created a military atmosphere at the university. 'The green grass of the campus,' it was reported, 'virtually disappeared as the fields became the drilling grounds for the volunteer force.'[7] Endowed with status as a regular contingent of the Canadian Officers Training Corps, that battalion provided a constant stream of officers and men for the Canadian forces throughout the entire period of the war. McGill also assembled, and was the first university to send into the field of active warfare, a medical unit, composed entirely of students and staff from its Faculty of Medicine.[8]

'The war has given a new connotation to the word "academic,"' said Sir William Peterson, principal of McGill, upon the declaration of the armistice. 'For the academic man – and woman, too – have done things in the great struggle and their practical achievements have reflected lustre on the institution in which they were trained.'[9] The war had infused the university with a purpose that many previously felt it had lacked, and in the years that immediately followed, its spokesmen searched for ways in which it could continue to make such a tangible social contribution. One such solution was found in the ideal of service. While the philosophy stemmed from the mid- and late nineteenth century, the idea that the university and its students had a duty to serve society was given renewed strength by the wartime experience and by the presence of hundreds of soldiers in its midst. The philosophy of service came to mean more than giving moral guidance to society; it implied providing the community with active leadership in almost every field of endeavour. Nowhere was the new conviction more evident at McGill than in the Board of Governors' choice of a successor to Peterson, who suffered a stroke in 1919 from which he did not recover sufficiently to resume his place at the head of the university.[10] His position was offered to a man who symbolized the very ideal of wartime service – Sir Auckland Geddes, at that point minister of National Service in the British government. Although Geddes initially accepted the offer, he was appointed British ambassador to Washington before taking up the duties of office, and the Board of Governors turned to another high-ranking military figure and man of action – Sir Arthur Currie, commander of the Canadian corps in France. Currie was not an academic, but the governors believed that his prestige, forceful personality, and esprit de corps – proven on the fields of

France – were qualities from which McGill could benefit. It was expected that he would manage the university's affairs in much the same way as a general ran an army, not by paying attention to the thousand technical details involved in its day-to-day administration but by delegating authority to his officers of staff.[11] More importantly, as in the case of Geddes, it was hoped that his presence at the helm of the university would serve as a reminder of its wartime accomplishments and give assurance to the community at large that McGill would continue to contribute to its well-being during peacetime. Indeed, very early in his principalship Currie signalled his intention to adhere to the philosophy of service. 'The world today,' he said upon his installation into office, 'needs the man who combines theory with fact, who fills his work with noble inspiration, whose methods are irradiated with high motives and whose lofty thoughts are translated into splendid action.'[12]

In an atmosphere where the idea of active service was exalted, academic detachment was held in low esteem. 'No university should be a place where the undergraduate obtains a certain modicum of learning,' Currie once argued. 'No undergraduate should leave our doors without realizing that he is a member of a community, that he has some responsibilities to others than himself.' He was not suggesting that McGill become another Oxford or Cambridge, where the individual was almost completely subordinate to his college and behaved in accordance with clearly developed precepts of what should or should not be done. In that system, he contended, the student was judged less by what he knew than by what he was. Despite the tyranny of class customs and the powerful conforming pressures of the British system, Currie nevertheless believed that it had some merit. It at least ensured that students had contact with their fellow men, learned to deal with others and serve their country. At the opposite end of the scale were what he called the American 'knowledge factories,' which set no higher goal, he claimed, than the production of skilled individuals. Perhaps they did so in the name of 'individual liberty' and 'academic freedom,' but as far as Currie was concerned, these were nothing more than much-abused catchwords, rendered meaningless because they no longer carried any sense of social obligation. The American universities had forgot, he concluded, that a university's most important task was to create good citizens.[13]

In advocating that the university pledge itself to community service, Currie had in mind a particular *type* of community, and it was implicit in his criticisms of both the American and British systems of higher education. In contrast to the class-consciousness and self-serving individualism that he saw as the respective products of those two systems, he proposed that every member of McGill – teacher and undergraduate alike – strive towards 'the high ideal of national duty.' While he acknowledged that the university had an obligation to serve mankind in general – 'to teach, inspire for truth amid the wonders of science, and seek new ways to aid the sick and suffering' – he argued that it would be a long time before the world was so ordered that nationality would be unimportant. Until that time came, he contended, there could be no higher duty for a citizen than to serve the country and community to which he belonged. [14]

The nationalistic strain in Currie's concept of service was a product of the wartime experience, reflective of the pride that many English Canadians derived from the country's contribution to the war effort. It also had a deeper significance. The war fostered an almost militant nationalism in Canada, as it brought military men, patriots, social gospellers, and reformers together in common cause. They saw in the war an opportunity for implementing their particular goals, and wartime propaganda absorbed their rhetoric, particularly the idea that the great struggle would mark the birth of a new society. [15] Although enthusiasm for the war died down as it dragged on longer than expected, these groups pledged themselves to the task of building that new society once the war was over, if only to justify its great cost in human lives. That objective was a major element in the nationalism that emerged in English-speaking Canada in the post-war years, but it also became entwined with another philosophy that was popular throughout the Western world at the time – 'reconstruction.' Depending upon the perspective of the advocates, discussions about reconstruction took on religious, philosophical, or economic overtones. The concept, however, revolved around two basic goals. One concerned the establishment of international stability (through the settling of national rivalries and the formation of the League of Nations). The other was the idea that each nation (or 'people') had to weave a new set of values from the 'strained and broken threads' of the old. [16] Institutions of higher learning obviously had an important role to play in the latter objective, and it was not surprising that many university spokesmen incorporated the slogan of 'reconstruction' into their educational philosophies in the post-war years. So it was that Currie combined his nationalist sentiments with a pledge to usher in a regime of 'optimistic reconstruction' at McGill, promising that during his principalship the university's facilities would be repaired and expanded and the institution would be infused with a philosophy that emphasized its national obligations.

Currie and some of his McGill colleagues did not rest content with upholding a vague concept of national duty, however. They elaborated the ways in which the university could best serve the nation, and if they tended to give priority to the utilitarian disciplines, it was partly because those subjects had always enjoyed a certain pre-eminence at McGill. Their importance was enhanced, however, by the economic philosophy of the period, some of it stemming from ideas about reconstruction. It was a commonly held belief in Great Britain, the United States, and Canada that the key to international stability was economic productivity. With a wider distribution of wealth and goods, it was argued in some quarters, the chances for national rivalries and class conflicts to erupt into war would be minimized. (For obvious reasons, the idea appealed as much to egalitarians and socialists interested in eliminating class divisions as it did to businessmen and financiers concerned with building up their own enterprises.) It was also recognized that such economic productivity would not be possible unless a large part of a nation's resources were mobilized for industrial development, wastefulness and inefficiency were eliminated, and human productivity was encouraged. 'We have almost succeeded in perfecting the inanimate machine,' said one eminent statesman; 'we have too much neglected the human machine, of all others the most complex because it is dominated by what may be called psychological forces. It has been possible in the case of animals to produce types exactly fitted for the service of man. Can something of this nature be achieved in the case of men and women by education, environment, and inspiration?'[17] In this atmosphere the cult of scientific management flourished: in Britain foundations and commissions employed investigators to visit trade and labour unions and encourage workers to be more efficient in their tasks: in the United States such individuals as Frederick Winslow Taylor and Hugo Münsterberg undertook studies to determine how that major impediment to human productivity – fatigue – could be eliminated, and then published manuals explaining how useless motions and wasteful efforts could be eliminated from most jobs. Universities picked up on the vogue to produce 'trained human doers' and implemented programs in applied science, vocational and industrial training, or simply courses designed to equip men and women for the practical affairs of life.[18]

At McGill the importance of economic productivity was not only recognized but blended with the philosophies of service, nationalism, and reconstruction to form one conviction – that it was McGill's particular duty to make Canada a front-ranking industrial nation. With such emphasis attached to that goal, science could not help but hold a high place – all the more so, as one McGill spokesman explained, because the war had demonstrated the importance of scientific research.[19] At the same time, he went on to argue, it also revealed that Canada had too few specialists in the area and could expect a dearth for years to come because of the large number of prospetive research students who had been killed in action. All those factors led many of the university's authorities to the conclusion that McGill must not only teach scientific research but science in all its branches. More than once they held up Germany's educational system as a model for Canada to emulate. One of the chief sources of that country's pre-war strength, they insisted, was the large number of men, thoroughly equipped in all branches of scientific work, whose services were available for the development of the arts and industries during peacetime and for the active and efficient prosecution of the war upon the outbreak of hostilities. They therefore concluded that an ever-increasing number of men, highly trained in the principles of science, with an ability to apply their knowledge to the needs of the community, was what Canada required for its industrial development.[20]

Despite the importance that McGill officials placed upon science, non-scientific subjects were not dismissed as useless. It was recognized that they could contribute to Canada's development in other ways. McGill had for some time supplied men for the strictly scientific branches of the civil service; Currie proposed that it establish a program in public administration so that the Dominion and provincial governments could call on the services of highly trained men for all their departments.[21] More generally, it was acknowledged that any discipline that dealt with social issues – or 'common life' – also fulfilled an important function. As Sir Arthur Currie told the participants of the Second Congress of the Universities of the Empire in 1921: 'The times have changed and our educational system must change with them if it is to serve the new environment; the deeper waters of ancient knowledge must still flow on as heretofore but they must be swelled by the streams of the new learning which have changed the face of the world in which we live.' In that respect, it was thought that social studies – the 'Realities,' as Currie once called them[22] – bore the same relation to the humanities as applied science did to scientific research: they represented the application of principles and ideas to the practical affairs of life. Just as instruction in applied science had enabled students to transform the physical environment, so it was expected that instruction in the social studies would enable them to interpret, adapt to, and perhaps even improve the social environment. In both cases the nation's progress was assured: the former contributed to its industrial development; the latter gave it social stability.

II

The belief that the university should offer courses that dealt with common life was a natural extension of McGill's utilitarian traditions and its desire to be of service to the nation. At the same time, it was also a response to the problems that the war had created. There was a fear, widely expressed in the years immediately following the war, that unless universities undertook to explain the evolution of social institutions to their own students as well as to the public, the social strife of the period was likely to develop into social upheaval. This was a concern that seemed to permeate the discussions of the Second Congress of the Universities of the Empire. The focus of that congress, unlike the one of 1912, which dealt with administrative matters, was the curriculum and new fields of study. Recognizing that the world had changed drastically since the Great War, the conference organizers asked the university representatives to focus on the question of how responsive institutions of higher learning should be to contemporary needs. Arthur Currie explained his position in the session on 'The Universities and Technological Education,' but he was not the only member of a Montreal university to speak at the conference. William Caldwell, professor of Moral Philosophy at McGill, and Edouard Montpetit, director of the University of Montreal's Ecole des Sciences Sociales, Economiques, et Politiques, participated in the session on 'The Universities and the Teaching of Civics, Politics, and Social Economics.' Fellow speakers included Sir William Beveridge, director of the London School of Economics, and Lynda Grier, a lecturer in Economics at Newham College, Cambridge. Taken together, their speeches depict a world in turmoil, desperately in need of assistance and direction from institutions of higher learning. Montpetit's opening address perhaps best conveys the atmosphere of the time:

Does it not seem like a reflection of our epoch that one of the questions asked at the very opening of the first after-war Congress of the Universities of the Empire be precisely one relating to the teaching of Civics, Politics, and Social Economics?

Human societies have been deeply impressed by the Great War. In political spheres, the solutions of peace have not yet acquired a character of absolute stability. Nations are uneasy and unquiet. International relations are not definitely sealed. It is felt that the problems which the war has revealed exact a renewed study. On the other hand, the social question clamours incessantly. The military hostilities are apparently followed by a social revolution whose prodromes are already in sight. An unrest, inevitable but singularly alarming, threatens to give rise to the violent reactions of a Commune with the entire world as a theatre ...

In the midst of general anxiety, Universities cannot remain unconcerned. In fact, they have not waited to set before the nations a line of conduct. They have performed works and formulated doctrines, and especially since the conclusion of peace, they have come forward to be of service to the nation.[23]

In different ways all the participants in the session on 'Civics, Politics, and Social Economics' saw the usefulness of what could be broadly termed 'social study.' Beveridge believed that the social sciences were the key to international peace because they provided insight into human relations, insight that could potentially remove the causes of war. Grier argued that rather than leave the interpretation of contemporary social conditions to politicians (who would twist and distort the information to suit their purposes), the universities should teach them in the detached and scholarly atmosphere that only they could provide.[24] Montpetit and Caldwell were more circumspect. While both saw the necessity for social study, they questioned the wisdom of allowing students to specialize in the area before they had acquired a philosophy of life.

Edouard Montpetit's concerns represented the traditional French Canadian antipathy towards specialization. He argued that the only way in which the university could deal with contemporary needs was to prepare an elite, with a thorough grounding in classical education, for action. He held up as an example the program for which he was responsible. In 1920, shortly after it gained autonomy from Laval, the University of Montreal instituted a course of study in politics, social administration, and journalism. The program, however, was more philosophical than technical: pupils were allowed to specialize in one of the areas only after they had received a classical education, and even then they were still required to take courses in social philosophy. (Moreover, in the section on social administration, instruction was almost wholly theoretical.) It was hoped that students trained in such a manner – 'steeped in a deep and general culture' and familiar with 'the ensemble of social questions' – would be able to adapt themselves to society's needs when necessary. 'Civism,' Montpetit explained to the audience, with a scientific analogy he must have thought they would appreciate, 'is like a moral radioactivity which arises from hidden energies dwelling in the inmost recesses of the heart. Empiric decrees, utilitarian arguments, occasional endeavours, partial reparations, tardy commands, all that is artifice.'[25] Montpetit did not think his views differed in substance from those of his 'McGill colleague,' William Caldwell, who had once argued that until such time as the universities introduced ethical considerations into their curricula, society could not expect to see all its citizens trained in the necessary moral and social habits.[16]

At the time he addressed the Congress of the Universities of the Empire, Caldwell was quite accustomed to dealing with the question of the proper place of social study in a university curriculum: he had studied and taught at institutions where that issue had been at the forefront of concern. Born in Cambridge in 1863, he graduated as a Doctor of Mental and Moral Philosophy from the University of Edinburgh in 1886. He taught Logic and Metaphysics at Edinburgh for a year, won the Shaw Fellowship (the highest academic distinction in Scotland) to do work on Schopenhauer, and then travelled to Germany and France for further graduate studies. In 1891 he was called to the Sage School of Philosophy at Cornell, the first American university to emphasize utilitarian education, and then in 1892 proceeded to the University of Chicago, where Albion Small was just setting up a department of sociology. Between 1894 and 1903 Caldwell taught moral and social philosophy at Northwestern University, and then accepted the position of Sir William Macdonald Professor of Moral Philosophy at McGill, where he taught courses in philosophy, psychology, and sociology.[27]

His views on the teaching of social science, Caldwell told the Congress in 1921, had basically not changed since 1898. In that year he had published an article that outlined his philosophy: while he had no objection to any discipline that purported to deal with facts, he did not believe it was wise for any student to do work in sociology – either theoretical or applied – without preliminary work in general history, ethics, economics, and philosophy. On one level his concern was that of a moral philosopher – he feared that without the understanding of the evolution of social institutions that those disciplines imparted, students would be incapable of integrating new information into a cohesive social philosophy. He did not agree with the pioneering sociologists that their discipline would fulfil such a function. 'It would not be difficult to prove from a dozen leading treatises on sociology,' he argued, 'that the stupendous task of correlating and organizing the facts bearing upon the essential nature of social organization and social evolution cannot but be the task of philosophy.'[28] In 1921 he adhered to that position for stronger reasons – he feared that unless students had a background in moral philosophy, there would be social upheaval: 'The more we study the sociological movements of modern times, and liberal and reform movements and their results, the more do we become convinced of the grave error and of the danger in allowing students to take social studies early in their careers, or of allowing anyone to speak out with regard to social problems without a sound philosophy of life and without a sound philosophy in themselves, and without an active sympathy with the great fundamentals, institutions of society, the family, the school, the Church, and so on.'[29]

Those reservations aside, Caldwell was not prepared to rule social studies out of the university – quite the contrary. He repeated to the congress a discussion he had recently had with Alfred Mansbridge, founder of the Workers' Educational Association, that even with the work of the WEA and university extension, the surface of industrial and social discontent had just been scratched. Under those circumstances the universities had to make themselves successful with the public, Caldwell argued, and the only way they could do that was by interpreting common life and proving that education was really 'the interpretation of and adaptation to the environment, the continual recreation of the environment.' He saw one major obstacle to that objective, however, and that was the academic superiority and aloofness of English university men. 'Sometimes in Canada we get men from England,' he continued, 'but they are apt to give the impression that they are superior to their surroundings and live "apart" from common life. Occasionally, we get men like our best Governor Generals who can go into the mining camps or the factories and interpret to people the life they are living ... When you interpret to a man or a woman the proper meaning of the life they are living at the moment, you take them into the atmosphere of what is called the university.'[30]

Caldwell more fully elaborated his educational philosophy in an article entitled 'A New Birth for Education,' which he wrote in 1918. It contained an argument so close to Currie's that one is led to wonder whether Caldwell counselled or perhaps even wrote the principal's speeches. Like Currie, Caldwell believed in the ideal of service – he had once criticized Americans for failing to understand that freedom could only exist when a person recognized his social duties, in addition to his own needs and privileges. In 'A New Birth for Education' he condemned the class biases in British higher education for the same reasons. 'The war itself began the work of "nationalising" or "generalising" the work and service of every individual, of showing to him and making him feel his value to the community,' he said. Nevertheless, the British establishment – clergymen, members of Parliament, magistrates, and schoolmasters – were perpetuating an educational system that never rose above a class conception of the country – 'the old gentleman, the Empire.' They continued to insist upon a 'stupid separation between information and active work, an educated smattering and the real work of life, preparation for life and life itself,' when Britain's well-being in the post-war age, Caldwell contended, depended upon its ability to see the relationship between the cultural and the useful. He conceded that Canada and the United States had had difficulty in producing true intellectuals but thought that Britain could learn from their example that the study of common life and common activities was a natural sphere for acquiring all the culture and learning one could – particularly with the extremes of Bolshevism and radicalism in so many places.[31]

Caldwell has been seen as something of an anomaly in Canadian intellectual life because his ideas represent one of the few incursions of pragmatism into Canadian thought. Moreover, it has been argued that he had little intellectual influence because of John Watson's dismissive criticisms of his work *Pragmatism and Idealism*, published in 1913.[32] Nevertheless, Caldwell did have an influence on the shape of early sociology at McGill; his concerns about social science were shared by many academics in Canada, and his fears about social unrest reflected some of the factors that shaped educational policy at McGill in the aftermath of the First World War.

It is not surprising that Montreal academics at the Second Congress of the Universities of the Empire spoke so much about social unrest. The war had created severe economic problems in Montreal, and those conditions were making it even more difficult for McGill to recover from the wartime disruptions. They were also perceived as obstacles to the goals that the university was trying to reach in the post-war years. In the first decade of the twentieth century McGill had expanded, responding to the favourable economic conditions that stimulated the growth of Montreal itself. Though not all of its residents shared in the benefits, the wheat boom of the period made the city prosperous:[33] the new-found wealth was most evident in the transformation of its downtown core into a predominantly commercial centre. Montreal became so modernized with the construction boom of the time that it turned, according to one obsever, Colonel William Wood, into a 'second New York City.' Old landmarks disappeared as office structures, apartment houses, factories, and schools rose all over the city. Churches moved westward with their congregations, and the vacated buildings became houses of commerce. The suburban population increased rapidly as new towns and suburbs sprang up around Mount Royal and on the south shore.[34] The construction boom ceased, however, with a depression that began in 1913. Although the war stimulated a high level of production in the city's factories as well as creating new war-related industries, it did not bring renewed prosperity. When it was over, the economies of Canada and the United States went into a slump because of the inability of the war-improverished European nations to purchase exports from abroad. The United States was able to recover by mid-1920 because of its large domestic market, but the Canadian economy was far more dependent upon the export trade and did not revive until 1923.[35]

The fluctuation between high production and depression had a strong effect upon the standard of living in Montreal. The wages of workers increased during the war, but inflation eroded their earnings in real terms: between 1915 and 1918 the cost of living rose by more than 40 per cent in the city, and it continued to climb throughout 1919 and 1920. The inflationary spiral wound down in mid-1920, but the post-war depression created widespread unemployment, and it remained at high levels until the middle of 1922.[36]

Post-war economic conditions created an atmosphere of instability in Montreal. 'Bolshevism was in the air,' commented one prominent Montrealer. 'It affected not only some disgruntled soldiers who wrecked restaurants but even the citizens and the city's employees.'[37] Although Montreal did not experience a general strike, there were widespread work stoppages. Perhaps the most serious was the one that began on New Year's Eve 1918–19 when an accident at the aqueduct precipitated a strike by the employees of the water and incineration departments, and a sympathetic strike by the police and fire brigades ensued. Fearful of the destruction that might result from the lack of water and danger of fire – not to mention the suspension of law and order – a group of citizens met in the Board of Trade and set up a committee to deal with the impasse. At first they considered asking the mayor to read the Riot Act, but then they decided to invite representatives of the striking services to explain their cause. Eventually a civic commission was established to conduct an investigation, and the men returned to work. Their grievances were looked into, and it was concluded that the strike arose because their wages had not been sufficient to meet the city's high cost of living.[38]

McGill officials were acutely conscious of the problems that the high cost of living was creating in their midst. Prior to the war, salaries hardly gave professors and their families more than the bare comforts of life; later, the abnormally high costs made it impossible for them to maintain themselves and their families in conditions of modest decency and comfort. During the war there had even been reports of professors who 'tented' around the city. Although the university granted a 'war bonus' – or direct salary increase – to every permanent member of the teaching staff at the beginning of the 1918–19 session, they found it necessary to provide them with another increase in August of that year. That made the salaries of McGill professors, on the average, 33 per cent higher than they had been in 1914 but still not very adequate. With another increase in 1919–20 their salaries were comparable to those of faculty in many American universities and higher than any in Canada. Nevertheless, at three thousand dollars per annum a professor's salary was reportedly less than that of a locomotive engineer, while the wages of an instructor were well below the annual earnings of a mechanic or an artisan. This was a situation that the university's authorities considered unsatisfactory for two reasons. They wished to raise the quality of education at McGill by attracting the best professors, but they also wanted to ensure the stability of the 'new era' that the world was entering.[39] That would only be made possible, they believed, by providing every faculty member with an income high enough to enable him to maintain a family comfortably 'in such a city as Montreal ha[d] come to be': 'Harassed in many cases by debt, is it any wonder that the able men in their thirties are foresaking the teaching profession and the ablest men in their twenties are no longer entering it. Very many of those who remain are compelled to eke out the exiguous incomes by devoting time, that should be spent in study and leisure, to work outside the university. In some Universities, members of the teaching staff, embittered by their poverty and despairing of the future, have turned to the heresies of socialism and communism. May this not happen at McGill!'[40]

In 1920 the university was compelled to launch an endowment campaign to raise its revenues. Normally, McGill officials relied upon the gifts of individual benefactors to provide for whatever the university needed, but they did not think they could depend upon traditional sources of support to deal with the university's post-war problems. Since the money was required for salaries and not expansion, they could not memorialize a donor's generosity by dedicating a building in his name. Since student fees were already higher at McGill than anywhere else in Canada, they could not raise tuition to cover the additional expenditures. And no one expected the likes of a John D. Rockefeller to come forward with a sum of fifty million dollars, such as he had recently donated for professorial salary increases in the United States. Instead, pointing to the millions of dollars that Yale, Princeton, and Columbia had raised from public subscriptions, the one million that Dalhousie University had received from its constituency in the Maritimes, and the five million that the francophone population of Quebec had recently given for the establishment and endowment of the University of Montreal, McGill officials asked the Canadian people to contribute five million to McGill. The university needed at least that amount to overcome its war-related problems or they claimed, it would fall behind in prestige and never recover. They hoped that in view of the great services that the university had rendered to Montreal and to the country in general, Canadians would rally to its aid.[41]

Thanks to gifts of one million dollars from the Rockefeller Foundation and the Quebec government (which gave matching sums to Laval and the

University of Montreal), McGill was able to raise $6,320,000 during the endowment campaign. More than two-thirds of that went into a salary fund; the remainder was spent on construction, in fulfilment of the Rockefeller Foundation's request that the university spend an amount equal to its donation on buildings for the biological sciences.[42] There was still not enough money, however, to provide for the construction of student residences, a scheme that had been planned for some time but had to be abandoned during the war. Only a small minority of students who came to McGill from outside Montreal were able to find university-affiliated accommodation – either in Strathcona Hall, in the dormitories of the theological colleges, or in the Greek-letter societies. More than two thousand of them lived instead in boarding houses that were scattered throughout the city and even beyond its limits. During the 1920 endowment campaign the university engaged the services of Stephen Leacock to awaken public interest in the problem. He recalled the horrible experiences of his undergraduate days, when, as a student at the University of Toronto, he lived in seventeen different boarding houses. 'I was not alone in the nomadic life I led,' he wrote. 'There were hundreds of us drifting about in this melancholy fashion from one habitation to another. We lived as a rule two or three in a house, sometimes alone. We dined in the basement. We always had beef, done up in some way after it was dead, there were always soda biscuits on the table.' Canadians were just waking up to the idea of what a university should be, Leacock continued. Where they had once thought that the student should be a pallid creature who burned the midnight oil and worked himself to death for some measly scholarship, they now realized that what he needed was the right kind of environment. Students should be allowed to live together, smoke together, and eat together, he insisted, and then proclaimed: 'If I were founding a University – and I say this with all seriousness I can muster, just think of that – I would found first a smoking room; then after that, a decent reading room and a library. After that, if I still had more money left over I couldn't use, I would hire a professor and get some textbooks.' He also admitted that if Toronto had offered the kind of dormitory life that was available at Harvard, he never would have graduated.[43]

Despite Leacock's sarcasm, there was real concern at McGill about the university's lack of student residences. Because of the code of behaviour that they instilled in their students, they were regarded as essential to the development of a true collegiate spirit.[44] More importantly, it was believed that they provided a necessary shelter against the bad influences of city life. A scheme for student residences under strict university supervision had been a pet project of Sir William Peterson, who worried about the moral perils that a large city like Montreal, with its public-health problems, overcrowding, and vice, posed to students who came to the university from small towns, villages, and farms.

In the last years of his life social conditions in Montreal increasingly troubled Peterson. They not only stimulated his interest in student dormitories but contributed to his conviction that McGill should establish a department of social service. 'He beheld the city from his uptown coign [sic] of vantage,' said the speaker at his memorial service, 'and the vision troubled him. The social evils of the great commericial centre challenged him to do something for the alleviation of distress, the improvement of housing conditions, the prevention of such slums as are a blot on the fair city of Edinburgh which gave him his birth, the reduction of that infant mortality which is a scandal to our population.'[45] Peterson was moved by more than Victorian notions of uplift; he believed that Montreal required a department of social service more than any other city on earth because its numerous social-welfare agencies were too wracked by religious and racial divisions to be effective in alleviating its problems. He hoped that the university would be able to succeed where those agencies had failed – that it would not only inspire a passion for social redemption nor simply act as a school for the scientific training of social workers but become a centre where the work of existing agencies would be 'strengthened, stimulated, and coordinated.'[46]

III

Sir William Peterson did not act single-handedly in implementing McGill's Department of Social Study and Training, nor were his views about the role it should play unique. The department was established in response to three different currents of thought regarding social welfare, and its program of study reflected those influences. Through their participation in such wartime organizations as the Red Cross and the Patriotic Fund, the social-welfare leaders of the city's anglophone community saw how effective large-scale effort and financing could be for the practice of social work and were anxious that the university – a non-sectarian agency – should assume a leading role in co-ordinating the city's social-welfare efforts once the war was over. The theological colleges affiliated to McGill, concerned with 'the social question' since the turn of the century, had become more interested in practical social work in light of the problems that the war exposed in Montreal, and were accordingly willing to support a program in social service when the idea was proposed. Although the war served as a catalyst to the development of McGill's Department of Social Study and Training, the idea that the university should serve as a centre for training social workers in addition to co-ordinating the work of existing agencies was an extension of a trend that had been developing over a much longer period of time: social work evolved as a university-accredited course out of the links that two institutions – the Charity Organisation Society and the university settlement – forged with institutions of higher learning in late nineteenth-century Britain. Many social-work programs in the United States developed in accordance with that pattern, as in some respect did McGill's.

The organization that became the McGill University Settlement was founded in 1891, and the Montreal Charity Organization Society a decade later. Both, however, were adaptations to North American conditions of the principles and methods of the British models. Though different in their approaches to the treatment of poverty, the Charity Organization Society and the university settlement were products of a movement that began in Britain around the middle of the nineteenth century, whose aim was to make the organization of philanthropy and the distribution of charity more effective than the traditional forms of alms-giving or parish relief. In fact this movement represented one of a number of responses to the social and economic conditions of that period in which the ideology of national efficiency had its roots. In the second half of the nineteenth century philanthropy was organized in Britain on a wider scale than ever before, but the rapid population growth of the period and the exposure of massive destitution led many people to question its effectiveness. It was thought that by scrounging from a number of charities, the poor were both evading and disrupting the operation of the free-market economy, and that the wealthy, by doling out their money indiscriminately to so many different agencies, were losing the intimate contact with the poor that was considered a necessary part of the philanthropic exchange. To serve as a corrective to this situation a number of approaches to more disciplined philanthropy were formulated. Each of them rejected the idea of direct material aid in favor of measures calculated to have a more long-lasting effect. Reformers such as Edwin Chadwick fought for control of factory hours, popular education, and the extension of the franchise. Robert Owen, Elizabeth Fry, and Mary Carpenter advocated personal contact with the poor, believing that global changes would result from such small beginnings. Under the leadership of Charles Loch, the Charity Organisation Society set forth as its objective to restore the recipient of charity to as much dignity, self-sufficiency, and personal responsibility as possible and worked out a number of principles and methods by which those goals could be accomplished.[47]

All these groups left their mark upon the character of social work: Chadwick, by demonstrating that it was possible to combine social reform and social control, shaped the administrative arm of the practice; Owen, Carpenter, and Fry infused it with an evangelical ethos that indirectly influenced the settlement movement. None, however, was more influential than the Charity Organisation Society. It laid the foundation for what was to become the major technique in the practice of social work – casework – by insisting that the causes of poverty and distress be understood, that a methodical investigation of every applicant seeking aid be undertaken, and that assistance other than monetary be rendered. Moreover, because it insisted that all the social and psychological factors in the life of a client be taken into consideration, the Charity Organisation Society introduced the scientific mode of thought into social work, as well as contributions from the disciplines of sociology, economics, and biology.[48] Finally, since it was a tenet of the Charity Organisation's philosophy that its objectives could only be accomplished with the co-operation of all social workers, it was responsible for instituting the first program in social work.

In 1896 the Charity Organisation Society, in alliance with the Women's University Settlement of Southwark, London, began offering a series of lectures in London on such broad issues as 'the scope of charitable work' 'the family,' and 'social worth.' As the work of the Joint Lectures Committee grew rapidly, extending even outside London, the Women's University Settlement withdrew, and the impetus behind the lectures was channelled more specifically into practical training. In 1901 members of the committee decided that it might be wise to combine their courses with university work and considered affiliating with the London School of Economics for such purposes. Because of the lack of social and ethical content in its teaching, however, as well as its 'conspicuous association' with one school of thought, the committee rejected that idea and invited one of their own tutors, E.J. Urwick, to draw up a course of training. His plan was implemented, and in 1903 the School of Sociology opened in Southwark, London. The two-year training program covered such subjects as the natural history of society, social philosophy, social economics, individual and social psychology, law, history, and theories of the state. Courses dealing with sanitation, education, and the treatment of the sick and the imbecile made up the practical side of the program, and there was a small start made in field-work as well: upon Urwick's suggestion students were sent out to observe social conditions in the city under the guidance of an experienced administratior of social work. (In 1912, hampered by financial difficulties, the London School of Sociology finally decided to merge with LSE's Department of Social Science and Administration. Urwick followed the school in its move and maintained control of his program for two years. Ultimately, because LSE was so much larger an institution than the London School of Sociology and lacked sympathy for the kind of charitable work the Charity Organisation Society favoured, changes were instituted and Urwick departed. He went on to become chairman of the Department of Political Economy at the University of Toronto, acting director of its Department of Social Service, and critic of 'scientific' sociology.)[49]

The first American Charity Organization Society was established in 1879, during a period of industrial depression, by the Reverend Stephen Gurteen, an Episcopal clergyman from Buffalo, New York.[50] Economic conditions proved conducive to its expansion, and the Charity Organiza- tion Society flourished in the United States. It also stimulated the development of many university-affiliated social-work programs – the Columbia University Graduate School of Social Work, for instance, began as a six-week summer course offered by the Charity Organization Society of New York in 1898.[51] It was the American variant of the charity organiza- tion, in fact, that influenced the social-welfare leaders of Montreal's anglophone community: although such individuals as Sir Herbert Ames and Jeffrey Burland had been familiar with the work of the Charity Organisation Society from their travels abroad, it was only when they started attending welfare conferences in the United States and saw how its principles and methods were adapted to North American conditions that they considered forming a COS in Montreal. The Montreal Charity Organization Society was founded at the turn of the century, largely owing to the efforts of the Montreal Council of Women, whose board of directors included such individuals as Lady Julia Drummond and Helen Reid.[52] Reid, one of the first women to graduate from McGill, had also been instrumental in forming the Women's University Settlement of Montreal and would go on to play a major role in developing McGill's programs in social work and nursing.

What distinguished the charity-organization movement in the United States from its British counterpart seemed to be the greater emphasis it placed upon elevating the social worker to professional status, not simply by endowing him – or her – with the necessary qualifications to be a professional but ensuring that the community perceived him as one. The

Charity Organisation Society initiated the professionalization of social work in the nineteenth century by treating charity as 'efficient service,' but it was the growth of bureaucratization and specialization, resulting from the rise of an urban industrial society, that was the more important stimulant. Employed in such institutions as hospitals, where they worked alongside other professionals – nurses and doctors – who had special claims and qualifications for practising in their fields, American caseworkers attempted to define and clarify their own vocation, its techniques and requisite knowledge, in order to legitimize their interference in people's lives.[53] It was not surprising, then, that the practice of social work in the early twentieth century was full of medical terms and analogies.[54] This was certainly true of the publicity that the Montreal Charity Organization Society produced, and it was only natural that it should be so, given that throughout the twenty years of the Montreal COS's existence it hired American workers and organizers.

The objectives of the Montreal Charity Organization Society were identical to those of the original British movement: to restore every client who came to its doors to a state of independence and self-reliance by some means other than monetary. Material relief, the Montreal COS argued, only encouraged laziness and mendicancy. 'Organized charity,' its pamphlets repeated over and over, 'provides a channel not for your dollar bill to reach the pocket of the poor fellow you wish to help – you could see to that yourself – but for your dollar bill to be converted into a service more effective than could the cash alone.' Typifying the professional ethos that had come to characterize American charity-organization societies in the twentieth century, the Montreal COS explained why it was the agency that could provide the most efficient service in the treatment of poverty. Its members called themselves 'trained practitioners in the art of family rehabilitation' – men and women who would determine by careful investigation what an individual client's (or perhaps an entire family's) difficulty really was. 'The physician does not accept the patient's statement of his ailment, nor does the Charity Organization Society think the applicant, however truthful, is able to give a correct diagnosis of his own difficulty.'[55] By visiting his family, friends, relatives, church, physician, and employer, the charity-organization worker would attempt to ascertain the true problem. Once the cause of the client's 'maladjustment' was diagnosed, the social worker would attempt to rally to his aid all his 'natural resources' – his friends, family, church, or lodge – and try to keep him off relief by finding him a job, perhaps moving his family from an unsanitary house or a bad environment, strengthening his church ties, and ensuring that all children of school age attended school. Occasionally, in dire emergencies, direct material aid was rendered. Relief, the Montreal Charity Organization Society explained, was as drugs to the physician. 'At times necessary, and often as a means of saving [a] life, but by no means the most important element in [the social worker's] art, and to be used with the utmost discretion.'[56]

In addition to casework the Montreal Charity Organization Society undertook a number of specific projects in the impoverished areas of the city. One was to prevent overcrowding in the immigrant quarter; another was to remove families from basement dwellings. There was a city by-law that made it permissible for basements – but not cellars – to be rented out as habitations, but since there was a fine line between the two, the law was often broken. Indeed, one cos worker reported that he had discovered many families living in basements that were nothing more than damp, filthy cellars: 'I have seen the blue mould inches thick and vermin crawling up the walls.' No sooner would one family be convinced to move from such a dwelling, he complained, than an unscrupulous landlord would rent it out to another.[57] The Montreal cos also had difficulty in overcoming the obstacle that stood in the way of co-ordinating social-welfare efforts in Montreal: the fact that its social agencies, like the city itself, were sharply divided along religious and racial lines. The cos did make some attempts at co-operation with the francophone community: it invited a number of prominent French Canadians to serve on its board of directors, and a few of them obliged – one such individual was Edouard Montpetit. In 1912 and then again in 1915 it worked with the Municipal Assistance Department on a project that was aimed specifically at improving conditions in the francophone districts of the city: to abolish street-begging. For reasons cos never elaborated on but that must have been connected with the economic depression of the time as well as animosity on the part of the French Canadians, the project was not very successful.[58]

In 1915 the Montreal Charity Organization began to hold public lectures at McGill, but that was not the avenue through which it became linked to the university. It was its wartime work that provided that foundation. By organizing sewing classes for poor and unemployed women and by distributing Red Cross work rather than giving direct material relief, the cos was able to pursue its policy of restoring the impoverished to a state of self-reliance, in addition to contributing to the war effort. But more importantly the war provided the organization with the opportunity to co-ordinate the work of other social-welfare agencies and to strive for the greatest efficiency of funds and effort in social-work practice. Some years prior to the war the Montreal Charity Organization Society began to keep a register of all its cases so that other social agencies could see who had come to its doors for assistance, and would not treat the same individuals. With the onset of the war the cos argued that further economy of efforts and funds was necessary and suggested that Montreal's social-welfare agencies follow the example of many American cities and establish a Confidential Exchange – a list of all those who were on relief or seeking it. This would allow one agency to know if a family it was helping had registered with another and thereby enable 'all those interested in the family to get in touch with each other and work out an intelligent plan for the betterment of the family.' The cos's suggestion was taken up by the Montreal Women's Club, who invited the registrar of the Boston Confidential Exchange (reportedly the first and best of its kind in the world) to visit Montreal and advise the city's social workers on how to set up theirs. The cos started to organize the exchange in December 1915, and it began operating two months later, with sixteen thousand cases registered. Included among the participating agencies were the Patriotic Fund, the Meurling Refuge, the Montreal Hospital and Sheltering Home, and the Victorian Order of Nurses.[59]

Through their experience with the Confidential Exchange and the co-ordinated work of the Red Cross and the Patriotic Fund during the First World War, a number of Montreal's anglophone welfare leaders were convinced that some non-sectarian agency would have to take control of the city's social-welfare efforts when the war was over so that the policy of efficient service could continue to be pursued. They accordingly undertook a plan to investigate the possibility of forming a federation of all the city's social-welfare institutions, and looked to the university as the agency that through training and research, could provide the personnel for it. When Sir William Peterson framed the proposal that was to be put before the McGill Board of Governors regarding the establishment of the Department of Social Service, he had the assistance of an individual who was involved in all these efforts – James A. Dale, professor of Education at McGill.

James Dale came to McGill in 1908 as the first occupant of the Chair of Education, but prior to that he had been closely connected with the movement for popular education in his native Britain. In fact Dale's activities over the course of two decades reflected that evolution from reformist convictions to 'action,' from an almost evangelical impulse to a drive for efficiency, that seemed to characterize the work and ideas of many reformers in the early twentieth century. In 1901, after graduating from the University (at that time, the College) of Birmingham and, afterwards, Oxford, Dale was appointed to the staff of Isleworth Training College for

Teachers. His interest soon turned towards the movement for adult education, one that had as its essence the belief that social improvement was possible only through knowledge. In 1902 he was hired to teach courses in literary and education movements as an extension lecturer at Oxford; he also travelled throughout England, France, and Belgium to confer with leading educational authorities on matters of common concern. Dale was one of a circle of people who worked with Albert Mansbridge, founder of the Workers' Educational Association in Britain, and was connected with Ruskin College, another working-men's educational insititution, in the early days of its existence. (He was also secretary of the Ruskin Society and editor of its literary organ, 'The St George.') Once at McGill, in addition to his work in education, Dale was a member of the Charity Organization Society and president of the School of Education. It was in the latter connection that he began to strive after the mental and physical efficiency that was later channelled into his social-work efforts; caught up in the desire for action during the First World War and probably the hope that the struggle would bring great social change, he trained with the McGill battalion during the war. Ill health made it impossible for him to fight overseas, however, and he was released for educational work with the Khaki University in Germany, France, and Belgium. Prior to the war, however, Dale was chairman of the committee that reorganized the University House and incorporated it into the National Federation of University Settlements. In fact, it was largely through Dale's efforts that McGill students and Montreal social workers gained an understanding of the settlement movement.[60]

Like the Charity Organisation Society, the settlement movement was a middle-class response to the social problems of late nineteenth-century England. The 'founder' of the movement was Samuel A. Barnett, who became convinced, through his experience as vicar of St Jude's in one of the worst areas of east-end London, that urban and industrial change had undermined the ability of both the parish and traditional charity to deal with poverty. He thought a more effective method lay in broadening the horizons of those who lived in industrial slums, a strata of society that the university extension movement with which he had been involved had failed to reach. With the encouragement of such men as John Ruskin and T.H. Green (and a number of other professors and clergymen who were critical of the excesses of economic and social individualism), he conceived of a scheme whereby university students would live and participate in the daily struggles of an underprivileged neighbourhood. At his invitation a group of Oxford and Cambridge students set up a residence (which they named after

Arnold Toynbee) in the Whitechapel district of London and organized a number of educational, cultural, and recreational activities for the community. They also became involved in investigating the labour conditions that led to the dockers' strike, and undertook the research that resulted in Charles Booth's study *London Life and Labour*. Following the example of Toynbee Hall, a number of other settlements were formed in London, but the movement attained even greater success in the United States. Transplanted to America, it became more flexible, a little less academically oriented, and, most importantly, shifted the emphasis of its work from class to race relations. Hull House, established in 1889 under the leadership of Jane Addams, became the model that many American settlements followed.[61]

When James Dale arrived in Montreal, he found a University House that was quite different from either the British or American models. In 1891, the Alumnae Society of McGill (an organization that a small group of McGill female graduates formed in 1889 for the improvement of their own literary interests as well as to further the interests of women in Montreal generally) undertook a project to help the working women of the city. Renting a house on Juror's Street in the heart of the industrial area and naming it the Women's University Settlement, they set up a lunch-room to provide meals at moderate prices to female factory and shopworkers in the district. The project was obviously intended as a means by which the graduates could learn the techniques of philanthropic organization, not as an arrangement whereby they threw in their lot with the dwellers of an underprivileged neighbourhood. By hiring a cook and a housekeeper to take care of more mundane matters, they freed themselves to attend to the supervisory tasks of managing the project, purchasing the food, and planning the meals. In the first year of its operation the lunch-room attracted forty to seventy clients daily, but the number grew so rapidly that within two years the Alumnae Society was forced to move to larger quarters on Bleury Street. At that point, the members decided to diversify their operations and began to provide evening classes, sewing classes, Christmas parties for poor children of the district, as well as a fund for ill and unemployed women. With two more changes of locale in 1902 and 1903, they opened their facilities in the evenings to boys and girls of the district. They were, therefore, compelled to invite male graduates to help supervise the work, a change that led them, in the short space of two years, to abandon the Girls' Club and allow the administration of the settlement to pass out of their immediate control. In 1907–8 they discontinued the lease on the house and moved into new quarters with an even more diversified program, one that very closely resembled that of Hull House. Renamed the McGill University Neighbourhood Club, it provided a workshop, courses in needlework, drawing, and a kindergarten class. In 1910 it became the University Settlement of Montreal upon the suggestion of J.A. Dale and was recognized as part of the university proper by the Corporation of McGill.[62] (At the time that it was incorporated into the university, the settlement was providing instruction to about two hundred children in the industrial district. In 1912 it moved operations to two tenements on Dorchester Street, one of which was a residence for university volunteers. It remained at that site for many years, successfully attracting students from particularly the social work and sociology programs until about 1928, when, because the number of volunteers was dropping off so drastically, the settlement was forced to recruit older boys and fathers from the district to work as supervisors.[63] The sudden apathy on the part of McGill students may have had something to do with the fact that by 1928 the Protestant churches had by and large lost interest in practical social work, and sociologists no longer believed, as they initially had, that the settlements would provide them with data for their theories.)

IV

The announcement that McGill would begin offering courses in social service during its 1918–19 session was made with a flourish. 'Experience has shown,' the report proclaimed, 'that such schools of social science can best be established in connection with a university, of which the University of Edinburgh [Peterson's alma mater] is the most recent example.'[64] There was also an acknowledgment that McGill lagged behind a sister institution in establishing such a program. In 1914 the University of Toronto inaugurated what was, with the exception of some lectures organized by private individuals at the University of Manitoba, the first department of social service in Canada.[65] (In 1920 James A. Dale would accept the invitation of Robert Falconer to serve as its director.) Prior to that, Canadian students who were interested in social-work training were compelled to go to the United States – an unsatisfactory situation, as far as University of Toronto officials were concerned, because those students did not learn about Canadian needs and problems or, worse still, found jobs in the United States and never returned to Canada. The University of Toronto's program attained instant success. In its first year of operation it attracted approximately two hundred students from all parts of Canada.[66] That seemed to bother McGill officials, and the fact that students from eastern Canada were enrolled in the program was a particular annoyance. They promised that their program, once established, would supply 'the constant demand for trained social workers in Quebec and the Maritimes,' a demand that had been met in the past by hiring American social workers, who usually returned to the United States after a few years' employment in Canada.[67] With all those considerations – the need for trained social workers, the rivalry with Toronto, not to mention the importance that McGill had attached to the philosophy of 'service' and practical education in the aftermath of the war, the position of a department of social service at that university should have been secure. It was not. While the university's authorities were willing to establish the program, they were not as interested in finding the funds for its operation. It was true that the university was experiencing financial difficulties because of the wartime disruptions, but that was not the root of the problem. McGill's traditional concern with developing the scientific disciplines had been intensified by the war, and because of that, non-scientific disciplines were given short shrift. A department of social service was eventually established but only on a trial basis, and was highly vulnerable to the criticisms – and whims – of its sponsors.

When Sir William Peterson placed his proposal for a department of social service before the Board of Governors in 1918, he intimated that he had been approached by two private individuals who offered to give the university an annual subsidy of two thousand dollars for the establishment of a department of social service if it could raise a similar sum. The Board of Governors nevertheless told him that they would only authorize the establishment of the Department of Social Study and Training, as they called it, if sufficient funds were available, and Peterson was thereupon compelled to ask members of the Corporation to beseech their friends for assistance so that the program could at least be established on a trial basis until a permanent endowment was secured. His plea was not very successful, but ultimately the Graduates' Society and the Joint Board of the theological colleges affiliated to McGill came forward with annual subsidies of two thousand dollars each for a period of three years.[68]

For the four Protestant theological colleges affiliated to McGill – the Congregational, Presbyterian, Anglican, and Wesleyan – the proposal to institute a department of social service at the university could not have come at a more appropriate time. Since at least 1912, when they allied to offer a common course of instruction, the colleges had been requiring their students to do work in theoretical sociology. In a course entitled 'Individualism and the Modern Social Consciousness' (which was really Christian sociology), theology students learned about the practical principles in Christ's teachings that could be applied to some phases of contemporary social problems, such as wealth, the care of the poor, and the industrial order. However, there was another course that dealt with more specific aspects of social welfare – criminology, the 'Boy problem,' the rural community, temperance, the white-slave traffic, and the problems of a city. In the 1917–18 session students began to take William Caldwell's 'Studies in the Principles of Sociology,' which added some new dimensions – discussions on the evolution of social institutions, industrial relations, and immigration. They were also required to do some field-work: under the guidance of John Bradford of the YMCA they investigated social conditions in the city and efforts at social reform. [69] The representatives of the theological colleges therefore indicated to Peterson that they would be happy to subsidize the program in social work; they had for some time recognized the need for lectures on social-service subjects in Montreal, not just for the general public but for their own students as well. But they offered the money with two provisos – that their students be allowed to take three courses annually in the department free of charge, and that some of those courses be in theoretical sociology. Their requests were necessarily complied with. [70]

Once the funds were found to establish the Department of Social Study and Training, it was set up on a trial basis for a period of three years, beginning in August 1918. A committee of management, composed of reprsentatives from the university (among whom were William Caldwell and Stephen Leacock) as well as from the theological colleges and the city's social-welfare agencies, was appointed to work out the structure of the program and oversee its work. It was decided that the Department of Social Study and Training should be a separate entity but that the Faculty of Arts should co-operate fully in allowing social-work students to attend any such lectures as the department advised. In the first year of operation the department offered a one-year experimental course, on a full-time basis or as a series of extension lectures, to anyone who worked (or was seeking employment) in social-welfare agencies, prisons, hospitals, or ministries. In the second it offered a two-year diploma course as well and in the third year added a month of intensive field-work training on to the diploma course. (The program, as it turned out, attracted more part-time than full-time students: 200 people attended the extension lectures offered in the first year, and in the third year, when the extension courses were dropped, 104 people registered as partial students. However, no more than 12 students ever took the diploma course). [71]

At J.A. Dale's suggestion John Howard Toynbee Falk came to Montreal in the summer of 1918 to serve as director of McGill's Department of Social Service. Falk had worked with the Red Cross and the Patriotic Fund during the First World War and through that connection had got to know Montreal's charity leaders.[72] They in turn had been very impressed by him. Like Dale, Falk had been intimately connected with social-reform movements in Britain but had also worked closely with Canadian and American reform leaders. Perhaps more importantly, he had gained through the course of the war the same strong commitment to efficiency that almost all of them shared.

Howard Falk was born in Liverpool in 1881 to a family of social workers: his mother was a sister of Arnold Toynbee's and a descendant of John Howard; his father came from a family that in 1813 established the first philanthropic society in Danzig as well as an institute for the care and education of neglected children. The elder Falk, a German-born chemist who became a successful industrialist in the northwest of England, cultivated ties with the great social-welfare leaders of the day when he first arrived in England. Not only did he marry Toynbee's sister, Rachel Russel Everard, but he set up one of the first employment-placement services in Britain for technical and industrial workers. Many of England's social reformers were frequent guests of the Falks, and it was at his parents' house and later at Balliol College, Oxford, where Howard Falk became acquainted with Colonel Barnett, Charles Booth, Sidney and Beatrice Webb, Octavia Hill, and Harold Laski. Falk selected Balliol for his university education because of its close connection with settlement work. He had no formal training in social work but as an undergraduate worked at Toynbee Hall and there met some of the founders of the first American university settlements, who told him of the great need for social-welfare work in America.

After leaving Oxford, though greatly interested in social work, Falk was apprenticed to a firm of grain merchants in Liverpool and spent two years working for the firm in Odessa, South Russia. In fact, he was there in 1905 when the revolution broke out and only managed to flee on the last foreign vessel to leave the port before it was closed. After spending another year in Liverpool, he crossed the Atlantic to work for the Northern Grain Company in Winnipeg but did not remain there for long. Shortly after he arrived in Winnipeg, some Americans whom he had met on the boat coming over from England and who were impressed by the way in which he handled the collection and distribution of funds and clothing for the Russian refugees on board offered him a position as director of Boys' Work at Christadora

House in New York. Falk accepted the job, and while in New York also became assistant secretary of the Tenement House Committee and acting secretary of the Tuberculosis Committee of the New York Charity Organization Society. True to the restless pattern that would characterize the rest of his life, Falk soon returned to Winnipeg. While in the Grain Exchange ambit he had met J.S. Woodsworth, and Woodsworth, greatly impressed by Falk's abilities, invited him back to Winnipeg in 1908 to undertake a survey of the city's local charities, with a view to federation. When the survey was completed, Falk became the first director of the Winnipeg Associated Charities. He was also the first secretary of the Welfare Commission and of the Manitoba Mothers' Allowance Commission; he helped to organize the province's Department of Public Welfare and obtain amendments to the Criminal Code. Moreover, Falk worked with J.S. Woodsworth to organize the social-work lecture series at the University of Manitoba, a program in which prominent individuals such as J.W. Dafoe were invited to speak on selected topics and students visited the CPR shops, the Children's Aid Society, the City Milk Depot, and the meetings of the Trades and Labour Council for their field-work. [73]

In 1918 Falk was 'drafted,' as he put it, by the American Red Cross to serve as chief of staff of the Rehabilitation Committee in Halifax after a shipload of munitions exploded in the harbour and destroyed a large section of the city. (Falk would later brag about how he carried out the task; confined to bed by phlebitis, he used his bedroom as his office, and the adjoining room served as the headquarters for the rest of his staff.) When the Halifax operation was complete, he returned to Winnipeg and shortly thereafter received the invitation from J.A. Dale to become director of McGill's Department of Social Study and Training. [74]

Falk's philosophy of social welfare was an intricate amalgam of all the reform influences to which he had been exposed prior to his arrival in Montreal. His argument that public opinion had to be educated before reform was possible stemmed from his connection with the settlement movement and his familiarity with members of the Fabian Society; his insistence upon economy of effort and funding in social-work practice was obviously a product of his work with the Charity Organization Society, the Winnipeg Associated Charities, and the Red Cross. There was even an element of evangelicalism in his view that social workers should be imbued with 'religion' in its broadest sense. [75] Nevertheless, there was one overriding conviction that shaped his social philosophy and his understanding of the purposes of social work – the belief that industrial society required all of its members to be productive. The notion, which may have initially come from his industrialist father, blended well with western progressivism, and if it was not a product of the national-efficiency movement, it was certainly strengthened by the popularity of that ideology in the aftermath of the war. Moreover, it accorded perfectly with the educational philosophy and objectives of McGill University in the years following the war.

Just after his arrival in Montreal, Falk explained the necessity for a department of social service. His line of argument was identical to the one put forward by the advocates of national efficiency in Britain during the First World War. The war had shattered certain assumptions in the mother country, Falk wrote, by placing an enormous demand on manpower for four years: it revealed that the manpower of the country had been severely weakened by deplorable social conditions. 'You can't have an A-1 nation with a C-3 population,' he said, quoting Lloyd George. 'We in the Dominion must squarely face this fact.' Canada did not have the same social problems, he conceded, because its virility had not been sapped by three hundred years of the English Poor Law and the demoralizing effects of the Industrial Revolution. Nevertheless, it still had some of the worst elements of British society in its social fabric – high infant mortality, child labour, commercialized vice, bad housing, and corruption in public office. The time had come to eliminate these social ills, Falk argued, because of the financial burden they were beginning to cause. History had demonstrated, however, he continued, that the task was too difficult for private individuals or groups to accomplish from a financial point of view, and the introduction of public effort did not improve the quality of work done. One need only look at the example of England, he insisted, to see that this was so: it spent an excessive amount on public assistance in the form of state insurance and education. The key to the solution, he believed, lay with the social-welfare agencies. 'Social agencies,' he explained, 'deal with the C-3 part of the population and their success depends upon their ability to raise people from the C-3 class to a higher plane.' But in order to be successful, social agencies had to have properly trained personnel. In the last five years, Falk concluded, English-speaking countries had realized that their efforts to alleviate social problems were often fruitless 'owing to the inexperience and lack of general and special education of those engaged in social work.'[76]

Falk also saw another effect of the war, and it infused his otherwise severe views with a certain idealism. The war had forced men and women of different classes into contact with each other on the battlefield, he said, and opened their eyes to the way the other half lived. That spirit of co-operation gave rise to dreams of a future in which class strife could be eliminated. Nevertheless, like many people of his generation, he believed that the only way in which that new society would come into being was through economic productivity and human efficiency. The wealth and prosperity of the Dominion, he contended, depended upon two things more than anything else – increased production and the right relations between capital and labour. (His argument was similar to that of William Lyon Mackenzie King, who argued in *Industry and Humanity* [1918] that economic growth and a wider distribution of wealth and goods would mitigate the potential for class conflict.)[77]

Because Falk placed such faith in economic productivity, he could not help but see the impoverished, the handicapped, the sick, and the imprisoned as anything other than parasites. 'We are apt to overlook the fact,' he said, 'that every person in poverty, hospital or gaol is not only a consumer but also a non-producer,' and as such 'a direct loss to the nation.' He did not think that the blame for the 'maladjustment' of such individuals could be placed upon a particular person, group, industry, community, or social phenomenon. If it could, he argued, then that particular industry or community could be made to bear the financial burden of caring for its victims and in the future would avoid producing these 'expensive parasites.' He simply wanted it remembered that the rest of society was compelled to expend vast sums of money paying for the people who attended the wants of these consumers and who, in turn, were non-producers themselves.[78] Unfortunately, human society did not function in the same way as industry. Industry, Falk once explained, was very careful in the selection of its machinery, and when it was worn out and ceased to be productive, sold it as scrap, and the raw material was re-created into productive machinery. The scrapped machinery of the industrial world cost nothing for further maintenance, but human machinery could not be scrapped so long as it lived, Falk argued. Society demanded that it be kept in working order – fed, clothed, and housed, though it might produce nothing for the rest of its life:

A licentious man co-habits for a single night with a feeble-minded woman who has slipped past the lax medical inspection at the point of entry, and an imbecile child is born. For forty years or more that human machine is a direct charge on the productivity of industry. In a drunken fury, a man kills a chance acquaintance, and society gives him life imprisonment in gaol where he produces nothing. An ignorant mother is confined by an untrained midwife and her child is blind for life because of the lack of simplest precautions at birth; and industry pays out of its productiveness for the care of this child in an institution for twenty years, and then gives it a license permitting it to shake a tin can in your face every time you pass it in the street.[79]

This view of the need for productivity highly influenced Falk's ideas about the role of social workers. He thought they could facilitate economic productivity by restoring the maladjusted to productive states and by bringing capital and labour together. He made it clear, however, that he was not forwarding this argument simply in the interests of social justice but for the material prosperity of the nation. In fact, he even suggested that the two objectives were not mutually exclusive. 'There is no real conflict between the action demanded by humanity in the name of Justice and the action demanded by industry in the name of efficiency, but the recogntion will only come with a change in the hearts of men.' And who was in a position to bring about a change in the hearts of men? According to Falk, it was the social worker, because he was in a strategic position to be the interpreter between class and class. 'He (one should almost write she, for there are few men in social work) has nothing to lose by telling the truth. Capital and management will praise and reward him if he can prove to industry that anti-social conditions are costly to industry. The wage-earner for the most part despises the social worker today for not telling the truth, and will welcome the day when the social worker shows signs of living up to his oft-vaunted motto, "prevention rather than cure." '[80]

Falk's beliefs about the benefits of economic productivity provided the broad outlines for his ideas about the purpose of social work, but he also had to set out a philosophy for social-work training, and it was similar to those of many other social-work directors in the early twentieth century. Falk was, first of all, a strong advocate of professionalization; he hoped that college-trained workers would eventually drive out the volunteers who were holding back the status of the profession. While he acknowledged that the task of alleviating poverty could most successfully be undertaken by someone who could bring to bear upon the maladjusted 'courage, hope, ambition, perseverance, cleanliness, honesty, faith in humanity, and belief in the coming of the Kingdom of Heaven upon earth,' he nevertheless argued that there was a limit to the amount of 'personality' that any one social worker could give to another individual. It was more important, he argued, to add to the number of fully trained professionals in the field because their number was 'totally inadequate for the work to be done.' In that respect he was critical of the paltry number of professional social workers in Canada and of the attitude that Canadians seemed to bear against the few that did exist. Able young men were staying out of the field, he claimed, because social workers were ridiculed if they worked for money. 'No one wants to be criticized for working because there is a salary check at the end of each month,' Falk proclaimed. He recalled the cold shiver he experienced when a newspaper published an article on his salary, divided it up into so much per month, day, and hour, and finally insinuated that he was robbing the poor of the very clothes they were wearing on their backs in accepting it.[81]

In order to qualify as a professional social worker, Falk believed, an individual had to be trained not only in the methods of treating poverty but in research and knowledge of other disciplines. 'The word philanthropy means nothing,' he said, 'if it does not imply that our philanthropic activities represent our love of our fellow man; there can be no love where there is no knowledge.' Accordingly, he believed that a social-work program should be composed of two elements, one that dealt with the more or less theoretical study of casework and the other that consisted of practical field-work. In the former, students would be taught about diagnosis and after-care (which would require some background in physiology, psychology, history, and economics), as well as social legislation, methods of research, statistics, and the techniques of organization and administration. The latter would require them to work under the supervision of trained and experienced workers in order to acquire knowledge of the social resources of a community. Since Falk also believed that it was necessary for social workers to influence public opinion, he suggested that McGill's program include a public-speaking course.[82]

Following Falk's advice, students enrolled in McGill's Department of Social Study and Training took a wide range of courses. The one he instructed, on the treatment of poverty, taught them the techniques of casework as well as encouraging them to make use of the Confidential Exchange, with its list of applicants seeking charity in Montreal. In a course on community development taught by James Dale, students examined such issues as the churches' role in social life, recreation, leisure, the rural community, the univesity settlement, and social surveys. Caldwell continued to offer his course in the principles of sociology; optional courses covered such topics as crime and delinquency, the social aspects of disease, laws affecting social workers, child-welfare problems, statistical research and surveys, business principles in social work, the economic theory of social reform, industrial and social history, social philosophy, the principles of biology, public health and housing, neuropsychiatry, and the elements of political economy (taught by Stephen Leacock) and elementary psychology (taught by William Tait).[83]

As far as the provision for accommodating the theological colleges was concerned, Falk suggested that their students be required to give one hour weekly in each of their three years to social work. He suggested that in their first year they take a course that would give them a comprehensive view of the social problems of the community and introduce them to the social agencies of the city. In the second year, he thought, they should take his course in the treatment of poverty. The course was necessary because no congregation could absolve itself from caring for the poor. Without the proper guidance from the minister of the church, he said, based upon his ten years of experience, much relief work could be done but with the worst results. Finally, he suggested that in the third year theology students take two half-courses, one in community development and the other either in the social aspects of disease, crime, and delinquency or in the study of laws affecting social workers. (Ultimately, what they did take was Caldwell's course and 'Social Research in the City' in their first year; second-year students were compelled to take a course in social service, an elective course in social research, and a half-course in rural sociology; third-year students were assigned to do work in economics, rural economics, and social research.)[84]

Directing the Department of Social Service was not Falk's only task. It had been the intention of Montreal's anglophone charity leaders to have McGill serve as the co-ordinating centre for the city's social-welfare efforts, and in that regard Falk was instructed by J.A. Dale that he would have to become acquainted with and do a report on Montreal's social agenies.[85] Because of the personal contacts he had made with Montreal's social-work leaders prior to his arrival in the city, it was not long before Falk was invited to take part in the survey of non-sectarian social agencies in Montreal that was being undertaken by the Montreal Charity Organization Society. That report eventually led to the creation of the Montreal Council of Social Agencies and to Falk's departure from McGill.

The stimulus to the development of the Montreal Council of Social Agencies came partly from the Charity Organization Society, but it was also a response to a suggestion on the part of the Social Service Council of Canada. By 1918 the organization was at the peak of its influence. Complete with full-time employees and its own journal, *Social Welfare*, it proclaimed itself ready to solve the economic, moral, and political problems of Canada. Moreover, it was determined to give specific attention to social welfare: it stood for the ultimate abolition of poverty, lobbied for mothers' pensions, care of defectives, dependents, and delinquents, proper housing and health measures, a system of social insurance against accidents, sickness, employment, and old age, the prevention of crime, and the redemption of criminals. It also encouraged the application of scientific means to the discovery and solution of social-welfare problems and to community organization and decision-making.[86]

Reflecting these new interests, the Social Service Council formed a Quebec branch in the autumn of 1918. A little later it was suggested by J.G. Shearer, the head of the national council, that a separate branch of the provincial organization be established in Montreal to deal specifically with social-service work. A preliminary conference was held to discuss the proposal, but the social workers in attendance pointed out that a major problem stood in the way of its realization. In other provinces and cities where religious and racial lines were less marked than in Montreal, such councils had been organized on non-sectarian lines (though nowhere had they been able to involve the Roman Catholic Church). The Montreal social workers believed that the only way in which a body for co-operative action could operate in their city (and attract the Roman Catholic as well as the Jewish social-welfare agencies) was for it to be independent of both the national and the provincial wings of the Social Service Council. Accordingly, in January 1919 representatives from twenty-five of the city's charitable agencies met to discuss the possibility of forming a Montreal Council of Social Agencies, and in March they decided to undertake a survey to determine what the scope of its work should be. They also engaged the services of Howard Falk as secretary of the survey.[87]

After his survey of eighty non-sectarian social-welfare agencies in Montreal, Falk recommended that a Council of Social Agencies should be organized to carry out surveys and do research work in the city, conduct a social-service directory, and hold an annual social-work conference for the city of Montreal and the province of Quebec. He did not, however, recommend co-operation with the francophone community, partly because he did not think that it would be possible to get several hundred agencies to work together. Records of his discussions with francophone welfare leaders on this issue are non-existent, but there are hints at other problems contained in some of his remarks in the report. He thought it appalling that Montreal had only one 'outdoor' non-sectarian agency – the Charity Organization Society. In no other city in Canada, he claimed, did such an immense proportion of the burden of caring for the poor in their own houses fall upon a private agency: 'It is a case of the municipality refusing to accept its proper responsibility.' Though he contended that he had no desire to emphasize racial or religious distinctions, he suggested that, because of language differences, it was necessary to form three separate councils in

Montreal – one Roman Catholic, one Jewish, and one non-sectarian. He recommended that each group appoint five delegates to a central standing committee on co-operation, whose sole function would be to secure simultaneous action in dealing with any social agency. He thought that the Montreal Council of Social Agencies should otherwise make no attempt to care for French-speaking dependent families, that rather they should remain the responsibility of the parish church. At the same time he believed that the Catholic Social Guild (which dealt with English-speaking Catholics) should join hands with the Montreal Council of Social Agencies, so that there would be one agency to deal with each major division in Montreal.[88]

Falk's report was not well received. While *Social Welfare* agreed that his specific recommendations deserved a fair chance, they complained that the report was full of destructive criticism.[89] In fact, Falk himself confessed to a social worker to whom he had shown the manuscript that he expected its publication to sign his death-warrant among people in the city who were interested in social work. Though somewhat harsh, Falk's criticisms of social-work practices in Montreal stemmed from his philosophy of social work. He chastized social workers for taking curative rather than preventative measures in dealing with the city's social diseases. He did not accept as an excuse that they were hampered in their attempts to co-ordinate their efforts by religious divisions – the English agencies could at least have co-operated among themselves, he argued. Neither did he think they were right to blame their inadequacies on the businessmen who controlled the agencies. He said that he could not estimate the degree to which social workers in the city were influenced in their daily tasks by the example of the life of Jesus but could not help remarking 'that there was little evidence to show that any large number had constantly in mind the fact that Jesus not only healed the sick and helped the poor, but also denounced the Scribes and the Pharisees and forcibly drove the money changers from the House of God.'[90]

Falk was at his most venomous when dealing with the members of Montreal's upper middle class who became involved in charity work only for the purposes of social climbing. First of all, he was critical that social-welfare agencies chose as members of their managing boards people with 'money-attracting power,' to whom such a position was but a step up the society ladder. Because they were only interested in fund-raising, such people rarely attended meetings, or else they held them without informing the chief executive. This was because they considered the social worker to be 'inferior,' fit only to carry out instructions but not to be consulted. (That attitude grew out of an old custom, Falk explained, in which social workers and domestic servants were graded together on the social scale.) Usually, however, businessmen left charity work to their wives, who, like their husbands, Falk complained, had no idea about the specific economic and social conditions that necessitated the existence of their institution and read very little in the way of history. They merely organized tag days, bazaars, balls, and cabarets to raise money for their favourite charities.[91]

Falk's impatience with the social pretensions of the upper middle class and their apathetic civic conscience grew worse as time went on. Incensed by a speech that Governor-General Lord Byng gave in Toronto in December 1921, during which he praised Canada for its lack of slums, Falk suggested to Arthur Currie that he invite Byng to Montreal. If Byng agreed to make the visit, then he should be taken to see some of the city's slums, Falk added, 'slums which an apathetic civic conscience has permitted to come into existence ... Since Earl Grey,' he continued, 'we have not had a governor general who seemed to care about the Dominion's social welfare.' Falk thought the Byngs showed potential but needed their eyes opened to reality.[92] Currie followed Falk's suggestion and invited Byng to take a tour of the city with Falk as a guide. He added that while he found no fault with the city's well-to-do giving money to charity, more than that was necessary: 'There must be real concern regarding conditions of living, housing, child welfare, the unmarried mother, etc., and before we can get that concern there must be knowledge. A great many women are interested in these things and there is much good work done, but we want the interest of the men as well.'[93]

After Byng accepted Currie's invitation and went on Falk's tour, Montreal's social-welfare leaders found the leadership they had been seeking. When Byng spoke at the Women's Canadian Club of Montreal, he admitted that he had been upset by what he had seen on the tour and had been searching his soul about it ever since. While he conceded that Montrealers were right to be proud of their city, he also told them that everything was not right in 'the best of all cities.' 'You have some slums in Montreal and I am not sure Montreal ought to have slums. We in the old country have them ... much worse then you have; but they are very old and deep-seated, and we do not see daylight for getting rid of them. But in Montreal you have some new slums. Why do you have new slums?' Moreover, he reported with shock, some of those slums were nothing more than converted stables, where manure smells arose through the flooring. He also commented on Montreal's shameful infant-mortality rate and its lack of care for children of less privileged backgrounds, especially the absence of playgrounds in which such children could play: 'You have the most glorious playground for children up the hill; but you don't take them there until they are dead; then you take them to the most lovely cemetery I have ever seen. I am not quite certain that some of the children in the murky atmosphere between St. Catherine Street and the River do not sometimes look up there at that happy Utopia, knowing that they will not go there until they are dead.'[94]

Falk won a minor victory with Byng, and his recommendation for the formation of a Montreal Council of Social Agencies was followed; but his days at McGill were numbered in any event. In October 1920 Falk was hired to direct the Montreal Council of Social Agencies. It had been difficult for the executive council of that organization to find the right person for the job – they sought a Canadian or British-born individual who lived in Montreal, knew its problems well, and had an instinct for administrative social work.[95] Falk obviously filled the bill, and an arrangement was worked out whereby he would spend half his time with the council and half at McGill. The university's officials did not object to the scheme, especially since Currie assured them that Falk's new job, rather than interfere with his work at McGill, would strengthen it, since he would be coming into daily contact with the city's social problems. Moreover, the Montreal Council of Social Agencies agreed to pay Falk a salary of two thousand dollars (representing half of what he got from McGill), and this relieved the university of having to pay him a full salary at time when there were already grumblings about what the social-work program was costing the institution.[96] Once in a position of power, Falk set out to implement the recommendations of his report and immediately found himself under attack. 'While it has been said before that communities waste too much through the uneconomical distribution of funds for philanthropic purposes and multiplication of effort,' *Social Welfare* reported, 'to come out openly and tell the community that a muddle-headed conception of its social needs and a fumble-fingered handling of relief grants, however inspired the spirit stimulating to action, is "poor business" and constitutes a failure in social treatment – this is a different programme of action, but that is just what Mr. J. Howard T. Falk of McGill University has had the audacity to tell the people of Montreal.' *Social Welfare* thought Falk's recommendations were admirable but warned that any intention on his part to implement them 'would be fraught with toil and turmoil, with the clipping of claws and the dropping of heads in more quarters than one.' There would be no peace and harmony attendant upon the new regime, the magazine added. Indeed, there were instant criticisms, the most significant of which came from the representatives of

Montreal's religious bodies, who attacked the Montreal Council of Social Agencies as 'lacking in Christian principles, in its constitution, and plan of co-operation.'[97]

These criticisms could not have come at a more inopportune time as far as Falk's future at McGill was concerned. He had taken on the position of director of the Montreal Council of Social Agencies just as the three-year trial period for the Department of Social Study and Training was ending and the structure of the program was under reassessment. Whether the criticisms that the theological colleges expressed against it had anything to do with Falk and his new position is not absolutely certain but seems likely. In February 1921 representatives from the theological colleges held two conferences with university authorities in regard to the program and clarified what they expected. They wanted their students to be instructed in three courses in the Department of Social Study and Training. The one for first-year students was to be 'The Principles of Sociology,' or social ethics, taught by William Caldwell. The objective of the course, they insisted, was 'to prepare men for the Ministry to understand the great social problems of the day and to give them a good idea of Social Ethics and Social Philosophy.' They wished it to be kept in mind that the men were being trained primarily for the Christian ministry 'and not merely as Social Workers or Directors of Social Service.'[98] For the second-year students they wanted W.D. Tait, a psychologist with conservative views, to direct a course in the study of the city's problems. Finally, they made it clear that their third-year students were to take a course on rural sociology, where they would learn about the problems of rural communities and perhaps come to regard such work as a permanent ministry rather than as a stepping-stone to larger urban centres. The Joint Board of the theological colleges recommended that Reverend Gordon Dickie of the Quebec Social Service Council be invited to give that course and that he be paid five hundred dollars for his work – the amount was to be deducted, they insisted, from their contribution to the department.[99] By such means, the theological colleges removed their students from Falk's influence and strengthened their ties with the Social Service Council.

Not only did the university assent to the theological colleges' specific demands, but one month following the meetings Currie informed James Smyth, dean of the Joint Board of the theological colleges, that the university intended to arrange for some well-known educational authority to replace Falk as director of the Department of Social Study and Training. The department was expected to grow rapidly in importance, Currie said, and Falk would not have time to supervise it because of his work with the

Montreal Council of Social Agencies.[100] (This was a seeming contradiction of the promise that Currie had earlier made to the Board of Governors.) He also admitted that the program was proving to be a problem for the university: it was not giving the theological colleges all they desired and was being maintained at a serious net loss to the university. As of September 1920 the net cost to the university of carrying on the department for one academic session was fifteen hundred dollars. But if the arrangement with Falk continued, Currie predicted, the cost would increase somewhat. Moreover, since the grant from the Graduates' Society was to expire at the end of the three-year period, McGill would incur even greater expenditures.[101] (The 'expense' of the Department of Social Study and Training was a constant source of complaint for the university's officials. When the Board of Governors decided to close the school down in 1931, they recalled that it had shown a deficit from the second year of its existence. The problem was partly related to the state of the economy: Falk complained in 1920 that the financial depression was retarding the development of social work and predicted that once the country recovered from it, the department would attract a greater number of full-time students and an increasing demand for their services. The university, however, willingly tolerated other deficits during the early 1920s: McGill managed to expand and progress during that period, Currie once admitted, because the Board of Governors sanctioned deficits. Starting from $4000 in 1923, those deficits mounted steadily until they reached $338,000 for the year ending 31 May 1931. Nevertheless, the university was never in debt; it simply had to sell securities to cover the deficits, but the Board of Governors did not like 'to suffer each year a lowering of [their] income-earning power.')[102]

Although the grant from the theological colleges allowed McGill's Department of Social Study and Training to come into being, it also tied its fate in with the Protestant churches' interest in social work. The Protestant churches became increasingly worried that their leadership in the field was being usurped by secular organizations and that perhaps they were even losing their own students to secular social work. With hindsight we know that they had something to fear: in the second half of the 1920s the influence of the Social Service Council declined, 'compromised by the emerging tensions between religious and secular social work.'[103]

Once the three-year trial period for the Department of Social Study and Training ended, Sir Arthur Currie appointed a special committee to consider its future.[104] Falk in the meantime was allowed to stay on as director for another year, but as the committee began to deliberate, he may have sensed that he was being eased out. The committee, whose members included William Caldwell, Stephen Leacock, and two representatives from the theological colleges, were faced with these factors: university authorities were not willing to support the program in social work for financial reasons; social workers in the city, however, considered it a tragedy for the university to abandon it. When word got out that the university intended to reorganize the department, perhaps even shut it down, Currie received a spate of letters in protest, all of them pointing out that the city desperately needed trained social workers.[105] The theological colleges did not wish to see the department entirely dismantled since they believed that some knowledge of 'social science' was essential to the Christian minister, but they did want the program revised, not simply for the sake of their own students but for others seeking training in social science. Finally a new arrangement was mooted, one that Stephen Leacock played a large role in formulating. It was suggested that the university appoint an assistant professor of social science (either as head of a new department of sociology in the Faculty of Arts or as an associate professor in the Department of Economics); the appointee would also serve as director of the Social Study and Training Department. It was also recommended that the university establish in the Faculty of Arts a certain number of courses leading to a BA in social science and that those courses deal with such subjects as social economics, industrial and social legislation, poverty, social pathology, immigration (including ethnology and land settlement), and urban and rural problems. It was hoped that this new course of study would meet the needs of undergraduates intending to enter the ministry as well as some other fields of public or social work, but it was also suggested that Arts students be permitted to elect courses in sociology, with the purpose of taking their BA in the field, or after two years be allowed to do work in the Department of Social Study and Training, with the possibility of getting a BA in that field.[106]

Upon hearing the committee's new scheme, Falk was irate. He objected to the idea of hiring a theoretical sociologist when there was such a great need for practical training in social work.[107] On 20 February 1922 he submitted his resignation at a meeting of the Committee of Management; at the same meeting Leacock more fully elaborated on how the social-work program could be saved through the establishment of a department of sociology. Behind Leacock's scheme was more than just administrative manoeuvring. A new direction in social research was emerging, and in the ruins of the social-work program the Faculty of Arts had the opportunity to implement it. Leacock explained why there had been no sociology courses in the Faculty of Arts previously: the staff was limited in numbers and the subjects offered seemed to meet the students' needs; it was also in dire financial straits and could not afford the additional expense. By the academic session of 1921–2, however, all that was changing. The numbers of students had increased; the university's finances were more secure. Now it was time, Leacock suggested 'to deal with the pressing nature of every social problem' that the war and its aftermath had brought to light. 'There is a great need,' he insisted, 'for the application of intensive study and trained intelligence in the urgent social questions of the moment, and an open field for the kind of effort only a university can undertake.' While a beginning had been made with the establishment of a department of social service, Leacock continued, its scope was too restricted; it formed no part of the essential curriculum of any faculty and offered no course leading to a college degree.[108]

Despite the attempt made by the committee to placate all those who had been involved in the original social-service department, the new recommendations met with the objection of social workers in Montreal. Helen Reid insisted that they were being made from the point of view of the Faculty of Arts and did not take into consideration the community's need for trained social workers. The new program was being instituted at the expense of social work, she charged, and that was an unwise and retrograde step 'in these days of strained and rapid social adjustment in industry, commerce, and society ...' Throughout Canada and the United States, she continued, increasing recognition was being given to the need for social workers. One such program had just been instituted at the University of Western Ontario in London. 'Is McGill going to drop out of the world group of universities which is giving training to social workers, and by so doing admit her incapacity or unwillingness to give this training?'[109]

Despite these and similar protestations the committee's recommendations were accepted, and the search for a sociologist began. Among the numerous letters sent out was one seeking the advice of Albion Small, then professor and head of the Department of Sociology at the University of Chicago, on an appropriate candidate. McGill had received a letter from a C.A Dawson, then working at the YMCA in Chicago, who expressed interest in the new position, although he had offers from a number of American universities, because he wished to work in his native country. Dawson had actually received his degree in divinity from the University of Chicago but had worked closely with E.W. Burgess, Ellsworth Faris, and Robert Park. Small and Burgess gave him the highest of commendations, and Ellsworth Faris indicated that among one hundred students at Chicago, Dawson ranked third or fourth.[110] McGill had found their sociologist. On 8 May 1922 Dawson was conditionally hired as assistant professor of Social Science and director of Social Study and Training at McGill for a period of three years.[111] Details of courses were worked out, and then panic struck. Two representatives from the theological colleges, Ernest M. Best and Gordon Laing, had heard stories about a Dawson who worked for the Chicago YMCA, misappropriated some funds, and ran off with another man's wife. Was this the man the university had appointed? An investigation was carried out and it was discovered that the man in question was not C.A. Dawson but, ironically, J.W. Dawson.[112] His slate clean, Dawson was officially appointed by the Corporation in August.

Dawson's arrival at McGill has been seen as portending the end for social work at that institution, the first step in a process that culminated in the closing of the school in 1931.[113] The interpretation is not entirely correct: social workers who trained under Dawson frequently commented that he gave them a sense of being involved in an emerging profession. Indeed, Dawson was instrumental in establishing the Canadian Conference on Social Work and the Canadian Association of Social Workers. Moreover, when McGill closed the Department of Social Service in 1931 and forced it to operate independently, Dawson remained on its board of directors until it reintegrated with the university in 1945. The difference between Dawson's approach and that of Falk was that Dawson emphasized the primacy of research in gaining an understanding of Canadian social conditions and institutions. His convictions partly stemmed from his sense of Canadian nationalism, but they were also a hallmark of the Chicago school of sociology.

McGill's Department of Social Study and Training was established during what proved to be a difficult period for the university. In the years immediately following the First World War McGill had to recover from the stresses and strains of the wartime experience: it was compelled not just to recoup its financial losses but to build an educational philosophy that would enable it to play as visible and as useful a public role during peacetime as it had done throughout the war. The Department of Social Study and Training fit in well with the emphasis on service, action, and efficiency that dominated the university in the early 1920s, but because funds were lacking, it was vulnerable to the demands of benefactors. As economic conditions began to improve in 1922 and memories of the war receded a little, greater emphasis was placed upon research, rather than immediate action, as the key to solving social problems.

3

Carl Dawson and the Chicago School

In appointing C.A Dawson to succeed Howard Falk, the individuals involved in reorganizing McGill's Department of Social Service made a better choice than they may have realized. Dawson was selected for the position because of his academic credentials and training as a sociologist, but by virtue of his background and intellectual convictions he was ideally suited for solving the conflict over practice and theory that had almost destroyed the social work program. Prior to his arrival at McGill Dawson had been a minister and, while a student at the University of Chicago, a specialist in practical theology. At some point after the First World War he lost interest in the religious vocation, but he nevertheless retained a belief that some members of Montreal's theological colleges shared. When Dawson presented his ideas regarding Christian service to the Alumni Conference of the Presbyterian College of Montreal in October 1922, he was enthusiastically received. He asked the audience on that occasion to remember that they were just as much members of a city as they were of a church. 'Though we know that evil cannot ultimately prevail over the righteous,' he proclaimed, 'yet it is true that vice can vitiate the virtuous. It is our task not only to redeem man but to redeem the forces that will help men realize the best ends of life.'[1] While Dawson may have appeared to be invoking the social gospel, he was actually advocating something more subtle than that. He did not think that social reform was the most effective means for improving social conditions; it was his belief that social research – the extensive investigation of urban and rural communities and their institutions – would provide men and women with the insight to create a better society.[2]

Dawson's conception of social research had the potential for attaining widespread support at McGill. In its inherent antipathy towards action it accorded with the views of those who had criticized the practical emphasis that characterized the social work program under Falk's direction. There was also an element of the efficiency ethos in it, and it was in that respect compatible with the attempts of social workers to encourage productivity and thereby eliminate the necessity for reform. Shortly after his arrival at McGill, Dawson reiterated the complaint that Montreal social workers had been making for some years regarding the expense of reform, and he held out the promise that research would ultimately make such measures unnecessary. 'Reform and cure are costly,' he said. 'I wish we could develop such scientific understanding of life that it could be controlled and directed according to standards and ideals making [them] unnecessary. A resolute, patient, and extensive search for concrete and definite facts about Canadian communities is a fundamental need.'[3]

Dawson's conception of social research and his faith in its results may have accorded with the philosophy of science and efficiency that had attained such popularity at McGill in the aftermath of the First World War, but there was at that time little understanding in Canada of what social research entailed. Dawson was well aware of the problem: he complained that even those people who supported the idea of social research tended to confuse it with 'practical programmes for doing good.' The social surveys and studies of crime, vice, and delinquency with which Canadians had some familiarity, he noted, lacked depth, focused too much on the pathological, and were too closely connected with reform causes to constitute an 'objective and scientific quest for facts.' While he conceded that all research must eventually serve some useful purpose, he insisted that it could only be effective if it were carried out in detachment from practical ends. Work in the natural sciences, he asserted, demonstrated the value of research pursued for its own sake.[4]

Dawson spent much of his early years at McGill explaining what social research was, shifting the work in social service in that direction, and destroying the widely held assumption that sociology was a reformist discipline. He was in this respect more than the founder of modern sociology at McGill; he was rather one of a handful of Canadian academics who in the 1920s laid the foundation for the kind of investigation not taken seriously in Canada until the Great Depression, when governments turned to institutions of higher learning for assistance in dealing with the economic and social crisis.[5] Unlike those academics who became members of the League for Social Reconstruction, however, Dawson opposed political activism even then, still adhering to the belief that solutions would emerge out of detached research and investigation. His ideas were rooted in his education, his early career in the ministry, and his years at the University of Chicago. An examination of those aspects of his life provides some insight into the origins of social science in Canada.

I

Carl Addington Dawson was born in 1887 in Augustine Cove, Prince Edward Island, then a small farming community consisting of about fifteen families. He was raised in a strongly religious home – his parents were devout Baptists, and his great-grandfather, a Scotsman who had settled in Prince Edward Island in 1803, had been the first Methodist minister in the British North American colony.[6] Dawson's decision to enter the ministry was not an immediate one. After attending Prince of Wales College and Normal School in Charlottetown, he taught for three years.[7] He then enrolled in a Bachelor of Arts program at Acadia College in Wolfville, Nova Scotia, where he took a few courses useful for a prospective minister – Bible study, which was compulsory for all first-year and sophomore students at that institution, sacred oratory, and theology.[8] (Why Dawson chose not to pursue a BD at Acadia is unclear. Part of the reason might have been that the Faculty of Theology offered an irregular course for the certificate: by the early 1920s it had reportedly granted the divinity degree to no more than a dozen students.[9]) Nevertheless, upon his graduation in 1912 Dawson was sufficiently qualified for the ministry to serve as pastor of a Baptist church in Lockeport, Nova Scotia. He remained there only until 1914, when he decided to pursue his theological education further at the Divinity School of the University of Chicago.[10]

Once in Chicago Dawson did not devote all his time to academic pursuits. The university operated on a four-quarter system, enabling mature students to take their degrees part-time,[11] and from 1915 to 1917 Dawson was an assistant pastor at Englewood Baptist Church. In 1918 he recessed from graduate studies for war service, and as a member of the Canadian contingent of the YMCA Transatlantic Staff was in charge of organizing shipboard activities of an educational and recreational nature for the Europe-bound troops, as well as helping to transport some of the men back to Canada when the war was over. It was a job that entailed twelve crossings of the Atlantic.[12] Dawson resumed his studies at the University of Chicago in 1919, but by then it was clear that his interests had veered sharply towards sociology. Chicago's strongly service-minded Divinity School was, for reasons to be discussed below, closely tied to the Department of Sociology. Divinity students were permitted not only to enrol in an array of courses offered by that department but to take sociology as an elective for the BD and as the major subject of the PH D.[13] Dawson followed that option, and completed his BD in 1921 and PH D in 1922, both with concentration in sociology.[14] Furthermore, while appointed a Fellow in Practical Theology for the academic session 1920–1, he chose to work as a teaching assistant in the Department of Sociology and then as head of the Sociology Department at Chicago's YMCA College.[15] By the time he arrived at McGill, he no longer considered himself a minister, though he would always feel that his background had been valuable for his career as a sociologist.[16] That conviction underlay the particular kind of interest he took in the theology students under his supervision at McGill. One of them has recalled that in his early years as a minister, and later when he was posted in Rosemount – an area of Montreal badly affected by the Depression – Dawson would frequently visit, and always inquire in his kindly fashion, 'What have you discovered of Sociological Interest in your work as a Minister? Come in and tell us about it.'[17]

In explaining the reasons for Dawson's decision to turn from the ministry to sociology, it would seem logical to point to the factors in his background that were similar to those of many of the pioneering American sociologists. Like Dawson, many of the advocates of the new discipline – Albion Small, Franklin Giddings, Charles Henderson, to name a few – came from rural, pious homes. Witnessing in the growing American cities of the late nineteenth century a social disintegration that conflicted with the values with which they had been raised, they turned their attention to the study of society. Some championed reform or, wishing to build a sense of community in the urban settings, analysed social institutions with the intention of finding substitutes for those that had given rural society its cohesiveness.[18] Dawson's rural upbringing left a similarly strong imprint on his pursuits. All his life he was an avid gardener: in Chicago he kept a vegetable patch in the backyard of his Drexel Avenue home and grew pumpkins practically on the doorstep of the university. In Montreal he prided himself on having the largest garden in his Victoria Street neighbourhood. When not away on field trips he spent the summers swimming and fishing and the winters skiing in the Laurentian Mountains with his family.[19] His academic interest in rural sociology and in the development of social institutions in marginal areas of settlement reflected his continuing concern with rural life. Then too, while he abandoned his commitment to the ministry, his advocacy of social research and the faith he placed in its results evinced an almost religious zeal. Anyone who knew Dawson at McGill marvelled at his tireless efforts to establish sociology as a scientific discipline, worthy of respect from the Canadian academic community. More than one of his former students has remarked that the atmosphere of the Sociology Department in the early days was almost militant because of Dawson's insistence upon research and investigation.[20] Dawson was 'like a man who had received the call to expound the doctrine of sociology,' S.D. Clark once commented. 'He never wavered, no matter how hostile the reception, in his assertion of the claims of sociology.' What bothered Clark, however, and turned him into a critic of his former supervisor was that Dawson followed, as Clark put it, the 'teachings' of the University of Chicago.[21]

It is true that Dawson's theories regarding Canadian society were derived from Chicago sociology. The ideas and teachers with which he came into contact at the University of Chicago were indisputably strong factors contributing to his decision to become a sociologist. Moreover, at the time he became involved with Chicago's Sociology Department, efforts to make it scientific were intense, and he took part in laying the groundwork for some of those approaches. While he never quite freed himself from the Chicago influence, it is not entirely correct to see the discipline he established as an American 'import.' McGill sociology grew out of traditions that differed from those that influenced the mainstream of Anglo-Canadian thought, but it was a Canadian product none the less. The circumstances that drew Dawson to Chicago, and to sociology, reveal that there are deeper connections between the University of Chicago and the development of at least one aspect of Canadian social science than have been recognized.

II

When Dawson departed for the United States in 1914, he was following a well-travelled route. The poor economic conditions that had always intermittently afflicted the Maritime provinces reached the peak of their intensity in the early twentieth century, and from 1910 to 1929 a steady stream of people left the region in search of better prospects to the south. During the same period the lack of doctoral-level programs in certain fields within Canadian universities compelled many students to attend graduate schools in the United States. Because of its strong reputation as a research centre, the University of Chicago was a popular choice for many of them, but the Divinity School was particularly attractive to those of the Baptist faith. The University of Chicago was formally a Baptist institution: it had been founded in 1892 by the American Baptist Education Society with the assistance of a large endowment from John D. Rockefeller. Although the Baptists did not exercise a great deal of control over the university once it opened – as soon as sufficient operating funds were secured, it was given financial autonomy; no religious tests were imposed on faculty and students, and the first president, William Rainey Harper, ensured that interference in the curriculum was minimized[22] – the Divinity School was a Baptist stronghold and remained so until the middle of the twentieth century. It was also an influential school, providing theological educators for many other Baptist seminaries. More significant in the context of this discussion is that it included a large number of Canadians. Four of them were Baptists, appointed to teaching positions after receiving their doctorates from the institution. They included Allan Hoben, a native of New Brunswick (who taught a sociology course on the rural church while Dawson was at Chicago); Shirley Jackson Case, another New Brunswicker who taught at the academy level in New Brunswick and New Hampshire before being appointed to Chicago; Archibald G. Baker, who was born in Ontario and educated at McMaster; and Charles T. Holman, who was born in England but did his preparatory collegiate work at McMaster. In addition to these men, several other Canadians who received their doctoral degrees from the University of Chicago taught at the Baptist-affiliated Rochester Theological Seminary and Crozer Theological Seminary.[23]

The strong representation of Canadians within Chicago's Divinity School reflected the institutional ties that linked Baptists in Canada and the northern United States: the University of Rochester and Rochester Theological Seminary were founded in 1850 with funds partly contributed by Baptists in Canada West; the first Baptist institution of higher learning in the United States, the College of Rhode Island (Brown University), was intended to serve members of the denomination on both sides of the border.[24] For cultural and historical reasons the bonds between Canadian and American Baptists were, however, strongest in the Maritimes. Many of the region's inhabitants were converted to the Baptist faith in the eighteenth- and nineteenth-century religious revivals that originated in the United States. Thereafter, the statements of faith adopted by the Maritime Baptist churches were based on American examples, and the educational institutions founded by members of the denomination in the nineteenth century were patterned on those in existence in the neighbouring American states – for example, Colby College in Maine, Albion Small's alma mater, provided the model for Acadia.[25]

This deep influence persisted for many years. In 1921 two investigators commissioned by the Carnegie Foundation for the Advancement of

Teaching to survey educational conditions in the Maritimes found that Acadia offered a better balance of instruction than all the other outlying institutions in the region, having separate chairs in economics, history, psychology, education, and social service.[26] They commented, as some ten years later did Robert Falconer, president of the University of Toronto, that it was in that respect highly influenced by American trends.[27] That Acadia had so strong an American character was understandable, given its origins. Most of the early settlers in western Nova Scotia came from Massachusetts and Connecticut and most were of the Baptist faith. Feeling themselves excluded from King's College in Windsor, which was founded on Church of England traditions, they petitioned for a charter to establish an institution of their own at Wolfville. In spite of strong opposition in the legislature they were successful, and opened Horton Academy, a preparatory school, in 1829 and Acadia nine years later. Throughout its history Acadia maintained close relations with institutions of higher learning in the United States, particularly with Yale, which was only a short distance from Yarmouth, and with Harvard, where many prospective faculty members were encouraged to study. Artemas Wyman Sawyer, a native of Vermont and graduate of Harvard who was president of the college from 1869 to 1893, implemented the American system of electives. His successor, Thomas Trotter, continued the practice of following American trends by introducing courses in scientific and practical subjects.[28] (An incident that occurred during Trotter's presidency, moreover, indicates that Acadia also had financial ties to the United States: in 1903 Trotter received a call to the pastorate in Dayton, Ohio, but before accepting the position consulted with John D. Rockefeller Jr and Sr and Frederick Gates, corresponding secretary of the American Baptist Education Society. Upon receiving a guarantee from them that Acadia would be the recipient of some funds, he decided to stay on as president.)[29]

Perhaps the strongest example of American influence at Acadia was the college's course offerings in the modern fields of political science and economic history. Throughout the 1890s, for instance, the course in economic history covered such topics as railroads, commerce, and bimetallism in the United States. (Bimetallism was dropped from the calendar description after 1898, however, obviously in response to the defeat of the populist cause.) Acadia also offered instruction in sociology at a somewhat earlier date than most Canadian universities. In 1898 lectures on sociology and the ethics of citizenship constituted the course in moral philosophy; required reading included *The Ethical Import of Darwin* (1888),[30] written by Jacob Gould Schurman, an Acadia graduate and political-science instructor who went on to become president of Cornell University. In 1900, however, sociology was offered as the honour course for seniors under the rubric of 'Economic Science' – significantly, the same name Albion Small attached to it when he first taught the subject at Colby College. It was taught by John Freeman Tufts, a professor of history who had been largely responsible for introducing the modern subjects at Acadia after returning from a year's study at Harvard in 1874. While still reflecting some of the traditional concerns of moral philosophy, the new course seemed to be more concerned with problems of a pressing nature: it examined social evolution, poverty, co-operation, socialist theory, and contemporary socialism.[31] During the years that Dawson attended Acadia, it was mandatory for senior students to take a half-course in both sociology and political economy. The subject-matter of those combined courses continued to reflect a concern for contemporary problems in that they dealt with such issues as social tendencies, conditions of human progress, the function of reason and religion in the evolution of society, Western civilization, modern socialism, labour organization, co-operation, profit-sharing, panics, and depression.[32]

Along with two other Baptist-affiliated institutions, Brandon and McMaster, Acadia was one of the first universities in Canada to include a form of sociology in its curriculum. It probably took its lead from the American Baptist colleges, for they were also among the first institutions in the United States to offer instruction in the field.[33] While sociology emerged in response to the problems created by urbanization and industrialization in the late nineteenth century, its rapid acceptance into the college curriculum between 1890 and 1920 stemmed from the demands that urban reformers, settlement-house workers, and social-gospel ministers placed upon institutions of higher learning to deal with those problems. Because of their large endowments, private institutions could initially afford to resist the pressure, but land-grant institutions and colleges affiliated with the Congregational, Baptist, Methodist Episcopal, and Presbyterian denominations acted quickly to introduce courses in social science, social welfare, and sociology.[34] Those denominations were the ones most influenced by the progressive religious ideas of the late nineteenth century, and the early institution of sociology in their colleges illustrates how closely the discipline was linked to the rise of the social gospel.

That many of the pioneering sociologists were ministers or sons of ministers is only a partial explanation of the relationship that existed in the United States between sociology and the social gospel. More important was the fact that both sociologists and social gospellers formulated similar solutions to the problems of the late nineteenth century. Social gospellers placed great store in the socially applicable utterances of the Old Testament prophets and in the teachings of Jesus. They also had an evolutionary view of history that included a belief in progress and in the immanence of God in the historical process. Like the early sociologists they believed that through the social sciences they would be able to understand their society and perhaps create an improved social order. Moreover, both groups assumed that because men and women were beings shaped by social forces and customs, social conditions could be ameliorated through rational plans.[35] Their faith in that regard stemmed from the popularity of certain collective theories during that period: some people pointed to Herbert Spencer's depiction of society as an organism governed by the law of the survival of the fittest to justify the existence of poverty, but for others there were such examples as Henry George's *Progress and Poverty* (1877), which employed the same organic and evolutionary concepts to argue in favour of social reform.[36] Struck by the scale of hardship created by urbanization and industrialization, some religious leaders were all the more convinced that sin was not so much a product of an individual's shortcomings as it was a condition forced upon that person by his or her position in society.[37] They accordingly emphasized the need for churches to shift their attention away from individual salvation towards the improvement of social conditions. In the realm of social action the majority of social gospellers advocated economic and social justice and the alleviation of distress in the cities, where the greatest hardships existed. Some of their efforts were channelled into the settlement movement, where social gospellers worked hand-in-hand with sociologists for basically the same ends: the first generation of American sociologists may have regarded themselves as theoreticians, but they were primarily interested in applying their findings in such a way as to ease the social crisis. This is why most sociology courses offered before the First World War emphasized social problems and pathology.

The link between the social gospel and sociology in Canada has been traced to some extent by A.B. McKillop in *A Disciplined Intelligence*. Focusing primarily on the Queen's tradition, he illustrates that the social gospel as formulated by George M. Grant, John Watson, George Blewett, and S.D. Chown laid the foundations for social service. The 'Queen's spirit' of the 1890s inspired numerous individuals – among them Adam Shortt and O.D. Skelton – to become civil servants; it also influenced the ideas of Salem Bland, though he was radicalized later by what he saw in Winnipeg. It is McKillop's basic contention, however, that the gospel of active social service as developed by Grant was directed towards a spiritual end – moral elevation – and that Chown similarly hoped that the establishment of a systematic sociology would usher in the perfect moral state.[38] This argument is part of McKillop's more general hypothesis about the nature of Canadian social theory – that it developed within the moral-philosophy tradition as derived from Great Britain and continued to reflect the influences of that tradition well into the twentieth century.

While McKillop's analysis has a certain validity with regard to the development of sociology, it is based entirely on an examination of the social gospel as advocated by Presbyterians and Methodists in central Canada and does not take into account ideas expressed by other denominations in different parts of the country. Unfortunately, no comprehensive treatment of the Baptists' involvement in the social gospel exists, and the extent of their social concern is minimized in the general literature on the subject,[39] but there is sufficient evidence to suggest that they, too, placed an increasing emphasis on the social gospel as a solution to the economic and social problems of the late nineteenth century, and yet adhered to a different conception of it. In his examination of the *Canadian Baptist*, the official journal of the denomination, for instance, John Moir has found that the Baptists displayed an awareness and sympathy for the social gospel as early as the 1880s but adopted a far more pragmatic and less idealistic view of it as an instrument for social reform, more like that of the Presbyterians than that of the Methodists. They thought of it as, and frequently called it, 'practical Christianity.' They talked about improving the social environment as a way of preventing the production of criminals; they advocated prison reform, sabbatarianism, prohibition, and justice to native Canadians; they also argued for inner-city missions, purity in politics, profit-sharing, protection for children, and women's rights.[40]

In an article on the prohibition movement in Nova Scotia, Ernest Forbes has demonstrated the strength of the social gospel in the Maritimes, another aspect of the social gospel in Canada that has been overlooked. He finds that the success of the prohibition movement in that region was attributable to the widespread acceptance of social-gospel ideas: prohibitionists in Nova Scotia, he argues, were primarily motivated by a desire to eliminate the roots of human unhappiness, to create a society in which crime, disease, and social injustice would no longer exist. As proof of that contention Forbes points to the fact that the Maritime Synod of the Presbyterian Church adopted the social gospel and prohibition simultaneously.[41] The Baptists similarly linked temperance and the social gospel: in 1903 the Temperance Committee of the Maritime Baptist Convention issued a report that viewed the temperance problem in social-gospel terms. '"Christ's mission," it stated, was both to "save souls" and "to save society." "Christ was the greatest social reformer that the world has ever seen."'[42] Forbes attributes the rise of the social gospel in the Maritime region to the economic and social dislocations of the Laurier era. While that argument has some merit, it is also clear that the social conscience of the Maritime Baptists was awakened by the contact of some of the younger ministers with exponents of the social gospel in American theological schools, as well as by the widely read writings of those same men. Walter Rauschenbusch of the Rochester Theological Seminary was perhaps the most important of those individuals, but others included George Burman Foster, who taught at Acadia before going to Chicago, Washington Gladden, Franklin Giddings, and Albion Small.[43]

The argument could be made that with respect to their educational and religious ideas, the Maritime Baptists – and the Baptists of northern North America more generally – developed an intellectual tradition that differed from the one McKillop has traced, and it was that legacy that Dawson's brand of sociology reflected. He was a minister in the Maritimes at the height of its economic and social difficulties and at a time when interest in the social gospel was at its peak. It made a certain amount of sense for him to go to the University of Chicago: as his involvement in the YMCA and his appointment as a fellow in practical theology indicates, he was interested in 'practical Christianity,' and Chicago was noted for its work in that area. It was also a prominent institution, and one where Canadians of his faith had been welcomed and had fared well. Unlike some of his countrymen, however, Dawson did not become an eminent theological educator. In the aftermath of the First World War he was drawn out of the ministry by the inherent logic of some of the ideas he came into contact with at the University of Chicago. His transition to sociology is impossible to understand without tracing those ideas and the particular reasons for their development at that institution.

III

In attending the Divinity School of the University of Chicago, Dawson found himself at an institution that was at the forefront of change in theological doctrine. The northern branch of the American Baptist church produced many liberal and radical theologians, and their leadership was centred at the University of Chicago, where the major journal for the propagation of their ideas, *The Christian Oracle* (later named *The*

Christian Century), was published. Under the presidency of William Rainey Harper, a biblical scholar who encouraged a critical approach to the study of the Scriptures, and the influence of the dean, Shailer Mathews, the Divinity School had become, by the time Dawson arrived, a centre for liberal Christianity, higher criticism of the Bible, and social service.[44] Prominent among the ranks of the more liberal faculty were the Canadian members, and none was more influential than Shirley Jackson Case. Appointed in 1908, he went on to become an eminent social gospeller, the author of numerous books and articles, including *The Social Origins of Christianity* (1923). He also served as chairman of the Department of Church History, in which capacity he gathered around him a strong group of liberals, and was dean of the Divinity School between 1933 and 1938.[45]

The emergence of the Divinity School as a leader in progressive religious thought was inextricably bound up with the factors that shaped educational philosophy at the University of Chicago in general. From its very opening the institution was dedicated to discovering social needs and solving social problems through research and investigation. For that reason it developed not only a strongly service-minded divinity school but influential social-science departments. The service ethos stemmed partly from the university's Baptist origins and from Harper's attempts to build a graduate school that would combine scholarship with community service. It acquired even more importance because the university was situated in a booming metropolis that had a multitude of ethnic groups and suffered all the consequences of rapid industrialization and urbanization. (These problems had already given birth to a large and dynamic social-reform movement, whose members inside and outside the university co-operated for similar ends.) While it had initially been Harper's intention to create an institution that was strong in the traditional areas, when he failed to attract established scholars in classics, Semitics, and philosophy, he hired individuals whose careers were just on the rise, in addition to some eighty department heads from various colleges.[46] In the invigorating atmosphere of a new institution and under a president who wanted to establish Chicago as a research centre like Johns Hopkins, where students would be pushed along new lines of investigation, a very different kind of scholarship developed. Although Harper did criticize the sort of education that the traditional colleges offered, he tried during his presidency to combine the old and new learning in the service of religion. For example, the last of the colleges opened during his tenure of office was the College of Religious and Social Science. It offered a program that combined work in philosophy, psychology, and Christian sociology and was designed for prospective ministers who could not afford separate undergraduate and divinity courses and for those students who intended to do philanthropic work in the YMCA and other charitable institutions. The college closed after the university was reorganized in 1910, but the Divinity School remained closely linked with the departments of Political Science and Sociology. Not only did the Divinity School offer extensive courses in social problems and social welfare in order to train ministers to work for the betterment of society, but individuals such as Charles Henderson forged tighter links between the school and other departments. A sociologist, Henderson came to reform and social science through his deep religious convictions. University chaplain throughout his career, he was also actively involved in methods of charity organization and government.[47]

To celebrate the tenth anniversary of its founding, in 1903 the University of Chicago issued a series of publications explaining the work and philosophy of a number of its fields. An article on practical theology contained the clearest statement of the theories and concerns that shaped the university's philosophy of service. It explained that the object of practical theology was to formulate Christian truth in such a way as to emphasize its value for life. Accordingly, rather than dwelling on the archaeological, historical, and speculative elements of Christianity, practical theology was dedicated to uncovering its spiritual meaning and applying it to the problems of life. The article indicated that this approach was only partly necessitated by the pressing nature of contemporary social problems, however. The other major concern was to ensure that Christianity was aligned with scientific thought. In order to be genuinely scientific, the author insisted, practical Christianity must address itself to the present world – 'not an outgrown cosmos.' Only in that way, he continued, could the minister embody 'the ripest conclusions of theological scholarship' in his preachings and guarantee that practical Christianity 'did not suffer the reproach of crudity and of failure to stand before the bar of scientific criticism.'[48] The argument demonstrated the importance of science at Chicago, the way in which scientific investigation became an integral part of its educational philosophy, and the conviction that seemed to be widely held at the institution, that only with the 'ripest conclusions' of scientific research could the community be served. It also revealed the strength of modernist ideas within Chicago's Divinity School.

Modernism was an international religious movement that developed in the late nineteenth century and attempted to reconcile historical Christianity with the findings of modern science. Although it could be argued that it consisted of a set of ideas within liberal Protestantism, its implications were potentially more damaging to religious faith. Liberal theology expressed a general humanistic optimism about the world: it emphasized the presence of God in nature and in human nature and stressed the universal religious sentiments in the Scriptures. Modernism stressed the immanent rather than the transcendent nature of God and held that humam society was moving towards the realization of God's kingdom. In that regard its tenets not only gave a certain legitimacy to the analyses of society and culture on the part of theologians but required that the study of religion accord with modern empirical methods.[49]

Modernist ideas were accepted, at least in part, by the Baptist, Congregational, Presbyterian, and Methodist Episcopal denominations in the United States, but nowhere during the early twentieth century was the empirical approach to the study of religion more popular than at the University of Chicago. The presence within the Divinity School of such eminent modernist scholars as Shailer Mathews and George Burman Foster only partly explains the importance that modernist theories acquired at Chicago. More integral were the ideas that the divinity school and social science departments shared regarding the development of human society, culture, and morals.[50] In 1927 J. Davidson Ketchum, a University of Toronto psychologist once involved with the Student Christian Movement, visited the University of Chicago in the hope of finding in the social-science departments ideas he could employ back in Toronto. He was impressed by much of what he saw – the trip, he said, marked his 'conversion' to the sociological point of view – but what particularly struck him was the large degree of co-operation and mutual interest that existed among the social scientists. Each department went its own way, he noted, but there was a strong feeling among all the men that they were attacking social problems as a group and could count on as much assistance as any of their colleagues were able to render in solving social problems. 'Whether this is to be put down,' he commented, 'to the general "social" influence or to the beneficent influence of the Baptist faith, I do not know.'[51]

The 'social influence' to which Ketchum referred was the cluster of ideas regarding human psychology that members of the Chicago Philosophy Department had been formulating since 1894. So adaptable were their theories to the study of society and so in keeping with the science and service philosophy of the university that they were influential in several departments and their proponents were branded 'the Chicago school.' Although the term applied to the work of numerous academics in philosophy, political science, economics, sociology, and divinity, the nucleus of the Chicago school consisted of John Dewey, who came to the

University of Chicago in 1894 as head of the Department of Philosophy, his former University of Michigan colleagues George Herbert Mead, James Hayden Tufts, and James Rowland Angell, and Edward Scribner Ames, a theology student who received the first PH D from Chicago's Philosophy Department. Their ideas constituted part of the revolt against formalism that became prevalent in American intellectual life in the late nineteenth century, particularly among academics battling against the dominance of the patrician universities on the eastern seaboard and the entrenched humanistic studies. In contrast to the dualism inherent in the old physiological psychology, which had argued that mental life had a material basis in the nervous system and the brain and that the human mind was a fixed structure that arrived at truth through logic or intuition, the Chicago philosophers upheld a theory of mental development that implied, first of all, constant change, and secondly that there was no distinction between mind and material things. They argued that mind and society were two factors in a process and that both constantly evolved in conjunction with one another towards ends that were neither fixed nor absolute but ever changing. Although it was a form of pragmatism, they preferred to label their philosophy 'functionalism' or 'instrumentalism,' believing that such terms more adequately conveyed the sense of activity or process that was so integral to their theories.[52]

The Chicago philosophers derived their ideas regarding evolutionary and organic change from Darwin, and they regarded themselves as his true intellectual heirs. It was well known, John Dewey proclaimed in an essay, 'The Influence of Darwinism on Philosophy' (1910), that the publication of *Origin of Species* marked an epoch in the development of the natural sciences. It also embodied an intellectual revolt, he went on to argue, by introducing the phenomenon of transition into life. Dewey explained that the idea of movement or change had been accepted in the physical sciences ever since the sixteenth and seventeenth centuries, owing to to the work of Newton, Galileo, and Kepler. But in the natural sciences, species continued to be regarded as a fixed and final form until Darwin undercut that argument. In doing so, Dewey contended, Darwin allowed the philosophy of fixity as it applied to human life and philosophy to be questioned.[53]

Although other philosophical schools accepted Darwinian concepts of evolutionary change, they did not carry them to the same conclusions as did members of the Chicago school. Some American and British idealists adopted pragmatic concepts while continuing to insist that there was a fixed absolute, distinct from the activities of life.[54] William James, for example, employed the idea of process to attack philosophies of fixity but did not go as far as Dewey and his followers,[55] to argue that men and women were themselves capable of changing the world for the better. Dewey believed that the inherent logic of Darwinian knowledge introduced *responsibility* into intellectual life. 'If all organic adaptations are due simply to constant variation and the elimination of those variations which are harmful in the struggle for existence that is brought about by excessive reproduction,' he once said, 'there is no call for a prior intelligent causal force to plan and preordain them.' Since there was no higher order that planned and pre-ordained things, Dewey concluded, and ends were always subject to change, then it was possible for men and women to manipulate their environment to meet their needs.[56]

The inherent logic of Chicago philosophy demanded a new approach to the study of society and culture: its organic and evolutionary precepts required that society be seen as an organism whose members were socially constituted, not as a collection of individuals who were somehow externally connected. The individual primarily responsible for working out these ideas was George Herbert Mead, a social psychologist who greatly influenced the sociologists. Mead explained that the behaviour of an individual could only be understood in terms of the social group of which he or she was a member, and moral ideals therefore similarly developed out of a social matrix. Morals and ideals, he insisted, were not imposed from some external source by man or God but were responses to problems and their particular circumstances. Whether religious, aesthetic, or political, they were erected by man as objectives, considered valuable to invoke in the hopes that if he acted upon them, more promising circumstances might come about – but that was all. 'Democracy is preserved in the form of our political institutions,' he pointed out, 'though it is never achieved.' 'The religious goal of the brotherhood of man is maintained in our churches full in the face of man's inhumanity to man.'[57]

As Mead's statement reveals, the Chicago philosophers were prepared to concede that religion was significant as the bearer of certain principles. But apart from that, they were reluctant to deal with it: religious doctrine and culture, it has been argued, were too close to ways of thinking from which they were trying to dissociate themselves to permit them to examine it intensively. Nevertheless, in his annual course on the psychology of religion and in his book *The Psychology of Religious Experience*, published in 1910, Edward Scribner Ames formulated a set of arguments to explain religion's social origins and functional purposes. He explained that religion was related to the evolutionary life-process and that it grew out of the social development of a people and constituted one of the ways in which they adapted themselves to their environment and their environment to themselves. It was the primary means by which they promoted their highest ideas and attempted to make their lives fuller and richer. As such, he argued, religion should be analysed as representing the most important group interests of a particular time.[58]

In a book outlining the contribution that members of the University of Chicago had made to social thought, Ellsworth Faris once commented that Ames's work, which dealt with the social character of religious behaviour, 'added a strong structure to the tower of the temple ... When religion is defined as the consciousness of the highest social values,' Faris explained, 'there is made possible a study of religious experience through social psychology that was not previously available.'[59] Such advances in social psychology also explain modernism's efflorescence at Chicago. The theories of the Chicago philosophers, especially their conviction that there were no fixed or absolute ideals, accorded with the desire of modernists to shift their attention away from the doctrinal aspects of Christianity to study its cultural origins and purposes from the standpoint of modern empirical methods.

The strength of modernism and social psychology at the University of Chicago were to influence C.A. Dawson's atttitude towards religion profoundly. While never rejecting religion outright, he came to believe that research, which allowed one to see behind the values held dear at certain times, presented the best possibility for social improvement. His faith that research would provide men and women with the potential to realize their highest ideals was inherent in Chicago philosophy: one of its basic tenets was that it was possible for man to understand and change the world. 'The world men strive to know and to bring under their control is no longer an array of indeterminate objects outside the minds of men, towards whose eternal order men's ideas move by accident or magic,' John Dewey once said. 'The world, as known, is a product of knowing activity. That activity moves forward to meet new problems raised by data, and the world as known changes.' It was that precept that led Dewey to conclude and others (including C.A. Dawson) to concur that philosophy could be used for reformist ends. 'Philosophy must in time become a method of locating and interpreting the more serious of conflicts that occur in life, and a method of projecting ways for dealing with them,' Dewey argued, '– a method of moral and political diagnosis and prognosis.'[60]

IV

The University of Chicago had been founded in a decade when admiration for German *Wissenschaft* – the emphasis upon research and investigation rather than teaching – was at its height in the United States.[61] Throughout the late nineteenth and early twentieth centuries most scientific departments at the university were dedicated to research and investigation. The central preoccupation of Chicago philosophy with ascertaining the origin and function of certain social beliefs made the research orientation equally popular in a variety of non-scientific fields. This was the atmosphere that Dawson encountered when he first arrived at Chicago in 1914, and when he returned after fulfilling his wartime duties, the research emphasis was even stronger. The war had generated a great deal of support for nationally approved scientific research, and in the post-war decade private and public funds continued to pour into institutes supporting scientific endeavours. In some quarters the unrest and turmoil caused by the war led many people to question whether 'action' was the most efficacious method of dealing with social problems: the managerial revolution of the pre-war years had been channelled into wartime management, and a number of academics thought the same efficiency techniques could be successfully employed to achieve social progress during peacetime. For those reasons, not to mention their desire to divert some of the wealth and attention away from the sciences and towards themselves, social theorists were all the more determined to make their disciplines scientific in the post-war years in order to prove that they could halt social fragmentation by means of scientific investigation. Therefore, along with engineers, social workers, and scientists, they strove to make their own activities more productive; they undertook team investigations and publicized their findings, hoping to be noticed by governmental agencies and institutions.[62]

When Dawson became involved with the University of Chicago's Sociology Department, its members were beginning to lay the groundwork for such scientific endeavours. Indeed, in 1921 Robert Park wrote that sociology was just being transformed from a philosophy of history into a science of society by entering into a period of research and investigation. Although Albion Small and Charles Henderson, the pioneers of the department, had been advocates of research, they had been too preoccupied with promoting the discipline to do much in the way of specialized research. Then, too, they had seen sociology as an instrument for social reform, and while they argued that the success of reform measures depended upon the availability of reliable scientific knowledge, they were still basically concerned with applied sociology and with the construction of a more co-operative society. Albion Small had worked closely with Shailer Mathews (a colleague from his Colby College days) and had been impressed by the work of the Chicago philosophers. He had found Dewey's educational and social theories particularly useful for the study of society, and published a few articles jointly with the leading light of the Chicago school. But it was primarily the second generation of Chicago sociologists – William Thomas, Robert Park, Ellsworth Faris, and Ernest Burgess (a native of Tilbury, Ontario) – who developed a research orientation for the discipline and a theoretical framework that differentiated it from the other social sciences. Thomas had studied under Dewey and Mead, and his book on Polish peasants set out an approach for immigration studies that dominated Chicago sociology for some years. Park was responsible for creating the research program that the department followed thoughout the 1920s. Taking up a suggestion that Small had made before the war he decided that Chicago should be used as an area for investigation. Prior to his appointment to Chicago, however, Park had worked as a journalist, and, witnessing at first hand how social surveys and investigations had failed, because they were either too concerned with social problems or too influenced by practical ends, he told his students that they could not be activists or crusaders. Moral and political commitments, he warned them, would make them incapable of empathizing with all kinds and conditions of men.[63]

C.A. Dawson was intimately connected with the efforts of Park and his colleagues to work out a new approach for sociology. He belonged to the Community Studies Executive Committee, an organization formed at Park's suggestion to map out plans and ideas for urban research. (In addition to Park himself, other members of that committee included Erle Fiske Young and Roderick D. McKenzie, whose work on dominance and world organization would become extremely important for all the social sciences.) Dawson was also a teaching assistant in the introductory sociology course, where Burgess and Park first formulated the theories elaborated in their influential textbook, published in 1921. (Among the other assistants were men who became quite eminent in the field – Louis Wirth, Herbert Blumer, E.T. Kruger, and Frederic Thrasher.[64]) Finally, at both Chicago and the YMCA College, Dawson taught a course on social research and the collection of data.[65]

While not an example of urban research but a theoretical study, Dawson's PH D dissertation, 'The Social Nature of Knowledge' (1922), reveals how strongly Chicago theories had come to influence his way of thinking. It opened with a paean to the Chicago school. Whereas eighteenth-century writers had depicted the individual 'much more atomistically than present-day scientists treat the atom,' Dawson said, the Chicago school and its followers recognized that man was not 'a self-centred, self-contained unit ... the supreme architect of his own fortune and master of his own destiny.' Industrial development and the problems of social control occasioned by those advances had given rise to the idea that human nature was a social product, and that in turn had stimulated a new interest in the social aspect of mental life. 'It is now seriously considered,' he attested, 'that there would be no individual mind if it were not for social contact and interaction.'[66] Then, in a discussion that ranged over politics, art, literature, and religion, Dawson demonstrated that all culture and knowledge, morals and ideals, had social origins. He thereby laid the foundation for the crowning argument of his thesis, that even fact could not be regarded as a priori or fixed truth, but stemmed from the common experiences of individuals who constituted a group or a society. Adopting his typology largely from Emile Durkheim's work on collective representation, Dawson explained that in a process that started with collective excitement and evolved into symbolic representation, facts represented nothing more than the decision of individuals to agree on certain points and issues. Carried to its logical conclusion, his argument implied that by undertaking research, itself a collection of 'facts,' it was possible to ascertain why a group of people behaved the way they did and, armed with such understanding, to help them to realize their ideals.

In accepting the basic premises of Chicago philosophy, Dawson was compelled to dismiss any notions he might have had that religion was revealed to man by some divine authority. By the time he published his sociology textbook in 1929, he was quite forthright about religion's social origins and purposes. Religion, he said, was simply a form of behaviour born of insecurity: 'Confronted by natural phenomena of a startling nature – life, death, the enigma of a future after death, defeat – or anything that inspired in him fear of the unknown,' man 'searched his environment for an answer to the problem and erected an ideal which, for the time being, was beyond the verification of science.' That ideal elevated the level of human conduct by giving man something to aspire towards; it also acted as an effective instrument for social control, but it was nothing more. As far as religious practice was concerned, it was to Dawson's way of thinking just another form of social behaviour. 'Man was born into a worshipping community just as truly as he was born into a farming or industrial community,' Dawson said. There was, then, no real difference between evangelical religions and those that were more orthodox. One might emphasize intense and individualistic religious expression; the other was more concerned with ritual; but both required conformity to an accepted pattern of behaviour.[67]

In his thesis Dawson similarly dealt with religion's social origins but focused primarily on the concept of inspiration and revelation. As far back as the 1860s Horace Bushnell, a Unitarian, had contended that because of its emphasis on conversion American evangelicalism had underestimated the way in which education and socialization affected man's religious behaviour; as part of their desire to treat religion scientifically some modernists had been equally critical of revelation.[68] Dawson not only agreed with their convictions but argued that the entire notion of original inspiration was fallacious. He insisted that inspiration, whether religious, literary, or artistic in nature, merely arose from the social rituals, attitudes, and sentiments of the group in which the 'gifted' individual was a member. 'No man gets inspired with any very original conception,' he said. 'The voices that speak to him, the visions he sees, get their form and content very largely from the community about him.' Sensitive to life about him, stirred by the defeats and futilities of others, an inspired person simply puts himself in 'a highly emotional and suggestible mental state by brooding over them in isolation.' When he voices his ideas, he is sometimes regarded as a prophet revealing the proclamations of the unseen and the eternal, but he is in fact merely prophesying what is already in the popular consciousness in an inarticulate form – the hopes and fears of other people.[69] That conviction necessarily carried Dawson to the conclusion that religious inspiration, possession, and spiritualism were all the same thing. All were products of group life. Whether they assumed a divine or diabolical form simply depended upon the temper of the time in which an individual lived, for that is what determined the sentiments that emerged in his character. In the Middle Ages, Dawson explained, people were highly influenced by the conventionalized terms God, Spirit, and Devil, but because so many ordinary human motives were repressed and attributed to Satan, conditions were ripe for 'the contagious phenomenon of diabolical possession.'[70]

Dawson saw an inherent danger in all spiritual and inspirational phenomena. Their very 'impersonality' – the belief that they stemmed from some supernatural source – he warned, could lead to tyranny. He explained that when in the throes of diabolical possession or religious ecstasy, people are controlled and directed by an urgency so novel that they do not attribute it to their own personal capacities. They believe that they are being driven into strange missions by alien powers. As the contagion spreads, others yield to it, and are often drawn into the vortex against their wills.[71] 'However sophisticated,' Dawson said, 'we have all had some feel of it in movements of great collective emotion. "Seizure by the war-spirit," is a modern personalization of collective excitement on a large scale and few escaped during the Great War. They were ushered into a strange and compelling experience.'[72]

It was particularly in the allusion to war hysteria that 'The Social Nature of Knowledge' revealed Dawson's reasons for departing from the ministry to pursue a career in social science. His decision was obviously prompted by something more than just the influence of the modernists and social psychologists. Underlying his negative attitude towards social action is a war-weariness and a fear that collective action would lead to tyranny and violence. Because of what he witnessed during the war and the upheaval that followed, Dawson probably found Chicago philosophy appealing: it suggested that social progress was the inexorable result of the evolutionary process and simply had to be nurtured through rational observation and investigation.

For Dawson the war presented the starkest example of how people could be swept up in a tide of emotion to participate in something of which they had little understanding; this was an argument that he and his McGill colleague Warner Gettys elaborated more fully in *An Introduction to Sociology*. Believing that war was ineffective and utterly wasteful, they nevertheless pointed to the commonly held view that it was a biological necessity and politically inevitable. The problem, as they saw it, was that the literature on war was voluminous, and stories relating to the glory of battle were entrenched in many cultures. In addition there were the powerful rituals and dogmas of war; an emphasis on military training that had turned into national fetishes; propaganda, bogies, and alarms that endowed militarism with all the fervour of a religious cult; and patriotic organizations that aroused people's fears by taking up and popularizing myths, legends, slogans and symbols of patriotism, hymns of national sentiment, and hymns of hate. 'In modern times,' Dawson and Gettys argued, 'the war cult has become a way of escape from the morbid subjectivism of everyday life. People find release and satisfaction in the pomp, splendour, and parade of militarism and thrill and adventure in time of war.' The antidote, as Dawson and Gettys presented it, was to probe beneath 'the superficial romance' of war and discover its causes – war, they contended, stemmed from institutions and customs of long standing, personalities, international intrigue and hatreds, the breakdown of inhibitions, economic tensions, and population pressure.[73]

Despite his negative comments about collective excitement, Dawson was not entirely critical of crowd behaviour; he could not be if he believed that humans were essentially social beings. He merely wanted to demonstrate that knowledge could develop out of a crowd that *thought* rather than one that *acted*. In that respect his arguments were an extension of Robert Park's work on the crowd and the public, first formulated in his thesis, *Masse und Publikum* (1904). As Fred Matthews has explained in *Quest for an American Sociology*, Park attempted in *Masse und Publikum* to generalize crowd theory into a social psychology that would demonstrate the way in which men were influenced by the excitement of others. He thought this was a phenomenon that was ever present but sometimes submerged or channelled into more acceptable forms, such as social rituals and institutions.[74] Most nineteenth-century European and American crowd psychologists believed that individuals were transformed by joining crowds, and while Park drew heavily on their work, he did not share their antipathy to crowd behaviour. He believed that the crowd and the public could be 'the crucible of a new order.' As he saw it, the social unrest expressed by the crowd would eventually manifest itself in an organized movement, and when that movement petered out, it would leave behind its essence in the form of an institution. Since Dawson formulated his theories upon the foundation laid by Park, he frequently employed the same arguments. He, too, criticized nineteenth-century crowd psychologists, particularly Gustave Le Bon, for assuming that when people met, they necessarily became a two-thousand–headed monster. A crowd could be noble or vicious, Dawson contended, depending upon the reasons for its existence. During a crisis a crowd would unite for common action, its aim ephemeral. But when the same individuals met repeatedly, customs, traditions, and folkways developed. These traditions in turn formed the vantage-ground from which symbols were erected from time to time to arouse emotions that had been submerged. They could take the shape of objects, myths, or rituals. Frequently, usually earlier on in the social development of a people, these symbols would be highly emotion laden and could be utilized to incite the crowd to action once again. For instance, Dawson explained, the Bastille incited the fury of the French mob, but a myth, slogan, or word could be employed to the same effect. A modern example, he said, was the orator 'who metaphorically waves the flag and demands with unction, "that the World Be Made Safe for Democracy."'[75] When symbols were that highly charged emotionally, he explained, they were too close to an individual's experience to be analysed; there was still a tendency to identify life with the symbol – it called out a wealth of sentiments, provided a sense of security and a place in the sun, 'just as the native with his totem.' But when finally abstracted, stripped of their colour and vividness, Dawson concluded, symbols became 'the coldly precise objects of science.'[76]

Much of Dawson's thesis concentrated on explaining the mechanism by which knowledge, or science, emerged out of a crowd: the most important factor therein was man's ability to communicate vocally. In their capacity to be stimulated and controlled by collective excitement, Dawson said, humans were similar to animals. He alluded to the buffalo herds on the western plains who merely 'milled,' seeking an outlet for their discontent. A flash, a sound, or a disturbing smell would plunge them into the rush of a stampede.[77] The same thing could happen with a human crowd, but because man had the ability to communicate, that 'biological variation' allowed for the emergence of common meaning. Through words and symbols, human beings were able to put their experience in terms that others could understand, and by such means they built up a community of experiences. Their experiences were thus transformed into symbols of common meaning, and the existence of those symbols allowed man to express his feelings with reference to something that was relatively impersonal or objective. Therefore, even when experiences lost their original concreteness, they could still be identified with because they were a common product. And that product – or 'social objectification,' as Dawson called it, using Durkheim's terminology – was culture and science.[78] By this logic Dawson proceeded to argue that facts, which constituted the body of science, also represented common understanding and agreement. All objects of scientific research, he insisted, were observed and stated in terms of experience. 'The world is broken up into objects which are the products of experience. They emerge as common denominators out of the interplay of conflicting experiences.' Once agreed upon, however, the experiences became facts: 'Fact is a common agreement that has arisen out of conflicting interests and points of view. In the matching of stories and pooling of relevant experiences, statements of fact get clipped, pared down to certain definiteness ... Fact is just so much the rigid selection of incidents,' Dawson concluded; 'Time is taken to make them square with every possible situation and known exception. They are pursued to the limit in order that there may be a consistency and completeness to their establishment.'[79]

The emergence of fact was dependent upon one more factor that Dawson was compelled to explain: facts could only develop out of a public, not a crowd. Picking up from Park's hypothesis once again, Dawson explained that to be a member of a crowd one needed only to feel and to empathize,[80] but to be a member of a public one had to participate in a rational discussion. A public was composed of individuals who criticized one another, whose opinions clashed and then were modified. The process of criticism and modification, however, had to be continuous, or the public would degenerate into a crowd. That said, Dawson made sure his readers understood the difference between a public and a school of thought. A school of thought, he explained, started 'under the influence of some original genius,' who, 'mulling over the knowledge of the time hit upon a new slant – a different concept.' He preached it to his friends and followers, who embraced it with enthusiasm. The problem with a school of thought, however, was that it was a reaction against something and so usually contained a great deal of dogma of its own. Dawson cited as an example, the Enlightenment school of free thinkers, whose members strove to detach themselves from the religious doctrines of their time but fell victim to their own dogmatism. Dawson's attitude towards pragmatism was more favourable. While a purely philosophical school of thought, pragmatism was not specifically dedicated to fighting against 'antique religion.' It was a reaction against the absolute in philosophy and therefore a point of view for dealing with the whole field of knowledge. Schools of thought nevertheless served a useful purpose by serving with conflicting schools of thought as 'conflict parties' in 'that most disinterested of publics – science.' Only those ideas that ran the gauntlet of criticism and got accepted by common agreement, Dawson insisted, could be regarded as science. 'Science has no crows to pick,' he concluded. 'It stands for precise analysis and description. It is remote from bickerings and rests upon the integrity of its facts in the face of the widest possible publicity.'[81]

His veneration for science and fact, and the process of continual discussion and criticism out of which they emerge, reveal why Dawson preferred research to social action as a method for solving social problems. Facts were for him 'an emancipation from immediacy ... It is through fact,' he explained, 'that we get hold of ourselves under disturbing circumstances. Fact guides us beneath the surface stimuli of superficial opinion and suggestion which tend to call out precipitate responses.'[82] By contrast, he believed, reform movements were based upon false assumptions and mobilized people for action by invoking myths – usually in the form of historical predictions. At the time that Dawson wrote his thesis, the Winnipeg General Strike was probably fresh in his mind, and so he pointed to the general strike as an example of such travesty. 'The General Strike envisions a time when the proletariat will be so prepared that they will have the power to take over and administer economics and social affairs and their wishes will be clothed in a new kingdom of humanity ... This hope is clothed in vivid and arousing imagery. It spontaneously appeals to and formulates the experiences of the working class ...They have been through many strikes and these conflicts have left painful memories and desires.'[83] Once at McGill, Dawson attacked all manner of Utopian thinking in a similar way and for similar reasons. The writers of apocalyptic literature, he charged – and he included Marx – envisaged history as broken up into a series of stages, principally for the purpose of getting at the next stage ahead. They depicted the present stage as a period of crisis, the next as an inevitable outcome of the preceding, and continued on in that pattern until Utopia was achieved. 'That wished-for new era is idealistically pictured ... From the confusion and bitter suffering of the present, a new and utterly different day will be spectacularly ushered in.' Dawson insisted that such reform movements were doomed to failure because they had their impetus in times of disturbance and defeat; more fundamentally than that, their basic assumptions were unsound. They were not the products of scientific observation and cautious investigation but the outcome of feeling and wishing. 'Utopias have generally gone to pieces,' he proclaimed, 'because they are based too much on idealization and too little in a knowledge of human nature. Much precious idealism is poured out without stint to be broken on the rocks of cynicism on the morrow because facts did not have a sufficient place.'[84]

Dawson's arguments about research and social action were rooted in the very origins of sociology. A product of the French Revolution, sociology as formulated by Auguste Comte was a meliorative, predictive discipline intended to establish social stability. The maxim attached to it then, 'savoir pour prévoir pour pouvoir,' continued to influence later forms of the discipline. The Chicago theorists believed that social progress was guaranteed in the evolutionary process but that it was incumbent upon sociologists, by observation and investigation, to discover the laws of that process and aid in its development: 'The final stages of evolutionary development would have thrown off the irrationalities of previous stages and be in tune with the teachings of science.'[85] It was for that reason that Dewey, Park, and Dawson, too, taking their cue from Emile Durkheim, attached so much importance to reflection, discussion, and deliberation. As far as they were concerned, those were the things that would facilitate social progress and ensure the well-being of democracy.[86]

Dawson's insistence on the need for continual investigation, criticism, and discussion remained just as intense once he was at McGill. The advocates of national efficiency had claimed that they were motivated to encourage productivity after witnessing during the First World War 'the way the other half lived.' While Dawson sympathized with their objectives, he considered their approach, especially in regard to research that concentrated on social pathology, much too partial. 'Democracy can come into its own on a basis of fact,' he insisted, 'for it is related to facts at every step, not only facts as to how the other half lives but also as to how this half lives ... What will serve the social and democratic cause in this connection – provided we are zealous and earnest in our quest and service – will be a conservative and unshaded presentation of facts – all the facts.'[87]

Another Canadian social scientist who shared Dawson's convictions about research and would have concurred with his statement that facts represented 'an emancipation from immediacy' was Harold Innis. The similarity of their views was no mere coincidence. Like Dawson, Innis was a Baptist who went to the University of Chicago to study political economy after wartime service. There he came into contact with some of the influential ideas of the Chicago school. The affinity between Dawson's and Innis's outlooks lends credence to the argument that the Baptists played an important role in the development of social science in North America during the early twentieth century. It also confirms that it was partly Dawson's Baptist faith that influenced his antipathy towards collective excitement and turned him towards Chicago. There was a strong anti-authoritarian and anti-hierarchical strain in the Baptist faith, which Learned and Sills, for instance, noted about Acadia in their report on education in the Maritime provinces.[88] It was also something of which Innis was intensely aware: in his preface to *The Letters of William Davies* (1945) he stressed that there were differences among the Protestant denominations in Canada and that the significance of the Baptist faith lay in its individualistic and non-conformist traditions.[89] That tradition may have caused academics like Dawson to eschew political involvement, but it did not lead to their absolute abandonment of social concern. While individualism was at the heart of the Baptist faith, there was also a tendency within it to communitarianism. It developed in the Maritimes during the period of social disintegration that followed the American War of Independence: the New Light faith of Henry Alline caught hold of the popular imagination at a time when traditional institutions and forms of authority were collapsing. Though it emphasized individualism, its acceptance manifested a form of community-seeking. In the period after 1820 this religious culture was transformed into one concerned with social reform, but it emphasized that social regeneration could be achieved by freeing individuals from institutions and precedents.[90] The years following the First World War constituted a period of widespread social upheaval, also marked by a questioning and rejection of traditions and institutions. The new science of sociology, particularly the brand being developed at Chicago, offered an individual detachment from active social concern, at the same time providing the observer with the opportunity to analyse and understand the forces that led to social fragmentation and social cohesion.

V

In his search for facts regarding human society C.A. Dawson was guided by a theory that Chicago sociologists formulated throughout the 1920s and 1930s and that eventually became synonymous with the Chicago school. The theory, known as human ecology, was an amalgam of ideas borrowed from plant and animal ecology, physiology, and cultural anthropology. Modelled on natural-science procedures and concerned with the way in which human society evolves and functions as an organic entity, it was faithful to all the major tenets of Chicago social philosophy, particularly the notion that an understanding of society's natural evolution would provide the insight to guide social development towards the best ends. Human ecology was the framework within which all McGill sociology courses were taught, and the frame of reference for all research projects undertaken by Dawson, his colleagues, and his students throughout the 1920s and 1930s.

Although Robert Park suggested some of the ideas that were incorporated into human ecology in his article 'The City' (1915) and in his textbook, *Introduction to the Science of Sociology* (1921), he himself was not reponsible for working out the full dimensions of the theory. He was reputedly too imaginative and too impatient with details to be bothered. An article that he wrote on the subject for the *American Journal of Sociology* in 1936 was a much more cogent exposition of the theory than he ever presented in the 1920s.[91] Ernest Burgess, for his part, was too devoted to specific investigations of Chicago to be side-tracked into theoretical endeavours. Instead, it was Park's students, primarily Roderick McKenzie (and later, Louis Wirth), who systematized the theory: McKenzie formulated the ideas on community organization, dominance, and succession, and Wirth laid the foundations for what would become a new field of urban sociology.[92] While he never attained the eminence of either Wirth or McKenzie, Carl Dawson also made some contributions to ecological theory – enough, at least, so that an analysis of Chicago sociology that appeared in 1938 identified him as one of the 'younger' ecologists and referred numerous times to a chapter on human ecology that he had written for L.L. Bernard's *The Fields and Methods of Sociology* (1934). Moreover, Dawson and Gettys' textbook, particularly the second edition, which was published in 1935 (and was second in popularity only to Park and Burgess's

Introduction to the Science of Sociology), was the first such work to be written using human ecological concepts for its basic organization.[93]

Human ecology dealt with the process of change in human communities, and it derived from a scientific theory that gained popularity in the American midwest at the turn of the century, at a time when that region was being transformed by human settlement and Chicago was emerging as its dominant urban centre. As a theory of function and change its spirit not only befitted Chicago's dynamism but represented that major shift that occurred in American intellectual life in the late nineteenth century when mechanistic and abstract philosophies were rejected in favour of those that conceived of social development as the product of individuals interacting with a moulding environment. This new intellectual conviction has been described as a form of Social Darwinism, but more recently historians of social science have argued that Social Darwinism was part of a general way of thinking that should more appropriately be called 'evolutionary naturalism,' to signify the evolutionary, developmental, and naturalistic explanations of man and his culture that were formulated throughout the late nineteenth and early twentieth centuries. In the period 1890 to 1920, it has been noted, one generation of intellectuals strove to carry an updated Social Darwinism and science of man to a logical conclusion, but a second generation, who matured in the 1920s and 1930s, were more concerned with reconciling views of human nature with new scientific ideas that touched upon the problem of man and society raised by the theory of evolution. It is to the second category that human ecologists belong.[94]

We have seen that in their attempts to create a science of society, early twentieth-century social thinkers decided to employ the scepticism, rigour, and laboratory experimentation of the scientific disciplines in their own work. Sociologists turned primarily to biology for guidelines because, among other things, they found in that discipline suggestions for explaining the flux and mobility that seemed to characterize human society. Biology had long rejected a static, morphological view of nature in favour of a dynamic and experimental one, and though theories of process were popular in the physical, chemical, and geological sciences as well, sociologists depended upon biology because they assumed that man was an animal and that behaviour in human society likely paralleled that of animal societies. Moreover, the new dynamic approach in biology tended to stress the complex relations prevailing between organisms and the environment, and that idea was very compatible with early twentieth-century views of human society, particularly those in vogue at Chicago.[95] Indeed, it was for that reason that Chicago sociologists found ecology, an offshoot of biology concerned with plant and animal communities, particularly instructive for their understanding of human society. Ecology considered plants and animals as they existed in nature: it dealt with the formation of individual organisms, but it also focused on the relation of each kind and individual to its environment, as well as on the ways in which one organism depended on another. Furthermore, it analysed the ways in which plants and animals were distributed in their communities, but it went beyond a simple description of those communities to explain the processes that endowed them with their structures and caused changes within them.[96]

In his essay on human ecology Dawson traced the origins of plant ecology back to the work of Darwin and his followers.[97] One of the two components of ecological theory – the idea of interdependence in nature – was actually older than that and had found prominence in the work of Swedish botanist Carl Linnaeus and plant geographers Alexander von Humboldt and Augustin Pyramus de Candolle. Darwin's hypothesis – that the competitive struggle for existence was an agency of change in nature – provided modern ecologists with the means to explain change in communities of plants and animals. Although Darwin was not the first to put forward the idea that competition was endemic in nature,[98] the significance of his work was that it explained the mechanism by which evolution was accomplished, and it was by means of combining the themes of interdependence and competition, in effect, that Darwin came up with his theory of the origin of species by natural selection. Darwin saw nature as an intricate web of interrelations that was finely balanced – he believed that species were prevented from fully realizing their powers of increase by many checks, some of them presented by physical conditions but many more arising from the presence of other species. This conception led him to conclude that speciation occurred when a slight shift caused a new place to open up in nature, and a favourable variation that arose and was able to take advantage of the new place quickly seized it. The important element in his theory, and the one that human ecologists fastened on, was that speciation occurred because all beings were bound up in a web of relations with other beings, not because they were bound to the physical environment alone.[99]

Plant ecology first emerged as an academic science in northern Europe in the late 1800s. While continuing in the tradition that Linnaeus, Humboldt, and de Candolle had established, it employed Darwinian theories to describe the interdependence of plants within zones or communities.[100] The specific term for such an approach to the study of plants, *oecology,* defined by E.H. Haeckel, the major exponent of Darwin's theories in Germany. Haeckel adopted the term to describe the new science because it meant the study of households; he thereby implied that the living organisms of the earth, constituting a single economic and interdependent entity, resembled a family or household. Haeckel did not go much beyond giving the science a new name, but in so doing he stimulated the emergence of self-described professional ecologists.[101] The first generation of ecologists were European botanists who attempted to apply physiology to the study of plant adaptation. The work that finally gave ecology recognition throughout the scientific world was *Plantesamfund* (published in 1895, then revised and translated into English in 1909 as *The Oecology of Plants: An Introduction to the Study of Plant Communities*), written by Eugenius Warming, the Danish professor whom Dawson described as 'the father of plant ecology.' What was significant about Warming's work was that it called attention to the fact that different species of plants tended to form permanent groups or communities in fairly well-defined physiographic areas. It also described a kind of mutualism that operated among the different species in those communities, showing that plants that formed one community either had to practise the same economy, making approximately the same demands on the environment with regard to nourishment, light, and moisture, or one species had to depend upon another for its existence. Warming even went so far as to claim that it was not unusual for one or more species to be dominant in a particular formation and, if it was destroyed, for the whole community to disappear along with it.[102]

In the late nineteenth century many American scientists began to be influenced by the work of European botanists, and by the early twentieth century they had assumed the lead in ecological studies, producing a new theory that remained dominant in the United States and Great Britain until 1940. Called 'dynamic ecology,' it was concerned with the phenomenon of successional development, first described by Warming. It emerged particularly out of the new midwestern universities, fostered by men who were not initially ecologists but who took a keen interest in the new science. They included the University of Chicago's John Coulter (who had studied with Asa Gray at Harvard), C.E. Bessey (another of Gray's students), E.A. Birge, a zoologist at the University of Wisconsin, and S.A. Forbes, an entomologist associated with the University of Illinois, whose work 'The Lake as a Microcosm' (1887) was a landmark in American ecology. These men influenced the careers of many of the biologists who established ecology as a recognized science in the United States, most particularly Henry C. Cowles and Frederic Clements.[103]

Henry Cowles and Frederic Clements undertook the first major studies of succession in the United States and were chief spokesmen for the new dynamic ecology. Although they did not collaborate with each other, their ideas were remarkably similar, so much so that one historian of science has concluded that 'their thinking flowed in the same channel, one marked and dredged for them by the western movement of pioneering settlement across the North American continent.'[104] Judging by the kind of studies they undertook and the conclusions at which they arrived, there is some merit to the argument that the new model of dynamic ecology owed much to the example of human settlement on the frontier. At Nebraska, for instance, Clements participated in a seminar that C.E. Bessey organized specifically for the purpose of recording the indigenous vegetation of the state before it disappeared with the clearing of land by new settlers. (Another member of the seminar was Roscoe Pound, who abandoned botany a decade later to study law at Northwestern, after which he became dean of Harvard Law School and a major advocate of sociological jurisprudence.)[105]

It had been Cowles's intention to study geology and physiography – the study of landforms – when he first came to Chicago. Coulter, however, convinced him to do ecological work, and he undertook a study of the plant life growing along the shores of Lake Michigan. In what became an important paper in American ecology he employed Warming's concept of succession to describe the different zones of vegetation located on the shore, beginning with the water-tolerant forms on the edge of the water and ending with the climax forest. Cowles's later work was not as path-breaking: he received his doctorate in 1898 for a study entitled 'Ecological Relation of the Sand Dune Flora in Northern Indiana,' and once appointed to the faculty of the University of Chicago began a major study of the vegetation and physiographic ecology of the Chicago region. Perhaps his most important contribution was the influence he had upon a generation of Chicago science students, and in turn upon the university's sociologists.[106]

Frederic Clements received his PH D from the University of Nebraska in the same year as Cowles completed his doctorate. He first taught at the University of Nebraska, moved on to Minnesota, and was finally appointed to the Carnegie Institution of Washington. It was Clements' book *Plant Succession*, published in 1916, that Park called attention to in the *Introduction to the Science of Society* when he suggested that plant ecology could serve as a model for studies of human communities.[107] In *Plant Succession* Clements described the process by which plants were distributed in their characteristic formations, and the concepts and language he used became a major part of the Chicago sociologists' vocabulary, particularly in their description of cities and regions. Clements argued that plant formations were arranged in a succession of zones constituting successive stages of evolutionary growth: the higher life-forms succeeded the lower ones by pushing – he called it 'invading' – the existing population out of an area and forcing it to settle in a zone on the rim of its original habitat. As more- and more-evolved forms succeeded each other, he showed, the displaced plants congregated in a sequence of zones. Clements believed that the sequential arrangement of the zones was only partly determined by environmental conditions such as the water content of the soil; more important, he thought, was the reaction of the plants upon their habitat. He argued that as each plant-form modified its habitat, it created conditions making that habitat less favourable to itself and more conducive to the invasion of higher life-forms. This was a process that he believed continued until the final stage of vegetation, one most suited to the particular climate and soil of an area, became the dominant life-form. Able to keep the conditions of the habitat favourable to itself and so prevent further invasions, that form of vegetation constituted 'the climax stage.' Stable and permanent, it was open to disruption only by external factors such as changes in climate.[108]

In effect Clements considered the plant community itself to be a complex organism that passed through the same stages of growth as any individual organism. Indeed, this assumption led him to describe plant succession as a process of continual interaction between the habitat and the life-forms of a community and to depict that relationship as occurring in a cause-and-effect sequence until a state of equilibrium – the climax community – was achieved. In that respect, his ideas were shaped by the work of earlier plant geographers, as well as by Herbert Spencer, who had argued, particularly in his essay 'The Social Organism' (1860), that society was not an article of manufacture but a self-evolving organism.[109] Clements' theory illustrates that he shared with Spencer a conviction that the war of each against all ultimately resulted in the development of a more harmonious organism. Many ecologists concurred with Clements' view that despite the fierceness inherent in nature and in the struggle for existence, natural selection was a positive force, restoring an equilibrium that ensured the maximum common good.[110]

Park and his students were particularly attracted to ecology because of its underlying assumption that there existed a dynamic, changing, yet orderly process among organisms. If there was one factor that they thought characterized modern society, it was mobility.[111] The very opening of Dawson's article on human ecology in *The Fields and Methods of Sociology* described how modern invention had accelerated a world-wide movement of human beings, with social institutions either following at their heels or lagging behind. Indeed, with the migrations of people everywhere, the extension of transportation and communications networks, the interwar period was a mobile age. The Chicago sociologists adopted ecology to analyse the forces involved in that distribution of people and institutions; the theory was, as Dawson put it, an approach that gave a new emphasis 'to the ground march of human phenomena.'[112] At the same time, it also suggested that there were inherent natural forces that endowed society with a semblance of order.

Basing their work upon an understanding of plant ecology, Park and his students conceived of a human social order that transcended individuals and groups and was founded on a natural – or as they called it, 'biotic' – base.[113] While recognizing the role that morals and culture played in shaping society, they believed that physical and vital ties were the more fundamental factors tying it together. Specifically, they concluded that the primary basis of social organization in human society was impersonal and based upon interdependence and competition for scarce resources.[114] The mechanism by which 'the [ecological process] distribute[s] human units and determine[s] their function,' Dawson and Gettys argued, '[is] impersonal and almost completely unconscious – like a huge and continuous experiment.' Departing somewhat from the scientists, however, the human ecologists preferred to give more weight to the idea of interdependence – as Dawson and Gettys noted, the evolutionists used the phrases 'struggle for existence' and 'survival of the fittest' to describe the ecological process, but interdependence was just as important. In fact they thought that Darwin's theory had been somewhat distorted by later generations and that, though he never explicitly stated it, the basis of his theory was that all life on earth was socially determined.[115] Robert Park, for instance, began his article on human ecology with a discussion of 'the web of life.' He explained that the naturalists of the nineteenth century had been intrigued by their observations of the interrelations and co-ordinations among numerous divergent and widely scattered species because it seemed to shed light on the origin of species. 'The web of life,' said Park, 'in which all living organisms, plants and animals alike, are bound together in a vast system of interrelated and interlinked lives,' was a fundamental biological concept and 'as Darwinian as the struggle for existence.' Moreover, he claimed that it was by accepting the idea of interdependence, a sociological principle, that Darwin got his first clue to the theory of evolution. To Park, Darwin's web of life signified that all organisms – plants, animals, and humans – unwittingly toiled to maintain a vast, interlinked structure. 'By this means,' he explained, 'the numbers of living organisms are regulated, their distribution controlled, and the balance of nature maintained.' And by this means of competition, 'the existing species – the survivors in the struggle – find their niches in the physical environment and the division of labour between the species develops.'[116]

Human ecology envisaged a social order in which human beings laboured, without knowing it, to sustain a complex international structure based upon a division of labour and any other economic links that existed between individuals and groups in modern society. To explain the role that competition played in this scheme of things, human ecologists preferred to use the term *competitive co-operation* because it conveyed the idea that, even while pursuing their own needs and wants, individuals contributed to a common good through a mutually beneficial exchange of goods and services. The human ecologists labelled this competitive co-operation, which they saw as quite different from *conscious* social effort, *symbiosis*. (A biological term, symbiosis signified the living together in intimate association of two dissimilar organisms, especially when the relationship was mutually beneficial; in human ecology it referred to the division of labour and the impersonal mutual services arising from the exchange of goods and services.) Their use of the term symbiosis to describe the natural order of human society highlights the Chicago sociologists' belief that people, like plants and animals, came together because they were useful to one another, and they envisioned this symbiotic web as covering the entire world.[117] Their use of the term also illustrates that they imbibed the spirit of international co-operation so prevalent among intellectuals in the interwar years. While others sought political means to avert another international catastrophe, the Chicago sociologists showed that co-operation was inherent in the natural order of society.

There were, of course, practical reasons for Park to choose plant ecology as a framework for the study of human society. In the early years at Chicago he had been searching for a way to make social research quantifiable and to arrive at some generalizations about society on the basis of widely collected data. When he first arrived at the University of Chicago, ecological theory was fairly well entrenched and only grew in strength in the years that followed. Chicago's Biology Department became one of the strongest centres of ecology in the United States, and it profoundly influenced the work of other departments, to the extent that by 1940 ecology permeated the life sciences at that institution. Throughout the 1930s and 1940s, moreover, a group of Chicago scientists – Warder Allee, Thomas

Park, Alfred Emerson, Karl Schmidt, and Orlando Park (from Northwestern University) – provided the leadership for all of American ecology. Frequently joining 'the Ecology Group' at their bi-weekly meetings were Robert Park and anthropologists Robert Redfield and Alfred Louis Kroeber.[118]

Practical considerations notwithstanding, there were many respects in which the underlying ideas of plant and animal ecology were intellectually compatible with Chicago social philosophy, and also explain its appeal to Park and his students. Ecology suggested the idea of harmony, management, and efficiency. The notion of management was implicit in the discipline even before it had a name and was more generally called 'the economy of nature': both ecology and the older term derive from the Greek word *oikos*, which, narrowly defined, means house, though it was used more broadly to refer to the work of household management and, later, the political administration of all the resources of a community or nation.[119] One of the tendencies of ecology was to show that nature was harmonious and that everything within it had a function and a purpose. While such individuals as Forbes and Clements emphasized the element of competition in nature, they nevertheless demonstrated that its ultimate outcome was stability. Competition was central, for example, to the phenomenon of succession described by Clements, but in his scheme competition was gradually reduced, since one of the results of succession, as he saw it, was to establish dominance hierarchies among the plants of a community as the process evolved towards the final climax stage. In sum, all the ecological works illustrated in one way or another that the ultimate goal of nature was to produce stable, well-balanced societies. Armed with such convictions, twentieth-century plant and animal ecologists claimed that there was a practical side to their studies, that an understanding of nature's orderly sequence would enable scientists to manage it – to solve problems, for instance, in agriculture, forestry, or fish culture.[120] Park and his students held the same convictions about their work. By studying the natural order of society and attempting to understand its development, they would claim that they were helping to guide it to a stable state, beneficial to all its inhabitants, without intruding as activists or reformers.

VI

Chicago sociologists were adamant that their approach to the study of society was the only one that could purport to reveal true social development. C.A. Dawson's review of the studies that anticipated human ecology, to the extent that they treated social and environmental conditions quite extensively, illustrates that belief very strikingly. Dawson contended that the British regional survey was the first example of the cross-fertilization of sociology and plant ecology. The modern survey continued in the same tradition, employing techniques that had been developing since the sixteenth century, adopting some concepts of plant ecology as well as the regional approach that had been worked out by French geographers. He also argued that Charles Booth's sixteen-volume study of London (*Life and Labour of the People of London*, published between 1889 and 1903) contained by implication many aspects of the ecological approach. It observed and discussed population mobility, occupational and class segregation, family means and modes of living, poverty, and dependency. Moreover, it used maps, charts, graphs, and tables freely to define and present the areas over which these phenomena spread. It was, like the American social survey, a cross-sectional examination, attempting to look at the total situation.

Whatever their merits, however, to Dawson's way of thinking all these studies had shortcomings. First of all, they had not developed along the lines of pure science. The British regional survey, he contended, while contributing to the scientific study of human regions, was too influenced by reform interests: its predominant purpose was to guide education, town planning, and civic improvement. The American survey, as he saw it, was not much better: its prototype, the muckraking study, merely drew attention to the exploited and submerged tenth in the larger industrial centres by using the techniques of impressionistic journalism. While the social survey employed more objective methods, it did not break radically with the earlier work. It generated a great deal of data, but this was secondary to the reform interest; the case studies and statistics were used to mobilize all the forces that might improve conditions in a community. Booth's study came closest in its comprehensiveness to being the kind of study that human ecologists were aiming at, but Booth and his students did not refine their research methods, Dawson contended, nor did they define the processes they were observing and attempt to trace their role in determining diversification within the city's structure. [121]

Largely because they had not developed along the lines of pure science, Dawson found the antecedents of human ecology to be flawed in another, more fundamental way. They lacked, he said, the concept that communities and institutions had 'their own inevitable forms of natural history.' [122] Dawson's explanation of natural history and how it differed from ordinary history – the mere chronicling of events – reveals more clearly than anything else the Chicago sociologists' belief that they had discovered the means to understand the underlylng forces that shaped human society and, having done so, could guide social development along the correct path. History described events in all their uniqueness, Dawson argued. In that form, events occurred but once and history did not repeat itself. But the sociologist, he explained, extracted from specific situations incidents that repeated themselves, and this reduction of unique events to typical events, which were then given a generalized description, was the first stage in the scientific process. After reducing a biography or autobiography to a case-study of the typical events in the life of an individual, for instance, the sociologist was able to anticipate in some measure later events. 'Such is the nature of scientific control,' Dawson concluded. 'All our institutions may become more effective agencies for social control when they accommodate themselves to the results of scientific observation ... In this manner we can expect to bring more mastery and less drift and waste to the whole frontage of social control.'[123]

Dawson's use of the term *natural history* to describe human ecology is significant in another way. A number of historians have noted that scientific ecology was a descendant of natural history, an attempt, in light of the fragmentation and specialization of the life sciences after Darwin, to look at nature as an integral whole. Particularly in the 1930s, in the midst of general concern about specialization in higher education, sociologists would claim that their discipline was an integrative one, filling a vacuum that had been left after the decline of moral philosophy. Chicago sociologists must have felt they had particularly good reason to make such an assertion, given that human ecology was, in effect, a stepchild of natural history.[124]

There was one antecedent of human ecology that escaped Dawson's criticisms, and that was human geography. As a branch of geography that developed in the late nineteenth century, human geography was concerned with the interrelations of man and nature. Moreover, a number of its exponents, particularly Friedrich Ratzel, defined some of the concepts that human ecologists employed in their studies of society – specificially, 'natural areas' or regions, and 'natural boundaries.' Ratzel, the leading member of the environmentalist school, believed that man was shaped by the physical world and succeeded only to the extent that he adapted to his environment. Accordingly, he argued, every clan, tribe, state, or nation embodied two ideas – a people and its land; one was unthinkable without the other. What Dawson found significant about Ratzel's studies was that he compared typical people of all races and all stages of cultural development living under similar geographic conditions: in *Anthropogéographie* (published in two volumes in 1882 and 1891), Dawson explained, Ratzel's unit of investigation had been the natural area as opposed to the artificially defined political area. Following Ratzel's lead, Jean Brunhes subjected certain well-defined natural regions – 'the island of the desert' and the 'the island of the high mountain' – to systematic study and clear definition. He, too, defined an area's boundaries, not in accordance with the political map but as the line at which one type of phenomenon ceased and another commenced.[125] A conception of terrestrial unity and of the interdependence between man and nature was also central to Paul Vidal de la Blache's *Principles of Human Geography* (1922, a book influenced by Ratzel's work as well as Haeckel's *History of the Creation*, 1876). Believing that the environment was a composite, capable of grouping and holding heterogeneous beings together in mutual vital interrelations, Vidal de la Blache suggested that the study of man should follow plant ecology. 'A cleft in the rocks, provided a little dust has settled there,' he argued, 'is carpeted with moss, and soon a variety of plants take root, chance seeds borne by the wind. And it is not long before a world of buzzing insects is swarming about the plants.'[126]

Although there was little contact between human geographers and sociologists in the period after Park and his students formulated human ecology, there was a great deal of similarity between the two fields, as Park himself recognized. He was well versed in geographic literature and reviewed for the *American Journal of Sociology* a number of books in human geography, including the classics by Brunhes and Vidal de la Blache as well as the newer works of Ellsworth Huntington and Isaiah Bowman. His textbook, like that of Dawson and Gettys, included reproductions of work by Ellen Churchill Semple, particularly her *Influences of the Geographic Environment* (1911), by and large a restatement of the principles contained in Ratzel's *Anthropogéographie*, and of work by Jean Brunhes and Elisée Reclus. In the 1930s Park worked out a method to distinguish human ecology from human geography. He argued that the disciplines were similar but not identical: geographers were interested in the relationship of human beings to their physical environment, while sociologists focused on the relations of man to man as affected by the environment – that is, the definite and typical patterns that populations assumed in natural areas.[127] Dawson pointed to another element that distinguished the two disciplines. Human geographers were to a large degree aware of 'the ground march of human phenomena,' he said. They illustrated the distribution of population units and social phenomena with reference to natural regions and represented these facts by political maps and charts of settlement routes. Nevertheless, he contended, the definition of the processes by which human beings and their institutions came to form typical patterns in space and time awaited the researches of human ecologists.[128]

The University of Chicago's location in a city that was becoming the centre of a rapidly expanding region and served as the head of a vast communications network both contributed to and enhanced the theories of dynamism, succession, and dominance inherent in ecological theory. Human ecology, which was predominantly concerned with the growth of cities and industries, the extension of railroads and highways, immigration, and the movement and distribution of people, was as much an outgrowth of that dynamic ethos as of the scientific theory from which it derived. Not surprisingly, its major promoters were themselves products of the midwest – Robert Park, for instance, was born in Pennsylvania but grew up in a prairie town in Minnesota.[129] R.D. McKenzie, who presented the first clear statements of ecological theory in 'The Ecological Approach to the Human Community,' an article that appeared in the *American Journal of Sociology* in 1924, and in 'The Scope of Human Ecology,' which appeared in the same journal two years later, was a product of the Canadian west.[130] After making the first attempts to systematize and synthesize ecological theory, McKenzie considered its deeper implications for the study of human society and went on to formulate regional and world concepts, which he introduced in 'The Concept of Dominance and World Organization,' an article published in the *American Journal of Sociology* in 1927.[131] There were a number of important intellectual influences that affected McKenzie's ideas, but the fact that he was educated first in Winnipeg, which on the eve of the First World War appeared to be emerging as the dominating metropolitan centre of the Canadian west, and then in Chicago undoubtedly had a great influence on his thinking. His ideas of dominance not only became an integral part of human ecology but penetrated into Canadian historical writing: it was partly from Chicago sociology that Canadian historians derived their ideas about metropolitan dominance.[132]

Roderick McKenzie was born in Carman, Manitoba, in 1885 and grew up on a prairie farm. As a young man he enrolled at the University of Manitoba to do a bachelor's degree in classics, spending his summers working as a teacher at a rural school and as an employee of a Winnipeg business firm. There was also one extended interruption of his education when he taught at Manitoba Agricultural College. Although he completed his classics degree in 1912, McKenzie had by that point lost interest in a career in the humanities and sought a different academic pursuit. He finally chose sociology and entered the University of Chicago in 1913, intending to study interracial and inter-ethnic relations with W.I. Thomas, the trail-blazer in that field. After Thomas's abrupt departure from Chicago in 1914, however, McKenzie turned to Robert Park and, while remaining interested in immigration, considered it more important to understand the process of assimilation of people from diverse cultural backgrounds in the context of expanding territorial organization. In 1915 he was appointed a full-time instructor at Ohio State University, where he was a colleague of Ernest Burgess (who left shortly thereafter to take up his position at Chicago) and an instructor of Warner Ensign Gettys, who would join the McGill Sociology Department in 1925. While at Ohio McKenzie researched and wrote his doctoral dissertation, *The Neighborhood: A Study of Columbus, Ohio* (1923), and it became the model that Chicago sociologists employed to explain the spatial structure of all communities. During the First World War McKenzie served as director of Civilian Relief for the American Red Cross at Camp Sherman, and in the fall of 1919 accepted an associate professorship at the University of Washington, where he did his most important work. After ten years at Washington McKenzie moved on to the University of Michigan. Although that university did not have an independent department of sociology when he first arrived, largely because of McKenzie's efforts it became another major centre for sociology in the United States, continuing in the Chicago tradition.[133]

McKenzie's article on ecological theory opened with an explanation of plant ecology and its concern with the ways in which the struggle for space, food, and light affected the nature of plant formation. He went on to suggest that sociologists should recognize that the same processes of competition and accommodation were at work determining the size and organization of human communities, but added that there was a factor that made human communities more complex. The difference between the plant and animal organism, he argued, was that the animal had a greater power of locomotion, enabling it to gather nutriment from a wider environment; the human animal, in addition to the power to move in space, had the ability to contrive and adapt the environment to meet his needs.[134] Once again, the factor of mobility indicated that studies of communities should more appropriately focus on natural areas rather than politically defined vicinities.

The general focus of Chicago sociological studies was the natural area, a region that was thought to have its own internal division of labour, which served as the basic mechanism in the selection of population elements as well as marking it off from other areas and integrating it into a larger unit. The best illustration of how this 'symbiotic' process worked was the Chicago sociologists' understanding of how a city was structured. As a city grew, they believed, it was differentiated into natural areas that specialized in certain functions – the financial region, for instance, was concerned with the administration of industry and commerce, while the suburbs were predominantly residential. Nevertheless, all of these areas were interdependent, and their close proximity in the larger area was advantageous to each unit.[135]

An article by Charles C. Galpin entitled 'The Social Anatomy of An Agricultural Community' (1915)[136] furnished Chicago sociologists with concrete methods for delimiting natural areas. Galpin was not a human ecologist but was interested in making local governing groups more self-conscious and effective and accordingly defined a community in a way that did not strictly accord with political jurisdictions. Using the records of village storekeepers and administrators, he plotted on local maps the fringe of the most distant points from which farmers came regularly to the village.[137] His work indicated to Chicago sociologists that every community had a centre, tributary areas, and boundaries. Roderick McKenzie, in turn, built the theory on how natural areas changed over time. Taking his basic ideas from plant ecology, he argued that the structural growth of human communities proceeded by successional steps, evolving from primitive and agricultural stages to industrial and commercial phases. The formations, segregations, and associations that emerged at every stage, he argued, were the products of invasion, just as was the case in plant communities. As he saw it, invasion in the human ecological process was the means by which a type of industry, residence, or population entered a region or a neighbourhood already occupied by a different type or possessed for a different use. Invasions that could alter the structure of communities included changes in forms and routes of transportation, obsolescence resulting from physical deterioration or from changes in use or fashion, the construction of important public or private buildings, institutions that attracted certain elements and repelled others, the introduction of new types of industry or changes in existing ones, changes in the economic base of an area that affected income and necessitated a change of residence, and finally, real-estate promotion that created demands for special location sites.[138] Just as was the case in plant communities, the impact of these invasions was to create instability until such time as some sort of equilibrium was attained.

The most important component of McKenzie's theory was the concept of dominance. In principle, dominance in the human ecological process referred to the controlling position that one or more units succeeded in acquiring over other competing elements; it involved the idea of survival of the fittest as well as the control exerted by the fittest over less able competitors. Moreover, there was an assumption that once dominance had been achieved in an area, competition would cease and a state of equilibrium would be reached.[139] In application the theory suggested that people and institutions in the symbiotic organization of society were held together and distributed by the principle of dominance. In that regard each community was thought to have a centre – usually the business district – around which other areas located, their character and functions determined by the relative pull (usually determined by distance) that the centre exerted over them. It was also thought that when anything occurred to disturb the balance or equilibrium of the community, competitive forces would increase and lead to changes in the area of dominance, usually in the natural areas related to it.[140] Because human ecologists contended that the factor of mobility made human communities different from plant societies, however, they were compelled to alter the concept of dominance somewhat. In human ecology, accordingly, dominance was seen as the outcome of the process of centralization or concentration. As McKenzie explained and Dawson was careful to point out in his textbook, under modern conditions of rapid communication, centres of dominance emerged at focal points in transportation and communication. Whether in local or world centres of dominance, transportation links ensured that the dominant sector had a wider constituency of subordinate areas and centres.[141]

The Chicago sociologists' conception of dominance was, of course, derived from Darwinian ideas, but it was more directly influenced by the work of University of Chicago physiologist Charles Manning Child. (Along with R.D. McKenzie's 'Concept of Dominance and World Organization,' Child's book *Physiological Foundations of Human Behavior*, published in 1924, furnished Dawson and Gettys with almost all of the material and themes for the section of their text entitled 'Centres of Dominance in World Organization.'[142]) Child was an ecological physiologist and as such believed that changes in an organism were caused by its reaction to the environment. His ideas were evident in Dawson and Gettys' statement that 'the distribution of institutional units, and their complex integration take place with reference to the centre of dominance somewhat after the manner in which a higher organism has its parts co-ordinated and controlled by means of the specialized and central cerebral cortex.'[143]

In his account of the structural development of an organism, Child argued that any organism developed its centres of dominance at the point of greatest stimulation, and from that point its subsidiary parts were arranged and integrally related to each other. Furthermore, he contended that every organ was incorporated into an 'organismic pattern' that developed in the process of reaction to the environment. These organismic patterns could vary from the single to the multicellular or from the simple to the more axiate patterns, there being a more centralized point of dominance in the more complex patterns. In the case of the human organism, for instance, Child argued that the head – primarily the brain – developed from the most active region of the polar axis and that the regions of the central nervous system posterior to the head developed from the most active regions of the axis of symmetry; other organs in turn arose in definite order along these axes. The most significant point in Child's theory, however, was his argument that whether it was a simple or multicellular form (perhaps the difference between an amoeba or man), the primary physiological factor connected with an organism's reaction to the environment was the relation of dominance and subordination between integrated parts, cells, tissues, and organs. As the organism developed from the simple to the multicellular, he contended, the integration of parts became more complex and the relation of dominance and subordination more pronounced and localized.[144]

Since ecology permeated the life sciences at Chicago, Child's ideas, while intriguing, might have been overlooked by the sociologists as just another example of such theories had it not been for his suggestion that there was a relationship between the concept of dominance in the physiological sense and the structure of communities. He pointed out that social groups, whether animal or human, seemed to develop spatial patterns similar to organismic ones. This was a point that Dawson and Gettys were quick to pick up on and use in their textbook. All living 'units,' they argued, became integrated into a dynamic relation of dominance and subordination, leaders and followers. 'This is the pattern of the pack, the herd, the flock of migrating birds, as well as that of all human groups.' McKenzie took Child's argument even further, illustrating how it could be made to apply to human communities. 'As we ascend the scale of human life,' he said, '… we find an increasing differentiation of parts and concentration of the area of dominance, until we reach the human animal, in which the brain or cerebral cortex has become a specialized centre of dominance co-ordinating and controlling the complexly integrated parts of the body.' In social evolution, he concluded, somewhat similar steps stood out in the spatial patterns characteristic of human aggregations. 'It is common knowledge that all the spatially fixed aspects of our communal structure, such as roads, homes, shops, factories, institutions, become integrated into rather definite pattern forms with the relation of dominance and subordination as the dynamic organizing principle,' McKenzie proclaimed. Furthermore, he argued that as communities evolved, they became more differentiated and the points of dominance more concentrated. He believed for that reason that the primitive human community – a village or a walled city – could be compared to an 'interior-surface' organismic pattern, and the modern city to the more evolved axiate pattern. In that respect the modern city, like the human organism, had a centre of dominance somewhat similar to the brain: the city's centre was where the intelligence was received and transmitted and where the community was most alive.[145] This notion might help to explain why Chicago sociologists, though leery of the city (particularly the downtown core, which they saw as an area of deterioration), nevertheless argued that with all its impulses and stimuli it provided the individual with more freedom than he might find in a smaller community.[146] It certainly explains why they saw centres of dominance as vibrant areas, that dynamism diminishing as distance from the centre decreased.

C.M. Child's organismic theories accorded well with the conviction adhered to by Park and his students that the world was evolving into one large symbiotic network. Eventually and inevitably, argued McKenzie, the whole world would be led into a web of dominance and subordination. As the agencies of communication improved and impediments to movement were overcome, the world would be organized on the pattern of a spider's web, he insisted. 'The entire physical shell through which civilization functions is becoming a complexly related entity in which the fundamental relation of parts is that of dominance and subordination ... All the old boundaries, both local and national,' he continued, 'are gradually losing their significance; routes rather than rims are becoming the subject of stressed attention.'[147] While it could be argued that McKenzie's statements typify the attitudes of an expatriate who, having abandoned his homeland, felt the need to minimize the significance of national boundaries,[148] we have already seen how ideas such as his evolved naturally from scientific ecology. More than that, they reflect the Chicago sociologists' certainty that social improvement would only occur when social scientists recognized and scrutinized natural areas rather than artificially defined political jurisdictions.

VII

Part of the attraction that physiological theories such as C.M. Child's held for Chicago sociologists was the place they gave to environmental factors in determining the structure of an organism. Members of the Chicago school, particularly the sociologists, were opposed to extreme hereditarian interpretations of human nature and all those scientific theories that shaped them.[149] W.I. Thomas, for instance, was one of the first American social scientists to reject the idea of inherited racial differences in mental capacities. His massively researched *Polish Peasant in Europe and America* (published between 1918 and 1920) introduced the idea of disorganization and reorganization in the adjustment of the immigrants and illustrated that the immigrant could be assimilated to the predominant culture through the agency of primary groups. His work not only served as a model for Chicago and related immigrant studies but was thought to have influenced the way in which social workers handled immigrants in the cities.[150]

Largely responsible for such a redirection in social-science theories was the German biologist and theoretician August Weismann, who began to publish in the 1880s the ideas that would transform traditional conceptions of heredity. Before that, natural scientists tended to follow the so-called Lamarckian principle of the inheritance of acquired characters. This theory argued that biological reactions to events in the life-experience of an organism necessarily passed by hereditary means into the native endowments of its descendants. It also suggested that impingements upon the organism that persisted through several generations would effect changes in the biological inheritance of descendants. These inherited traits ranged from physical traits, which, after Darwin, were thought to be adaptive and attributable to the struggle for survival, to habits and attitudes, which were manifested in instincts, mental sets, and – according to some writers – ideas. Because Lamarckianism stressed that any change caused by the environment would become part of an organism's racial heritage, it enabled scientific thinkers to use purely biological theories to explain all human cultural phenomena, and psychologists and intellectuals in general to assume that heredity and environment could not be treated as independent factors in explanations of human nature. However, since laboratory workers had not successfully proved that induced deformities in organisms produced defects in descendants and because scientists had had difficulty defining what a trait was, Weismann began in 1883 to criticize Lamarckian theory. He argued that the germinal material – or germ plasm – of an organism could not be affected by the life-history of the organism. His ideas were accepted immediately by many American scientists, particularly animal psychologists. His work also suggested to many social theorists that they could treat heredity and environment separately, and this encouraged them to elaborate views of human nature that played up the importance of environmental conditioning.[151] Of course this did not represent a return to Lamarckian theories: the new view emphasized that man's social development depended upon continual interaction with the environment; it denied that acquired values were passed down from one generation to another by means of heredity.

By the end of the First World War most American sociologists had arrived at the conclusion that nature and culture should not be confused, for they represented entirely different elements in social development, and within a few years most American social scientists – particularly the social psychologists – concurred. Instinct theories were rejected in favour of the idea of culture and cultural determinism; human nature was seen to be flexible, subject to change in response to environmental conditions.[152] Illustrating their accordance with such views, C.A. Dawson and W.E. Gettys reprinted in their textbook a bulletin from the Society for Social Research that set forth the new theories. The bulletin explained how each organism began its life as a distinct individual entity in the form of a fertilized egg, or spore, or something similar, and then developed by an orderly process into an individual of the particular species, with all its characteristic structure and functions. The bulletin commented, too, that this development had once been regarded as a process predetermined by something in the protoplasm but that it was now held that an organism's development could be profoundly altered by external factors. Dawson and Gettys elaborated on the argument, explaining that at one time there had been a number of biologists who conceived of the organism as a fixed mechanical system that, like a machine, did not vary from the original plan in the performance of the specific functions for which it was constructed; these biologists did not recognize the importance of extrinsic stimuli in the physical and social environment that could determine the character of an organism. This did not mean that the social milieu could make 'a silk purse out of a sow's ear,' Dawson and Gettys were quick to assert. The organism had certain potentialities that the environment could not alter: 'From the moment of conception, the minute organism develops into an elephant, a hyena, a cockroach, or homo africanus – but what sort of elephant?' they asked. Hereditarians had a definite answer with respect to plant and animal life, Dawson and Gettys asserted, but they were not so sure about man. Whether the human organism would become 'a flapper, a babbit, a sheik, a grouch, a psychopathic inferior, a superior individual, or just plain moron' no one could predict. The general organic pattern for the human species was in the cell, they reiterated, but the type of personality that developed depended upon the continued interaction between the organism and its physical and social environment. 'The behaviour tendencies of natural man in reponse to his social environment are highly modifiable,' Dawson and Gettys concluded. 'In the biological sense, life is reaction to the environment. In the psychological and sociological fields the reaction of life to the environment is still more complex and extensive.'[153]

By the late 1920s American social scientists had indeed succeeded in achieving a complex theory of social development, and it permeated studies of personality, race, and community. It was a dynamic interpretation of human nature, founded upon the idea that human nature was a product of interaction between original nature and social environment, but it also held that man had undergone biological *and* cultural evolution and that it was the latter that distinguished him from animals. Although they argued that culture and nature interacted, American social scientists were nevertheless careful to stress that this development arose from many different factors and that culture and nature, while interdependent, represented entirely different processes, neither of which could be explained by the other. The creation of this new concept stemmed partly from the fact that social scientists did not wish to reject – or appear to deny – the doctrine of evolution as it applied to organic phenomena. It was also a self-protective move to prevent natural scientists from making any further incursions into what the social scientists regarded as their areas of expertise: by arguing that culture distinguished humankind from animals and that it grew from an entirely different order of things than did his biological evolution, they attempted to deprive their scientific cohorts of the right to explain human behaviour.[154] As early as 1923, for instance, L.L. Bernard, a behavioural sociologist, noted that American sociologists were attempting to rid their discipline of all its natural-science determinants, having realized that this was the only way in which they could build an autonomous discipline.[155]

The new understanding of social development could have been very problematic for Chicago sociologists, since much of the theoretical basis of their discipline was derived from ecology, but that did not prove to be the case. Chicago sociologists were among the strongest exponents of the new theory. While Park and his students believed that the primary organization of human communities was determined by interdependence and competition, just as was the case in plant and animal communities, they never denied the importance of culture and morals in shaping society. In fact, they had always claimed that human beings were different from plants and animals because they could modify their natural environments and, within limits, their habitats:[156] the division of labour and the exchange of goods and services released them from dependence upon their local habitat, and invention and technology enabled them to construct on the basis of the 'biotic' community an institutional structure rooted in custom and tradition. As Park saw it, moreover, culture could be as much of a controlling mechanism as competition: while competition served as the primary check upon the territorial expansion and dominance of plant species and instincts controlled relationships among animals, intelligence and communication, customs and inner morals regulated human contacts, so that in human society competition declined with cultural development.[157] In short, Chicago sociologists believed that the cohesion of human society stemmed from two processes: one was the biotic or natural organization, the other the social – culture, morals, values, and institutions. Park used the term *symbiosis* to refer to the first and *consensus* to refer to the second, a contrast similar, it has been suggested, to Tönnie's *Gemeinschaft* and *Gesellschaft*.[158]

In 1938 Milla Alihan argued in her critique of human ecology that the dualistic conception of society inherent in the theory was a product of Park's own ambivalence about human nature. She contended, in a point that Fred Matthews picked up and elaborated upon, that Park was attempting to reconcile the conflict between a Hobbesian and an Aristotelian view of human society by seeing it as both: the symbiotic interaction of human beings was based upon competition for scarce resources, while their social relations developed from values not specifically related to the quest for survival.[159] There are portions of the Dawson and Gettys' textbook that lend some credence to this viewpoint. In a section dealing with the formation of personality, for instance, Dawson and Gettys explained how the natural man (whom they also called 'the biological individual,' 'the organic identity,' not to mention 'the human unit') was incorporated into society. They depicted this 'candidate for personality' as a detached, unsocial creature who, in becoming a member of society, was compelled to give up his natural independence. Like Park, they implied that as society became wider and deeper, the individual was more repressed, but they also insisted that social organization, while imposing limits on the natural wishes of individuals, had certain advantages. Society was simply a network of patterns that made it possible for the individual to live and act, Dawson and Gettys explained. Without those patterns, they concluded, the activities of men would largely be attempts to avoid or frustrate each other.[160]

The political philosophies of Hobbes and Aristotle were evident in human ecology, but its inherent dualism cannot be attributed merely to an attempt to solve the age-old conflict between those two theories. Human ecology grew out of a particular intellectual milieu. The new concept of human nature forged by American social scientists in the 1920s was partly prompted by changes in anthropology, and it was from that discipline that sociologists increasingly adopted their ideas about social development.

Anthropology evolved in the United States as an adjunct of natural history, but a major rift developed between the two disciplines in 1917, when Robert Lowie, assistant curator of the American Museum of Natural Science, began to challenge the right of natural scientists to interpret cultural behaviour. Denying that discoveries in evolutionary science held the key to understanding human nature, he argued that culture represented all the values that men acquired as members of society. Language, myth, religion, social institutions, and values were the things that shaped human nature, Lowie contended. Instincts, genes, and land-forms had very little to do with it.[161] Along with Franz Boas, a German scholar initially trained in physical geography (another field from which anthropologists were striving to detach themselves in the early twentieth century), Lowie helped transform anthropology into an academic science, moving it from the museum to the university. Boas, in turn, was responsible for making Columbia University into a strong centre of anthropology but more importantly than that, he emerged as one of the most influential social scientists of the twentieth century, his work having a great impact on several disciplines.[162]

It was specifically from Boas, cultural geographer Clark Wissler, and Chicago anthropologists Alfred Kroeber and Edward Sapir that Chicago sociologists derived their ideas about culture. By the early 1920s, it has been noted, Chicago sociologists already understood the Boasian dictum, 'omnis cultura ex cultura.'[163] Though the calendar listings of sociology courses offered at McGill show little direct evidence of anthropological influences until 1930, the contents of Dawson and Gettys' textbook indicate that the culture concept was understood and incorporated into human ecological theory somewhat before that. There was little reason it should not have been. Cultural anthropology easily accommodated itself to the ideas that had been shaping Chicago sociology since the 1890s. The statement 'Human society, unlike animal society, is mainly a social heritage created in, and transmitted by communication,' reprinted by Dawson and Gettys from Park's textbook, flowed from the arguments of Chicago social philosophers regarding the importance of social contact and primary groups in moulding the human personality, and hence, society.

'The life of a society depends upon its success in transmitting from one generation to the next, its folkways, mores, techniques, and ideals,'[164] Dawson and Gettys elaborated. Although they saw the family as the chief agency in this process, and the foundation upon which society was built, they regarded language as more important still. Without language, they contended, the mental development of a human being was virtually impossible, and no social institution could exist. Language gave the experiences of family members direction, form, inheritability; it was the chief means for the maintenance of the social order, the most pervasive of all elements of man's cultural life 'and woven into every phase of the natural history of society.'[165]

C.A. Dawson had little difficulty accepting culture as part of ecological theory. Whereas Park had suggested that the distinction between the biotic and social aspects of human organization could be maintained by using the word *community* to refer to the former and *society* to the latter, Dawson used the terms interchangeably.[166] As far as he was concerned, a community *was* a society in so far as it had a collective, inherited way of acting. Each individual and institution within a community, he argued, embodied both the biotic and social – or, 'the distributive and societal phases,' as he put it – of that community. One needed only to look at the way families differed in accordance with the forces of mobility at work in various communities, he thought, to see that this was true. In the rural community members of the family were closely knit and formed an economic unit. In regions of high mobility and diverse cultures, by contrast, where family members worked at different jobs and belonged to different groups, there was a great deal of instability, reflected in mounting divorce rates. Carrying the argument even further, Dawson contended that all the institutions of a particular community would eventually be integrated into a pattern that reflected the character of that community. In an agricultural community, he insisted, rural attitudes and rural ways are woven into a pattern of 'ruralism' that pervades every social institution.[167]

Dawson's ideas about institutional patterns were obviously derived from Child's *Physiological Foundations of Human Behavior.* Dawson managed, in a similar fashion, to weave the cultural concept into a number of other theories that sociologists had adopted from ecology and physiology. Most significant, perhaps, was his illustration of the similarity between 'natural areas' and 'culture areas.' As Dawson explained it, a culture area was a geographic area within which were distributed a number of culture traits sufficiently distinctive to mark the area off from other culture areas. In that respect the United States, England, the Western European nations, and some of their colonies – Canada, Australia, and South Africa – constituted one vast culture area. The people were much alike – Christian, highly mechanized, and nationalistic with democratic tendencies; their art and literature conformed to the same plan. In short, they were 'Western nations.'[168] Nevertheless, Dawson showed that within one vast culture area there were many major and minor regions with their own cultural traits and practices. These developed, of course, through the agency of dominance. Each culture area, Dawson explained, had a centre from which traits originated and pushed outwards in concentric circles 'like ripples on the surface of a pond when a pebble was dropped into it.' Traits in adjacent areas spread the same way; eventually the two waves met, and a mixed type of culture appeared at the margin. The metaphor of ripples in a pond was an allusion to Clements' concept of succession or zonation in plant communities, but gilding the lily, Dawson threw in a little more from Child. He argued that the role of the centre of dominance in the origin and diffusion of culture traits could be depicted as a 'gradient' showing the greatest number of dominant traits at the centre and flattening out towards the circumference. For example, he added, 'Pioneer belts, not yet under the dominance of any one local or outside centre, allow for the diffusion of culture traits from the circumference towards the developing areas as well as from the centre forward.'[169]

The adoption of the major tenets of Chicago social philosophy and dynamic ecology led Dawson to perceive society as an order that transcended its individual members and progressed in accordance with the principles of successional development. Although he believed that social evolution was achieved though the mechanism of competition and the principles of dominance, he saw no reason for society to be riddled by struggle and war. The ultimate end of the evolutionary process was to establish an equilibrium and a harmonious social order:

The spatial distribution of man and his institutions is the result of the process of competitive selection, a continuous, impersonal and largely unconscious process. Through social interaction, the spatially distributed units of mankind are brought under the bond of common practices and experiences that constitute society. Physical and social distances are overcome by means of communication, and the social order is woven within the framework of the ecological order. The linking of these two orders sets before us the web of life in its completeness. In ecological interaction, mind penetrates mind and social groups interchange some of their inner life. Human society takes on form and organization when its mobile units participate in the system of common aims to which they have contributed.[170]

Such convictions shaped not only Dawson's understanding of human society in general but his beliefs about the way in which nations, regions, cities, villages, and parishes developed; his research on Montreal and other parts of Canada were guided by these principles. The significance of these theories was that they emphasized the influence of the environment in shaping the social structure, and, in turn, the values, culture, mores, and institutions which any group of people constructed. In so doing, they rejected the idea that genetic predisposition or inherited traits could explain the character of nations or ethnic groups and the nature of their institutions. Armed with these convictions, Dawson would set out to investigate different parts of Canada, and within the framework of a theory that emphasized transition would strive to explain and describe the changes occurring within Canadian society in the early twentieth century.

4

Metropolis and Hinterland

Throughout the 1920s Carl Dawson, his colleagues, and his graduate students devoted their attention to examining the ecological history of Montreal and the social conditions of its segmented districts. Towards the end of the decade Dawson also began to frame the theory that would shape his investigation of the Canadian west in the early thirties. The agenda of McGill's Sociology Department in the first years of its existence reflected a number of influences. Dawson had been brought to the university specifically for the purpose of researching the problems besetting post-war Montreal. In keeping with the tenets of Chicago sociology, particularly its indifference to reform, he chose to undertake that task not by focusing on social pathology but through the broader investigation of the structure of the city and the way in which it moulded the behaviour and institutions of its inhabitants. From this concern with the urban environment, the step to examining the development of the Canadian west was an easy and logical one to take. A concern with the expanding metropolis and the influence it exerted over contiguous regions was a component of Chicago sociological theory, a natural extension of its interest in dominance, derived from its biological antecedents. The nationalist ethos that pervaded McGill University and so much of English Canadian intellectual life in the 1920s also contributed to an interest in regional sociology, as it had, in a sense, to the development of sociology at McGill in general. Dawson and his colleagues hoped that by means of research they could assist in making community development – whether it was in Montreal or the west – a smooth and stable process. That was as much an expression of the nationalist consciousness of the period as was the emergence of numerous patriotic and professional associations and artistic movements.

I

The task set before Carl Dawson when he first arrived at McGill was quite onerous. In compliance with the stipulations of the Committee of Management he was required not only to build a sociology program but to direct the School for Social Workers. He put an equal amount of effort into both tasks: in his first two years at McGill he established new sociology courses on immigration, rural life, and social research; he wrote to government agencies for information from which he began to compile data on Canadian society;[1] he ably directed the social-work program and was involved in organizing the Canadian Association of Social Workers and an annual Canadian conference on health and social welfare.

Dawson seemed to take on his social-work reponsibilities with great eagerness at a time when most American sociologists were attempting to dissociate themselves from the reform- and practice-oriented discipline. But he saw no inherent conflict in being a scientific sociologist and serving as head of a social-work program, and his Chicago teachers would not have disapproved of his activities. While they were leery of social action, they were never absolutely opposed to it: John Dewey believed that an unbiased social science would ultimately build a foundation for social action; Robert Park, even though he feared that social action would fail through the ignorance or corruption of reformers, also held the same conviction.[2] Dawson inherited that belief, and nowhere was it more evident during his early years at McGill than in his activities as director of the School for Social Workers and as spokesman for the larger social-work community in Canada.

Within a few months of his arrival at McGill, Dawson wrote an article for *Social Welfare* that outlined all the fallacies and dangers inherent in reform movements and all the shortcomings of social surveys and investigations of social pathology. He was careful to explain that he was not criticizing the studies that existed, that, on the contrary, he was impressed by what busy people with a multitude of tasks had managed to do, 'coupling spade work with construct[ive] action.' Much time had necessarily been given to the pathological side of social life in Canada, he said, and probably even more studies on the insane, delinquent, and degenerate were required. But he believed that it was more important, despite the alarm that Premier Drury had recently expressed over rural depopulation in Ontario, to push research into *ordinary* areas. Canadians tended not to study a social situation until a crisis arose, which was understandable, Dawson conceded, given that it had a psychological basis. But he proposed that they 'problemize the unproblematical' by seeing potential crises before they occurred, 'just as the engineer [did] in his blueprint bridge or tunnel.' Accordingly, he suggested that social workers and researchers undertake studies of rural and urban communities in typical sections of Canada and ascertain, through careful observation, the social changes that were caused by advances in communication and transportation, what people were interested in and what they were contented about. With the knowledge of how attitudes and sentiments were produced, Dawson promised, and with insight into those factors that gave rise to crime and vice as well as joy and contentment, those who had to deal with the specialized problems of welfare, family aid, and social hygiene would have a better balance and approach to their particular problems – they would be able to deal with them in relation to the soil in which they grew.[3]

Dawson's convictions regarding the necessity for social-science research were evident in the way in which he revamped McGill's social-work program. Instruction in casework, administration, and statistics continued to comprise a fundamental part of the program, as did field-work in Montreal's social agencies and hospitals. May Reid, a graduate of Brandon College, former work instructor of the Summer School for Social Workers at Columbia, and personal-service secretary of the Montreal Council of Social Agencies, was hired as assistant director and supervisor of field placement. Howard Falk and a number of other individuals recruited from the community continued to provide instruction in such specialized areas as public hygiene and neuropsychiatry. All the practical and technical courses, however, were given in close association with the social sciences, and students in the two-year diploma course were required to take university courses in psychology, economics, and sociology. Courses offered by the Department of Social Science, renamed the Department of Sociology in 1925, included Introduction to the Study of Society, which examined social interaction, communication, competition, war, racial and cultural conflicts, social control, and collective behaviour, The Community, which focused on the nature of urban and rural communities and the modifications they experienced in modern development, and Social Pathology, which surveyed contemporary social problems, dependency and poverty, defectiveness and degeneracy, social unrest and disorder, the pathology of play and amusement, crime and its treatment, delinquency and the gang. In 1923 a course on immigration dealt with social, industrial, and political aspects of the immigration problem, types of migrations, immigration laws and policies, assimilation and Canadianization. In 1924 Dawson instituted a fourth-year seminar in his area of greatest interest – social research on Canadian topics.[4]

The new format of McGill's social-work program obviously conformed to the wishes of the Committee of Management as well as with Dawson's own views regarding the necessity for research. In some respects, too, it did not break radically from the groundwork established by Howard Falk. Calendar descriptions continued to contain the dictum that 'the public is spending larger and larger sums of money on social welfare and has a right to expect that only those should be appointed who have made every effort to attain efficiency by careful training.'[5] Dawson agreed with his predecessor that the amount of money wasted on welfare was shameful, and in 1924 delivered an address to the Social Service Council attesting to that. 'Not many years ago,' he proclaimed on another occasion, 'hundreds of thousands of dollars were being expended by philanthropic agencies in which the spirit of co-operation and standards of work were not in keeping with the ideals of a small group of experienced social workers and intelligent guardians of the purse. Into such a situation, the McGill School for Social Workers came, in a tentative way, in 1918.'[6] In their attempt to deal with the whole problem of waste in welfare as well as the economic and social problems of post-war Montreal, Dawson explained, Falk and a number of other social-welfare leaders had attempted to create a group of trained professionals. Their efforts were laudable, he thought, but represented only a beginning. Under Falk's direction the school for social workers offered merely a specialized phase of social-work practice, Dawson insisted, while under his own it was attempting to produce social workers with a broad conception of their task, offering them 'a chance and a challenge to contribute to the building of Canadian life on a broader and more enduring knowledge.'[7] What Dawson only implied in this context but said more directly on other occasions was that it was the program's emphasis upon social research, based upon the Chicaco 'naturalist' conception of social organization, that was giving it that more solid foundation.

It was not until the late 1920s, and much more so in the 1930s, aided by recruits from Chicago and a large number of graduate students, that Dawson was able to get the important research projects for which the McGill Sociology Department was noted – the Frontiers of Settlement, the unemployment and immigration studies – under way. Nevertheless, from very early on, Dawson encouraged his undergraduates to investigate the communities in which they lived. We have seen how important the concept of community was to Chicago sociology: in its territorial aspect the community was regarded as the fundamental basis of society, the structure that determined population aggregations and the character of all institutions; in the social realm it was seen as the matrix in which the human personality, social values, and culture were all formed. For that reason Dawson and Gettys began their textbook with a description of the community. It was, they said, the sociological conception that stood first in the experience of the individual, but they also hoped that the description of the community contained in the early chapters would call out the student's interest in his own community, sharpen his powers of observation, and introduce him to the tools of social analysis.[8] Accordingly, in their first sociology course McGill social-work, theology, and sociology students were introduced to Chicago ecological theories as they related to the community, asked to apply them to certain typical human situations and to analyse 'some small bit of reality' during the year – perhaps a family, perhaps a community. Not only was this intended to serve as a substitute for lab work and to teach them about the rules of group life; it also enabled them to contribute to the data on Canadian society that the faculty members were compiling. Everett Hughes, who joined the department in 1927, once expressed dismay that McGill students had no understanding of the naturalist approach to social organization, though they had a grasp of the concept in biology, physics, and economics. He recalled that in the department's early years students used to ask with some impatience why the data on the immigrant, on race relations, and on type of communities was all drawn from the United States. '"Give us time," we would tell them, "and you will be the people who develop the Canadian data."'[9] With the institution of the graduate program in 1925 this information-gathering became a more serious enterprise. Masters students were assigned to study various aspects of Montreal life: theology students tended to undertake church-related investigations; social workers examined some facet of social welfare; and sociology students studied natural areas within the city.

In 'The City as an Organism,' which Dawson wrote for a Montreal town-planning publication in 1926, the structure, lines of argument, and purpose of the Montreal studies became evident. First and foremost Dawson asserted that his interest in the city was not that of the reformer or town planner but that he merely wished to show that all cities grew in charateristic ways and that any attempt at planning or reform would have to reckon with the 'forces' that shaped a city's structure. The city, he said, was essentially an organism. It had a centre of dominance – the business sector – around which were arranged a number of zones in concentric circles, their use and occupants varying in accordance with the value of the land and the distance from the centre. Each zone in turn was divided into subsidiary 'natural areas,' marked off from each other by natural or artificial boundaries and distinguished by their own characteristic institutions and populations. Inhabitants were 'sifted' to these areas by a selective process, and their attitudes and behaviour were shaped by it. Segregated though they were, the residents of a city functioned – symbiotically – as a single unit, as did the business, residential, and industrial areas. Change in any one area, accordingly, had ramifications in all other parts of the city.[10] Then, curiously, after disclaiming all interest in reform, after arguing that spotty, patchwork, and haphazard city planning would only prove to be futile in Montreal because, like all cities, it grew in certain natural directions, Dawson proceeded to argue that a thorough investigation of the city, similar to the type that public utility bodies were undertaking in their attempt to predict the rate and direction of the city's growth, could prove to be useful to planners and reformers.[11]

Chicago-trained sociologists regularly denied interest in reform, but they were also convinced that their research investigations would either lead to improvement or help those interested in reform to implement the correct measures. Dawson, it appears, adhered to this conviction quite strongly. While he agreed, for instance, that the growing pains of modern cities were chronic, he was not prepared to concur with the 'pessimists' that they were 'well-nigh incurable.' 'The city left to itself,' he argued, 'grew naturally in certain directions but grew wildly, and while every city suffered from this wild growth, deterioration and change were outstanding in certain areas.'[12] It was his belief that a city plan based upon adequate study would not work against the natural forces making for city growth but would direct them in the production of more stable, healthy, and wholesome neighbourhoods. Such a plan, he contended, '[would] mitigate the slum by aiding in the decentralization of manufacturing and business and by forecasting the needs of the central district. It [would also] prevent the shacktowns or slums at its circumference which are the most inexcusable of all ills of a city; it [would] bring to every area of the city more [stability] and amenity of life by preventing industrial and commercial invasion.'[13] Moreover, once all the areas were studied and the data accumulated, Dawson promised, the efforts of people who attempted to improve deteriorating areas would be more effective.

While Dawson held out great hope for the future of the city, he made it clear that the key to its well-being lay in research. Nothing but research, as he saw it, would uncover the 'mysterious forces' shaping the city's structure to which Dawson was constantly alluding: 'cities which at first seem to be pure artefact, with their checkerboard streets and angular blocks,' he said, 'are found on closer examination to be moulded for forces only partially apparent and they become something no one foresaw or intended.'[14] Interestingly enough, Dawson brought his Chicago urban theories to Montreal at a time when the interest in urban reform in that city – as well as in the rest of Canada – had dissipated and the movement was fragmented. At the turn of the century Montreal had been the great battlefield for urban reformers trying to break the hold that corrupt politicians and entrepreneurs held on the city, but, as in so many other causes, the zeal for urban reform died in the years after the Great War. Only the passion died, however, since in a fashion that paralleled developments in sociology, utopian visions were replaced by a faith in management and efficiency. Moreover, the organic and collectivist strains of thought that had been strong in reform ideas remained: now, a concept of the public interest based upon the notions of civic community, social order, social justice, and good government was upheld. Reformers had impressed upon the public the idea that the city was an organic community, 'resting upon the interdependence of all its citizens.'[15] Dawson's ideas meshed well with these in every respect: human ecological theory showed the interdependence that naturally existed in society and held out the promise that the revelation of these interconnections, by means of research, would ease social problems.

II

By the mid-1920s members of the Chicago Sociology Department had formulated a number of theories about the city, theories that they thought constituted a natural history. For them the city was a symbol of civilization and an example of the way in which the web of life functioned in microcosm. It was these ideas that Dawson and his students adopted and applied to their studies of Montreal.

When Robert Park suggested that the city be seen as a social laboratory in which human nature and social processes could be examined, he was not expressing an entirely new view in sociology. He believed that with their incessant conditions of mobility and change, cities lacked the customary networks that characterized traditional communities, and so they accordingly exposed the processes of social control for dissection.[16] This was an easy enough conclusion for Park to come to, living in Chicago with its wide-open streets and neighbourhoods.[17] But interest in the city was deep-rooted in sociology: classical sociologists were drawn to the subject because they thought the city represented modern society, and this was a conviction that Park's teacher, George Simmel, also shared. In general sociologists were concerned with how the moral order of society could be maintained and human beings integrated into what had become a highly complex and technological civilization. They regarded the city as an excellent means by which to approach this question because the city, in its complexity and differentiation, exemplified modern society.[18] It was partly for that reason that Louis Wirth once remarked that the history of civilization could be written in terms of the history of cities.[19] Of course, the exalted place that the city held as a symbol of modern society also stemmed from the scale of urban growth in the early twentieth century. Chicago had, for instance, grown to a large and diversified city in a short period of time, and its problems tended to be attributed to that rapid development. 'No student of the American scene could be oblivious to the fact that what was challenging the public attention in the form of urban turmoil was in part a symptom of the growing pains of an order that had taken the leap from a simple agrarianism to a complex urban industrialism in the short span of a few generations,' Wirth noted.[20] To Dawson's students the growth of Montreal seemed no less spectacular. One of them noted that while the growth of cities was an outstanding feature of modern civilization, nowhere was the change more profound than in the new land. 'Within a little more than a century,' she remarked, 'America had changed from a rural to [an] urban civilization.'[21]

Although urban research was not its sole interest, the Chicago sociology Department became famous for its urban sociology; throughout the 1920s and 1930s its graduate students published about two dozen monographs on the subject.[22] In addition to R.D. McKenzie's *The Neighborhood: A Study of Columbus, Ohio*, other important studies were Nels Anderson's *The Hobo* (1923), Frederic Thrasher's *The Gang* (1927), Louis Wirth's *The Ghetto* (1928), and Harvey Zorbaugh's *Gold Coast and Slum* (1929). As ecological studies these examinations of particular urban groups attempted to prove that the behaviour and social values of human beings and their institutions were products of environmental forces.

There were a number of earlier studies from which Park and his students could have drawn inspiration in their efforts to examine the structure and growth of modern cities. But they found such works as Robert A. Wood's *Hull House Maps and Papers*, the social surveys of Pittsburgh, Cleveland, and Springfield, not to mention the work of the Benthamite reformers in Britain, much too reform oriented for their tastes. Closer to what Park had in mind was a series of studies that Franklin Giddings had supervised at Columbia: with no underlying objective to stimulate government action, these examinations were merely attempts to describe the society of small, defined regions. This was the approach that Park envisaged in 'The City,' took over, and made the symbol of the Chicago school.[23]

Although the Chicago studies were mainly theoretical, built upon the precepts of plant ecology, they were also based upon extensive data. The sociologists and other members of Chicago's Local Studies Executive Committee set out with their students to examine the social, political, and cultural life of metropolitan Chicago and, to some extent, Illinois and the midwest generally. They observed and took notes on such phenomena as industrial development, transportation innovations, immigration, housing, labour organization, crime, juvenile delinquency, family disorganization, welfare work, and child labour.[24] They then plotted the data they gathered on base maps in order to see the distribution throughout the city of certain groups, institutions, traits, and practices. There was, as Fred Matthews has noted, a concreteness to Chicago sociology that came from its visual, spatial quality, most strikingly expressed in this heavy reliance upon maps.[25] The technique, borrowed from earlier community studies, was developed by E.W. Burgess. With methods similar to those employed by Galpin in his study of an agricultural community, Burgess attempted to delineate the natural boundaries of Chicago communities by reference to zoning ordinances, land values, and nationality of population. Towards that end he and his students plotted railroad property, industrial and commerical frontage, parks, boulevards, and physiographic barriers on maps of the city. If they discovered that one or more of these features rimmed a natural area, they relied upon land-value maps to delimit it more specifically. These areas then became the focus of their investigations, replacing wards and census districts, the artificial political jurisdictions that Chicago sociologists considered so unsuitable.[26] Upon his visit to Chicago, University of Toronto psychologist J.D. Ketchum was awestruck by Burgess's map room in the university's social-science research laboratory. The walls of the room, as he related it, were covered with forty maps showing inhabited and industrial areas; plotted on them were such things as the residences of those who attended dance-halls, poolrooms, and houses of prostitution, the location of various nationality groups, and the distribution of suicides and murders in any given year. 'Burgess was very anxious to have similar work done in other cities in order that comparative data could be secured,' Ketchum remarked, 'and the vagueness of many answers which I could give him about Toronto made me realize how valuable such a study would be [in Toronto].' When he returned to Toronto

Ketchum recalled that it was seeing those maps, which made Chicago one of the best-known cities in the world, that brought to his attention the fact that Toronto had no sociology, and he wondered why.[27]

Through their investigations of Chicago, Park, Burgess, and their students found that the city's natural areas were distributed in a definite pattern, and since Chicago had relatively few physical barriers, they concluded that its structure, with some modifications, was likely typical of all cities.[28] By the mid-1920s Park and Burgess had formulated a systematic description of cities of the same character as Chicago, a description that argued that every city was a constellation of typical areas, geographically and spatially defined; the areas were 'natural' to the degree that they came into existence without design and they experienced typical cycles of development as well as performing specific functions in the economy of the city as a whole. These factors, in turn, determined their institutions, populations, and moral climate.[29]

The idea that a city was divided into specifically defined regions and natural areas received its greatest impetus in R.D. McKenzie's *The Neighborhood*. There, indebted to an earlier study entitled *Principles of City Land Values* (1903) by Richard M. Hurd, McKenzie advanced the notion that the city was a configuration of business, industrial, and residential areas. Following the lead of Hurd, he showed that the city expanded radially from the business area, an area that, with few exceptions, was the geographic centre of the city. He then went on to argue that the business area, occupied by a complex of highest land-value uses, was surrounded by a fairly disintegrated area inhabited by immigrants with low buying power. Out from these areas were arranged other industrial and residential districts composed of population groups who had been attracted to neighbourhoods best suited to their economic status and racial sentiments.[30] In 'The Growth of the City,' which appeared in *Publications of the American Sociological Society* in 1924, E.W. Burgess extended McKenzie's arguments and cast them in more ecological terms. He observed that Chicago had grown in concentric circles and that this represented the tendency of any city to expand radially. The first and central circle was the business district – 'the sensitive focal point in the total life of the city.' Encircling it was 'the transition area,' a residential district in the process of being encroached upon – Burgess used the term 'invaded' – by the business and light-manufacturing enterprises. The third zone, 'the area of working-men's homes,' was inhabited by industrial workers who had escaped the second zone but for economic reasons were compelled to live close to their workplaces, and the fourth, labelled 'the residential zone,' was an area containing fashionable apartment dwellings and exclusive districts with single-family residences. Lying within a thirty- to sixty-minute streetcar ride from the central district, finally, was 'the commuter's zone,' an area of dormitory and industrial satellite cities.[31]

The concentric-circles structure was considered an ideal pattern, based upon a city with a flat surface and absence of topographical barriers. As such, it could be modified by geographic factors and physical structures.[32] As Dawson and Gettys explained in their textbook, with not a great deal of profundity, cities located on lakes tended to expand in semicircles rather than circles; topographic elevations, such as existed in Seattle and Montreal, attracted higher-income residents, as did lake-front sites; natural and artificial barriers, such as rivers and railroads, served to divide a city in half.

Concern with the city's structure only constituted part of Chicago urban sociology. Contained within the concentric circles were numerous communities and natural areas upon which the sociologists focused much of their attention in research and writing. They saw and described each area as a distinct unit, specialized with respect to land use for business, industry, play, and cultural interests; they also believed that each area attracted to itself the appropriate age and sex groups and repelled those that did not fit into its 'web of life,' but they concluded that each area, whether it was an apartment district, a Greenwich Village, or a satellite city, constituted part of an organic whole. They were connected to each other not only by means of transportation and communication but through a chain of sub-business centres and the institutions that clustered about them; they were also interdependent parts – a regional division of labour – playing a part in the economic and social life of the metropolis.[33]

The idea that a city could be so segmented and yet function as a unit was a logical conclusion for anyone who lived in the ghettoized Chicago of the early twentieth century to draw.[34] The notion that populations could be attracted and conditioned by physical factors also illustrated that Chicago sociologists followed geographers in assuming that populations settled at or near, and were affected by, natural resources.[35] The most important influence upon Chicago urban sociology, however, was clearly post-Darwinian biology: the concentric-circles theory was modelled upon Clements' description of the formation of zones in plant communities; it also incorporated from the plant ecologists and the physiologist C.M. Child the idea that communities could be likened to organisms with centres of dominance that determined their structure and change.

The influence of plant ecology was particularly discernible in the manner in which Chicago sociologists explained the process of growth and change in urban communities. Twentieth-century plant ecologists believed that the changes, or successions, that occurred in plant communities resulted from a series of invasions that distributed plant life in a sequential arrangement from lower to higher life-forms. Human ecologists believed that the city grew and expanded in much the same way, and they depicted zones as representing successive stages in the city's growth – areas that evolved through different stages of land occupancy and use until a dominant form established itself. They believed that the process of change started in the business district, that as the area expanded, commerce encroached upon the areas lying outside its boundaries and disturbed their equilibrium.[36] Although the Chicago sociologists regarded the expansion of commerce as the major factor causing change, they recognized that other sorts of 'invasions,' such as changes in transportation routes or the introduction of a new type of industry, could also play a part. The first indication of an invasion was a drop in land value, a decline in construction, business failures, the emergence of numerous service institutions, and automobile service rows. Invasions also had an important effect upon the city's population: when an area was used for a new purpose, Chicago sociologists observed, new types of population were attracted to it and others forced to withdraw.[37]

As had been the case in his adoption of ecology generally, Park applied the succession theory to describe the growth of urban centres because it was a logical way to explain the great mobility and transiency of a city's population. Instead of attributing the phenomenon to economic circumstances, he conceived of the city as the great sorting mechanism that determined where people resided and in what jobs they worked.[38] Park was fascinated by the subject of mobility: not only did he see it as the critical factor that distinguished and caused differences in natural areas, complicated social relations, and created change; he believed that it freed the individual from the mores in which he was raised and subjected him to a wide variety of new stimuli.[39] Certain individuals survived what he called this process of social and personal 'disorganization' better than others, and that was another area of investigation upon which he put his students to work. A large number of Park's students investigated subjects in what was regarded as the city's most extreme area of mobility – the downtown core. Nels Anderson's *The Hobo* and C.R. Shaw's *The Jackroller* (1929) and *Delinquency Areas* (1930), for instance, examined the impact that the invasion of industry, physical deterioration, and breakdown of social control had upon the occupants of the area of transition. They concluded that delinquency and other types of social and economic maladjustment could all be attributed to the physical conditions of the area.[40]

In their tendency to attribute social problems such as juvenile delinquency and crime to conditions in particular urban environments, the work of the Chicago sociologists was of historic significance. Many other sociologists and biological scientists, as well as the general public, had been convinced by the arguments of late-nineteenth-century geneticists that slums were the product of the selective breeding of defectives, and hence that crime, poverty, and disease all resulted from ethnic or individual proclivities. The Chicago sociologists preferred to see the extremes of poverty and disease as the product of social disorganization – indeed, their studies showed that each racial or national group that had been compelled to live in a slum area suffered the same problems, but as they prospered and moved into more settled residential districts, the symptoms of disorganization declined.[41]

The Chicago urban studies depicted a harsh and impersonal selective process at work in the city, creating within it, as Dawson attested, many areas of great human suffering. The selective process, he also admitted, was crude, in that at a given point in history it eliminated as failures certain types that the order might find indispensable at a future date.[42] He nevertheless believed that it was the most efficient and, in some ways, the most democratic system, for after a series of invasions and periods of destabilization the 'human units' would ultimately attain a position of equilibrium in relation to each other. While no one claimed that the impersonal mechanism of selection operated wisely or well, Dawson concluded that the only alternative for this competitive selection was 'status,' and status was 'conservation' – 'a makeshift to avoid the inconveniences of continual readjustment in the social structure.'[43]

III

By the mid-1920s developments and conditions in Montreal made it a fertile ground for studies similar to those that Park's students had undertaken in Chicago. In fact, Dawson was not averse to comparing Montreal with the great midwestern American city. 'In the United States,' he said, 'the railroad centre is Chicago, but the Laurentian Plateau has thrown the Canadian center 1,000 miles east, and has made it Montreal.'[44] As Dawson and other observers then and since have noted, a number of additional factors contributed to Montreal's position as Canada's dominant urban centre. Located at the head of deep-water navigation and owing to the extensive improvement of its harbour at the beginning of the twentieth century, Montreal was the leading Canadian port. With the growth of the Canadian west, moreover, it had become the main centre for wheat exports to Europe, though its position was weakened when Vancouver began shipping the commodity through the Panama Canal in 1922. Montreal was the head of extractive industries in central Canada, and concentration in the banking field enhanced its economic position. Two of the most powerful banks in the country – the Bank of Montreal and the Royal Bank – as well as two institutions owned by French Canadians, the Banque Canadienne Nationale and the Provincial Bank, made their headquarters in the city. Moreover, with an ever-growing number of commercial and financial institutions springing up in the city – insurance companies, brokerage houses, and specialized service institutions, such as universities, large hospitals and cultural establishments – Montreal had extended its influence over neighbouring regions.[45]

Perhaps more so than Park, Dawson was interested in the effect that dominant urban centres exerted over their surrounding regions, and that became an integral part of McGill sociology, but his attention was first devoted to Montreal and how its status as the metropolis of Canada affected its internal structure. From the standpoint of urban sociology, the fact that a city was dominant in a region guaranteed that it would be diverse, vibrant, and complex. In the case of Montreal, Dawson argued that its role in organizing finance, markets, and transportation facilities across Canada endowed it with extensive divisions of labour and other specialized services.[46] Indeed, by 1928 Montreal had no fewer than fourteen hundred industries, among which were included the manufacturing of locomotive and railway cars, structural iron and steel, electrical appliances, machinery, rubber goods, tobacco, boots and shoes, clothing, sugar refining, silk, cotton, woollens, paints, furniture, carriages, confectionery, flour milling, and pulp and paper. It also had, by one observer's account, the greatest stockyards, abbatoirs, and packing-houses east of Chicago; it was a district rich in power-plants, and its population was increasing yearly, making it by 1928 the fifth largest city in North America.[47]

After the problems it experienced in the aftermath of the First World War, Montreal saw tremendous growth and expansion in the second half of the 1920s. The Canadian economy began to recover in 1923–4, and in 1925 there was an enormous increase in investment and production. For Quebec province as a whole the 1920s was the peak of industrial growth, partly stemming from the success that the Taschereau government had had in attracting foreign capital for natural-resource development. The pulp and paper, aluminum-textile, chemical, and asbestos-mining industries grew impressively, but the mainstay of the Quebec economy remained the production of manufactured goods, as it had been since the late nineteenth century. As for Montreal itself, its growth in the second half of the 1920s continued to be attributable to its diversified industrial structure, as had been the case in the fifteen years prior to the war. Although the shoe industry declined, other traditional industries, such as clothing, textiles, tobacco, iron and steel products, continued to grow, and new industries – electrical appliances and petroleum – developed. By 1929 Montreal not only housed 63 per cent of all manufacturing in the province of Quebec; it also increased its exploitation of natural resources in the forest, mining, and hydroelectric industries.[48]

The offshoot of industrialization in Quebec was urbanization: at the turn of the century a little over one-third of the province's population were urban dwellers, but during the war years the cities attracted large numbers of rural inhabitants, so that by 1915 50 per cent of the population lived in urban areas, and by 1931 the figure had risen to 63 per cent. The hydroelectric, aluminum, chemical, pulp and paper, and copper-mining industries were responsible for giving birth to such towns as Arvida, Shawinigan, LaTuque, and Kenogami, but urban growth was more pronounced in Montreal than anywhere else in the province. Its port, industries, and services drew migrants and immigrants by the thousands every year, attracting not only Britons, southern and eastern Europeans, but also rural Quebeckers. Between 1901 and 1931 Montreal's population increased by more than six hundred thousand, making it a city of three-quarters of a million people in 1921 and one million in 1931. This increase in population was partly attributable to the fact that the city's boundaries were extended to include two groups of suburbs that had grown up in a belt around Montreal towards the end of the nineteenth and the beginning of the twentieth centuries. Electric streetcars, first introduced in 1892, partly contributed to the expansion of the city's territory – they enabled thousands of workers to move out of the city's inner core into the numerous residential neighbour-hoods and suburbs that were springing up all around the city.[49] The pattern of Montreal's growth and the factors that contributed to it accorded with Chicago urban theory. As Dawson explained it, the growth of cities, especially in the new world, depended upon modern means of transporta-tion, which facilitated a greater concentration of population – with its streetcars and status as a railway centre, Montreal was a case in point. Perhaps more important, the city's structure conformed to the concentric-circles theory of expansion, as Dawson pointed out in 'The City as an

Organism' after outlining the general theory. He was sure, he said, that there were people who could remember when the inner circle of the city contained all the concentric areas between Sherbrooke and the river. Since then the city had grown enormously: while the main tendencies of expansion radially from the centre held true for Montreal, its topographic features distorted the concentric circles somewhat. As the city grew, it was squeezed between Mount Royal and the St Lawrence River, and that had turned the circles into 'concentric kidneys.' Other than that, with respect to their use and the character of their populations, the zones held true to form. Dawson explained that he considered the hotels, central stations, and very high land values at the intersection of Ste Catherine and Peel-Windsor on the one hand, and the tremendous movement of population at Bleury and Ste Catherine on the other, and decided that Phillips Square was the centre of Montreal;[50] what he made no attempt to account for, and what arguably was another distortion that Chicago urban theory could not explain, was the division of the city, straight through its centre, into French and anglophone groups. (See Figure 1.)

Telling them that a city's streets could be read 'as a geological record in the rock' – that churches, street signs, and storefronts were all symbols of passing decades[51] – Dawson sent his students out into the neighbourhoods of Montreal to observe and record information about their structure, social institutions, and moral climate. These studies displayed more than just the degree to which McGill sociology was wedded to Chicago ecological theory; they presented a fascinating picture of Montreal as it existed in the late 1920s. Furthermore, despite the contention of a number of its critics, they illustrate that McGill sociology did have a historical perspective, even if that perspective was conceived and presented in terms of a natural history.

Most of the sociological studies of Montreal opened with a review of its history. The city's location on a river was seen as extremely important, not only in providing it with a transportation route but in enabling it to exploit a hinterland – a factor that would determine the city's growth from the fur trade through the nineteenth and twentieth centuries. Montreal was described as growing phenomenally since 'the Industrial Revolution,' from a fur-trading village to a modern metropolis, with its growth particularly notable since the building of the Canadian railways. The transportation links of river and rail were regarded as crucial in an additional way, making Montreal part of the interdependent web that constituted civilization.[52] 'Not many generations ago,' one student said, 'inhabitants of Canada lived in small communities and towns which were homogenous and relatively

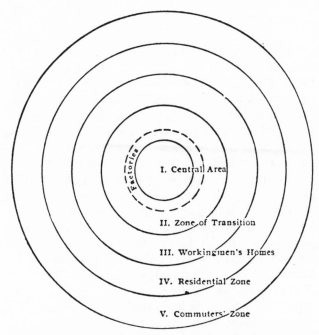

Diagram I. Ideal Expectation of a Pattern of Urban Expansion

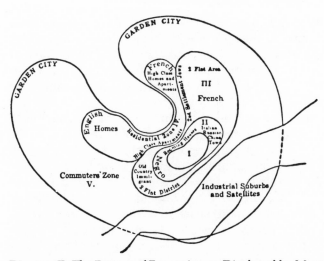

Diagram II. The Pattern of Expansion as Displayed by Montreal

Figure 1
From C.A. Dawson and W.E. Gettys, *An Introduction to Sociology*
(New York: Ronald Press 1929, 1935), 130

stable. Life was simple and intimate while contacts with other settlements and the outside world were few and far between. Today we live in a greatly changed Canada.' Since the Industrial Revolution and the subsequent improvement in transportation, 'we find the small communities which had formerly existed in isolation now being linked up with the outside world; now in place of isolated settlements and towns, there is a connected and mutually influencing series of modern industrialized urban centre.'[53]

Viewed from the perspective of social ecology, Montreal's growth from a small town to a major industrial city was most apparent in the changes that occurred in its central area. As attested to by its street names, the city was cradled in religion. In what became its business district once stood the old walled town of Ville Marie, founded as a religious community by priests and missionaries. Its location on the banks of a great river established the city as a centre of religious dominance during the French regime, and it maintained that status after Protestantism was brought with the British conquest, but even in the early days Montreal was more than a religious colony. The other purpose of its founding had been for the exploitation of the fur trade, and the interests of that trade, as well as the other commerical enterprises the city developed, soon superseded those of the gospel. Although the subordination of religion to the needs of commerce was more pronounced after what one of Dawson's students described as the Industrial Revolution of the 1850s, business began to take priority even during the French regime. As the fur trade grew, the business institutions that had initially located near the river encroached upon the residential district – the walled area of the city – and it was ultimately turned over to trade.[54] At that point it became the centre of dominance for the entire city, and the area in which an urban culture took root.

According to Chicago theory, one of the first signs of a community's passage from a small town to an urban centre was the introduction of public utilities. One of Dawson's students accordingly noted that the first indication of Montreal's evolution into a city was the installation of street lighting in 1815.[55] More significant, however, was the city's territorial expansion, which began in earnest in the 1820s and was manifested in the levelling of the city wall to give more space to commercialized interests. The signing of the Annexation Manifesto by 325 merchants in 1849, the repeal of the Navigation Laws to allow foreign ships to enter the St Lawrence, the deepening and widening of the channel, the incorporation of the Grand Trunk Railway in 1852 (and the completion of the Montreal-Toronto section in 1855), not to mention the opening of the Victoria Bridge in 1860, all turned Montreal into a centre of trade and commerce, and an era of construction and suburban growth ensued. It had been a discovery of the Chicago school that population followed the lines of least resistance, which in Montreal meant along the river with a gradual easing towards Mount Royal. To accord with that movement, tramway lines were laid in the centre of the city and extended to outlying districts following the lines of settlement.[56]

One of Dawson's students examined the effect that the construction of transportation lines had upon population settlement in a study of the St Antoine district, an area of Montreal that in the 1920s was on the verge of becoming a slum. The district as the student described it was a natural area of the city that had been created by the expansion of the business section; its boundaries were defined by tramway lines, and its population, which included a large portion of Montreal's black community, had been drawn in by the railway. The area first developed when the growth of the city's business district and the construction of the Grand Trunk and Canadian Pacific Railway lines forced the residents of the city's centre to settle in contiguous zones. At first, when the railway lines were laid, they created social disruption because they acted as barriers that divided people on one side of the tracks from those on the other. After a short period of instability, however, a community emerged and took on the pattern of urban growth. A centre emerged where the tramway lines intersected and hotels were built around the railway station. All this activity drove the home-lover out of the area, but St Antoine's days as a residential district were numbered in any event, the student reported. When Windsor Station was constructed, all the houses on the point of the district were given over to the railway; by 1927 there were no more houses or churches on the district's main street – the railway corporation owned all the property on St Antoine and was holding it for the day when it needed to increase its yard capacity. At that point, Dawson's student predicted, another period of demolition would ensue. As it was, the area's more successful residents had already moved above the hill and to the west; only those workers who needed to be close to their places of employment remained behind, to be joined by the unskilled groups who were increasingly taking up residence in St Antoine.[57]

The part of Montreal that experienced the most severe disruption as the business centre expanded was Dufferin district, a neighbourhood that lay in the city's transitional zone. Constituting a little more than half of the western portion of the St Lawrence ward, bounded by Ste Catherine Street on the north, St Lawrence on the east, Craig Street on the south, and Bleury on the west, the district was the slum of Montreal, a slum whose conditions were reportedly as bad as those of any European city.[58] Robert Percy, the master's student who undertook the study of the area, noted that the slum was a *fact* that sociologists had discovered in their investigations of social phenomena: 'it has been found,' he said, 'that slums grow up when the downtown area begins to invade the area immediately surrounding it.'[59] Indeed, in terms of its physical boundaries, spatial location, and social conditions, Dufferin district fulfilled all the criteria that the Chicago school had identified as characterizing a slum. The area was 'encircled by the tentacles of industry': on the four major streets that formed its boundaries were streetcar lines; these same streets were almost wholly occupied by commerical enterprises, some of which were invading the intersecting streets. Lying outside the district and to the west were more business offices, printing establishments, and warehouses. To the south lay the financial and business centre of the city; to the east was an almost entirely French district, and to the north was Ste Catherine, the great retail street of the city. Its social composition was similarly typical of transitional zones – a patchwork of immigrant groups. In fact, Percy contended, the area bore certain similarities to the old Indian village of Hochelaga. 'Cartier found two races,' he said; 'today in Dufferin district we find twenty – each differing from the others in tastes, characteristics, and modes of living, and even as Hochelaga had to give way to fratricidal war, racial animosities and foreign invasions, so, too, we believe will Dufferin district be eventually displaced by commercial invasion.'[60] Percy predicted that the district was in its last stage as a neighbourhood because the area was the favoured site for a new railway station and it was expected that the widening of St Urbain and Clark streets would rid it of its residents and turn it over entirely to commercial enterprise.[61]

Using street directories that illustrated changes in land use, Percy traced the history of Dufferin district up to the point at which it had become a slum. Only a few minutes' walk from the old Ville Marie, the district was originally a forest lying north of a brook along what became Craig Street. Gradually people built houses on the road that led to the country north, and the forest was transformed into a settlement, for many years known as the St Lawrence suburb. One of the first suburbs of the city, it was the place of residence not for the wealthy, who preferred to live within the city limits, but primarily for working men: the first city directory of 1801 listed its population as including labourers, bricklayers, and carpenters, a variety of different craftsmen and artisans, schoolmistresses and notaries, tavern-keepers, merchants, grocers, and the rector of the English church. By 1851, when St Lawrence Street had become the main street of Montreal and the dividing line between the eastern and western parts of the city (and

Dorchester separated uptown from downtown), Dufferin district was still a relatively stable area.[62] As Percy was to show, however, its proximity to the heart of the city ensured that it would become a transitional zone, invaded by industry and the point of entry and first settlement for newly arrived immigrants.

According to Percy's calculations, Dufferin district became a slum at the turn of the century, when the commercial sector of Montreal expanded and a flood of immigrants poured into the city from Asia and Europe. As its boundaries were invaded by machine shops, warehouses, and light manufacturing, the more successful among the English, Irish, Scottish, and French families who lived in the district departed. Their vacated homes began to deteriorate, were remodelled into flats, and occupied by the less prosperous, who rented but did not own them. The first large influx into the area was of Chinese, predominantly single men, who arrived in Montreal in 1893 and settled around Lagauchetière. Jews fleeing from the pogroms in Russia also settled in the district in the 1890s, for a while making it into the ghetto of Montreal. By the 1920s its population included, in addition to the remaining members of those two groups, Russians, Greeks, Italians, Germans, Poles, and an ever-increasing number of blacks.[63]

While stable residential neighbourhoods were well equipped with such institutions as churches and schools, Dufferin district did not have these in any great number. What it had, instead, was a number of 'imposed' or 'elevating' institutions – another index, according to Chicago theory, of an area's deterioration. According to Percy, rescue missions first made their appearance in Dufferin district in the 1890s, when, in order to counteract the influence of crime and all the other evils of the so-called demi-monde, 'the good people' from 'uptown' established museums, settlement houses, and playgrounds in the area. At the time of Percy's writing, in addition to McGill's university settlement, the district had a Chinese mission and Sunday school operated by the United Church, a Chinese YMCA and kindergarten run under the auspices of the Presbyterian Church, and a Catholic mission supervised by the Sisters of the Immaculate Conception. English missions to the French had ended in failure because of their attempts to proselytize, but the Protestant House of Industry and Refuge, which had been situated on Dufferin Street for fifty years, was a thriving enterprise. Subsidized by the city, it operated along the lines of an English workhouse, providing breakfast to the long line-ups of men, both Catholic and Protestant, who appeared at its doorstep every morning, but requiring them to work in the woodpile for a few hours before being dismissed.[64]

In at least two instances Percy remarked upon the existence of racial tensions in Dufferin district, noting that the area was 'torn asunder by racial animosity and cultural clashes.' He did not attribute those problems to any inherent antipathy the different ethnic groups might have felt towards one another but to the disorganized physical environment in which their poverty had forced them to live:

Crowded up to a deteriorating tenement there is a machine shop – next to it a factory, across the road, a tavern, beside it a Greek Coffee House or a Chinese barbershop – everywhere one looks there seems to be disharmony. The clash of interests, cultural and economic, the conflict between old ways and new, the discord of individuals and groups, all reflect to marked degree, the disunity of the district.

A seething mobile polyglot population lives here. An old Jewish patriarch with white flowing beard is jostled by a huge Polish labourer, a Chinaman steps out of the way of a passing Italian – a negro youth loiters in a door-way – a crowd of boys hurry to the Public Bath, a group of girls scamper off the roadway where they have been skipping.

Throughout the day and into the night, he continued, there were car jams and gangs of youths hanging around the street. To the north, by contrast, was an area of private homes and apartment houses where there was no clash or noise; to the south was the business sector, where, at least at night, it was quiet. But in Dufferin district, Percy concluded, there was constant noise, dirt, stimulation, vice, despair, and 'exaggerated life.'[65]

As an unstable area lying close to a business district, a slum, according to Chicago theory, was open to all manner of evil influence, and Dufferin district was no exception. Just to the east of it lay a red-light district and an area of commercialized vice, and in Percy's estimation these contributed in no small way to its problems. The notoriety of Cadieux Street was recognized world-wide, he contended. Not only was white slavery practised there, but the city was reputed to be the headquarters of the traffic; practically every house between Craig Street and Ste Catherine was a house of prostitution; solicitation was carried on in the streets wherever there were crowds, as well as in theatres, hotel lobbies, and Salvation Army gatherings. Newspaper boys, taxi-cab drivers, and bellhops all played a part in directing clients to the right houses. In 1925, Percy continued, the police attempted to clean up the area in response to public outcry. The backbone of the district was broken, but the Cadieux Street, Ste Elizabeth, and Hôtel de Ville residents simply moved out of their old habitats to establish places of business in other parts of the city. Although the majority left the area entirely, several located near McGill because of all the street-walking on Sherbrooke; others stayed downtown and flourished on Mayor Street, one block north of Ste Catherine, and on Inspector Street, adjacent to the railway station and hotels.

Through his own investigations Percy determined that there were in Dufferin district several houses of prostitution that catered to immigrants and homeless men. He believed these dated from the break-up of the red-light district – one section on Dorchester Street was, in fact, known as 'the Red Light Block.' He remarked, however, that none of the girls who worked in the district was attractive, that instead many of them were slovenly and unkempt and, even when they dressed up, displayed a penchant for showy, flashy, cheap attire and ornaments. Tourists, men-about-town, and visitors did not patronize these establishments but ones that claimed to be quiet and respectable, Percy explained, where procurers said they could secure 'Parisian girls' and French Canadians. In those houses the inmates commonly showed medical certificates of health; in Dufferin district the houses did not claim to offer freedom from infection to the patrons, 'who [were] themselves as dirty and as unattractive as the prostitutes.'[66]

In prostitution as in other illegal enterprises, vice existed in Dufferin district, but it was not highly organized. The street-walker was not usually in the control of a madam but was, rather, free-lance and knew where to take her client if she did not wish to bring him into her own home. There were in addition blind pigs and taverns open after legal hours, and some street traffic in narcotics. Although Chinatown catered almost exclusively to the Chinese population, Percy added, there were many Caucasians who frequented it after dark. 'They were generally members of the underworld or "pigeons" – the dope fiends, dope peddlars, and gamblers.'[67]

Two sociological studies that examined subjects commonly associated with social pathology – gang behaviour and dependency – verified, as did Percy's thesis, the Chicago theory that environment shaped behaviour. Although these were undertaken by social-work students under Dawson's supervision, they were also written in an ecological perspective and employed all the techniques of Chicago sociology. Interviews were conducted and information was obtained from settlement and playground workers, but all the data were plotted on maps to illustrate the spatial distribution of the particular problem under investigation. In 'Mobility and Boy Behaviour' one student found that juvenile delinquency was much more prevalent in such areas as the St Lawrence ward and the North End, Verdun, and the intersection of St Denis and Ste Catherine than it was in the less mobile residential areas of Westmount and Notre Dame de Grace.[68] A study on child dependency similarly found that families in need of assistance showed the greatest preponderance in 'areas of transition'; their highest degree of concentration was centred in an area west along Ste Catherine and east along Ontario Street, north along Park and Park Extension – all of which were arterial highways and main tramway lines. There was also a minor group of dependency cases in two suburbs of Verdun in the southwestern part of the city, and in Rosemount in the northeast. (The Rosemount suburb, which had grown up around the CPR Angus shops, was an extremely poor area of the city. What Dawson's student found particularly distressing about it, however, was that the houses showed no variety but were all alike 'with their long outside staircases, presenting the appearance of a bad dream.') From Mansfield west to Jeanne Mance and from Sherbrooke on the north to Craig Street on the south there was an almost solid block of dependency, and only less solidly did it spread as far west as Dominion Street and as far east as St Denis. This, of course, was the business area of the city, and also part of the slum; the cases above Sherbrooke Street, stretching from University on the west to Hôtel de Ville, were similarly in an area of transition. Once the site of single-family dwellings, by 1931 the district was composed almost entirely of apartment houses, flats, tourist accommodations, and boarding houses. (The study on child dependency was undertaken by a native Manitoban, who was able to compare her Montreal findings with a similar investigation of Winnipeg. The student discovered that the dependency cases in Winnipeg followed the same general pattern of distribution as in Montreal. The greatest number were located in areas invaded by business and industry – they were concentrated around the CPR tracks, extended south to Chinatown, and from there spread into the wholesale district, covering the area from Princess Street west to Sherbrooke and south to Portage Avenue.)[69]

Whether they examined topics that fell under the rubric of sociology, social work, or theology, all of Dawson's graduate students believed that the structure, growth, and expansion of the city had a tremendous impact on the social life and value of its residents. While they understood that industrialization and transportation, trade and commerce were the forces that determined the city's character, they were not prepared in the 1920s to attribute its problems to unregulated capitalism. The city loomed large in their eyes – they saw it, and not some economic system, as the mechanism that sifted and sorted the population and determined its values and institutions. In fact, they regarded it as such a powerful force that they did not think anything could escape its control. Nowhere was this more evident than in the studies that dealt with the subject of religion. In an ecological history of the Protestant church in Montreal, for instance, one of Dawson's students insisted that as an institution that reflected particular forms of communal organization, the church was constantly being modified by changes incident to city life. The church, he said, was an institution with goals and ideals that changed and adapted, 'but neither its tradition, nor its power for good [could] save it from the disintegrating influences of city life.'[70] He grouped the churches of Montreal into three categories, all of which accorded with the different concentric zones in the city. He found a downtown pattern, consisting of missions maintained by one denomination or another in behalf of submerged souls and the immigrant population; inner-city area churches that behaved like downtown churches, attracting transients and appealing to lost souls; and suburban churches, which had moved from their initial location within the city in response to their congregants' acquisition of wealth. Moreover, he argued that the differences that divided the Protestant churches and missions in Montreal stemmed not from doctrinal divisions but from their need to adapt and readjust to the city's growth.[71]

In a study of the Montreal YMCA another of Dawson's students illustrated how quickly the conditions of city life eroded the religious impulses that underlay the development of that social institution. As the student explained it, the YMCA was at birth a city product, founded in London, England, in the 1850s in response to the problems caused by the Industrial Revolution. The founders of the organization attempted by religious means to ease the problems of social adjustment that the young men who had come to the city looking for jobs were experiencing. Their methods were evangelical, Dawson's student contended, because they were religious and knew no other methods: 'they believed in the doctrines of the church, that man's immortality was due to original sin, and could only be prevented by conversion to membership in the Christian church.'[72] Nevertheless, as the decades passed, the religious impulse was submerged in favour of a social motive, and this, too, was apparent in the history of the Montreal organization.

The Montreal Young Men's Christian Association was founded in the 1850s, but it did not have much of an affiliation with the London organization, nor was it required to deal with the same social conditions that afflicted London. Montreal's population at the time was only 57,715, about half of that number English. The Y's early work consisted of mental improvement: it opened a library stocked with primarily religious books, held weekly prayer-meetings, and operated a Sunday school. By the 1860s, however, under pressure to give more attention to social problems, its members inaugurated cottage meetings in various parts of the city, went on house-to-house visitations, and worked with sailors on the wharves and vessels; they also visited soldiers' barracks, hospitals, jails, and the female refuge.[73] By 1871 Montreal's population had grown to 107,225, and the emphasis on the social motive intensified. Though the YMCA moved to a new building, complete with spire, gothic windows, and room enough for large evangelistic meetings, its primary purpose was to provide a pleasant environment that would serve as a counterpoise to the ills of the city found in Montreal's 357 licensed and 116 unlicensed saloons, billiards, and clubhouses. The shift away from a religious orientation was even more noticeable by 1881: because the city had no public libraries, museums, educational classes, or recreational facilities for men of moderate means, the organization instituted lectures in philosophy, hygiene, chemistry, American history, the first principles of machinery, arithmetic, and bookkeeping.[74]

Evaluating the Y's program up to the 1880s, the McGill sociology student noted that although Darwin was probably unknown to most workers of the organization, they seemed to be attempting 'to work out the theory of evolution in relation to the development of the human personality' – after all, their activities concentrated on the growth of the body, mind, and spirit. In the late nineteenth and early twentieth centuries the idea of salvation by education of the body, mind, and spirit became a way of life rather than a creed, he contended, and after the First World War education played an even larger role in the YMCA's program. In 1919 the educational department, which included a boys' grammar school, became known as the YMCA School; in 1920 it instituted what turned out to be a very popular evening class for students preparing for university matriculation. These schools were made into a distinct branch of the organization in 1925, when a separate board of management was appointed to administer them. In 1926, in order to honour the man who had initiated similar activities in the London association, the name of Sir George Williams was adopted in place of the Montreal YMCA School, and this was the beginning of Sir George Williams University.[75]

The Montreal YMCA placed such emphasis upon educational programs in the early twentieth century because of the city's increasingly problematic social conditions, made all the more difficult with a large immigrant population and the absence of legislation enforcing compulsory education. Its recreational program was equally affected by the conditions of modern industrialism: in the interwar period, the evangelistic motive was almost completely abandoned in favour of human engineering and efficiency, and questions were raised as to the beneficial results of certain of the Y's activities. It was believed that the difficult problems with which the association had to deal would only yield to careful and skilful treatment and that its success as a social institution would depend upon its willingness to acquire and use new educational social techniques based upon experimental science. Consequently, a new emphasis was placed upon staff training and surveys: in 1923 an extensive investigation was undertaken to determine what needs the organization had failed to meet among the boys and young men in the city; information was gathered on population, industries, commercialized amusements, churches, schools, and other social agencies. A decision was made in light of the survey to restudy YMCA services and to adopt an even more scientific approach. The distance the YMCA had travelled from its initial religious motives was even more evident in the public's reaction to its new direction. In 1927 a series of lectures on the general theme of 'Science, Philosophy, and Religion in the Modern World' was given under the auspices of the Young Men's Forum. The lecture on evolution incited controversy, complete with an article in the Montreal *Gazette* that deplored the organization's commercialization and secularization.[76]

These studies of Montreal were among the few such investigations undertaken of the city in the 1920s. However much they were derived from the themes of Chicago sociology, they reveal something of the pressures that the city experienced during a period of rapid growth and industrialization, and that, after all, was the reason why scientific sociology had been instituted at McGill.

IV

In the late 1920s, while his students were still investigating Montreal, Dawson began to turn his attention towards explaining the general pattern of settlement in Canada. In so doing he was not departing from the major tenets of Chicago sociology, neither from the emphasis that it placed upon the community as a focus of study nor from the importance that it assigned to the city as a symbol of modern civilization. Ecological theory suggested that human society was organized on the pattern of a spider's web. Dawson similarly described it as 'one great community,' and that, in addition to the migration movements that were giving the world the appearance of being, as he put it, 'one huge directory,' provided him with all the justification he needed to focus on areas other than the local community. More importantly, Dawson's fascination with the city, like that of a number of other Chicago sociologists, entailed an interest in more than just its internal structure. He regarded the city as a spatial pattern of a fixed centre of dominance with tributary subordinate districts whose expansion and control over surrounding regions was facilitated by improvements in transportation and communication.[77] Not surprisingly, this led him to conclude that the entire history of Western civilization could be explained in terms of an ever-increasing metropolitanism, a phenomenon that brought more and more areas under the control of great cities. His understanding of Canadian society was shaped by a conviction he shared with many other Chicago sociologists – that North America, a product of the overseas expansion of the great European centres of dominance, was a striking example of the process of metropolitanism at work.

Before he had the opportunity of undertaking his own investigations for the Frontiers of Settlement project, Dawson's views of Canadian settlement were largely derived from ideas he found in the work of R.D. McKenzie and another Canadian academic teaching in the United States, N.S.B. Gras. McKenzie had first introduced into Chicago sociology the notion that the expansion of Western civilization was the product of metropolitan dominance in 'The Concept of Dominance and World Organization' (1927). With reference to the writings of John Wynne Jeudwine, he argued that throughout history all effective expansion had begun from a town and that the extent and success of that expansion depended upon the factors that linked the metropolis with its hinterland. From that perspective he illustrated that the ancient empires of China, Greece, and Rome, representing military and political forms of dominance centred in fortified cities, had operated through their ability to utilize whatever crude forms of communication and transportation were available to them. Their expansion had been limited, McKenzie argued, because 'tribute' defined their relation to subordinate regions. With the rise of trade centres on the Mediterranean and Baltic seaboards, however, the relationship between cities and hinterlands shifted from political to economic dominance, and that stimulated improvements in transportation, which enabled centres of dominance to consolidate their power. The Spanish, Portuguese, Dutch, French, and English all competed to extend their commercial relations with Asia, Africa, and America, McKenzie explained, but England emerged supreme because she developed and managed to maintain between her own ports and the outlying ports of the world the most effective system of transportation and communication. England possessed the greatest merchant marine and navy, laid most of the cables of the world, and built and financed most of the ports and railways outside of Europe. To McKenzie's way of thinking the concentration of the main arteries of world communication 'in the little island of the North Sea' gave to England a dominance in international commerce that was 'very similar to the business centre of the city with respect to its local integrated districts.'[78]

Although McKenzie's work was not directly influenced by it, in his *Introduction to Economic History* (1922) N.S.B. Gras had outlined the stages involved in a town's rise to metropolitan status. These included the organization of a well-developed marketing system, the establishment of manufacturing enterprises in both the metropolis and its hinterlands, the construction of transportation routes linking the city with outlying areas, and the consolidation of financial power by means of a more sophisticated financial organization.[79] In their explanation of London's emergence as the market and organizing centre of a world economic order, however, Dawson and Gettys relied heavily upon Gras' typology. They outlined the manner in which London became the centre of a world securities market, the centre of trade routes and of telegraphic communication, the headquarters of great trading companies, and the most active agent in the mobilization of commodities and men. They described how, through the natural medium of London, new regional divisions of labour arose and within them, new spatial distributions of institutions and men. What they regarded as most important was Gras' discussion of transportation routes, and they elaborated in typical Chicago terminology that as London became the hub of growth and change, its influence was transmitted outward 'along the axial lines of transportation.' As they described it, when London expanded, it absorbed competitive but subsidiary cities that became links in the chain connecting its life to that of other regions. Each of these cities in turn became the centre of its own particular hinterland and served the needs of that hinterland in specialized ways.[80]

Neither McKenzie nor Dawson and Gettys' discussion of the centres of world dominance were intended to extol British imperialism or the virtues of the Anglo-Saxon race. They were meant to illustrate, rather, that particular civilizations predominated at certain points in history because of their resources and their ability to exploit them. As Dawson and Gettys saw it, the British were merely 'a functioning unit in an international order of interdependent parts,' equipped to take the greatest advantage of the resources and main trends of development 'to become the point where that order was most vibrant and most sensitive to change,' but this supremacy was ephemeral, and their powers and earlier advantages were bound to pass into the hands of their competitors and even their hinterlands. In fact, to Dawson and Gettys the course of contemporary events indicated that the centre of world dominance was shifting to the United States, which had itself begun as a series of frontier colonies, primarily of England. Not only was New York vying with London for the position of dominance in finance, but it had outstripped it in certain forms of industrial financing. The world now had two centres of dominance, they argued, and all other cities played a role in an international mechanism that revolved around London and New York.[81]

Perhaps not so ironically, Dawson's first tract on Canadian settlement appeared in the same issue of the *American Journal of Sociology* as McKenzie's 'Concept of Dominance.' Entitled 'Population Areas and Physiographic Regions in Canada' (1927), its purpose was to illustrate that Canada's pattern of settlement and economic activities were primarily shaped by the country's status as the hinterland of a succession of dominant centres, first of France, then of England, and more recently of the United States. The French began their overseas expansion in Canada, Dawson explained, entering the continent at its most accessible point from the east, the St Lawrence–Great Lakes system, which extended two thousand miles into the heart of North America and almost reached the Mississippi valley. This was a region that offered two outstanding resources for exploitation – argriculture and fur – but since the purpose of French expansion had been to consolidate the empire and extend the sway of the king rather than to establish a home, emphasis was placed upon the latter. Some settlement was encouraged because colonists were necessary for the conduct of the fur trade, and some agriculture was practised for the same reason, but both were meagre enterprises. The fur trade produced a wanderlust, Dawson explained, that mobilized the restless elements of the community, and this seriously limited the extent of the settled population. The Maritimes were similarly unimportant from the point of view of settlement. Although the fisheries produced some sparsely settled areas, since the chief market for their produce was in Europe, most fishermen lived in European communities. When control of the new-world colony passed into British hands, however, a policy of settlement was more actively pursued. Two main agricultural sections – the St Lawrence and Niagara regions – were developed, and they provided a base for expansion into other regions.[82]

In 'Population Areas and Physiographic Regions' Dawson illustrated that Canada's major urban centres were also products of the commerical interests of dominating metropolises, cities that linked the dominant centres with their hinterlands. Montreal and Quebec became important as centres of trade and protection under the French regime when, along with Trois Rivières, they became the depots to which fur traders brought their wares and the points from which were distributed the few articles of consumption that came from the outside world. After the British conquest Montreal continued to be an important centre because of its strategic location on the St Lawrence, but since the system of British colonial organization was designed to maintain the dominance of British centres, Montreal, along with the rest of Canada, was compelled to provide the raw materials for England's industrial production.[83]

A more thorough analysis of the way in which Canada's urban centres were affected by shifts in the country's centres of dominance was provided by S.D. Clark in a master's thesis done under Dawson's supervision at McGill. Clark's thesis, 'The Role of Metropolitan Institutions in the Formation of a Canadian National Consciousness' (1935), was undertaken in connection with the Canadian-American relations study launched by the Carnegie Endowment for International Peace.[84] Often ignored as part of the corpus of Clark's work, perhaps because of the opposition he later expressed against McGill sociology, it amalgamated the objectives of that project with the major elements of Parkian theory. The specific purpose of the thesis was to explain the manner in which Canadian attitudes towards the United States had led to the creation of a distinct Canadian national identity, but Clark saw nationalism as having two foundations, and these accorded with the distinctions that Park had made between community and society. Clark argued that nationalism had an ecological basis that stemmed from the attempt of cities to mark out an area of dominance for themselves, and a psychological aspect that was manifested in the development of a sentiment to accord with the area of political organization.[85] Specifically, he considered that Canadian nationalism was based, on the one hand, upon the integration of the economic life of the hinterland with local metropolitan organization, and on the other, with the creation in the minds of Canadians of symbols that distinguished Canada from Great Britain and the United States.[86] Of the two, Clark believed that the main 'thoroughfare' in Canadian national development was the attempt of Montreal and Toronto 'to bring the narrow, straggling strip of territory stretching across the fringe of the United States under their economic tutelage.'[87]

In his analysis of the efforts of Montreal and Toronto to weld Canada into a single economic and industrial structure, Clark did not merely catalogue the activities of the two cities' economic-interest groups. He illustrated the difficulties they faced in carving out for themselves an area of influence free from the commercial interests of Britain and the United States. From 1783 onwards, he argued, Great Britain and the United States competed for control of markets in the western hemisphere, and Canada's early economic history took the pattern of competitive struggle between the metropolitan interest groups of both those nations to control the hinterland market. He showed that within the framework of the imperial system there grew up in Canada certain economic groups interested in maintaining the imperial connection. Whether they were involved in the fur trade, lumber, wheat, or transportation, these groups were outposts of the British metropolitan structure and chains of communication between the frontier and the empire centre. Concentrated in trade and transport, they included strongly organized firms such as the Canadian steamship and railway companies, interests associated with Canadian ports, and exporting and importing merchants. All of them naturally favoured trade with Canada and distant countries – especially Great Britain – rather than the United States. At the same time, there were a number of internal trading groups that constituted an integral part of the commercial organization of the United States and accordingly favoured trade with that country. That these groups were strongly associated with the developing agricultural communi-ty, particularly that of the west, was not surprising to Clark. Ever since the opening of the American west and the rise of Chicago as the natural centre of transportation in North America, he contended, the Canadian west had been an extension of the great American plains. Later on, with the advent of large-scale production, the availability of abundant resources, and the rapidly expanding hinterland markets, the supremacy of the American metropolitan centres was strengthened all the more.[88]

As Clark saw it, when local metropolitan groups tried to assert their control over the fledgling nation's economic activities in the second half of the nineteenth century, they were forced to league together with imperial interest groups to combat the influence of the American centres. Their first priority was to create efficient lines of transportation and a fiscal policy that would encourage the flow of trade through imperial rather than American channels. The railway-building of the 1860s and 1870s, the port question, the agitation for a protective tariff, and imperial trade preference all seemed to Clark to be manifestations of these objectives. (He showed that the issue of transportation was extremely important to Montreal, which saw itself as the main port of entry into Canada and, therefore, the chief rival of the American seaboard cities. He also pointed out the displeasure that the Montreal Board of Trade expressed about the shortage of transportation facilities, which caused a large portion of the northwest trade to be diverted to Duluth, Buffalo, and other American channels.) The fiscal policy of protection, Clark argued, was designed to integrate the various regions scattered from the Atlantic to the Pacific into a national economy, and it was almost wholly directed against the industries of the southern republic. The insistence of the Canadian Manufacturers' Association that the policy was foisted upon them by the United States' refusal of reciprocity was, according to him, a justification and not a cause. Many local manufacturers did not want reciprocity, he contended, and in any event the tariff strengthened their position and made possible the expansion of the Canadian industrial community. The issue of imperial trade was more problematic. Although they were not initially willing to encourage the sale of British products that would compete with commodities they producted themselves, local manufacturers turned towards the principle of empire trade after the McKinley tariff destroyed the possibility of reciprocity with the United States. Such events as Empire weeks, British trade shows, and even the decision of McGill University to levy higher tuition fees on all students except those who came from Canada and parts of the British Empire reflected support for the idea. Since the British Parliament was wedded to the idea of free trade, however, the tariff preference of the Laurier government remained the lone gesture towards Empire trade until the 1930s, Clark noted, when the threat posed to Britain's free-trade empire by the Depression and the collapse of Canada's wheat market revived the principle and resulted in the convening of the Imperial Economic Conference in 1932.[89]

Clark concluded that for most of its history, Canada had been a frontier on two fronts, serving the metropolitan interests of both Britain and the United States. Yet it seemed to him from the vantage point of the 1930s that although the country was still tied to the metropolitan economies of Britain and the United States, the frontier relationship was changing and in its place was arising a relationship based upon local metropolitan organization. He thought that the institution of the protective-tariff policy augured the beginning of this reorientation and that the Ottawa Economic Conference marked its definite recognition in the politics of the Empire but that the factor that contributed the most to its realization was Canada's industrial progress in the early twentieth century.[90] Although Toronto had established the lead in industrial production, the exploitation of hydroelectric power in Quebec had widened Canada's industrial base and caused a realignment of regional relationships. 'Montreal drew nearer to Toronto,' Clark argued, 'and the ends of St. James and Bay Streets joined to become the heart of a new manufacturing centre.'[91] Together the two cities attempted to develop strong home markets and ensure that commerce ran in an easterly and westerly direction.

In the second part of his thesis Clark attempted to explain how and why the economic interests of local metropolitan groups had been translated into a nationalist ideology. He argued that Canadian nationalism was expansive – it began as 'a regional consciousness of rising industrial centres' based upon 'the ambitions of cabinet and machine manufacturers' who saw in the growing hinterland market the opportunity of securing greater profits. Although the railway-building of the 1860s and 1870s provided the framework for a metropolitan economy under the control of those manufacturers, it lacked a foundation, a sentiment tying together the provincial groups of the dominion. The British identity had been the cement that held together the disparate parts of Canada, but when that weakened, manufacturers and entrepreneurs contended that only intranational bonds of transportation and trade could save it from disintegrating.[92] Nationalism, as Clark saw it, was the mechanism by which metropolitan organization was justified and sustained. 'Industrialism had to seek support,' he said, 'in a conception of political relationships wide enough to permit the free operation of the forces of capital expansion and yet provide protection from the dominant industrial enterprises of outside centres. Such a solution was found in the idea of the nation state.'[93] By means of their close relationship with the urban daily press and through their own institutions in local communities, manufacturers and entrepreneurs were able to direct the currents of national thought, to institutionalize and give expression to metropolitan control. They tried to foster the notion that their interests and those of the general public were identical by depicting themselves as spokesmen for the urban community and the tariff as 'the sine qua non' of urban life. They also attempted to convince railway stockholders that they had a vested interest in supporting a field of activity that had grown out of local metropolitan organization. They strove to establish a rapport with labour by calling upon the Canadian public to buy Canadian goods and so ensure industrial employment. Agriculture did not conform as readily to the needs of metropolitan organization, but manufacturers tried to argue that they shared common interests with the farmers – most particularly a market that would be lost under a system of free trade.[94]

V

In its discussion of Canada's initial status as a frontier in which there gradually evolved strong local metropolitan centres, S.D. Clark's thesis reflected a major concern of Chicago sociology.[95] It also illustrates how well the theories of that school accorded with the nationalism popular in English-speaking Canada during the interwar years. The theory of metropolitan dominance was easily applied to describe and explain the attempts of Montreal and Toronto – the two powerful cities of central Canada – to consolidate their control over the development of the rest of the country. The same relationship was evident in a theory that grew from metropolitan dominance and that Carl Dawson increasingly regarded as integral to understanding Canadian society – regionalism. Because Canada was such a vast country and far less urbanized than either Europe or the United States, Dawson had found it necessary to formulate a set of concepts to define the growth and structure of its regions. He began working on the theory in the late 1920s and put it to its most extensive use in his contributions to the Frontiers of Settlement series. Although the theory ultimately attained as much importance in his work as the city held in Park's, it did not minimize the status that the Chicago school had assigned to the city as the motive force in the development of Western civilization. Metropolitanism and regionalism were two sides of the same coin; both stemmed from the ideas about dominance that Chicago sociologists had inherited from post-Darwinian biology. Where the former was concerned with the emergence, growth, and influence of cities, the latter focused on those areas that came under their control.

In the context of international organization, metropolitan dominance meant that the extension of the market through the development of transportation was believed to have brought large sections of the world under the control of great cities. Because the subordinate areas were compelled to serve the economic needs of the dominant centres, some parts of the world were given over to agriculture, cattle-raising, or wheat-growing, and some to the cultivation of cotton, coffee, spices, and rubber; other areas were devoted to mining and lumbering, while some, because of their proximity to raw materials, specialized in transportation and manufacturing.[96] The outcome of metropolitan dominance, in other words, was regional specialization, but this was not the issue with which Dawson was specifically concerned; his theory of regionalism dealt with the internal structure of regions – the metropolitan centres and tributary districts that developed around them. Even in that context, however, the concept of metropolitanism continued to be important. Rather than define a region in geographical terms – as an area distinguished by natural areas and topography – Dawson preferred to describe it as a constellation of communities at whose head stood a main city that served as the focal point in determining the structure, institutions, and division of labour of the area. While a region might well be bounded by topographical features such as mountains, large lakes, and rivers and might also differ from other areas with respect to its soil, climate, and natural facilities for transportation, Dawson argued that it could nevertheless extend beyond its topographical barriers to take in parts of other regions. This was because its unity was based not upon physiography but upon the functions that its constituent communities played in a division of labour that covered a much vaster area.[97]

Dawson first employed his general theory of regionalism in 'Population Areas and Physiographic Regions in Canada' to describe the country's structure. He explained that Canada had four clearly defined physiographic regions, which were separated from each other by great barriers; these same regions ran down into the United States, where the barriers running north and south were less distinctive. The most important among them was the central area, which included the agricultural lands of Ontario and Quebec. This region was almost a continual area of land, except that it was separated at Kingston, near the outlet of Lake Ontario, by a point of the Laurentian plateau that formed the Thousand Islands in the St Lawrence and then jutted down into New York State. On the west and north the area was bounded by the Laurentian highland or Canadian Shield, but on the south for some distance there was no natural barrier between Canada and the United States, and this had facilitated early connections between the valleys of the Richelieu and Hudson rivers. Lying to the east was the Maritimes, cut off from the central region by the northward thrust of the Appalachian Mountains. Except for New Brunswick the area was primarily island and physiographically part of New England. (In fact, Dawson explained, the Maritimes had shared in the expansive development of New England until the American tariff barrier of 1864 isolated it economically from the United States, as it was isolated by nature from central Canada.) The third region, the western plains, was separated from the central area by the Laurentian Shield, though only artificial barriers marked it off from a similar physiographic region in the United States; the fourth region, British Columbia, was separated and distinguished from the plains by a sea of mountains that appeared at the western edge of Alberta and extended westward to the Pacific Ocean, but again, Dawson noted, only artifical barriers divided it from the United States.[98]

While Dawson's description of Canada sounded like the typical continentalist interpretation, he was not attempting to minimize the differences between Canada and the United States. He believed that it was important for the sociologist to understand the physiography of an area in so far as it determined social distance, and since Canada was a country of far more marked physiographic regions than the United States, he said, it was to be expected that there would be a greater dissimilarity of its population groups and cultures. But physiography was not the only factor that shaped the character of a region. Though largely determined by topographic features, transportation and communication were equally important, since in conjuntion with an area's natural resources, they provided the foundation for its division of labour, the basis of its unity. In the case of Canada, Dawson argued, the conjunction of transportation and communication had determined that the central region would play the dominant role economically, politically, and socially in a system of 'decentralized centralization.' With that term he was not referring to the Canadian federal system, though he believed it mirrored the physical realities of the country, but to the fact that while Canada was socially and geographically stratified, it was tied together, however tenuously, by the economic interests of the centre. The Great Lakes–St Lawrence system had always been the heart and highway of settlement and the economic nerve-centre of Canada, Dawson said. Like all such dominant centres, it was the point from which expansion to other regions had been initiated and the area of industrial concentration. All this was reflected in its social structure: the provinces of Ontario and Quebec together possessed 60 per cent of Canada's population and 80 per cent of the persons employed in manufacturing.[99]

The most obvious example of the way in which other regions were drawn into the web of the central area's dominance was the west. The most specialized farming section in Canada, Dawson explained, the plains region was inhabited by approximately two million people. With the fringe settlement of ranching pushed back into dry areas, the region's central economic interest was grain, which yielded four million bushels a year, and germane to that were the railways and banks administered from the central area. 'Nowhere in Canada,' he said, 'with the possible exception of British Columbia, did the railroad so obtrude itself into the consciousness of a Canadian area of population.' The economic interests of the centre, manifested in the presence of the railway, had done much to shape the contours of the region. In the early nineteenth century the American frontier had rapidly developed: the cultivation of cotton and tobacco had given a market and an early impetus to the industrial and commercial progress of its eastern region, enabling it to organize resources and markets that in turn facilitated population movement into the central and western plains.

This was in stark contrast to Canada, which at the time had lumber and agriculture to put on the world market in the midst of keen competition, but no great staple like cotton. Wheat was only 'a vaguely suspected potential' of the Canadian western plains, and there was no way to export it except through the United States, 'for the Laurentian highlands formed a formidable rocky barrier of 1500 miles.' Nevertheless, despite the fact that the natural route lay south of the Great Lakes and that it was a difficult task to build and operate a railway through such a long stretch of rough and uninhabited country with no local traffic, a line was built across the Shield by the Canadian Pacific Railway company at a great cost in money and western land ceded to the company. The location of the railway lines, in turn, determined the path of population settlement. Where the earlier inhabitants had followed the buffalo trails used by the Indians, in the days of the railway surveys, with few obstacles to road-building, most of the early trails were ploughed up and obliterated. By means of the gridiron survey the people were set down in regular administrative areas; topography was not taken into account at all in the settlement of this relatively level region.[100]

British Columbia and the Maritimes were less solidly tied into the dominance of Canada's central region, but as Dawson explained it, this was a new development for the former and part of a long historical trend for the latter. Dawson argued that the rapid industrial progress of British Columbia during the early twentieth century, its access to the Panama Canal, and the fact that its Pacific ports were never closed by inclement weather had served to erode the power of the central area. The Maritimes, by contrast, belonging to an economic unit outside Canada, separated from it by American tariff regulations and by freight rates favouring central Canada, had always been a 'border region' and suffered from that status. The French had treated the region as an outpost guarding Canada's gateway, and after 1864 it developed subsidiary to the Great Lakes–St Lawrence region. It experienced isolation from within and without. Traffic went by it on two sides – either down the St Lawrence or by the short route to Portland, which had practically become Canada's winter port. Originally peopled by the same groups that had settled Ontario, for a long time the region had little or no immigration and a very slight population growth. Its fertile areas were separated by topography, its fishing villages by land configuration, and there was no particular urgency for improvements in transportation that might alleviate that problem. The cultural barrier of Quebec, Dawson concluded, only extended the social and physical distance that separated the people of the Maritimes from the central area.[101]

Dawson was not unaware of the grievances and alienation that the system of 'decentralized centralization' had caused in Canada. He noted that the outer areas were not well accommodated to the prestige and power of the central area and thought that perhaps the Fathers of Confederation had foreseen this 'when they attempted to put under the federal government twice as many items as were retained by the provincial governments.'[102] He alluded to the high freight rates levied upon the west because of the necessary haul through 'the no-man's land of the Laurentian highlands' and explained how this had generated criticism of railway policy and battles to revise rates downward. Moreover, he argued, the demand for banking autonomy in the form of rural credits being sought by rural farmers was threatening to undermine the central area's power. 'In Parliament,' he said, '[the prairie farmers] are more solidly represented than any area except Quebec. This liberal-progressive bloc knows what it wants.' Dawson was, of course, most familiar with the discontent of the Maritimes, his native region. He detailed how its sensitivity to a loss of status and its lack of financial and political power commensurate with other sections of the dominion had resulted in unrest and finally in an investigation by a parliamentary commission.[103]

Dawson's reason for dwelling on Canada's regional problems in an article written for an American journal is not entirely clear. It may, however, stem from the importance that all Chicago-trained sociologists attached to understanding issues in terms of their natural history or with reference to natural areas. As we have seen, Chicago sociologists believed that specific environments just as easily generated problems as they shaped institutions and culture. By 1937, after more than a decade of research on Canadian society, Dawson was arguing that all problems and issues with which sociologists had to deal had a regional context, were tied up with the life of that region and with the stage that the region had reached in its development.[104] In that respect, in 'Population Areas and Physiographic Regions' he had not only put forward his theory of regionalism but hinted at his future agenda, which was to study the different areas of Canada and the lives of the people within them.

VI

Given his belief in the principles of dominance, Dawson had to insist that every part of the world would eventually be drawn into the pattern of metropolitanism. With the extension of transportation and communication, he and Gettys once argued, 'the physiographic areas of the world could no longer exist in splendid isolation ... Barriers were crossed by goods and information.' People and their territories were drawn into a world-wide competitive system as older types of livelihoods and their methods of organization, devices of transportation, and ancient heritages were thrown into the maelstrom of the selective process. 'Fast mail, cable, telegraph, telephone, wireless, and radio [had] transformed the world into a vast whispering gallery.'[105]

Despite all the rhetoric about interdependence and interconnections, Dawson recognized that there were a few isolated regions left in the world, and of these Canada had two different types. The lower St Lawrence was one such region: the meagreness of its resources and a generally poor climate had prevented marked agricultural and industrial exploitation in the area; the means of communication by land and water were primitive, and as a consequence it was only slightly under the dominance of Quebec City. It had few divisions of labour; its scattered communities had little contact with each other and little interaction with the culture of other regions. For such reasons, Dawson and Gettys noted, the area was often called backward, impervious to new ideas, and culturally retarded. While they believed that it did suffer from isolation – contact with other people, they thought, was the path to cultural enrichment and individual development – they considered the stability of its cultural and social institutions to be remarkable. The inhabitants spoke as their fathers spoke, sang the old songs, and passed the ancient legends down from generation to generation, they reported.[106] At the time, Marius Barbeau was collecting folklore in the area for the anthropological section of the Canadian Geological Survey, and Dawson and Gettys reprinted in their textbook an article by Roderick Peattie, who had ventured into the lower St Lawrence region with him. Peattie noted that there had been some recent modifications in the area's isolation, with the development of transportation facilities and the cheese industry, but that Barbeau was able to collect several hundred old legends, ballads, and verses from the natives of the poorer and less accessible regions, who had preserved in old French the legends of northern France and passed them on to succeeding generations. He described how they went into the cabin of an old man noted for his versatility in the art of ballad-singing and how, as the man sang to them, at the far end of the room his daughter crooned the words to the baby nursing at her breast. 'Unless the railroad invades the town,' Peattie commented, 'the baby will grow up to know and love these songs. Should the railroad penetrate to Tadoussac, the chances are that the child will read the newspaper to the exclusion of the old ways.'[107]

Areas such as the lower St Lawrence region provided sociologists with as much insight into the development of society as they furnished anthropologists with information on the development of culture. The interest of those trained at Chicago was, of course, in observing how such isolated regions were integrated into the pattern of metropolitanism. Another type of area not yet woven into this pattern was the frontier. After studying Canada's historical development as the frontier of Britain and the United States, Dawson was ready to examine Canada's own hinterland. The theories outlined here provided him with the framework to study the internal structure of the Canadian west, its institutions, economic activities, and towns. The theories of metropolitanism and regionalism, however, had their limitations, and that only became clear to Dawson in his actual investigation of the west.

5

Frontiers of Settlement

The inception of the Canadian Frontiers of Settlement project enabled C.A. Dawson to apply his theories of metropolitanism in a study of the development of the Canadian west, but he was not the only social scientist for whom the project presented an opportunity to study a subject of long-held interest. As one of the first examples of co-operative research in North America, the Frontiers of Settlement project embraced the intellectual concerns of a great number of academics. It permitted Canadian social scientists to study the west from a number of different angles, including its ability to absorb new immigrants and its productivity in mining and agriculture. However, since the project originated in the United States, it also reflected the preoccupations of many American social scientists, particularly the interest they took during the 1920s in international migration and the battle they were waging with natural scientists over which group had the right to undertake migration research.[1] In fact, it was this issue and the determination of American social scientists to demonstrate the usefulness of their disciplines that gave birth to the project.

I

In their attempt to reach a wider audience, to gain financial support for their research, and to influence public policy, there was no better issue for American social scientists to turn to in the early 1920s than immigration. In order to win recognition as experts in the field, however, they were forced to compete with those of their colleagues in the natural sciences who had become involved in migration research during the First World War and had been able to continue their investigations after the war with considerable financial support. The most influential of these individuals were Robert M.

Yerkes, who had directed the army's mental-testing program; Charles Davenport, who had undertaken an anthropometric study of servicemen; and John C. Merriam, a supporter of eugenics. As president of the Carnegie Institution, Merriam had been able to convince members of that organization to sponsor a series of conferences on biological research through 1920 and 1921. Most of the participants in those conferences tended to share his views on eugenics, heredity, race, and biological anthropology; Yerkes in particular had concluded during the war that racial differences were important in human affairs and was determined thereafter to examine what ramifications race had upon public policy. Following the Carnegie conferences, accordingly, he decided to establish a major research program on race under the aegis of the National Research Council and its division of anthropology and psychology. A member of the NRC board, he persuaded his colleagues to appoint him chairman of a new committee on the scientific problems of human migration, following which he and the other committee members drew up a preliminary research agenda devoted to examining immigration to the United States as well as the movement of southern blacks to northern American cities.[2]

It was no accident that natural scientists became interested in migration research when they did. Changes were anticipated in American immigration policy, and they wished to be in a position to influence the new legislation. Yerkes's committee contended that the First World War and transportation improvements facilitating the movement of people and racial intermixture had created a complex pattern of migration and that more information had to be gathered on the physical, mental, and social characteristics and relations and values of ethnic groups and races before any new policies were implemented. Otherwise, they argued, the decisions of policy-makers would only be clouded by the prejudices and tensions arising from the immigration phenomenon.[3]

In the fall of 1922 Yerkes obtained a small grant from the Russell Sage Foundation to draw together a number of academics interested in migration research. Although the group consisted primarily of psychologists, biologists, and eugenicists, Yerkes also appointed two social scientists to the committee – Mary Van Kleeck, a former social worker who had become a director of industrial research, and Clark Wissler. Since neither of them was sympathetic to eugenics nor shared the racial interpretations of man adhered to by most of the scientists, there was tension within the group right from the beginning, and it broke open when the full committee met in January 1923. At that meeting Yerkes laid out a program of research that was geared entirely to the biological sciences. It dealt with such topics as methods of racial testing, studies of race mixture, individual case studies of immigrants, and better means of selecting aliens. Van Kleeck immediately suggested that the committee co-operate with the group of social scientists who were then organizing what was to become the Social Science Research Council. With no reason to disagree, Yerkes and the other committee members went along with her proposal, and that gave the social scientists the opening for which they had been looking. John Merriam's brother Charles, a Chicago political scientist and one of the major figures responsible for creating the Social Science Research Council, quickly appointed a social-science committee on migration research – this before the Social Science Research Council had even come into formal existence; he named Yerkes a member of that committee and arranged for a joint meeting to be held with the scientific group.[4]

The social scientists were enthusiastic about the potential of migration research, believing that it would enable them to deal with national policies that were being settled without consultation from representatives of their disciplines. Yet, aware that there was no clear demarcation between their academic interests in the subject and those of the scientists, they quickly realized that benchmarks would have to be established. The high stakes that both groups saw in migration research were evident when Yerkes first met with the social scientists. Not wishing to give the impression that scientists were encroaching upon social-scientific fields, he explained that members of his committee had no desire to intervene in matters in which they had little expertise, but the subject of migration was, by nature, interdisciplinary. The social scientists agreed that the subject demanded intellectual co-operation – even on an international scale – but they also turned the argument to their advantage. Columbia sociologist William F. Ogburn insisted that there should be a division of labour between the two groups, with the natural scientists studying the scientific aspects of human migration and the social scientists focusing on the cultural. Accordingly, Robert Park, contending that immigrants should be considered as subcultures and not biological individuals, succeeded in tearing the entire subject of immigrant communities away from the scientists. So skilful were the social scientists in forwarding their case that by the afternoon of the meeting one of the NRC members declared that natural scientists indeed lacked the training to study cultural behaviour and processes. Yerkes agreed and, with that, saw a substantial portion of the research that he had earmarked for the scientists taken away and given over to the social scientists.[5]

The understanding that the natural scientists and social scientists had reached fell apart in 1924. Yerkes had succeeded in obtaining a grant from the Laura Spelman Memorial Fund of the Rockefeller Foundation to finance co-operative research for three years, but while the Social Science Research Council was attempting to initiate its program, the National Research Council became involved in projects that included studies of Negro intelligence, human racial blood groups, and immigration – this at a time when the American Congress was debating the immigration-restriction bill. Not only did relations between the two groups deteriorate over this matter, but Yerkes, preoccupied with his new position at Yale and eager to begin the most important work of his career – research on primates – asked to be replaced as chairman of the NRC committee in the spring of 1925. At a meeting in April of that year Van Kleeck and Wesley C. Mitchell censured the scientific committee for slighting the social scientists, and pushed through a resolution insisting on joint co-operation in all further research projects. At another meeting in May Van Kleeck secured agreement from the scientists that all social-scientific work would henceforth be turned over to the Social Science Research Council; at the same meeting Yerkes's resignation was accepted, and the committee discussed dissolution.[6]

At its first major meeting at Dartmouth College the Social Science Research Council, at last sufficiently organized to handle the migration work, discussed areas that needed attention: committees were appointed to draw up plans for research on American blacks, labour, crime, mental defectives, and migration. While these were subjects of interest to the NRC, by that time its migration committee had weakened, was accepting no new proposals, had dropped many of its ongoing projects, and effectively left the field of race almost entirely open to the Social Science Research Council. Accordingly, the SSRC announced its intention to study a wide variety of topics, among them world statistics of migration, internal migration within the United States, emigration, conditions in Europe and other countries, immigration and the mechanization of industry, legal and administrative policy, and studies of immigrant communities, using Thomas's and Florian Znaniecki's *The Polish Peasant* as a model.[7] It was even pointed out that Canada would prove an interesting field of study, not only because of its proximity to the United States but because the lateness of its immigration movements ensured full and trustworthy statistics and because it could provide a foundation for comparing Canadian, American, Australian, and British immigration policy and administration. There were also some very pragmatic reasons for the attention the organization wished to give to the subject. It was expected that future immigration policy in Canada would be influenced more so than in the past by American example: because of the imposition of restrictionist policies in the United States, Canada was receiving more immigrants, and it seemed to the social scientists that the contemporary Canadian immigrant experience was not very much different from that of the American generations earlier. That, not to mention the fact that Canada had become the back door of entry for immigrants trying to get into the United States, suggested that investigations of Candian legislative history and policy concerning immigration, of specific problems in administration and control – such as the exclusion of Asiatics – as well as of European immigration to the United States via Canada were warranted. Neither did it escape the attention of some members of the SSRC that Canada was being 'invaded' by people from the western and southwestern parts of the United States and that studies of American immigrants to Canada, including blacks, and of methods of attracting those settlers would also be useful.[8] Having been excluded from influencing American legislation, it would seem, the social scientists saw and seized the opportunity to shape Canadian policy.

It was in this atmosphere that the Canadian Frontiers of Settlement project was conceived: it constituted part of a larger study on pioneer settlement throughout the world, a master plan that was tossed back and forth between natural and social scientists until the specific details of the study and the responsibility for its supervision were worked out. The initial proposal for the study of pioneer settlement was put before the National Research Council in 1925 by David White, an officer of that organization and home secretary of the National Academy of Sciences; the same plan was presented to the Social Science Research Council in 1926.[9] It was Isaiah Bowman, however, the Canadian-born founder and director of the American Geographical Society, who took over and guided the entire project.[10] Bowman envisaged a scientific study of settlement, undertaken by geologists, geographers, soil experts, economists, historians, and sociologists, that would show by what means men and women were occupying empty lands in the Canadian west, the far western prairie regions of the United States, Alaska, South America, South Africa, Australia, and Manchuria, and in so doing dispel the illusions and misconceptions surrounding pioneer settlement, replacing the haphazard methods used in the past with a more unified, wiser scheme of settlement.[11]

II

A number of ideas shaped Bowman's proposal for the study of pioneer belts, but overarching them all was the same concern with immigration that preoccupied so many other social scientists during the 1920s. Bowman alluded to the fact that this was a period in which the national policies of a dozen countries involved questions of immigration, land-use, and settlement. He argued that further settlement in the world's major urban centres should be discouraged because newcomers would only add to the cities' problems, either by undercutting the wage-earners or by adding to the number of unemployed. He pointed out, however, that many countries had unsettled farmland of good quality and that an intelligent immigration policy depended upon an assessment of those lands and an estimation of the number of immigrants they could sustain.[12] His proposal echoed the old American belief that the frontier could ease the pressure of urban centres by siphoning off the excess population. To the pessimists who claimed that the solution was no longer viable since the frontier was closed, Bowman argued that there were many distant, unsettled parts of the world to which people were migrating. Millions of people lived in pioneer lands, he claimed, and millions more could be accommodated there. Between 1911 and 1921 some twenty thousand people had settled in the Peace River country in the Canadian northwest; western Australia was in the midst of great expansion and rapidly acquiring population; the division of landed estates in Soviet Russia and in parts of central and eastern Europe had also thrown open vast tracts of land for settlement. Moreover, Bowman considered as contemporary pioneers the hundreds of thousands of Chinese annually settling in Manchuria; the Scottish, Welsh, and English sheep-herders and farmers living in the grasslands along the eastern edge of the Patagonian Andes; the thousands of different sects and nationalities – Icelanders, Scandinavians, Ukrainians, Dukhobors, Hutterians, and Mennonites – migrating to Canada; the Australians and other English-speaking people living on the grasslands of that continent; the Russians in Siberia and the steppe region.[13]

While Bowman was eager to promote settlement in previously uninhabited lands, he warned that the undirected and wasteful expansion of the past should not be allowed to persist. He advocated in its place a planned, scientific settlement that dealt with matters of production, transportation, and the marketing of produce.[14] In part he wanted to ensure that the new areas did not turn into 'slums of settlement,' as had happened in the case of the agricultural colonization of the barrier of the Laurentian. (Bowman related how 'a notorious rural slum' had developed in that harsh environment when the eastern Canadian lumber industry declined after 1873: the farmers who had settled in the Laurentian country north of Lake Ontario and in the region between Georgian Bay and Lake Huron were left stranded and without markets; their oats and potatoes could no longer be sold at good prices to the lumber camps, and after the forest was depleted, the soil cover was too light to withstand the rain-wash. Many people moved out of the area but the most shiftless and incompetent remained, Bowman argued, and social conditions deteriorated further.)[15] In arguing for a science of settlement, Bowman was not simply interested in ensuring the well-being of the individual settler; he stressed that frontier settlement was no longer just a way of life but that the frontier was rather a chief source of food and raw material for the rest of the world. Especially since contemporary settlement represented a new phase – most of the best lands had been taken up and the rest had to be occupied differently from commonly accepted practices – there was a need for experts who could devise schemes to make the newly opened landed estates and the previously unproductive pioneer belts of the world fertile.[16]

The assistance that science could be to the fringe of settlement had already been proven in the development of dry-farming in the United States and in the discovery of frost- and drought-resistant strains of wheat, but Bowman was advocating a much more ambitious scheme. Contending that it was no longer sufficient to examine a region here or there, he argued in favour of a world-wide survey of agricultural conditions and capabilities, a survey that would marshal the resources of numerous disciplines. 'The dry border of the prairie lands of every continent offers science an especially wide field of inquiry and exprimentation,' he insisted.[17] He thought that the question of the destiny of the pioneer would accordingly be of interest to geographers, economists, and colonial administrators, that it would equally attract the attention of biologists and eugenicists interested in improving the breed and aware of the higher birth rate among pioneers, and that the physical jobs that needed to be done – the dams and canals to be built, the hydroelectric power stations to be installed – would appeal to the engineer.[18] Finally, for sociologists and historians, he contended that frontier settlement presented an opportunity to watch nation-building in action. 'Pioneering to-day is not a mere farming venture,' Bowman explained, 'but a field of social engineering and agricultural experimentation. It is not a mere extension of farm population but a thrust of an entire civilization, with all its qualities – a new form of nation-building.' Such political significance, he promised, would become most obvious when the relation of frontier settlement to immigration policy in Canada and to empire-building in South Africa was examined.[19]

Bowman did not miss the opportunity to point out another respect in which the study of pioneer belts would benefit academics. The final result of their co-operative efforts would be the production not of a handbook to assist the individual pioneer in locating a productive farm or increasing his crop – such needs were already fulfilled by government bulletins – but a guide for the makers of public policy, just as a city survey aided city planners. Bowman argued that such assistance was invaluable to policy-makers since the issue of settlement was clouded by appeals to popular sentiment. 'Straight thinking in provincial assemblies,' he said, 'is often difficult because a noisy "expansionist-at-any-cost" regards himself as the highest kind of patriot. On the other hand, the conservative who has questions about methods and future earnings is looked upon as a weak-kneed citizen.'[20] The pioneer-belts study, Bowman insisted, would also ensure that the new regions promised enough permanence to justify the heavy capital investments that governments would be compelled to make. The pioneer did not want to live as in the past, he contended; no one was looking for 'rough fare or homespun.' In order to attract settlers to the new areas and encourage their productivity, the gap between city and country life would have to be closed, and towards that end governments would have to assist in building roads, railways, telegraph lines, and schools and in providing lower freight rates, mail service, and support in marketing produce.[21]

After two years' consideration by the National Research Council's special committee on pioneer belts as well as its division of geology and geography, the project was approved and passed on to the Social Science Research Council for its consideration. That organization's committee on pioneer belts, whose members included Robert Park – the chairman from 1926 to 1927 – N.S.B. Gras, Isaiah Bowman, Harvard historian Frederick Merk, government agriculturalist O.E. Baker, and University of Wisconsin sociologist Kimball Young,[22] similarly studied the proposal for two years before giving its approval and providing financial support for the first part of the plan – a five-year program of research, and publication of a series of volumes on Canadian settlement.[23]

Although it expected studies of other areas to be undertaken in light of the information and experience gained in the Canadian field, the ssrc committee chose Canada for the first phase of the pioneer-belts project because of its accessibility and because there were a number of Canadian investigators eager to undertake the necessary field-work and research: in 1927 a group of interested Canadian scholars had conferred with the Social Science Research Council at Dartmouth and pointed out the excellent opportunities that the Canadian west presented for a study of pioneer belts. The Social Science Research Council's work with respect to the Canadian phase of the project, however, and indeed to the rest of the program, was limited to organizational matters; once it presented its report at Hanover in 1928, the committee on pioneer belts disbanded with the understanding that the American Geographical Society, acting through its director, Isaiah Bowman, would take control of the project.[24]

Using funds provided by the Social Science Research Council, the American Geographical Society set up an advisory committee of geographers, historians, economists, and sociologists to formulate a detailed plan of research in the Canadian field. It also established a separate fund to support related work on a more limited scale in several other regions, contributing, along with the Social Science Research Council, to a joint fund for the publication of a series of papers on pioneer settlement, to be written by thirty specialists familiar with the problems of different regions.[25] When the machinery for the Canadian project was set in place, the geographical society's committee, which included Dr W.L.G. Joerg, secretary of the organization, Dr O.E. Baker, Frederick Merk, Kimball Young, and W.J. Rutherford, dean of the University of Saskatchewan's School of Agriculture, turned responsibility for the study over to a group composed exclusively of Canadians. Rutherford, one of the academics who had approached the Social Science Research Council in 1927 with suggestions for the Canadian study, had begun to organize the group, aptly called the Canadian Pioneer Problems Committee, at Ottawa in May 1928. For the next twelve months he and the other members worked on finalizing the details of the project; by 1930, when the research was finally under way, the committee consisted of D.A. McArthur, a professor of history at Queen's and vice-chairman of the group; Carl Dawson; Chester Martin, professor of History at the University of Toronto; R.C. Wallace, president of the University of Alberta (in place of an original member, D.A. McGibbon, professor of Economics at the University of Alberta, who resigned upon being appointed to the Board of Grain Commissioners in Canada), and W.A. Mackintosh, professor of Political and Economic Science at Queen's, who was appointed director of research; Rutherford, the chairman of the committee, died in May 1930. At its insistence, and apparently not without a battle, the committee was given full control over the direction of the Canadian study; it was instructed to consult with the American Geographical Society, however, on all essential matters of policy.[26]

Once the project was organized, W.A. Mackintosh began to search for Canadian academics working on topics related to general, agricultural, and land economics, as well as problems of the Canadian west. His announcement that funds were available for research in these areas must have been greeted with some degree of pleasure. Throughout the 1920s Canadian social scientists had been decrying the lack of financial support for research in their fields. Dawson, one of the most vocal critics, surmised that the problem stemmed from the fact that the social sciences, particularly psychology, sociology, and political science, were relatively new as organized departments and could not as easily place themselves at the disposal of the 'money-making interests' that supported the university as could the older, more entrenched natural sciences. He was irritated, however, that the social sciences were even more poorly endowed in scholarships, fellowships, and other incentives than the traditional humanities. In the mid-1920s he had helped to organize the Canadian Association of Social Workers and an annual Canadian Conference on Social and Health Work because he thought there was a need for an organization to co-ordinate a common plan of action amongst the various social-work interests in Canada. He was motivated partly by nationalist sentiments: he hoped that under the stimulus of a larger audience the work of existing organizations would be enhanced, that this would create more publicity, break up sectional and community isolation, and extend social services into areas where they were lacking. More importantly, however, he thought that the existence of such institutions would encourage the co-operation in social research so necessary for social action in Canada. Later, although he applauded the research efforts of the Canadian Council on Child Welfare and the Canadian National Committee for Mental Hygiene, he did not think them sufficient. He did not lay the blame at the doorstep of those institutions; he thought that as promotional and service organizations their primary purpose was to apply the results of research rather than to carry out painstaking, firsthand investigations. It was only within the universities, he argued, that a body of scientific knowledge could be built up, organized, and set in proper perspective, and it was to the universities, he concluded, that outside organizations should be able to turn for such resources. [27]

There were two factors underlying Dawson's preoccupation with the state of social research in Canadian universities. On the one hand he was worried that because the stimulus for sociological and psychological research in Canada was non-existent and because such research as existed was feeble and unproductive, superior students would continue to go to American universities, where they would study American problems and be lost to Canada – the efforts he made to deal with this problem will be discussed in the next chapter. His other concern was with the quality of public policy. Believing that research was a necessary prerequisite for any kind of reform, he warned that unless some kind of co-operative effort were made to develop opportunities and means of social research in Canada, 'the well-known game of meddlesome muddling would continue.' Accordingly, he insisted that university administrators interested in Canadian affairs were under an obligation to aid the social sciences and to help academics finance and carry out their research. Expecting that it would be difficult to win assistance from such quarters, he argued that the allied departments of social science in all Canadian universities would have to work out a scheme of co-operative research among themselves before they could hope to receive administrative and public support.[28] The goal was achieved with the pioneer-belts study, but the money came from the United States.

More than just financial considerations explained the eagerness of Canadian social scientists to undertake the pioneer-belts survey. Sharing with their American colleagues a desire to shape public policy, they were aware of the circumstances that made the post-war years an opportune time to carry out the study in western Canada. As Chester Martin explained, from a historical point of view the 1920s marked the end of one era in the administration of Canadian public lands and the beginning of another. After some fifty years of controversy, policies that had been instituted in a period of crisis were about to change. The transfer of western lands to Canada had signified the triumph of settlement over the fur trade, but the Metis's demands for protection against the onslaught of immigration resulted in an insurrection at Red River in 1870 and a rebellion in Saskatchewan in 1885; problems stemming from the land transfer of 1870 also created political turbulence in Manitoba and the rest of Canada in 1889 and 1896.[29] Now, however, responsibility for control of their natural resources, including ungranted lands, had passed from the federal government to the provinces of Manitoba, Alberta, and Saskatchewan. New settlement policies were anticipated, and it was expected that they would depart from the traditional policy of free land. With that, changes in the machinery directing and controlling immigration were inevitable.[30] In short, recognizing that the prairie provinces would henceforth take a more direct interest in colonization and immigration, Canadian social scientists knew that if they wanted to achieve an ordered, scientific settlement, there was no better time than the present for them to lend their expertise.

The degree of nationalist sentiment that infused the objectives of the Canadian Pioneer Problems Committee cannot be overlooked. Members were conscious of the international stature Canada had attained and the role western development had played therein. Duncan McArthur, for instance, related how the opening years of the twentieth century had marked Canada's emergence to prominence in the minds of Britons and Europeans. Queen Victoria's Diamond Jubilee had been celebrated with pomp and ceremony, and the extent of the empire had been demonstrated. Indeed, in their ability to share the burdens of imperial partnership – he cited Canada's participation in the South African military campaign as an example – the senior members had displayed their growth and maturity. Out of all this Canada emerged, as he put it, 'the new star on the transatlantic horizon.' It had gained a reputation for being a country of vigorous people, with endless stretches of excellent, uninhabited agricultural land that awaited settlement.[31] The nationalist euphoria did not even escape Isaiah Bowman, who excused Laurier for his grandiose exaggeration that 'the twentieth century belong[ed] to Canada.' After all, Bowman conceded, Canada had only reached its present stature after overcoming some difficult problems in the second half of the nineteenth century – the lack of a staple commodity to export and the obstruction presented to westerly expanding settlement by the Laurentian barrier. It was only after 1900, he explained, with the pressure of increased population and of world market conditions, that the natural resources of the prairies were exploited. Their development was aided by the extension of branch railways and the production of strains of early-maturing wheat and improved or adapted types of dry-farming.[32] As a result of that development, settled country in Canada was no longer limited to a narrow strip but covered a wide belt running to the north. Palliser's Triangle, designated as grazing country, had been homesteaded; the northwest forest was being cleared; settlers were moving as far north as the fifty-eighth parallel; and the discovery of rich mining areas in northern Saskatchewan and northern Manitoba promised to attract agricultural settlement. Population figures bespoke the northwest's rapid development: in 1870 it contained only forty-eight thousand people, but by 1926 its population was slightly over two million. The most remarkable growth had occurred between 1910 and 1921, when the population quadrupled, increasing by 75 per cent.[33] It was Bowman's opinion, however, that of all the factors that contributed to Canada's international status, the most important was the discovery Canadians had made of the necessity of 'following the isotherms': this had enabled Canada to double its wheat crop since the First World War, something no other country had achieved.[34]

Despite all the attention they gave to the west's record of achievement, members of the Pioneer Problems Committee were aware that its development had not proceeded without hardships, difficulties, and failures. The invasion of the dry-belt, for instance, had proved to be an error: in 1926 the departure had been recorded of 55 per cent of the farmers in Census District Number 3 in Alberta, an area approximately enclosed by the Red, Bow, and South Saskatchewan rivers northwest of Medicine Hat. In 1924 and 1925 there was a considerable exodus of post-war settlers out of the Peace River valley. Among those who had chosen to live in the bush country between Lakes Winnipeg and Manitoba, moreover, a very low standard of living was reported.[35] Carl Dawson, carrying a concern over from the early 1920s, thought all this illustrated that the west's development had been too rapid, and hence economically and socially wasteful. He pointed to the many evidences of the waste of unplanned settlement that the Grande Prairie region displayed – with only an insecure foothold on the land, many of its settlers had drifted away – and suggested that the western governments take heed.[36]

As much as they were interested in encouraging western development, the Canadian Pioneeer Problems Committee wanted to ensure that this would be a smooth process, resulting in a secure living for settlers and a success commensurate with Canada's new international status. For that reason they were interested in ascertaining not merely where the best settlement land was but where the most successful adaptations to the natural environment had been made; where failures and maladjustments had occurred; what shifts in location and agriculture would engender greater security in land occupation and higher standards of living.[37] Of course, the issue of secure settlement was inextricably linked to immigration – the number and types of newcomers who could be successfully absorbed into the region. The population expansion that the west had experienced during the late nineteenth and early twentieth centuries had slowed during the First World War: the land boom had ended, and the curtailment of railway construction brought a reduction in the number of foreign labourers entering the country. During the period of deflation that followed the war, moreover, there was a considerable movement of population out of Canada to the larger industrial centres in the United States, at one point making the number of emigrants exceed the number of immigrants. Around the mid-1920s the picture began to change. Owing to the implementation of restrictionist policies in the United States that were aimed at excluding southern and eastern Europeans, there was an increasing influx of immigrants from those regions into Canada. As far as McArthur was concerned, the emigration out of Canada raised questions about the number of new immigrants the country could accommodate. This was an issue that warranted examination, he thought – the results might reveal that Canada already had too many immigrants; at the very least, it would show the ones who were likely to remain permanently.[38] For another participant, R.W. Murchie, the important factor was to ascertain upon which lands immigrants could be placed in order to ensure an improvement in their standards of living. He suggested that if non-assimilable, illiterate people were placed upon marginal lands (such as those that lay beyond the southeastern Manitoba-Edmonton line) where they could not hope to have a higher standard of living, the difference between their way of life and the accepted standards of the country would be perpetuated. In turn, this would create future social problems. 'Only by a scientific survey,' he concluded, 'by fearless facing of the facts, and by carefully prepared programs of adminstration and development based upon these facts can these problems be met.'[39]

The committee divided its investigations into five categories. Much of the work on the first topic – a survey of soil and climatic conditions geared towards determining what unsettled land was suitable for occupation – was already being undertaken by the dominion and provincial governments. The second set of surveys, falling under the rubric of agricultural economics, was to deal with the different ways in which mature and newly settled regions were being utilized and also to assess their rate of progress. Primarily responsible for this task was R.W. Murchie, of the University of Minnesota's Department of Agriculture (but formerly of Manitoba Agricultural College), and his assistant. Although all aspects of research were to be examined historically, certain issues were assigned to historians under the supervision of Chester Martin, and these were intended to provide historical background for the whole series. In this context Martin extended his history of land policy, and Professor A.S. Morton of the University of Saskatchewan continued his study of early settlement; to Duncan McArthur was assigned the responsibility for the immigration study. In addition, special historical studies of particular racial and religious groups, such as Icelanders, Mennonites, Ukrainians, and Scandinavians, were also planned. A fourth category was devoted to examining the ways in which pioneer communities were economically deficient or paid more heavily for banking and credit institutions, railways and roads, marketing organization, and taxation. The last aspect was an analysis of the social structure of pioneer life. As director of the project's sociological studies, Carl Dawson had convinced other committee members that the pioneer fringe's most distinguishing characteristics were social ones – that its standard of living and lack of social institutions were often more distinctive than the types of farming or the sparseness of population. In co-operation with the agricultural surveys, therefore, Dawson intended to measure the deficiencies of new areas against the standards of mature communities. This was to be supplemented by studies of basic institutions – the family, the church, schools, health and social-work organizations, recreational facilities, the machinery of local government, the administration of justice – throughout the three prairie provinces.[40]

The Canadian Pioneer Problems Committee received assistance from many quarters. The Universities of Alberta and Saskatchewan as well as Manitoba Agricultural College participated in the field surveys and offered the services of their staff. Through the Dominion Bureau of Statistics, the Department of Agriculture, the National Development Bureau, the Topographical Surveys Branch of the Department of the Interior, the Dominion Meteorological Service, and the Geological Survey, the federal government participated in the project, as in other capacities did representatives of the three prairie provincial governments and the Canadian Pacific and Canadian National Railways. The final results of this co-operative enterprise were eight volumes, all of which, the Pioneer Problems Committee stressed, were not so much books on economics or agriculture as they were on frontier settlement.[41] They included an analysis of the geographical setting of western settlement and its economic problems by W.A. Mackintosh, a history of land policy and settlement patterns by Chester Martin and A.W. Morton, a study of standards of living and agricultural practices by R.W. Murchie, an analysis of the settlement of the mining and forest frontiers by H.A. Innis and A.R.M. Lower. Dawson and his research assistants were responsible for three volumes, one that dealt with the Peace River region, another that analysed the settlement of immigrant groups, and a third that investigated the social aspects of pioneering and the evolution of metropolitan centres within the prairie region.

III

The first of Dawson's studies dealt with the area of northernmost pioneer settlement in Canada. Noted by John Macoun for its luxuriant vegetation, fertile soil, and sufficient rainfall, the Peace River region consisted of approximately seventy-three thousand square miles of good farming land, almost all of which lay north of the fifty-fifth parallel, an area roughly corresponding to the northern tip of Scotland.[42] Its most remarkable feature, and possibly the one that attracted the attention of the Canadian Pioneer Problems Committee, was the rapidity with which it had been settled in the post-war years. In 1911 fewer than two thousand people, among them traders, Indians, and missionaries, lived in the Peace River valley, but with the advent of the railway in 1916 the area became more accessible, and by 1921 its population was recorded at twenty thousand, reaching sixty thousand a decade later. At the time of Dawson's study, despite the fact that only remote areas were available for settlement, people continued to pour into the region. With the use of rapidly maturing strains of wheat not restricting cultivation to the valley floor and with settlers willing to plant oats and barley, engage in mixed farming, ranching, hog-raising, and dairying, land fifty to sixty miles beyond the railway was being homesteaded and towns were springing up overnight.[43]

The purposes behind Dawson's study of this isolated region were twofold, and they reflected the general objectives of the pioneer-belts project as well as his own sociological convictions: the first was to determine whether the rush of settlement into the area should be discouraged until more was known about its economic potential and limitations; the other was to use the region as a model for explaining the social evolution of all pioneer communities.[44] As we shall see, the two objectives were linked, for by ascertaining what stage the Peace River region had reached in its natural history, Dawson thought he could better explain its conditions and predict its future.

With respect to the first objective, Dawson contended that his intention in the Peace River volume was not so much to advise readers as it was to furnish them with enough information to draw their own conclusions about the area. As for personally influencing administrative policy, he insisted that his only wish was to see that it was formulated on a scientific basis. Towards that end he devised a master plan of research. It saw him spending the summer of 1929 in a reconnaissance survey of the Peace River region – he was not completely ignorant of conditions in the Canadian west, having taught in a pioneer school in central Alberta before he went into war service[45] – and the summer of 1930 in more serious endeavours. Having identified the area's more mature settlements, transitional districts, and fringe regions (with the aid of R.W. Murchie, W.A. Allen of the University of Saskatchewan, and four student assistant field-workers, one of whom was the son of Alberta's deputy minister of Agriculture),[46] Dawson made a detailed survey of the Peace River area. Information was sought on farm business expenditures, family budgets, family histories, and forms of community social organization. Some of the data was acquired from the provincial departments of Agriculture, Education, and Public Health at Edmonton, the Dominion Bureau of Statistics, and public

officials in Peace River, but much more of it was obtained from questionnaires, consisting of several hundred standardized questions put to the
heads of approximately four hundred farm families, as well as administrators of schools, churches, hospitals, and other social institutions.[47] In
devising the questionnaires for this first piece of large-scale social research
in Canada, Dawson had the assistance of C.C. Zimmerman, a prominent
Harvard rural sociologist who spent a few days in the field with the
students, explaining the general purpose of social surveys and then helping
them set up questions for their own study. While the students handled the
farm surveys, making their way to the homesteads by car, or packhorse and
saddle, Dawson took care of the town districts, obtaining interviews from
the prominent citizens of about twenty-five settled communities. Moreover, he took responsibility for analysing and interpreting the data, which
he ultimately set in the framework of human ecology.[48]

Before the publication of Dawson's work for the Frontiers of Settlement
series there was almost nothing that dealt with the social development of
western Canada.[49] For a variety of reasons, not the least of which was that
its size was limited enough to enable familiarity with the region, Dawson
and other members of the Canadian Pioneer Problems Committee considered the Peace River area to be an ideal case for studying the social side of
pioneering. Its definite physiographic barriers and distinctive soil and
climate made it a subregion of the North American plains, but it was also
thought to be as representative as any area could be of the settlement of the
prairie provinces as a whole. On a smaller scale and with differences that
accorded with modern conditions, the Peace River area, described as 'the
last great agricultural frontier of the Western Canadian plains,' was
undergoing all the experiences that had characterized North American
frontier settlement since the late eighteenth century. These included the
premature beginning, the anticipation of transportation links, land booms
and collapses, the search for suitable agricultural methods and products to
market, the development of mature and stable settlements.[50] For Dawson,
moreover, its conditions made it like the control in a laboratory experiment. Although well-settled areas had fringes of settlement that could be
studied for the purpose of understanding the social evolution of the prairie
region, Dawson did not think that examinations of these older districts
would show pioneer life in its entirety. They were too much under the
dominance of contiguous settlements to reveal how the agricultural
conquest of the wilderness had proceeded; true pioneering conditions could
only be evident, he insisted, in the settlement of new, isolated regions
where the hazards that pioneering presented were pronounced, even

though access could be had to agricultural science and modern equipment. Separated from the rest of the prairie provinces, with its own fringe and mature centres, Dawson argued, the Peace River area had a regional life of its own. Its remoteness and isolation from older districts meant that it had not yet fallen under the dominance of an outside centre, and this would permit investigators to observe the natural history of the prairie region as it had actually evolved.[51]

We have seen in other circumstances that Dawson was adamant about the scientific verity of human ecology as an explanation of the development of human society; he was no less determined to assert that point in the Peace River study. In a sketch of the district that he wrote for the preliminary volume of the pioneer-belts project, he outlined the basis of the theory, explaining that it saw the social structure of a region as the product of geographical factors that determined the lines of transportation, and, in turn, occupations, divisions of labour, population selection, and centres of dominance. He added that these factors also determined the direction and extent of communication in a region from which there developed the less concrete aspect of its social structure – forms of culture. Then, in what seems to have been an attempt to make his readers see that the task of the social scientist was just as formidable as that of any scientist, and indeed justified the interdisciplinary approach of the pioneer-belts project, he stressed that the cultural element was the more difficult part of the social structure to understand. It could only be seen, he said, 'by means of the scientific imagination,' but it was 'a structure quite as real as the physical and quite as worthy of scientific study ... Those who ignore it,' Dawson cautioned, 'find themselves confronted by its persuasiveness at every turn.'[52] He explained in simple terms that wheat farming had an economic as well as a social aspect, and on a more complex level that, while population groups initially imposed upon a region their traditional social structure, there was in due course an adjustment between natural conditions and the imported culture – 'a compromise between nature and nurture.'[53]

To explain the evolution of prairie society, Dawson developed a concept that he called 'the life cycle' of the region. He employed it both as a hypothesis and as an analytical tool: in the former context it put forward the idea that regions of the same nature pass through similar stages of development, varying only with respect to the duration of their stages – in those regions with greater access to world markets, Dawson believed, the stages were briefer; in the latter context it was used to explain the social conditions and problems of a particular prairie region.[54] That Dawson could use the theory in both these fashions indicated that it was not derived from the data he collected about a certain region but was rather the framework within which the data was organized.[55] Indeed, it was built upon the principles of human ecology as well as Dawson's own regional sociology. Moreover, its characterizations of early frontier society were distinctly Turnerian, despite the fact that human ecological theory, with its fundamental concentration on metropolian dominance, was quite antithetical to the frontier thesis.

The Peace River volume contained the first full-length presentation of the life-cycle theory. In general terms it held that a typical agricultural region passed through certain successive stages, each of which was organically linked with its predecessor and in some fashion prepared the way for its successor. As in all ecological theory, changes were thought to be precipitated by invasions – new and disturbing factors that altered the struggle for existence in a region and made its social organization more complex. Of these the railway was the most common 'invader' and the one that brought about the most profound changes. In the first stage of the life-cycle of a region, the period of outpost settlement, lands were found and possessed by adventurers, explorers, traders, soldiers, and missionaries who joined forces at forts, unfortified outposts, or other strategic points on natural transportation routes. These primitive settlements had less contact with each other than with distant market centres, and this was manifested in the occupations of their denizens. The settlers engaged in the search for precious metals, hunted, traded, or, if conditions were proper, undertook large-scale ranching. Owing to these geographic and economic conditions, the population of the region at this stage was scanty, composed primarily of males – 'picturesque individuals,' as Dawson described them, who worked hard, drank hard, and fought hard. Since the region at this stage was considered unfit for white women and their children, alliances were made between white males and native women. The progeny of those unions did not create social problems until a later surge of settlement, when they came to be regarded as social misfits.[56]

The second stage in the region's life-cycle took root when agriculture was first introduced at the outposts as a secondary industry catering to the limited local market. Throughout the North American plains, Dawson argued, farmers were the first to make extensive use of the land; their operations formed the link between the outpost settlements and the more permanent forms of agriculture that eventually displaced ranching in areas where rainfall was sufficient for the growth of cereals. If the region acquired a reputation for being highly suited for cultivation, or if rumours of railway construction focused attention upon it, there would be a massive invasion of the land-hungry from remote regions. The introduction of the railway made farmland in fertile sections too valuable for ranching, and the cattlemen were pushed farther and farther back until they could utilize only those areas unsuitable for agriculture. Such development engendered some changes in the region's population structure: although the expectation of transportation facilities lured farmers from other lands, the population continued to be predominantly male. The early settler was usually unmarried, or had left his family behind until he succeeded in establishing a new home in the wilderness. If distances from the older communities were not too great, however, women would accompany their husbands, brothers, or fathers into the new areas. At the same time the ranchers, sensing that their old way of life was going to be threatened by the arrival of women, and ultimately of families and communities, departed. Small communities did develop in such regions, but they were separated from each other by vast tracts of unsettled land and developed on their own with the assistance of initial capital, some periods of work outside, and the surplus cash of more recent settlers. Their economic impediments and a social life that was quite elementary did not enable such communities to attain what Dawson saw as the primary objective of social organization – productive efficiency. They neither developed a division of labour nor rose above a low standard of living. Such goals were only attainable, he believed, when the railway got within at least twenty miles of a farm population.[57]

The catalyst to the development of the third stage in the life-cycle of the region – the integration of agricultural settlement – was, of course, the railway. Its construction and that of trunk roads provided temporary work to local settlers, made use of their local produce, and put more money into circulation. By connecting the local community with the world market, it also stimulated agricultural productivity, sped up the settlement process, and broke up the isolation that had once existed between the region's communities. Moreover, railway stations served as centres around which social and business institutions, and eventually towns, were built. Meanwhile, out from the railway on good land and bad, the fringe of settlement advanced and local communities developed once again but with a difference – roads and railways very soon integrated the isolated settlements into a new order of commercial and social life.[58]

The final stage saw the growth of regional centralization, and it was here that the principles of metropolitan dominance inherent in human ecology came most into play. One of the effects of the introduction of the railway,

Dawson explained, was to create a number of shipping towns strung along its route. As the result of an advantageous position or superior resources, one of the centres attained a dominant role in the region. It acquired a large population and certain types of goods and services unavailable in smaller towns; it became more urbanized, and its styles and social activities were imitated by the smaller towns. The dominant town and its subsidiary centres, he also argued, formed a single constellation and shared a division of labour: the small towns and hamlets retained their specialized local functions, while the large town provided expert leadership in various branches of agriculture, education, and religious and cultural life. By such means the agricultural communities reached their maximum in economic and social efficiency: agriculture expanded and reached a stability in production, modes of financing, and techniques. The social structure of the region became more balanced, with a standard distribution of population elements, predominance of the family unit, and an increasing birth rate. Finally, Dawson added, through the dominant centre the region achieved a self-consciousness and defined its interests in relation to other regions. While it did not immediately stop drawing upon the older regions for leadership, patterns of social organization, and financial aid, it developed its own economic and social capital and produced its own leadership. All this was in keeping with the principles of metropolitanism, but Dawson could not help noting how it accorded with another phenomenon then emerging in the Canadian west: he concluded that by means of their own leadership, inhabitants of the region had modified inherited and indigenous practices to suit the new spirit of regional autonomy.[59]

Using the concept of the life-cycle of the region, Dawson and his assistants investigated the Peace River area. Their examination of its population structure, standards of living, forms of social organization, and fringe districts led them to conclude that the region was in its very early stages of development. Nothing indicated that fact more than the composition of its population, which was youthful and predominantly male; indeed, the ratio of males to females was much higher in Peace River than it was in more settled parts of Alberta.[60] Dawson and his assistants were not content to stop at merely identifying what stage Peace River had reached in its evolution, however. Despite his claims to the contrary, Dawson was writing a guidebook for settlement, and even though ecological theory held that all regions must inevitably pass through a number of stages until they reach their most stable form, he looked for ways in which the earlier, more difficult phases could be shortened – or skipped entirely – and stable, productive settlement hastened. Adhering to the central tenet of Chicago sociology, that community was essential to social development, he argued that most of the hardships and failures endured in pioneer settlement were attributable to the absence of forms of community life such as religious and recreational activities in new regions and that such areas should be shunned in favour of those with established forms of social organization. To have even a bare minimum of life's amenities, he argued, settlers required a variety of institutional services – schools, churches, hospitals, clubs, societies, and recreational facilities. This was a costly business, he continued, made all the more expensive when the services had to be spread thinly to remote districts. 'A population of low density, isolated by lack of transportational facilities,' he concluded, 'has to endure social and economic disadvantages for many years.'[61]

Much of the data in the Peace River volume that attested to the importance of community was gathered by two of Dawson's assistants, both of them graduate students. Eva Younge, a Danish-born westerner whom Dawson initially recruited for the McGill social-work program but whom he found invaluable for the pioneer-settlement studies, undertook an analysis of the process of community development in the Peace River region;[62] Glenn Craig assessed standards of living in its fringe districts.[63] Younge handled her subject by looking at the accessibility of social facilities in Peace River as measured in the amount and variety of settlers' social participation and in the money spent on community activities and institutions such as halls, schools, churches, and hospitals. Surveying sample groups of farm families in the older districts of Peace River and adjacent areas, as well as the region's 'transition' and fringe districts, she not surprisingly found that it was the more settled parts of Peace River that were well equipped with community halls, music festivals, motion pictures, and other forms of entertainment. This illustrated to her, as it had to Dawson, the need for concentrated settlement. She conceded, however, that the high percentage of English-speaking people in some districts of Peace River made community organization easier than in areas with a more cosmopolitan population, such as parts of Manitoba's pioneer fringe.[64]

Craig's analysis of Peace River's newly settled fringe districts – Battle River, Hines Creek, and Clear Hills – areas remote from the railway and main highways, reinforced Dawson's argument about the need for settlements to be located near communication facilities. Craig found that fringe-district farmers had low incomes and spent a larger proportion of their money on farm operations and family expenditures than did farmers in other districts; with such a low standard of living their mobility was high and productive efficiency low.[65] In the Peace River volume Dawson elaborated upon Craig's arguments, noting that fringe farmers not only belonged to low-income groups but found it difficult to improve their standard of living. Long distance from the shipping point discouraged them from undertaking large-scale production, and more importantly than that, the majority of them had limited capital and found it more economically feasible to concentrate between seasons on clearing and breaking farmland. The more unfortunate ones were forced to look outside their small community for seasonal work to maintain and develop the family farm, a condition that Dawson saw as an even greater problem. Compelled to neglect their community and the property they owned in it, these farmers not only had little time for developing their homesteads but could not participate in the social life of the fringe.[66]

In arguing that areas lacking social and transportation facilities should be rejected for settlement, Dawson did not think he was contravening ecological theory, the notion that all communities had a natural pattern of development, including a first stage in which a scattered population, remote from the main lines of transportation, eked out their existence. Rather, he argued that it was possible to make a plan for settlement conform to the natural trends revealed by scientific inquiry into the process of settlement. As he saw it, the Peace River study showed not simply that stable settlement depended upon accessibility to social services and transportation facilities – agricultural output was small until communication links came closer to the farmer – but that there was a tendency for such services to be centralized in a constellation of villages, towns, and cities. He argued that this should provide certain clues for those attempting to promote stable settlement. For him, the data pointed to certain inescapable conclusions, the most important of which was that the settlement of the fringe should wait for the extension of settlement, transportation facilities, and social organization. By such means, he contended, the land would become valuable economically, attract settlers with the capital to utilize it properly, and ensure that they had access to the resources and services that would make their lives closer to what the sophisticated present-day settler expected and needed.[67]

Consonant with the conclusions he drew from the Peace River research, Dawson put forth a number of specific recommendations for the future settlement of the area. First of all he advised that land lying at a considerable distance from the railway not be considered, that instead suitable land should be settled in entire districts at a time, concurrent with the extension of transportation links if such facilities did not already exist. The scheme had obvious economic advantages; Dawson considered equally important that it would ensure large enough population groupings to encourage the rapid development of social organization and specialized services as well as influence the type of settler who came to the region. With regard to the latter, it was Dawson's belief that the extension of the railway would make raw agricultural land valuable enough to be bought rather than homesteaded and that this would increase the chances that the area would attract the kind of settlers likely to become permanent residents. He surmised that these would be native-born Canadians – the surplus population of the country's older agricultural districts – rather than new immigrants. His argument stemmed less from a nativistic attitude than from his conviction that future settlers of Peace River would have to have more initial capital than those who had settled in the area in the past, capital that poorer European immigrants were not likely to acquire through seasonal employment. With the mechanization of agriculture, opportunities for acquiring capital outside the settler's own farm had diminished. Furthermore, the great railway-building era had passed, and the construction of highway, telegraph, and telephone lines, as well as other public utilities, offered only limited employment at lower wages.[68]

The objectives that Dawson hoped to see achieved through his recommendations for Peace River settlement reflected a certain conservativism and rural nostalgia. He argued that it was the man who could devote all his energies to the development and operation of his own farm who would make true progress as a farmer and that his continued residence on the land would result in obvious gains to his own family as well as to local social institutions. It was a rule, he insisted, to which there seemed to be few exceptions in Peace River country. Nevertheless, his convictions also reflected an issue with which he had been concerned for many years. He considered it important that Peace River have permanent settlers, capable of supporting their own institutions, because this would result in a minimum of waste in human resources and a minimum of subsidization. If Peace River farmers had sufficient initial capital, adequate agricultural experience, and a temper for farm life, he was convinced that the districts they settled would pass rapidly through the early stages of development; attitudes of dependency would be less likely to emerge, and governments and public organizations would be able to spend the funds entrusted to them in wiser and more effective ways.[69]

There was another objective implied in Dawson's recommendations and it reached back to one of the purposes that underlay the creation of the pioneer-belts study at the outset – to ensure a role for academics, particularly social scientists, in the formulation of public policy. Dawson conceded that the responsibility for withholding lands, planning transportation facilities, and assembling accurate information to guide the settler belonged to the provincial governments and other bodies interested in western settlement. There was still a lot of land in the Peace River area, he noted, land that varied as to its conditions of fertility. He applauded the actions of the Alberta government in sending soil surveyors ahead of active settlement, thereby furnishing settlers with adequate knowledge of the land on which they proposed to settle and minimizing one of the greatest hazards in land settlement.[70] He stressed, however, that much more needed to be done, and for those tasks governments had to call upon experts. 'It goes without saying,' he explained, 'that governmental authorities are expected to protect the settler from exploitation of special interests who would promote land settlement for private gain and without thought of public good. The effects are far too significant to allow the free play of such interests.' He contended that in order for governments to be assured that the programs of private bodies were compatible with public welfare, they would have to employ specialists. He did not believe it would be easy for politicians, who liked to be popular with the electorate, to depart from the past policy of crude experimentation in land settlement; an increasingly intelligent electorate, he concluded, deserved the assistance of experts.[71]

IV

The Peace River volume was one of three studies that Dawson and his assistants undertook for the Frontiers of Settlement series. The second, *Group Settlement* (1936), which analysed ethnic communities in western Canada following the theories on immigration and assimilation elaborated by Robert Park and the Chicago school, will be discussed in the next chapter. The third, *Pioneering in the Prairie Provinces* (1940), though more ambitious in scope,[72] extended the ideas and recommendations put forward in the Peace River volume. It had been the task of W.A. Mackintosh in the first volume of the Frontiers of Settlement series to outline the physical factors that shaped the settlement process in the prairie west; in *Pioneering in the Prairie Provinces* Carl Dawson and Eva Younge treated the physiographic aspects. These included, in accordance with the precepts of social ecology, both the geographic as well as the less tangible social and cultural factors that affected the pattern, the quality, and the success of settlement in the prairie provinces.

Dawson and Younge decided that although the prairie west was composed of three major geographical subdivisions – the Red River valley and Manitoba lakes country constituting one, the area west of the Manitoba escarpment the second, and the area between the Missouri Coteau and the foothills of the Rockies the third – it was effectively a unit when the main physical and social controls that determined settlement were considered. The whole area was characterized by a relatively light rainfall, a fairly short growing season, and one dominant crop – wheat.[73] In keeping with that conviction Dawson and Younge devoted a large section of *Pioneering in the Prairie Provinces* to a discussion of the region's evolution as an area of almost continuous agricultural settlement. On the surface their treatment appeared to be nothing more than a conventional historical account, something for which they were sharply criticized – S.D. Clark, for instance, contended that by simply describing the history of the prairie west rather than attempting a sociological explanation, they provided no insight into the development of Canadian society.[74] What Dawson and Younge presented, in effect, was a natural history of the prairie's evolution. Their approach emphasized how river routes and railway lines had determined the pattern of settlement. They showed that apart from the casual and transitory settlements centred around trading posts, population groups entered the region along the most accessible and fertile river valleys. They argued, however, that despite its fertility, there had been no great stimulus to agricultural enterprise in the region before the advent of the railway, and this left the export of fur as the sole outside trade. One impediment was that the rivers were not sufficiently navigable for the transport of agricultural products, but even with the building of the transcontinental lines between 1871 and 1885 and the provision of the Land Act of 1872 that made farmlands available to persons with little capital, the region's true agricultural potential was not realized. The policies of Clifford Sifton, appointed to the Department of the Interior in the Laurier government in 1896, did not entirely explain the ultimate success that agricultural settlement achieved, they believed. Simply put, world markets did not favour western Canadian products until the end of the 1890s. At that point the continuing industrial expansion of England and continental Europe, along with the growing concentration of population in those regions, heightened the demand for a wide range of raw materials, including foodstuffs, whose movements had been hampered by tariffs. With only high-priced agricultural lands available in densely populated Europe, the availability of cheap frontier lands and the lowering of freight rates in Canada made the Canadian west attractive and an alternative to settlement in the United States.[75]

Aside from the historical account, *Pioneering in the Prairie Provinces* covered a wealth of subjects – farm-family expenditures, agricultural practices, the composition and social backgrounds of pioneer families, social, educational, religious, and health institutions. Some of this material was simply catalogued, but much of it was imparted in discussions of conditions in stable settlements, transitional areas, new pioneer fringe areas, and chronic fringe areas. Here, too, Clark was critical of Dawson and Younge's presentation, arguing that because they were so tied to the Chicago approach, they could not offer explanations, as he put it, 'outside a rigid ecological framework.'[76] Clark's contention bore some truth, but Younge and Dawson had specific reasons for conveying the information in such a fashion. It was part and parcel of metropolitan theory, an element of Chicago sociology to which Dawson strongly adhered, believing, as we have seen before, that all human communities were tied into the web of metropolitanism and that their evolution in that direction was an indication of maturity and a harbinger of stability. In *Pioneering in the Prairie Provinces* as in the Peace River study, Dawson showed that social institutions grew and stabilized in accordance with the community's growth. More importantly, he insisted, as he had in his earlier theoretical tracts, that by discerning the extent and limits of metropolitan influence, one could acquire an understanding of the region that it dominated and the character of its people and institutions.[77] Such an approach not only furnished Dawson and his assistants with an analytical tool for examining prairie society but gave them a foundation from which to offer advice to private and political bodies. Dawson continued to believe that knowledge of an area's true natural boundaries helped to endow with a certain efficiency whatever reforms or political measures were implemented within it.

The attention that was given in *Pioneering in the Prairie Provinces* to the evolution of urban centres in the Canadian west was a reflection both of Dawson's faith in metropolitan theory as a key to understanding regional development and of the strength of western regional consciousness. Dawson and Younge explained how Winnipeg, by virtue of its location at the junction of the Red and Assiniboine rivers, was the gateway city of the prairie region. Although its water routes were once used by fur traders, the city had since become an important railway centre, the regional headquarters of several communications systems – among them, telephone, telegraph, news publication, and radio – and had an internationally known grain exchange about which had sprung up the head offices of elevator companies and other grain-buying organizations. Further attesting to

Winnipeg's dominant position in the prairie region was the fact that it was the major provincial wholesale and manufacturing centre of the area between the Red River and the foothills of the Rockies, the administrative headquarters of several churches and other social organizations that functioned throughout the prairies, and the site of the provincial university.[78] Considering Winnipeg's attributes in the context of N.S.B. Gras' theories of metropolitan status, one of Dawson's students concluded that while the city lagged behind Montreal and Toronto, it was in the initial stages of a metropolitan economy: all transportation systems across Canada passed through it, and it was in a favourable position to influence a wider area; with the headquarters of the Canadian Wheat Pool, the Winnipeg Grain Exchange, and Union Stock Yards, it served as a distribution and marketing centre; it was growing industrially, with enterprises more numerous and varied than those of other urban centres in the prairies. Finally, its influence enveloped the whole region, while other prairie towns and cities served only tributary territories.[79]

When they turned to analysing Calgary and Edmonton, Dawson and Younge argued that while the two cities played an important role in the prairie economy, they were secondary to Winnipeg. Although Vancouver's growing importance as a centre for trade across the Pacific Ocean had resulted in a tendency to shift the distribution of many staple commodities away from Winnipeg to Calgary and Edmonton, the two cities remained primarily marketing centres for the western part of the prairies. Located at the junction of the Bow and Elbow rivers, Calgary was the centre of dominance for the southern part of Alberta, Dawson and Younge explained. Aided by the fact that the main line of the CPR passed through it, it had the advantage of being able to exploit the various resources of its hinterland. With most of the Alberta portion of the Palliser Triangle falling within its trade area, it was not only a centre of dry-farming but also of the irrigated areas of western Canada. Throughout its history, moreover, it had been the chief centre of the cattle- and horse-ranching industry in southwestern Alberta, and it had retained the atmosphere, Dawson and Younge argued, albeit more sophisticated, of its 'breezy frontier days.' (That spirit was kept alive by the development of two other important industries in its hinterland – coal mining and the production of oil.) Dawson and Younge believed that Edmonton, because of its strategic location with respect to natural resources and potential for expansion, was a more stable community than Calgary – it had fewer booms than that city, they argued, but it also lacked its colourful traditions. They calculated that its hinterland extended from Red Deer to the northern limits of settlement in the Peace and Mackenzie river basins; that its trade area included a portion of the fertile park belt, and that it was the wholesale centre for that part of Alberta lying north of the Red Deer. Although coal-mining, lumbering, and other industries had developed in its hinterland, Dawson and Younge considered that Edmonton's position as a regional centre of dominance stemmed from the industrial and commercial activities linked to agriculture. It was, moreover, the capital of Alberta and the seat of one of three universities in the prairie provinces. Finally, Dawson and Younge concluded that control of the trade area lying between the hinterlands of Winnipeg on the east and those of Calgary and Edmonton on the west belonged to Saskatoon and Regina, the two chief cities of Saskatchewan. Both had become manufacturing and wholesale centres, benefiting, they contended, from their location on the main line of a transcontinental railway system and serving, like Calgary and Edmonton, as focal points in a network of branch railway lines and motor highways.[80]

Dawson was influenced in his understanding of prairie trade centres by Nathan L. Whetten, one of his field researchers. A native of Canada, Whetten studied with C.C. Zimmerman at Harvard and, following his supervisor's interest in trends of centralization and dominance in rural regions, wrote a thesis on the social and economic structure of trade centres on the Canadian prairies.[81] Dawson also assigned one of his own graduate students to research news distribution in the region and from that study drew further insights into centres of dominance in the prairies. Robert Park had developed the technique of measuring the influence that cities exerted over a region by examining newspaper circulation. He believed that newspaper circulation was a reliable index of a city's trade area because it was closely linked to advertising: circulation departments of daily newspapers, he contended, usually concentrated their efforts upon the same territory that interested advertisers. In this and in an even more fundamental way he thought that newspapers mirrored the community; with the breakdown of primary relationships since the Industrial Revolution, he argued, the newspaper was an important socializing agency and a replacement for the town crier.[82] Not surprisingly, Dawson's student adopted Park's convictions in her own study, noting, for instance, how much isolated farmers depended upon newspapers to keep them informed of world events. Her more important conclusion, of course, was the discovery that the prairies had five regions, each of them centred around large cities and surrounded by small towns but all of them dominated by Winnipeg.[83]

Gladys Smith arrived at her conclusion about the regional divisions in

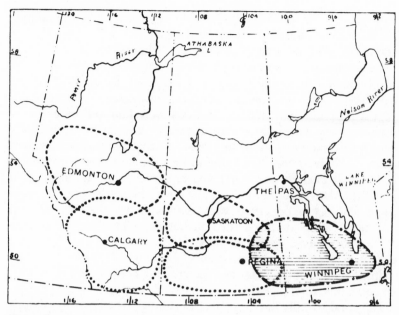

Figure 2
Adapted from C.A. Dawson and Eva Younge, *Pioneering in the Prairie Provinces*
(Toronto: Macmillan 1940), 45

the Canadian prairies by mapping out the circulation routes of different
papers. She found that from the five major centres of publication –
Edmonton, Calgary, Saskatoon, Regina, and Winnipeg – newspapers
were sent out in all directions along the lines of communication. They did
not travel the same distance in all directions, however, and in some cases
their circulation stopped abruptly – all of which Smith took as indicative of
areas of dominance and regional boundaries. Her map of newspaper
circulation in the prairie provinces indicated that the area that Winnipeg
dominated did not accord with political boundaries and was much larger
than that of any other region in the prairies. (See Figure 2.) Winnipeg's
dominant status, moreover, was reflected in the content of its newspapers:
while they featured news from all over the world, the greatest degree of
material was gathered from the centre of publication and its surrounding
territories.[84]

The conclusions that Dawson and Younge drew about prairie settlement
from their work on the pioneering project did not differ substantially from

those they presented in the Peace River study. Once again, they found that scattered settlement produced waste, inefficiency, and a low standard of living and impeded social organization as well. They pointed in particular to the adverse effects that sparse settlement had upon the development of health institutions. Although they praised local people for establishing the first health services in their towns and cities, Dawson and Younge noted that outpost hospitals and nursing missions were financed by hand-to-mouth methods, receiving little assistance until a crisis, such as a smallpox or typhoid-fever epidemic, motivated business and professional leaders into action.[85] Where *Pioneering in the Prairie Provinces* tended to differ from the Peace River study was with respect to its recommendations: while the Peace River study focused on providing advice for settlement, *Pioneering* was much more concerned with improving the functioning and administration of areas already settled. In that regard Dawson and Younge argued – in what was a favourite theme of Dawson's – that the region was in need of much larger administrative units to accord with its natural rather than politically imposed boundaries. The growing network of transportation and communication facilities, he contended, had divided the prairies economically and socially into a number of subregions whose peripheries were roughly indicated by newspaper circulation. Railway lines and roads served to link the large cities of these regions with the smaller centres of their constituent trade areas, each of these constellations of communities forming, Dawson argued, spheres of self-interest intermediate between the province and the local community. He thought that the growth of these subregions suggested a pattern that should be followed in organizing administrative units to superintend judicial, educational, and health services as well as to reorganize municipalities. Much of the problem of overlapping boundaries could be avoided, he contended, if town and rural village municipalities were extended to include the rural hinterlands that depended upon them for daily goods and services.[86]

In explaining the reason for his suggestions regarding the reorganization of administrative boundaries, Dawson revealed how strongly he continued to adhere to the principles and objectives of Chicago sociology. He believed that the substitution of natural territorial units for the existing municipalities, with their rigid, artificial boundaries, would strengthen the machinery of local government.[87] At bottom, then, his recommendations in *Pioneering in the Prairie Provinces* were intended to strengthen 'natural' communities, to draw together people with common interests, and to give them a voice in a government that would take care of their needs. In effect his intentions were not very different from the spirit of the Canadian west in the interwar years. Perhaps *Pioneering in the Prairie Provinces* did not offer an enduring theory on the development of Canadian society, but it stands as a reflection of a period.

V

By the time Dawson's contributions to the Frontiers of Settlement project were published, they were outdated, and his concern about the continuing haphazard and rapid settlement of the west needless. The research for his volumes had been undertaken through the years 1929 to 1931. Although economic problems had begun to plague prairie farmers at that point, farm deficits were much worse a couple of years later when the full effects of the Depression and the drastic drop in wheat prices were felt.[88] Dawson and the other academics involved in the pioneer-belts project nevertheless believed that their studies could be useful for dealing with the crisis then affecting the country. Harold Innis argued, for example, that the Depression merely served to bring out in sharp relief the problems that western Canada had been experiencing and that were documented in the Frontiers of Settlement series. He also thought that the series could be viewed as a preliminary attack on the difficulties of federal-provincial relations – western Canada was to Canada's industrial centre, he said, what the fringe was to the centre within the western provinces. Dawson drew somewhat different lessons from his research, and they reflected upon both his past and his future academic preoccupations.

In 1937, in an address dealing with the problems of rural communities, Dawson alluded to the popular belief that smaller centres naturally disappeared in favour of the larger and more resourceful areas in a region. The initial research in regard to that problem, he explained, had come from studies of the American and Canadian plains. What those studies showed, he contended, was that the popular inference was not correct – at least not without major qualifications. 'The smaller centres are holding their place and discovering more restricted functions under which they may operate effectively. The larger towns are growing larger not at the expense of smaller villages and hamlets, but ... at the expense of less favourably located major towns.'[89] Apart from revealing his loss of faith in metropolitan-dominance theories, Dawson meant to encourage further studies of community structure in Canada. Not only did he wish to know why smaller centres had so stubbornly survived in Canada, but he argued that such research was a necessary prerequisite for implementing special-ized institutions and services in the country's cities, towns, and villages. He warned that it was unwise to launch upon schemes of community organization until it was known what existed, what could be supported, or what was likely to be supported in communities with certain kinds of resources and traditions. There was nothing novel in that proposal; Dawson had long seen this as one of the purposes of sociology. What was new and had deeper implications for his sociological research was another conclusion he drew from the Frontiers of Settlement series – that Canada was, as he put it, 'a small fringe country ... Many say that Canada is a large country,' he elaborated. 'I should say, and there seems to be much to support the contention, that Canada is a small country from the point of view of possible settlement, and that population growth is likely to be very slow in the future.' His observation of conditions in the pioneer fringe of western Canada had taught him, moreover, that the phrase 'living off the land' was a fiction. To those who were proposing back-to-the-land schemes as a solution to the economic and social problems of the 1930s, he argued that the land was already oversettled and that on the basis of existing knowledge, land settlement could not possibly serve as a solution to unemployment. He proposed, instead, that unemployment problems be solved in the cities where they began[90] but added that research was a necessary prelude to any kind of action. In so doing he revealed the agenda of the McGill Sociology Department in the 1930s.

6

The Social Science Research Project

By 1930 ten years had passed since Sir Arthur Currie acceded to the principalship of McGill, and the university decided to mark the event by undertaking a survey of its past accomplishments in order to set the course for its future development. Committees were appointed to examine the work of each faculty, and their members were instructed to ascertain whether existing programs were training leaders befitting Canada's new international status, whether McGill was maintaining its 'proud place' in 'the friendly competition between French and English Canadian universities,' and whether it was adjusting to all new aspects of Canadian life.[1]

Currie was prepared to predict that some obvious conclusions would result from the survey. One of them would undoubtedly be that the university required more money in order to increase salaries, augment understaffed departments, establish new chairs, provide for scholarships and sabbaticals, and build professors' houses 'to keep them from "tenting" all over Montreal Island.'[2] McGill's student body had grown steadily since the end of the First World War, more than doubling in the Faculty of Arts, Pure Science and Commerce, where an enrolment of 529 students was recorded in the 1913–14 session, as compared to 1,331 in the 1928–9 session. The dean of Arts was warning that the faculty would soon have to end its expansion – there was, he claimed, room for no more students, not one more seat; timetables were so congested that it was impossible to move. The suggestion that the Faculty of Arts accept fewer and better students had been rejected as an unacceptable solution to the problem – Montreal was growing rapidly, with no evidence of any future interruption, and many more students were coming to McGill from other parts of Canada. As it stood, the university was not admitting all students offering the usual matriculation certificates – the dean estimated that probably half of those who applied were turned away.[3] The Faculty of Arts had been complaining about overcrowding and neglect for some time and likely had little reason to expect that the survey would improve the situation. Indeed, while Currie expressed confidence that more money would come the university's way, he also warned that there would not be enough to do everything faculty members would like to see accomplished. Accordingly, he recommended that a list be made of the priorities among its future objectives but advised survey members to be discreet about it. While criticism was permissible within the university's doors, he argued, common sense and loyalty had to dictate what was exposed to the public. Each committee was therefore instructed to make two reports, one a narrative of events, complete with statistics to be published for McGill supporters, the other a more searching and confidential report, such as department heads made to business directors.[4]

Largely because of worsening economic conditions, the reports were not published and most of the proposals recommending expansion were not implemented. Nevertheless, the confidential reports revealed that there was a great deal of doubt within the university as to whether the growth of social science had been beneficial. Concern over the popularity of sociology in particular took up much of the Arts survey committee's time. Carleton Stanley, a classics professor, drew attention to the fact that McGill was the only Canadian university with a full-fledged department of sociology. Since it was not the richest of universities, he wondered why it was so out of step and why sociology could not be studied in conjunction with economics or political science, as it was in other Canadian and British universities. The dean of Arts, Ira Mackay, shared Stanley's views, adding that sociology intruded into other fields too much; he did not think it was right to have one department delving into such issues as immigration, population, and land settlement. He also feared that students, rather than acquiring a sound knowledge of mathematics and history, were drifting early into political science, sociology, and psychology, and would continue to do so because they could get there without 'the necessary discipline and irksome work.' Of equal concern to committee members was the rate at which MA students were increasing in the Sociology Department. They feared that if the department grew too large, it would become a tremendous expense; they also questioned whether it was a subject warranting a graduate degree. Sociology on its own, some argued, did not constitute an education. It was a subject for mature minds, others argued, and could be taken in a student's final undergraduate years if it were done conservatively, thoroughly, and in a scientific way or if it were done in conjunction with history, mathematics, and other cognate subjects. After substantial discussion the committee recommended that sociology not be recognized as a basic subject and that its study be deferred until third year.[5]

In contravention of everything the Arts survey committee recommended, McGill's Sociology Department continued to expand in the 1930s. A grant in aid of the social sciences made by the Rockefeller Foundation enabled it to undertake a major project on unemployment and immigration in Montreal, a study the likes of which had never been done in Canada. In connection with the project members of the Sociology Department examined the problems that Canada was experiencing as it became more urbanized and attempted to absorb a large and diverse immigrant population into the economic mainstream and forge a national identity. The Sociology Department in that respect met the challenges mentioned in the survey announcement, and it was ironic that it emerged at the end of the decade in disrepute.

I

By 1930 American social scientists had done much to solve the problem of funding research in their fields. Largely through the aegis of the Social Science Research Council, which represented academics from psychology, anthropology, sociology, political science, and history, jurisprudence, public health, and psychiatry, they had obtained more than four million dollars from such philanthropic organizations as the Carnegie Corporation of New York, the Carnegie Institution of Washington, the Carnegie Endowment for International Peace, the Carnegie Foundation for the Advancement of Teaching, the Laura Spelman Rockefeller Memorial Fund, and the Rockefeller Foundation. The contributions continued, moreover, throughout the Depression years.[6] The provision of such handsome grants for social-science research stemmed from the attempts of philanthropists to find new and more socially and financially effective ways to dispense and organize charity in the interwar years. It was no less attributable to the ability of such academics as Charles Merriam, founder of the Social Science Research Council, to perceive the change in philanthropic objectives and to urge social scientists to restructure their research interests accordingly.[7]

Out of the belief that social improvement was being impeded by lack of knowledge about human behaviour, those responsible for administering the funds of philanthropic foundations decided in the 1920s to use the money to foster a program of national research and reform. They turned away from their former policy of funding individual scholars and specific institutions to give support to projects involving academics from different fields. Although both the Carnegie and Rockefeller foundations continued to select the strongest and most promising institutions as recipients of their grants, the Rockefeller Foundation's donation of fifty million dollars for salaries was one of the last grants given in the name of broad, strengthening purposes. The strong support the foundations gave to research projects during the interwar years shifted the emphasis in higher education from teaching to scholarly investigation and writing.[8]

One historian has noted that the philanthropic foundations were among the most influential institutions moulding the character of higher education in the twentieth century. Indeed, their influence upon social science was profound. The foundations' willingness to give money for specific research projects enabled organizations representing the social sciences, most particularly the Social Science Research Council, to go out and attract money on their own, but it also affected the nature of their research. Prior to the First World War the foundations had shied away from giving grants to potentially controversial topics, preferring to endow, for instance, medical research, which was socially beneficial and safer than anything that smacked of politics. Understanding their caution, Merriam attempted to convince them that it was possible to finance political reform without becoming politically involved.[9] This only strengthened the resolve of many social scientists to reject political activism, claiming, as they had been doing since the end of the First World War, that it was detrimental to pure research.

Merriam found the task of obtaining funds for social science easier when he acquired direct access to the philanthropists through Beardsley Ruml, a twenty-seven-year-old graduate of the University of Chicago. At the urging of Abraham Flexner and James Angell, president of Yale, Ruml, who had been involved during the First World War in the new field of pedagogical testing, accepted a position with the Rockefeller Foundation, where he was put in charge of launching new programs under its General Economic Fund. A loyal Chicago alumnus and an admirer of Merriam, Ruml opened the coffers to social-science research; in fact, as Merriam's biographer has noted, from 1925 on Ruml was the influence behind Merriam's attempts to reorganize the social sciences.[10] Indeed, the two shared many of the same convictions. Under Merriam's leadership one of the major tasks of the Social Science Research Council was to encourage and aid studies across two or more fields: it was not concerned with research projects falling within a single branch of social science. The council also attempted a systematic investigation of economic and social conditions in order to discover where research was required.[11] In managing the Rockefeller funds, Ruml made it clear that he believed that social research should have a practical end – to achieve concrete improvements in social conditions and to contribute to the public welfare. He thought that the scientific approach would generate a greater understanding of human affairs than would emotional appeals to traditional values. Perhaps more importantly, he believed that the divisions between the social sciences were artificial and that an interdisciplinary approach – a new synthesis and division of labour – could more effectively deal with social problems.[12] Accordingly, he backed yearly Social Science Research Council meetings held at Dartmouth College with the Spelman memorial funds. (Originally a conference of psychologists, these annual gatherings eventually brought together the major figures of American social science and university administration; their purpose was to give the Social Science Research Council and its financial backers an opportunity to decide upon the distribution of funds.) Under Ruml's direction, moreover, the Rockefeller Foundation financed joint studies, organizational devices, encyclopedias, publications, fellowships, and the construction of a social-science building at Chicago – all in an attempt to encourage more unity in the social sciences.[13] Eventually, Ruml moved to the University of Chicago to become dean of the Social Sciences Division; Merriam was succeeded as chairman of the Social Science Research Council in 1927 by Wesley C. Mitchell of Columbia University, and took over the Spelman fund (which was consolidated with the Rockefeller Foundation in 1929).[14]

Fortunately for McGill social scientists there was a small network of Canadian academics who had links with the American philanthropic foundations and used their influence to put McGill's case forward. Sir Arthur Currie, for example, was a member of the Advisory Committee on International Relations for the American Social Science Research Council and a member of the Institute of Pacific Relations, along with Joseph P. Chamberlain and James Shotwell. (Shotwell was responsible for directing one of the most extensive interdisciplinary studies involving Canadian academics – the Canadian-American relations series, financed by Carnegie funds.)[15] Edward A. Bott, a native of Ingersoll, Ontario, who taught psychology at the University of Toronto, was a member of the American Social Science Research Council's Committee on Problems and Policy – perhaps one of the organization's most important committees. In that capacity, along with fellow members Charles Merriam, Beardsley Ruml, and Wesley Mitchell, Bott was responsible for assisting the board of directors to formulate policies that would stimulate and improve research in the social sciences, for recommending projects that were feasible and scientifically important, and for supervising the organization and budgeting of research projects for which funds were appropriated by the board of directors. He was also chairman of the Social Science Research Council's Advisory Committee on Personality and Culture. Another member of that committee, C.M. Hincks, would prove to be the most important link in McGill's acquisition of the Rockefeller grant for social-science research.[16]

Clarence Meredith Hincks was a psychiatrist and physician, born in St Mary's, Ontario, in 1885, a nephew of T. Wesley Mills, the McGill physiologist. A pioneer in the field of mental hygiene, he introduced intelligence testing in Ontario schools, was a medical inspector for the Toronto public schools from 1912 to 1917, a psychiatrist for the Toronto Department of Health, and, in partnership with Dr C.K. Clarke, superintendent of the Toronto General Hospital, opened the first psychiatric clinic in Canada. Although Hincks's special interest was in mental defectives and the care and training of 'backward' and 'feeble-minded' children in school, he also lectured throughout North America to further the mental-hygiene movement and to stress its importance in the practice of medicine, teaching, social work, and anything else connected with individual behaviour and social relations. He founded the Canadian National Committee for Mental Hygiene and in 1931 was appointed general director of the American organization of the same name. He also helped to develop the University of Toronto's psychology program soon after the department was founded, attracting a team that included William Blatz, Bott, and J.D. Ketchum.[17] In most Canadian institutions of higher learning, psychology developed out of mental hygiene, and so it was only natural that Hincks should become involved with Toronto's program. But he took a special interest in the development of all the social sciences, believing that they were integral to the well-being of modern society. In fact, that conviction, his efforts to obtain grants for the new disciplines, not to mention his activities in the field of mental hygiene, led one journalist to describe him as a unique personality – 'the only generalissimo who [could] lead economics and the applied physical and chemical sciences, education and preventive medicine and the social sciences in the vitally necessary struggle for a resurrected civilization.'[18]

C.M. Hincks was well acquainted with C.A. Dawson and like the McGill sociologist was involved in the founding of the Canadian National Conference on Social Work and served as its chairman. In that capacity he also strove to make social workers understand that research was a necessary foundation for social improvement. In his presidential address to the Second Canadian Conference on Social Work in 1930, for instance, he spoke of the discontent that existed among social workers, particularly of their feeling that they were attacking social problems with ineffective weapons, patching up rather than offering constructive social effort. Canada was in its formative years, he explained, and its problems had not yet reached the magnitude of older civilizations. The only way to ensure that it developed a great civilization, he argued, was to see that social-science research was funded as generously by governments, industry, foundations, and the general public as the physical and natural sciences. Using the same metaphor as the Chicago-trained sociologists were wont to employ, he contended that with the community as their laboratory the social sciences could contribute more vitally to social welfare than the other two branches of science. 'They can lead us to a better understanding of the environment in which we live,' he said, 'of the way in which our social institutions affect mental and physical health, and of the factors that are requisite for the development of culture and the finer qualities of citizenship. At all cost,' he concluded, 'we must encourage the development of the social sciences. They are needed to offset the present tendency to materialism, and Canada offers the greatest laboratory in the world for convincing demonstrations of their value.'[19]

At the time he delivered this speech, Hincks was trying to negotiate a grant from the Rockefeller Foundation to fund social-science research at McGill University. Hincks probably became interested in McGill through his friendship with C.F. Martin, the university's dean of Medicine and officer of the Canadian National Committee for Mental Hygiene; he brought McGill's case to the attention of the Rockefeller Foundation through his acquaintanceship with Dr Edmund E. Day, director of the Social Science Division.[20] In late 1929, after discussing among themselves the benefits to be gained by supporting McGill, Hincks, Martin, and Day approached Sir Arthur Currie and urged him to apply for a large grant for the study of social science and human welfare. They suggested that the grant might be used to create at McGill something along the lines of Chicago and Yale's interdisciplinary social-research projects.[21] Currie took up their suggestion, first by making inquiries of those universities on how their projects functioned. He told James Angell that McGill was deeply interested in Yale's Institute of Human Relations and would be pleased to see not only information on the project but copies of any memoranda or speeches that the Yale president had made on the the subject.[22]

Yale's Institute of Human Relations was neither a faculty nor a teaching department but an agency that co-ordinated the research of different groups within the university. It began as an attempt to encourage closer work among the medical, biological, and social sciences and soon initiated co-operative research projects and acted as a clearing-house for data gathered from such investigations as the structure of public-utility companies and regional statistical analyses of family structure, technical improvements in industry, and the unemployed.[23] At Chicago the Local Community Studies project, which had been established in 1923, expanded to include social research that was not specifically local but still followed the same problem- rather than discipline-oriented approach. In order to facilitate this work and improve relations between the disciplines further, in 1929 the social-science departments at Chicago were housed in one building and organized according to research fields rather than along departmental lines.[24]

Both Chicago and Yale's programs, the Brookings Institution of Washington, and the Institutes of Social Research at North Carolina and Virginia were examples of 'intellectual co-operation,' an approach to social research that became popular in academic circles after the First World War but actually had its roots in developments of the preceding decades. Thorstein Veblen, in his problem-oriented approach to research, and John Dewey, in his call for co-operation among social scientists, had both espoused the principle, and their ideas were followed by other academics even after the two left Chicago.[25] In the interwar years intellectual co-operation was a response to increasing specialization in higher education, not only between disciplines but within them.[26] The desire to encourage intellectual co-operation on an international scale was manifested in the establishment at Paris of the Institute of Intellectual Co-operation to further education in arts and science; it was also exemplified in the Carnegie Foundation's support for a major study of the economic and social history of the war – 325 monographs superintended by James Shotwell.[27]

Many American academics found the idea of intellectual co-operation attractive because it evoked the spirit of national purpose and service to the state that had been channelled into the war effort. As one historian has noted, however, they either forgot or played down the legal and administrative restraints, social and intellectual pressures that compelled that co-operation.[28] For those who had been involved in the actual organization and administration of the war, the lack of knowledge about human behaviour and resources and the 'waste' that arose therefrom was dismaying. With representatives from social agencies repeatedly speaking about their inability to solve social problems, with the conviction that the Great War was the product of the breakdown of social control, many academics, especially social scientists, believed that the time had come for a kind of social engineering that had never before existed.[29]

An enormous amount of faith was placed in co-operative research, and social scientists made all sorts of claims about the benefits that would arise from their work. They promised to remove prejudice and stale custom, ease man's relationship with his fellow man, promote harmony and fairness, and exercise the social control necessary to 'keep the train from going off the track,' as it had done in 1917.[30] Sir William Beveridge envisaged a concerted world-wide movement – a league of universities – to bring 'light and research and knowledge into human affairs, to narrow the dark kingdom of blind chance, black temper, and self-will.'[31] Finally, in his dedication address at the opening of the social-science research building at the University of Chicago, Robert M. Hutchins declared, 'If this building does not promote a better understanding of our society, we shall know there is something wrong with the social sciences or something wrong with us.'[32]

This was the spirit that was to have infused the McGill project, and in the spring of 1930 Edmund Day and Beardsley Ruml prepared to visit the university and explain to Sir Arthur Currie the Rockefeller Foundation's interest in promoting the social sciences and to hear something of McGill's proposal. Anxious that the grant be given to McGill and that it stimulate developments in social science throughout Canada, C.M. Hincks took it upon himself prior to their visit to explain the foundation's philosophy to Currie and to elaborate on their reasons for selecting McGill as a possible institution upon which to bestow Rockefeller funds. Ruml and Day, he said, were interested in the contributions that McGill could make in the development of the social sciences and in the training of leaders. In an obvious attempt to flatter the principal, Hincks insisted that they favoured McGill because of Currie and Sir Edward Beatty's 'vision with regard to the possibilities of the social sciences contributing to human welfare.' He further implied that Day and Ruml were aware of the peculiar advantages that made McGill well suited for the task: it was a university with a national outlook, and a private corporation 'unfettered by the strictures of government control.' It had already given splendid leadership in the biological and physical sciences, and its close co-operation with the National Committee for Mental Hygiene ensured that it would make the kind of contacts with governments, industries, and other organizations that were necessary for research and for the practical application of research findings. Finally, he said, Ruml and Day realized that at McGill the social sciences could utilize all of Canada as their laboratory, a laboratory that was 'unrivalled' because the country was young, in the process of active development, and less bound by tradition than other civilizations. As far as specific projects were concerned, Hincks explained that the Rockefeller Foundation wanted to promote studies on racial and immigration policies, human relations in industry, and education, as well as to investigate problems of unemployment, delinquency, dependency, and government administration; and finally, to investigate the possibility of making health resources available for the entire population.[33]

Hincks suggested that Ruml and Day's visit might not amount to anything more than a general exchange of ideas, but in case the question arose of how McGill would foster social-science research, he took the liberty of recommending a policy. He thought it might be wise for McGill to consider organizing an institute of social science. It would not be necessary, he explained, for a building to be involved, but the university would need to hire a capable director – a man with vision and grounding in social-science techniques – to organize a small committee composed of department heads interested in the social sciences; the function of the institute would be to review and research training projects. If it became necessary to strengthen the university departments in order to accomplish this work, Hincks added, further Rockefeller grants or funds from other organizations could be obtained.[34]

Following Ruml and Day's visit, Currie held a number of conferences at his home with faculty and other individuals interested in formulating a grant appeal to be submitted to the Rockefeller Foundation. Among the faculty members who attended the meeting were Percy Corbett, dean of Law; Fred Clarke, chairman of the Department of Education; Grant Fleming of the Department of Health; William Tait and Chester Kellogg of Psychology; C.A. Dawson; Charles Hendel of the Department of Philosophy; John Beattie from the Department of Anatomy; J.W. Bridges, research director of the Canadian National Committee for Mental Hygiene (the organization's research division was located in Montreal); a professor of Industrial Medicine, a professor of Engineering, and E.W. Beatty. Operating under the mistaken assumption that the Rockefeller grant could be used to strengthen faculty ranks, the McGill professors came up with some grandiose schemes. A number of them liked the idea of establishing an institute of human relations and suggested a myriad of topics that could be pursued under that umbrella. These ranged from such pressing issues as unemployment, industrial relations, immigration, marital infidelity, desertion, divorce, and delinquency to more esoteric subjects such as supernaturalism, the psychology of belief (particularly rural superstition and unusual religious and political beliefs), the folklore of native peoples, and the classification and measurement of emotions. Several topics reflecting the growing popularity of scientific management were also mentioned: a new maze test for measuring intelligence, monotony and motivation studies for the workplace, and the more efficient organization of welfare.[35] (As material for those studies, J.W. Bridges offered the clients of the Committee for National Hygiene – in 1929 alone the organization had over five hundred new cases. These were individuals, Bridges argued, who in one way or another had failed to meet the demands of society.)[36]

Reflecting the initial enthusiasm for the project, John Beattie spoke in lofty terms about what McGill would accomplish with its institute of human relations. The university's national status, its strategic position at the portal of Canada in the midst of a cosmopolitan population, provided it with a rich and fertile field in which to work. With an agency co-ordinating research in sociology, law, psychology, economics, welfare, medicine, and public health, he predicted that it would not be long before the university was brought into public life and perceived by the Canadian people as a contributor to social welfare. Since the other universities were provincial, he argued, the only other means of tackling social problems on such a scale would be by government action – a contingency, Beattie guessed, that was not likely to arise for many years.[37] Despite his qualms about the social sciences, Ira Mackay also saw the benefits of the co-operative research program. He recognized that industrialization had created a new economy – a large economic machine, as he put it – that threatened to paralyse human interests, and that it was the university's duty to be awake to all the problems this had produced. After all, he said, quoting William Lyon Mackenzie King, 'Industry was made for humanity, not humanity for industry.'[38] Mackay nevertheless counselled against creating as large-scaled a project as Yale's. The effect of establishing an institute, he thought, would be to set up 'a counter-university within a university.' Instead, he suggested that the project focus on Montreal's particular economic and social conditions. Montreal was a unique city, he allowed. The juxtaposition of English and French communities and the sprinkling of races along the borderline between them offered 'a pattern in social studies peculiar to Canada.' Moreover, Montreal was surrounded by a number of towns and suburban communities that were unlike any others to be found on the North American continent. In some of them, MacKay argued, 'the economic and social history of the last three centuries may be read as clearly today as when it was written'; small holdings and primitive domestic economies on the one hand and large industrial communities on the other were found side by side in the same community. The study of a few typical examples of such communities, he suggested, would be of great value and interest to students in social and economic science.[39]

Mackay believed that initially the departments of Sociology, Economics,

Political Science, and Ethics should be involved in the project and that if the venture progressed, appointments should be made in social and industrial psychology, social ethics, and international relations. (A chair in international relations was long overdue at McGill, Mackay argued, and he looked forward to having the Rockefeller grant, if only to establish a position in that field.)[40] It was later brought to the attention of the McGill group, however, that the Rockefeller Foundation did not intend its funds to be used for strengthening faculty ranks; that was left up to the university itself. The idea behind the social-science grant was to assist staff in doing research by providing scholarships to postgraduate students who would do the spadework under the professors' guidance. The money could be put towards covering the cost of printing research findings, or for paying the travelling expenses of a great authority whom the university might want to invite to Montreal to interpret the data, but its primary purpose, as Day and Ruml explained to Currie, was to make it *obligatory* for a professor to do some research or to get out – that is, to make it impossible for him to claim that he could not do research because of the lack of facilities.[41] After a number of discussions, and partly because of this discovery, many of the McGill faculty agreed that it might be best for the social-research project to start with a small number of pertinent, practical problems of interest to the community – perhaps even old problems, which for the first time could be examined scientifically. Again and again it was the issue of unemployment in greater Montreal, particularly seasonal unemployment, that was mentioned.

Even before Currie had begun to hold conferences at his home, Stephen Leacock had argued that the McGill project should focus on something having to do with Montreal. He thought that the human, not the commercial side of the city's problems should be pursued and suggested investigations of housing, unemployment, and the absorption of immigrant families into the community.[42] Correspondence with Arthur Mathewson, a city alderman who was an economist and lawyer by profession, convinced him of the worthiness of unemployment as a subject of study. Mathewson had told Leacock that Montreal entrepreneurs would find useful an investigation of the effect of seasonal migration upon working men, especally in the shipping and ship-building industries. He alluded to the fact that longshoremen in the port of Montreal could not work during the winter months and so remained in the city unemployed or went to Portland, Maine, and Saint John, New Brunswick. From an employer's point of view, he explained, they were a difficult class of men to handle; Mathewson wondered, however, if they were rough by nature or whether their home life was to blame. Confused about the disloyalty that ship-builders and repairers displayed towards their companies, he wondered if their attitudes were also attributable to their extreme mobility.[43]

Chester Kellogg liked the idea of focusing on unemployment, too, but for different reasons. As a psychologist he was interested in the degree of unemployment that might stem from maladjustment, or the failure to employ people in accordance with their mental level and temperament; and in how much of it stemmed from lack of vocational education due to child labour, fluctuations in economic conditions, adjustment difficulties among immigrants, and overproduction. The factor of world overproduction struck him as a problem that was senseless to tolerate. If there was a need for goods, he argued, everybody should be busy producing them; if there was a surplus, no one should have to suffer for lack of them. 'Any system which treats the surplus of the property of the employers, gives employees only sufficient wages to cover subsistence while they are at work, and does not provide for steady employment,' he argued, 'is headed for trouble ... Can we find a way out,' he asked, 'or shall we wait for an insane solution by communists?' Kellogg also thought that the subject of unemployment lent itself well to co-operative research, and indeed that such research was the only way in which to solve the problem. Biology and medicine, he contended, could provide information on public hygiene; psychology could furnish an understanding of individual, sex, and race differences in intelligence and temperament, efficient methods of learning in education and industry, scientific management, and educational reform (the latter so that children were not driven out of school into unemployment); sociology could provide insight on social service, the preservation of rural community life, the treatment of immigrants, the effect that female labour had upon family life; economists could focus on industrial reorganization, co-operative ownership, conditions of employment, and unemployment-insurance schemes that would not 'penalize the industrious in favour of loafers.'[44]

In the conferences held at Currie's house there was also a great deal of support for studies on race composition in Montreal, particularly for an investigation of the changes in the city's racial composition since the end of the nineteenth century. Which races tended towards urban settlement, the sorts of occupations they pursued, and their crime records were also raised as subjects of interest. Ultimately, the McGill professors decided that unemployment should be the topic of investigation, with conditions in Montreal as the focus. They regarded unemployment as the best choice not only because it was pertinent but because its multifaceted nature made it well suited for interdisciplinary research. They also thought it was sensible to focus on Montreal because as an industrial city with an admixture of races, manufacturing plants, seaport associations, and pronounced seasonal unemployment, it furnished a cross-section of Canadian life not to be found elsewhere. Moreover, approximately one-seventh of the total wage-earners in the dominion lived in the city.[45]

The decision to focus on Montreal was in some respects a recognition of the need for urban research. Alluding to the fact that the rate of urbanization had been rising ever since 1891, reaching 50 per cent in 1921, the professors gathered at Currie's house noted that by 1930 Canada was no longer distinctly rural and city conditions were not unrepresentative of Canadian community life. A report of the McGill Social Science Research Project would note that by 1935 nearly one-third of the Canadian population lived in the country's fifteen largest towns and more than a quarter in its seven largest cities.[46] In the development of this new type of economic and social organization, as one of Dawson's students was later to point out, people were being mobilized into vast new aggregates, cut away from their moorings, whether thought of in terms of birthplace, social position, or established customs and traditions, and such an upheaval left few areas of life unchanged. What made Montreal all the more attractive as a subject of research, however, was that although it was industrial and urban in character, it was situated in a province that was still the chief region in Canada of small-scale farming and long-established rural life. That, in addition to the French-English division of its institutions, made the city's social and economic structure more complex than those of other Canadian cities.[47]

Before submitting their appeal to the Rockefeller Foundation, the McGill group decided to work out the administrative structure of the program. Towards that end they organized a social-science research committee and began to search for a project director. Owing to the paucity of social research in Canada, the committee was forced to look outside the country for individuals with the kind of experience necessary to direct their study. Aware that work of a similar nature had been undertaken in a number of centres in England, they asked Sir Josiah Stamp and Sir William Beveridge to suggest a qualified investigator. Upon Beveridge's recommendation they hired Leonard Marsh, a graduate of the London School of Economics.[48]

Marsh decided to take the McGill position because as a student he had established a close friendship with two Canadians and through them had become interested in emigrating to North America. Counselled against settling in the United States, he turned down a research grant from

Harvard; he was also passed over for a position in the Department of Political Economy at the University of Toronto, for which A. F. W. Plumptre was hired. A native of London, England, and from a fairly poor family, Marsh went through university on the scholarship system. He completed his BSC in Economics with first-class honours and received the Gonner Prize in Economics, annually awarded at LSE to the student with the highest mark in that subject. Upon graduating, Marsh was appointed to LSE's Department of Economics as a research assistant and lecturer. He also served as statistical secretary for the new survey of London life and labour. Directed by William Beveridge, the survey was a study of economic and social conditions in London – an update of Charles Booth's work, its objective was to show how incomes and expenditures, labour and leisure, wealth and poverty had changed since the time of Booth's investigation and, like the earlier study, to determine the geographical distribution of those phenomena throughout the city. In connection with the project Marsh spent about a year doing field-work – studying housing conditions and rents, the cost of living, working conditions, slum conditions, and unemployment in the East End, the poor part of London. He participated only in the research for the first book of the series, however, departing for McGill shortly before its publication.[49]

During his years as a student and through his involvement in the London survey, Marsh acquired the techniques of investigation and philosophy of reform – through the presentation of findings and statistics – that its Fabian founders had introduced into the London School of Economics. Those methods characterized the work he did for the McGill project as well as for the League for Social Reconstruction. In later years, when asked to assess the influence that the London survey and his contact with Beveridge had had upon his life's work, Marsh expressed frustration that the connection had led many people to conclude that his ideas for social insurance were copied from Beveridge's scheme. Marsh claimed that his contact with Beveridge was meagre, that the LSE principal merely edited the work that Marsh had done for the London survey, and argued that if there was any subject upon which Beveridge influenced him, it was unemployment, not social insurance.[50] In any event, that made him undoubtedly well qualified for the McGill project.

In late August of 1930, armed with a topic, a review committee, and a project director, Currie travelled to Dartmouth College and the annual conference of the Social Science Research Council to sound Day and Ruml out on McGill's plans. Cataloguing all the reasons that his officers of instruction had presented for studying unemployment, Currie also explained that the subject had never been investigated in Canada, and such studies as existed were loosely and unscientifically researched. He emphasized that since it was a local, national, and international problem, it had a very wide range of interest, touching life and living most intimately. He stressed, furthermore, how important it was that a Canadian university be given the opportunity to train people for social-science research. It was shameful, he argued, that when a group wanted to undertake such work in Canada, there was no one adequately trained to direct it; for such reasons McGill had had to engage the services of Leonard Marsh. Day and Ruml sympathized with the McGill academics' desire to focus on unemployment but warned Currie that the Rockefeller Foundation did not like to provide funds for the investigation of a particular topic; they preferred to encourage scientific research in the social sciences in a broad way. Nevertheless, they suggested that Currie request fifteen thousand dollars in funds for the first year, twenty thousand for the second, and twenty-five thousand for the next five years. That period of seven years, they assured him, would be ample time for McGill to demonstrate whether or not it was capable of doing worthwhile work.[51]

With this guarded encouragement the McGill faculty reconvened at Currie's house in the fall of 1930 to draw up the appeal to the Rockefeller Foundation. A new wrinkle was added, however, when it was suggested that in addition to an executive committee that included Currie, Corbett, Marsh, Clarke, Dawson, Carleton Stanley, and J.C. Hemmeon there should also be appointed a general council among whose members were a few prominent Montreal businessmen. The idea was that the executive committee would handle the daily operation of the project and the administration of funds, while the larger council would serve in an advisory capacity. When the issue was discussed, there was a general feeling that while the assistance of a few such men might be valuable, the inclusion of many businessmen – without careful selection – would make it difficult for professors and students to state frankly the findings of their investigations. An attempt was made to convince the dubious that such men would, on the contrary, welcome findings of a scientific nature; E.W. Smith and Julian Smith were suggested as appointees, and Currie was engaged to interview them.[52]

In the end, four powerful Montreal industrialists were invited to join the advisory council. Why such importance was attached to their inclusion at this late juncture is not entirely clear. Perhaps it was thought that the Rockefeller Foundation might be more favourably disposed towards the project if prominent businessmen gave it their blessing. The final draft of the appeal certainly emphasized the importance of their participation; it also indicated that beneath the shared enthusiasm for the project, McGill professors and Montreal businessmen had vastly different ideas about its purpose. The application was written primarily by Percy Corbett, with slight amendments made by Currie and more substantial ones by Beatty.[53] The reasons why the university chose unemployment in Greater Montreal were highlighted and need not be repeated here. At Beatty's suggestion, however, emphasis was placed on the factor of Montreal's attractiveness to research workers because of its diverse ethnic composition. Not only did the cleavage of its two main races complicate all social problems, Beatty noted, but representatives of every race, class, and industry found a home in Montreal. This was extremely important, he thought, in a country that was steadily admitting immigrants, the effect of which would be felt for some time. The fact that McGill's constituency was neither municipal nor provincial – 65 per cent of its population was from Quebec, but 20.5 per cent of the students came from other countries – ensured that it would approach any problem from both a local and an international standpoint. Not surprisingly, Beatty played up McGill's private status, as Hincks had done earlier. Its freedom from government control, he contended, ensured that 'no restrictions of policy [would] limit the scope of the investigation or the publication of findings.' Finally, he argued, McGill's situation in the largest city, the principal industrial and financial centre of Canada, meant that the Social Science Research Project could call on the assistance of the outstanding leaders of Canadian industry and commerce. These men would furnish investigators with entrées that might otherwise be difficult to obtain. 'Proceeding under the auspices of such men,' he promised, 'the investigators will carry with them a guarantee of good faith and a passport which will open doors that might be closed to the ordinary enquirer.' Moreover, the participation of the businessmen, as Beatty saw it, would do much to correct the public's perception of the university as an institution remote from real life.[54]

Appended to the proposal was a list of the qualifications of the industrialists interested in participating in the project. In addition to citing all his company directorships, the background information on Beatty added that as president of the CPR the McGill chancellor was interested in employment questions in Canada and Great Britain as well as 'all problems of man's relations with his fellow man.' Also included in the advisory council because of his 'life-long experience as an employer in the textile industry,' his 'thorough acquaintance' with conditions in that and other industries across Canada and the United States, was Sir Charles

Blair Gordon. A governor of McGill, Gordon was president of the Bank of Montreal and the Royal Trust and a member of the the the board of directors of both the Dominion Textile and the Dominion Glass Companies, among others. Julian Smith, president and general manager of Shawingan Water and Power Company (and a chief executive of all its subsidiary companies), vice-president of Dominion Engineering Works, president of the Quebec Power Company and the Montreal Tramway Company, as well as director of Montreal Light, Heat, and Power, was cited as an authority on the economic effect of the production and use of hydroelectric power. He was also said to be thoroughly acquainted with labour conditions in the hydro industry as well as in the city's traction and subsidiary industries. Thomas Bassett Macaulay, president of the Sun Life Assurance Company of Canada, director of Dominion Glass, Montreal Light, Heat, and Power, and the American Superpower Corporation, was added to the council for similar reasons. As president of Sun Life Assurance, the Rockefeller Foundation was informed, Macaulay controlled 'the largest group of Canadian and American securities held by any corporation in Canada.' He also claimed to have a wide knowledge of general economic conditions, particularly in agriculture, in Canada and the United States.[55]

Members of the executive committee, all academics (with the exception of Currie), were given second billing. It was noted, however, that Carl Dawson had participated in the pioneer-belts project, one of the most important enterprises undertaken by the Social Science Research Council, and that he had devoted particular attention to the many problems arising from immigration. Chester Kellogg's expertise in psychological testing was also highlighted: Kellogg had been a psychological examiner at Camp Devens in 1917 and at various other camps between 1920 and 1921; he had enlisted in the medical department of the American army and was a development specialist in testing and grading with the War Department Field Service. (Some of his test revisions were incorporated into the series used by the United States army in the 1920s and 1930s.) Percy Corbett was the house specialist on intellectual co-operation: the dean of the Law Faculty was a former assistant legal adviser of the International Labour Office of the League of Nations; he was also a member of the League of Nations Society, author of *Canada and World Problems* (1928), and a lecturer on the problems of political science at the Institute of Politics in Williamstown and the Harris Foundation in Chicago. Among the executive committee's members were also some experts on industrial conditions, though their qualifications were somewhat different from those of the industrialists. J.C. Hemmeon, professor of Economics, was a member of the Board of Arbitration for the Amalgamated Clothing Workers of America (International) and for the Lady Garment Workers' Association. He had, moreover, conducted a study of social conditions among Montreal textile workers for the ACWA. Frank Pedley, assistant professor of Industrial Hygiene and member of the Canadian Public Health Association and the Federated Social Agencies of Montreal, was, at the time McGill applied for the Rockefeller grant, involved in writing several works dealing with industrial conditions, one on chronic poisoning by tin, another by lead poisoning in the bronze foundries.[56]

The appeal was taken to the Rockefeller Foundation offices by C.M. Hincks, who had been visiting Montreal on his way to an appointment with Edmund Day in New York. With it Currie sent an accompanying letter explaining that McGill understood that the foundation's funds could not be used for paying professors' salaries but were to be offered as scholarships for postgraduate students, to enable professors to visit statistical bureaus at Ottawa, Toronto, New York, and Washington, and to publish findings worth publishing. He closed by noting that the McGill group was not only enthusiastic and capable but ready to proceed at the word go. Moreover, he assured the foundation that the work would not be interrupted by university vacations but would be prosecuted continuously until completed.[57]

Upon reviewing the application, Day informed Currie that while the memorandum of objectives was acceptable, the request for funds was inadequately developed with regard to prospective financial support after the initial effort. He explained that the Rockefeller Foundation was willing 'to carry the load' at the outset but that it expected at least a general assurance of reasonable support from other quarters as the program developed and demonstrated its value; he suggested that they have a meeting to discuss this further. Currie agreed to discuss the matter with Day at a meeting in New York in mid-November but assured him in no uncertain terms that the work would be continued after the Rockefeller grant lapsed. The fact that the university had taken the trouble to hire and pay a new member of staff, responsible only for the investigational work, had to be evidence of its earnestness, Currie argued. Marsh had already been supplied with an office and a secretary and was making contacts with a number of individuals and institutions necessary to obtain data for the project.[58]

Currie explained to Day that he could not absolutely promise a further contribution of funds until McGill's next endowment campaign, which was scheduled for May 1931 but was likely to be postponed because of the continuing economic depression. After that, he was sure that he could promise an appropriation of ten thousand dollars a year. Moreover, he had strong hopes – not without justification, he said – that the interest shown by such men as E.W. Beatty and T.B. Macaulay would ensure that the work was not dropped. He then added that there was another ground, an even more urgent one, upon which he was basing his plea for the grant. 'One day last week,' Currie said, 'it was announced by the government of Quebec that it would hold a survey into many of the questions which we contemplated studying, and that its survey would be presided over by Professor Montpetit of the University of Montreal.' Currie was sure that all those employed in making that survey would be officers of the University of Montreal. 'That is one way which this French-Canadian Roman Catholic government of ours has of helping the University of Montreal.' The fact that no McGill men would be employed, he declared, was just the sort of thing that made it harder 'for McGill to continue to stand as a bulwark for liberty and freedom against the encroachments of the Church ... I know full well,' he continued, 'that the government's investigation will not amount to a row of pins and that its findings will be just exactly what the government heads wish it to be, – a pat on the back which may serve a political use, and in other ways an excuse for any policy the government intends to put in force.' In closing he pleaded for a chance to make a truly worthwhile, independent investigation and pronouncement. 'Such actions by the government are, of course, a challenge to our English-speaking people,' he added, 'and we are made of that kind of stuff, I am pleased to say, that accepts the challenge.'[59]

After matters were straightened out at the New York meeting, Currie returned to McGill to work out the final logistical details of the project with members of the council. They decided that it might be better to take six months and refine their ideas still more, with a view to taking advantage of the grant for the first year on 1 July 1931. In the interim Marsh was instructed to make contact with statistical bureaus and other government departments and to travel to Chicago and West Virginia to observe the work being done in connection with those social-research projects. In addition, word was spread to other universities that McGill might soon be in a position to offer two-year scholarships to graduate students, leading to an MA in a number of social-science fields. The council members' plans were almost upset when Day informed Currie that while the grant was likely to be given to McGill, it would probably be scheduled to start on 1 June 1930, that being the start of the fiscal year. On a more serious note, Day told Currie that he was a bit disturbed by McGill's intention to offer scholarships. In that regard he explained that it was the foundation's policy in providing research grants not to permit any part of them to be used in support of announced scholarships or fellowships. This did not preclude the development of part-time research assistantships, which could be given to graduate students spending the rest of their time in candidacies for advanced degrees, but, as he pointed out, this was quite different from 'a programme of fellowships with all the publicity which is commonly attendant upon the administration of such awards.' Day expressed his hope that the restriction would not destroy the plans that McGill had been developing; indeed, he assured Currie that it did not create any real obstacles.[60]

In December 1930 the Rockefeller Foundation officially granted McGill University $110,000 for the development of research in the social sciences. (The grant was to cover a period of five years beginning on 1 June 1931 and ending 31 May 1936.) Although the foundation agreed to the project on unemployment, it did so with the hope that McGill would eventually open it up to broader fields.[61] The project was announced with much fanfare. An article in the *McGill Daily News* was typical of the reaction it received: lack of funds had been a stumbling block to the development of social-science research, it pointed out, but with the grant several McGill departments would be able to carry out work that might not otherwise have been possible.[62] A more unusual reaction was a letter of congratulations sent to C.F. Martin from Edward Bott.

At a meeting of the Problems and Policy Committee of the Rockefeller Foundation held in Toronto, Edmund Day informed Bott that the McGill appeal had been granted. Bott told Martin that he was delighted to hear the news – Day had explained to him that the grant was being given to McGill in order 'to give Toronto some competition.' Bott was seemingly not amused; he told Martin that what was needed in Canada was help, not competition, and he hoped that when the McGill committee was drawing up its plans, Martin would keep in mind 'a special point about psychology in which our Canadian universities can play ball together.' He explained that Day had been hoping that the Social Science Research Council would become a medium for co-ordinating certain fields of work at different universities throughout North America, work that his Rockefeller division could then liberally support. Hitherto the council had 'a rather nondescript policy of [supporting] miscellaneous projects, large and small, but with little cohesion and no continuity of plan,' Bott elaborated. At Day's urging, however, it had decided to cultivate a few fields until they were as firmly established as the natural sciences: the fields initially chosen were international relations and business relations and finance; a third –

behaviour and personality – was added later. Bott believed that any university aiming to develop the social sciences had to include the third topic and at Day's instigation had agreed to steer this job for the council. After turning down the opportunity of becoming council president, 'for the sake of sticking by Psychology (and Canada),' he told Martin, he could not refuse to help with the promotion of psychology at the main university centres across the continent.[63]

Bott also wanted to make sure that Canadian institutions got their share of foundation funds. Yet he was embarrassed by the fact that in Canada psychology was not only young but relatively lacking in unity. Advances had come in two or three institutions but only because those in charge had tied psychology in with a number of disciplines that shared a mental-hygiene interest. Bott was not certain that this was a wise policy, though it had brought vigour and opportunity. He argued that while it might initially have been a good thing for the Universities of Alberta and Saskatchewan, the mental-hygiene angle was not fully acceptable to Psychology at McGill. Yet no alternative means of uniting psychology with the other disciplines concerned with human problems had presented itself at that institution. He wondered how the new field of behaviour and personality could be made to fit McGill's needs, and he asked Martin to help him. McGill's assistance was necessary, he argued, for the development of psychology in Canada; he suggested that the major institutions create programs adapted to their own localities but offer a united front when seeking support or concessions from the outside. In fact, he wondered whether it might be worthwhile for Canadian psychologists to ask the National Research Council of Canada to act in their favour. 'It will certainly be anomalous for Canadians to devote themselves to building up American centres,' he concluded, 'without doing as much for all our friends on this side.'[64]

For a variety of reasons, among which were jealousy and suspicion, Bott was not very successful in his attempts to encourage intellectual co-operation within Canadian institutions of higher learning. There was enough hostility towards him at Toronto alone. His letter came into the hands of Carleton Stanley, who promptly wrote to G.S. Brett of the Department of Philosophy at that institution, asking why McGill was being invited to join Toronto in seeking financial support for studies on such issues as motivation and learning, family research, and deviant behaviour. Brett wrote back explaining in unflattering terms that there was a growing feud with Psychology at Toronto. That department, he elaborated, wanted to do everything and to boast about its numbers. 'Bott seems to be afflicted with the American (or late Chicago) idea of efficiency. He is a go-getter by nature. The result is that we have a nursery school, an educational programme and a social science programme all being engineered from one angle. Why or how the Rockefeller committee . . . became convinced that it should operate solely through Professor Bott we do not know.' The result, he said, was that the Social Science Research Council was wholly ignored by Toronto's other social-science departments, particularly Economics and History. They objected to being circularized 'and told to line up when Mr. Sharp [of the Rockefeller Foundation] comes to town: especially as something called the "Frontier Project" was organized with no reference to people like Innis (Economics) who really knows something . . . You can see that there is not much "co-operation" here,' Brett continued, 'and the only co-operation offered is loaded down by the connexion with psychology.' Then, in a ringing condemnation that partly explains some of the hostility the McGill project met, he concluded, 'This introduces the fact that the main part of the racket is Mental Hygiene – the Hincks organization wants to establish *independent* agents, with *independent* money, under the roof-tree of a University which gives the show prestige. The actual result is that the staff and students are both sides of the wall: the students can be bought with the money and the staff can acquire honour as getters of money.' He urged McGill not to be strung along by this but to set its own terms. Unlike Toronto, Brett argued, McGill had a professor of Sociology upon whom the problem could be unloaded. The topics that Bott mentioned – motivation, family research, and behaviour – Brett suggested finally, were nothing but jargon and 'psychological urgencies'; there were other topics, he concluded, that could be pursued.[65]

II

By January 1931 unemployment was widespread in Montreal and throughout the world, the subject of front-page material in almost every newspaper.[66] Although many of the students that it drew from upper middleclass ranks were immune to the effects of the hard economic times, McGill was not. During the academic session of 1931–2, as the university's revenues began to fall, the wealthy industrialist members of the Board of Governors decided to underwrite its deficits and rigidly curtailed expenditures in all departments. McGill's rate of progress slowed considerably from the 1920s as expansion plans were postponed; the School for Social Workers was closed; and faculty were asked to accept a reduction of salaries and wages (effective 1 June 1932) on a sliding scale, varying from 10 per cent on the highest salaries to 3 per cent in the lower ranks.[67]

Despite the fact that it was conceived in the atmosphere of the Depression and focused on unemployment, the objective of McGill's Social Science Research Project was not to offer remedies for the crisis. Leonard Marsh reiterated time and time again that periods of economic depression always produced some immediate problems of which the most pressing was relief – 'the ambulance work,' as he put it, of the unemployment situation. A problem of which everyone was aware, it necessarily coloured a great deal of thinking on unemployment. Nevertheless, Marsh argued, while much could be learned from handling emergency measures, such experience would not provide any insight into the causes of the economic malaise or help to solve it. The Depression had its roots in international problems of at least ten years' making. With all the distress it had created, it had at least destroyed the optimistic views of unemployment that prevailed in North America before 1929 by making people realize that unemployment was a recurrent problem. In light of that, Marsh explained, the McGill project was to be directed towards issues of which the current depression constituted only a part. The studies done under its auspices were to represent a stock-taking rather than a prescription of cures; they were to be examinations of employment and unemployment problems not unique to depression periods. There were many phases of the labour market, he explained, that could be improved whether economic conditions were good or bad. Impartial fact-finding was the necessary basis of such improvement and the object of research.[68]

In consultation with members of the executive and general council, Marsh drew up a large-scale and ambitious project that included in the first year of its existence the Departments of Economics, Sociology, Psychology, and Education; in the years thereafter Medicine, Law, Mental Hygiene, and Industrial Engineering also participated. It involved an extensive demographic survey of employment in Montreal – of industries and occupations in the city and of the composition of the work-force in each industry, paying particular attention to opportunities for unskilled labour in the dock, building, and railway industries. (Very early in its existence the Social Science Research Department was invited to conduct an industrial survey of Montreal by the Montreal Board of Trade and J.B. Baillargeon, head of the Civic Industrial Commission. The survey was supervised by Dr Meredith F. Burrill of the Oklahoma Agricultural College, who had made what was considered a highly accurate survey of the city in 1928 and 1929, financed by Rockefeller Foundation funds. [The demographic survey was likely part of this project.]) A statistical survey of unemployment and the organizations dealing with relief was also undertaken; subsidiary problems such as dependency, labour mobility, education, and juvenile employment were equally scrutinized. Information was gathered from trade unions, dominion employment indices, employment services, social agencies, and relief authorities, and firms in almost every branch of industry in the city were approached – the Board of Trade and the Canadian Manufacturers' Association willingly gave their assistance.[69]

The overall objective of the employment survey, as Marsh saw it, was to complete detailed studies of the major industries, their employment problems, and the possibility of stabilization on the one hand and the sources of labour supply, particularly from the schools and immigrant stock, on the other. He promised the members of the executive committee that this was a field capable of wide augmentation and development in later stages of the scheme but suggested that the project initially focus only on the issues of employment and unemployment. He felt that while extension in some directions might be desirable, it would hamper progress on the employment survey.[70] In order to co-ordinate and streamline the work, he recommended that the Economics Department look at unemployment problems in particular Montreal industries. (He himself intended to work on the topic of labour mobility and unemployment, something that he had begun in England and hoped to extend in the Canadian field.) To the Education Department he assigned the task of examining the permanence of school-taught knowledge and its relevance to employability. He suggested that the psychologists concentrate on the qualitative character and industrial aptitudes of unemployed as compared with employed groups and that they also examine literacy, aptitutes, and mental defects, relating these to factors such as age, race, periods of unemployment, and age of leaving school. Since Montreal was the dominant city of entry to Canada for immigrant groups and families, a very substantial element in Canadian unemployment, Marsh thought, was the success or non-success of the new entrant to the country. He accordingly proposed that the Sociology Department deal with the social and occupational adjustment of immigrant groups in Montreal, in the hope that such studies would unearth more information on the functioning of immigrant agencies and the comparative success, tendencies, and problems of particular groups.[71]

One of the reasons why the Sociology Department's task differed from those of the other departments was C.A. Dawson's objection to the single-minded focus of the Social Science Research Project. He felt that it was unfair to ask all the participants to concentrate on unemployment, particularly if they were equipped for or interested in studying some other subject. (Undoubtedly Dawson's keen interest in Canada's immigration policies and problems and the opportunity that the Rockefeller money presented for pursuing these further were added factors.) The other members of the executive committee concurred with Marsh on the need for efficiency and co-ordination and tried to dissuade Dawson from pursuing his own course, but he was intransigent. In order to appease him, they decided that each department would agree on one subject, preferably something having to do with employment, as the main focus of study for the first year and upon a secondary topic to be pursued if funds later became available. The Economics Department announced that it was only too happy to work on Montreal industries for the first year, particularly employment and unemployment problems in the rail-transport industry since the modern railway and its subsidiary operations constituted a source of employment for a large part of the working population. The industry, moreover, was affected by employment conditions special to Canada. The economists indicated, however, that they would look at the subject of unskilled labour in Montreal as a secondary topic. The others similarly went along with Marsh's suggestions, but Dawson continued to insist that the Sociology Department would make immigration its main field and problems related to unemployment – such as slum conditions and other factors contributing to the production of unemployables – its secondary interest.[72]

Graduate students were drawn upon as the main source of research assistance for the project, though salaried assistants were employed for short periods where this was considered preferable. (The Social Science Research Department was not itself a teaching department, though there were plans – never implemented – for it to offer an interdisciplinary seminar. It supervised and directed the individual researches of graduate students in the allied departments and special students not in pursuit of a degree.) Graduate students worked under the joint guidance of the director and a member of the department concerned with the study. The research was accepted as MA work, equivalent to work on a thesis, provided that the student spent two years in the program and fulfilled all other departmental requirements for the degree. In a number of cases the work was considered and approved for publication as part of the McGill Social Science Research Studies series.[73]

Throughout its ten years of existence some thirty-eight students were involved in McGill's Social Science Research Project, more than half of them from universities other than McGill. Dawson was involved in the attempt to recruit the best students from all over Canada, a task made easier by the ability to offer grants ranging from five hundred to seven hundred dollars a year in a period of economic depression. For students interested in pursuing graduate studies in the social sciences in Canada, the Rockefeller Foundation money was without doubt a great boon. The scholarships in those fields were meagre, poorer even than in the humanities.

In part because of the Rockefeller funds and because of Dawson's efforts to attract students from farther afield, by the academic session of 1937–8 Sociology had one of the largest graduate departments at McGill, with ten students.[75] A number of these were people who might not have gone into sociology under different circumstances; many of them had backgrounds in economics and returned to that field to do their doctoral degrees. By their own accounts they chose to study sociology at McGill because there were so few alternatives during the depression years; Dawson was more than willing to have them in the program because there were not enough graduate students in sociology in Canada to carry out the research program that he had envisioned. They were nevertheless an enthusiastic and spirited group and went on to become quite eminent in their fields. One of them was Oswald Hall, who recalled that when he graduated in economics in 1935, the market was considerably 'less than nil' unless one had a father in a business. In any event he was not eager to do graduate work in economics, and so when the opportunity arose to do research in sociology at McGill, he grabbed it. Unlike some of his colleagues, however, he continued in the field, proceeding to Chicago for a PH D and to a long and successful career as a sociology professor in a number of Canadian universities. Stuart Jamieson's background was in economics and history; he was studying at the University of British Columbia when Charles Topping, a classicist turned sociologist, informed him of McGill's Social Science Research Project and Dawson's inquiries as to whether there were any able students interested in coming to Montreal. Even though he was at the top of his class in economics, Jamieson felt he could not refuse the offer of $750 a year for two years' study in sociology at McGill. Lloyd Reynolds' story was similar to these. When he completed his BA in economics at the University of Alberta in 1931, Reynolds planned to work for a while in order to gain some practical experience. Since the best job he could find was a part-time one in the basement of the T. Eaton Company store in Edmonton, the offer of a graduate fellowship at McGill, despite the fact that it was not in his field, seemed, as he put it, 'a superior alternative.' Reynolds emerged as one of the top students in the program; afterwards he returned to economics, obtaining a PH D at Harvard, and then became very prominent in the United States in the field of labour economics. He once credited

McGill's Social Science Research Project with giving him a taste and competence for detailed fields of investigation that stayed with him all his life, as well as a broader perspective on economics, which many other academics in his field lacked. A number of other sociology students fared almost as well, many of them proceeding to doctoral studies at Harvard, Yale, and Michigan, complete with scholarships.[76]

Twelve projects were undertaken in the first year of the Social Science Research Department's existence, all of them in categories that the departments agreed to follow. Marsh was responsible for three of them – an analysis of the available statistics of industries and occupations in general for Canada and Montreal, trends of employment and unemployment in Montreal and comparative areas since 1921, and seasonal variations in employment in Montreal and Canada. By 1933 ten more studies were under way, and in 1935 the participants began to collate, write, and edit the material for publication.[77] A four-year extension of the grant was requested from the Rockefeller Foundation in 1936, Marsh stressing again that the participants were not looking for remedies for unemployment – indeed, they had found none – but were attempting to amass facts and train men and women for industry, government, or social agencies. The only way in which the results of their research could be applied, he told the Rockefeller Foundation, would be by educating and winning public opinion to their side. That was what made the project's continued existence at McGill important – it was a new experiment, a valuable and constructive one, according to all the members of the executive committee. For one thing, as the program proceeded, there was a marked improvement in research facilities for the social sciences.

In 1934 the university provided the project's offices with a home of their own on University Street. Nothing as grand as Chicago's social-science research building, it nevertheless had a statistical library, a room to house machines and maps, administrative offices, a small conference or seminar room, and a room where students could keep their books and other materials. There common basic data were compiled, and stenographic work, statistical tabulation, the preparation of maps and diagrams, and anything else required for publication was undertaken. Moreover, during the five-year period of the grant the committee had published three volumes and had planned four more. In addition to their own research members of the Social Science Research Department had been consulted in the drafting of the Federal Employment and Research Bill, prepared a report on the municipal relief situation for the Dominion Conference of Mayors, assisted in a report on housing and slum clearance in Montreal, and received various requests for assistance or to supply information. That was not to say that they were given complete access and co-operation in surveying social and industrial conditions in the city. A number of industries and certain governmental bodies refused to assist them when the research was so extensive as to require special arrangement, when criticism of some kind was feared, or when an especially controversial issue was involved. Marsh saw this as partly a problem of tact, also one of education: 'Beyond a certain point in our particular field of science,' he wrote to the Rockefeller Foundation. 'we cannot do research unless society wants us to.'[78]

The Rockefeller Foundation approved the four-year extension on the grant, and the McGill social scientists believed that they were on the road to seeing social research made a permanent fact at McGill. It was a belief that quickly dissipated, and the rumblings were apparent almost from the time the grant was initially made.

7

The Sociology of Unemployment, Immigration, and Assimilation

The initial interest that McGill officials took in the Social Science Research Project did not last much past the announcement that the Rockefeller funds had been granted. In the winter of 1931 Currie left on an extended trip to India; Carleton Stanley filled in as acting principal, and Marsh was left to handle the project on his own. Never finding it convenient to attend meetings and to submit to Marsh's long 'memo harangues,' the industrialists drifted away; Ira Mackay washed his hands of the whole thing, and Stephen Leacock refused to become involved. When Currie returned to McGill in the spring, he found the project well under way but following lines different from what he had envisioned. Although he attended a few meetings, he confessed that he found it 'all stuff and nonsense' and that it worried him. With the departure of the industrialists, Mackay, and Leacock, 'the socialist-sociologist-psychologist group,' as the principal's secretary referred to the executive committee, was left to its own devices.[1] Their work was tolerated until the late 1930s, when A.E. Morgan, Currie's successor, was forced to resign and was replaced by Lew Douglas, who was determined that McGill not become a centre for socialist thinking.

I

What Mackay, Currie, and the industrialists likely found objectionable about the Social Science Research Project was the 'collectivist' philosophy that seemed to permeate it from the start and found its strongest expression in L.C. Marsh. In January 1931, shortly after his arrival at McGill, he addressed an audience at the Montreal Forum on the subject 'Unemployment: An International and Community Problem' as part of the People's Forum lecture series. The speech received extensive newspaper coverage, and its contents had to rankle the industrialist members of the Board of Governors. It was replete with collectivist arguments, not simply in its perceptions of unemployment but in its recommendations for treating it. Marsh's central thesis was that unemployment was a community problem that could only be understood from an international perspective, that it arose from more than personal causes and had to be dealt with by more than individual effort. 'Personal causes go far in determining the incidence of unemployment, its duration, and its effects,' he argued, 'but the major cause of unemployment is the functioning or the failure to function of the economic system itself.'[2]

To bolster his arguments about the non-personal causes of unemployment, Marsh explained that because Canada was a growing country with a resource-based economy, a certain amount of unemployment was inevitable. Seasonal fluctuations and drastic changes in climate were especially problematic: the concentration of harvests in particular months, he pointed out, affected the mobilization and migration of labour. In the past the problem had been dealt with by co-operation with the Employment Service and the railways; in recent times the increased use of agricultural machinery had reduced its magnitude, but, Marsh contended, there was no evidence that labour was being successfully reabsorbed after the harvests were in. In addition, change and progress in industry were giving rise to a substantial volume of unemployment, affecting different individuals all the time. Since in Canada it was well known from experience which months were particularly bad and which would continue to be so in the future, Marsh argued that attention should be directed to providing for unemployment as a *permanent* element of social organization, and efforts should be made to provide for employment and maintenance in slack months. He knew that these views would not be readily accepted, but he was convinced that unemployment or underemployment could be reduced by improved planning within the industries or provided for on a sound actuarial basis.[3]

As far as the international causes of unemployment were concerned, Marsh adhered to the trade-cycle theory, the idea that there were alternate periods of boom and depression that extended over a period of years and affected all industries, though not necessarily equally. He told the forum audience that even though economists could not agree on why the economic system could not function continuously without maladjustment, they concurred that the real cause of recession was the inflationary aspect of the boom that preceded it. In this context Marsh saw the Depression of the 1930s as the logical consequence of the boom of the 1920s, exacerbated by world-wide maladjustments since the war – a war that he contended had not ended until 1920, at least from an economic standpoint. As he outlined it, a world-wide inflation, marked by the highest prices of a century, was followed by a catastrophic boom that broke late in 1920 and saw rapid returns to the gold standard between 1923 and 1925. Although that seemed to create stability, in reality it engendered substantial deflation and heavy credit. Such economic problems, in addition to a general increase in tariffs, reparations, and war-debt settlements served to impede the resumption of normal trade relations. If all of this were not enough to create chaos, war demands had caused world-wide overproduction by stimulating the production of raw materials in countries responsible for world supplies and manufacturing industries in those that depended upon foreign trade.[4]

Marsh's remedies for problems on the international scene smacked just as much of collectivism as did his advice for handling domestic problems. He emphasized the need for international co-operation in dealing with world prices; he argued that central banks had to be given greater power and freedom and that the League of Nations ought to be encouraged in its efforts to perfect international banking and financial operations. More-over, he suggested that every country establish a permanent advisory body on unemployment and that these agencies provide employment bureaus with information on the contemporary situation as well as undertake their own research and planning for long-range relief policies. In Canada, where four of five cities were the main centres of unemployment, he thought there was good reason to set up in each of them a body to co-ordinate the unemployment work of all existing agencies. More important than the provision of an efficient and nation-wide employment service, he argued, was a need for a permanent unemployment-insurance scheme to relieve the distress that inevitably arose from unemployment. In alleviating the unemployment that stemmed from all types of fluctuations and industrial changes, the scheme would assist normally employable workers, leaving social-welfare agencies to devote their efforts to their traditional spheres of interest. As for the problems within industry, Marsh called for a greater degree of scientific planning, proposing that production, marketing, and technical improvements be worked out in consultation with workers' representatives. He contended that this would ensure a steady output of production in spite of normal seasonal variations in demand. He did not think it would be possible to abolish seasonal fluctuations completely, but he believed that attempts could be made to alleviate its worst effects by publicizing general business conditions and undertaking the long-range planning of public works.[5]

Not everything that Marsh proposed in his unemployment speech became policy of the Social Science Research Project, although these were ideas that were certainly shared by his League for Social Reconstruction colleagues at McGill.[6] Marsh's connections (and those of a number of other participants) with the LSR and CCF did not sit well with McGill officials and certainly did not contribute to their understanding of the Social Science Research Project, but not all its members nor all its publications expounded collectivist political philosophies. What did characterize most of the work was a concern with social well-being and social cohesion, which might have seemed during the Depression years to have a leftist orientation, though this was not always the case.

Only a few of Dawson's students undertook economic studies; the majority examined issues having to do with immigration policy and immigrant groups. Each set of studies was devoted to different objectives, and in the case of the immigrant studies one of the major purposes was to assess the degree of assimilation that had occurred among the newcomers. They all nevertheless shared a concern that had characterized Dawson's own work since he arrived at McGill and that, despite the ecological trappings, had manifested itself in the pioneer-settlement series. Dawson's assessment of life on the fringe, farm budgets, and family expenditures was done with the intention of ascertaining whether the environment in which the settlers lived afforded them a decent standard of living. The studies done on Montreal in the 1930s, in one way or another, were devoted to the same issue. When it came to looking at conditions in the city during the Depression, however, attention had to be paid not only to environmental factors but to employment conditions. Dawson had nothing to do with the LSR, and yet for the reasons stated above, one of the earliest theses done under his supervision in connection with the Social Science Research Project ended by advocating the implementation of a social-insurance scheme.

Phyllis Heaton's examination of standard-of-living studies and their usefulness in Montreal began, mildly enough, by tracing the history of standard- and cost-of-living studies. It pointed to LePlay's research into the consumption and expenditure habits of nineteenth-century workers, to the numerous investigations, most notably that of Lord Shaftesbury, undertaken in Britain between 1880 and 1914, and to Charles Booth's survey of London life and labour. When it came to dealing with more contemporary studies, however, Heaton referred to the major impact that the war had made, introducing two new ideas – the first, that everyone was entitled to at least a minimum share of the world's goods (an amount that ensured something more than subsistence); the second, that wages or the share of production going to labour should bear some relation to the retail price level and the cost of living. Both of these, she noted, represented a tacit abandonment of laissez-faire ideology and gained currency during the war as a result of the tremendous rise in prices and the growing strength and power of labour. She added, however, that the upheaval that the war had engendered, causing a re-evaluation of long-held ideas, was another critical factor: in its wake laissez-faire was seen to result in misery and waste, and there emerged a conviction that society must be mobilized and controlled for the well-being of all its members, instead of allowing individuals 'to be swept along by the inevitable operation of natural laws.' To ascertain what that level of well-being should be, Heaton argued, was the objective of post war standard-of-living studies. [7]

Standard-of-living studies undertaken during the 1920s varied from extensive sociological surveys of entire cities to intensive inquiries into the habits of small, specialized groups. Such studies were meagre in Canada, though cost-of-living studies abounded. In 1913 a board of inquiry authorized to investigate the cost of living found an increase in the per capita consumption of a great number of articles and a rise in wages consonant with retail prices of food, fuel, and light but not rents. In addition, the Dominion Bureau of Statistics and the Department of Labour published cost-of-living indices monthly. But as far as studies of individual cities were concerned, Herbert Ames's survey in 1897 of a working-class section of Montreal stood as the lone tract – with the exception of a cost-of-minimum-health-and-decency study of ten Canadian cities undertaken by the United States Bureau of Labor Statistics, the Family Welfare Association's survey of Montreal in 1926, and the study of ten Canadian cities made by the Canadian Brotherhood of Railway Employees (in an attempt to show the arbitration board that the wages of railway workers were insufficient to maintain a proper standard of living). Working independently, Heaton undertook a necessarily small-scale evaluation of the standard of living of a group of English-speaking working-class families in Montreal during the period between January and May 1931. They were, she said, the sort of people whose standards of living were particularly sensitive to economic fluctuations: able to keep their heads above water in good conditions, they were forced to seek aid from philanthropic organizations during adverse times. It was her intention, she explained, to determine from the evaluation of this group what should be the *minimum* standard of relief-giving and to what extent unemployment insurance, wage increases, and other efforts 'to make life more liveable' were necessary. [8]

The discovery that almost half – seventeen – of the families that she surveyed had been compelled to seek aid from relief agencies led Heaton to conclude that in supporting these agencies 'the public ... [was] really going far towards subsidizing inadequate wage-rates.' Moreover, she found that a typical family, consisting of 2.5 dependent children with an average income of $1,027 a year, received only $200 from the Family Welfare Association, making its income well below the standard of health and decency, which had been set at $1,107.76 for Montreal in 1927. These revelations prompted her to recommend that wages should be raised, that minimum-wage legislation ought to be supported and extended, and that a much greater development of social-insurance schemes was mandatory. Furthermore, she contended that old-age and widows' pensions and health and unemployment schemes should be undertaken on a sound actuarial basis, that school curricula had to be reformed and vocational guidance offered to guarantee a supply of intelligent workers and ensure that fewer went into blind-alley jobs.[9]

Heaton's recommendations came close to being the kind of curative measures with which Marsh had promised the Social Research Project would not be concerned. They also reflected the reformist attitudes that Chicago sociology supposedly eschewed. Yet there was nothing contradictory in her suggestions for their implementation. For all their talk about the operation of natural laws, Chicago sociologists were not advocates of laissez-faire; they were interested in social improvement and social justice. In the 1930s economic circumstances had grown so bad that it was not surprising for someone trained in that tradition to argue for the necessity of a social-insurance scheme. Heaton's conclusions, drawn from E.I. Devine's *The Normal Life* (1917), illuminated that conviction: 'by examining the elements of a normal life and considering how far individuals fall below it,' she said, quoting Devine, 'we can arrive at a fair idea of the scope and nature of social economy ... the aim of the normal life is to anticipate and prevent tragedies which occur as a result of broken homes and exploiting industry.'[10]

There were a number of other studies that dealt with the quality of life or standards of living, but Heaton was the only one of Dawson's students to advocate so directly the implementation of social-welfare policies. In keeping with his conviction that it was preferable to prevent 'pathological abnormalities' from ever arising than to have to deal with them by reform measures, he assigned a number of his students to research demographic topics. The purpose of these studies was to gather information that would provide sociologists with insight into the effect that urbanization, industrialization, and immigration were having upon Canadian life as well as to furnish governmental bodies with the necessary information to formulate policies.

One such study was Oswald Hall's analysis of the Canadian family – of the difference in its size and structure in urban and rural areas. Hall looked at 584 two-parent families (in which the mother's age ranged from twenty-one to fifty) in three separate rural regions. (He was careful to ensure that all of them were far removed from the influence of large American centres: two lay up the Ottawa River near Renfrew; another was situated down the St Lawrence, across from Three Rivers.) These he compared with 1,849 families in both well-to-do and working-class sections of Montreal and Toronto. In the course of his investigation Hall discovered that French Catholic families – rural or urban – were almost always larger than anglophone Catholic and non-Catholic families. But more significantly, he found that there was a vast difference in family size and composition in rural and urban regions: rural areas had a larger percentage of older parents than metropolitan areas, and families there averaged 3.95 children per family, while in urban areas the average number of children was 2.14. Furthermore, among the younger age group the rural families were often twice as large as those in metropolitan areas: families with more than seven children were not uncommon in the former; they were almost non-existent in the latter, where it was not unusual to find no-child or one- or two-child families and women who tended to be between the ages of 21 and 30 when they bore their children. In commercial towns – Nicolet, Megantic, Iberville, and Rivière du Loup (Quebec), Arnprior, Pembroke, and Renfrew (Ontario) – families were larger than those in metropolitan areas – 50 per cent had more than five children – but smaller than in rural regions.[11]

His data led Hall to conclude that family size was a response to industrialization. The urban pattern of family life, he argued, followed close on the heels of industry. The fact that cities did not produce their own members but attracted people from other areas, especially the young and propertyless, was a major determinant in urban family structure. People transplanted from rural to urban conditions, he contended, did not remain unchanged during the process; they saw that families hindered them in an environment that placed a premium upon mobility and that, while a rural family might be an asset, an urban family was an economic liability. The more crowded conditions of urban life and the tendency of many women to choose careers over marriage were other factors that compelled people to reduce the size of their families in urban areas, Hall added. He also argued that urban professional families deliberately lowered their birth rate in order to maintain a high standard of living – they were more experimental in using contraception, he insisted, if they saw that having too many children conflicted with their attempts to achieve a coveted status. Finally, despite his discovery that managerial people had smaller families than clerical, commercial, or supervisory workers (whose families, in turn, were slightly smaller than those of skilled or unskilled workers), he contended that membership in a socio-economic class did not affect family behaviour as markedly as did the place of residence in a region. Pointing to the fact that urban francophones had smaller families than their rural kin, he concluded that membership in a racial group did not make one immune to the effects of industrialization. [12]

When the Social Science Research Project was being mooted and McGill professors expressed an interest in examining social conditions in Montreal, one of the issues raised was the effect that female employment was having upon the family. Another of Dawson's students, Mary Aikman, looked at this subject, and while she conceded that economic circumstances had done much to force women into the labour market, she also made the strong feminist argument that the development was beneficial, giving women independence and dignity. She noted that the employment of women outside the home was 'jolting' because it jeopardized old beliefs about the relationship between women and the home and raised questions about the duties of daughters to their parents, mothers to their children, and wives to their husbands, but she insisted that these concerns constituted a case of old mores persisting in a set of new circumstances. As proof, she traced how such factors as the needs of an expanding country and new inventions had stimulated the gainful employment of women in Canada, and how the Great War had created a situation in which 'the social disapproval concerning women working outside the home was abolished under the stress of patriotism and sheer necessity.' By the time the 1931 census was published, it revealed that the number of women employees in Canada was increasing more rapidly than the number of men in almost every occupation except manufacturing and personal service; by that time, too, Montreal had among the highest concentration of female employees than anywhere else in the country. Dawson's student insisted that this resulted from two factors, the strongest of which was economic necessity. Women, especially those who were widowed or whose husbands were ill, unemployed, or poorly paid, entered the labour market in order to keep their families together and free from want. There were others who worked because they wanted more material comfort or because feminism had become a popular movement, but in either case, having once been employed, they discovered that there was prestige in holding a job. They saw their importance rise in the family, Aikman argued, or they developed a sense of liberty and independence from the authority of their parents and past conventions. She criticized the older generation for regarding this new liberty as licence and for not realizing that many of the women in Montreal worked out of economic necessity.[13]

Perhaps the most important of the demographic studies undertaken by Dawson's students was one entitled 'The Peopling of Canada.' It examined the influence that natural increase, immigration, and emigration had had upon Canadian population development in all five of the country's regions. In effect, it laid the foundation for all of the immigrant studies, and more particularly Dawson's views on immigration policy, by illustrating the degree to which the country was capable of absorbing newcomers. Like his supervisor, John Berry was critical of the lack of planning in Canadian settlement: no consideration had been given to Canada's resources or to opportunities available within its frontiers; instead, settlement policy had consisted of 'muddled reactions to existing circumstances.'[14]

Berry made it clear that in the debate that had been raging throughout the 1920s as to whether or not massive immigration had been essential for Canada's development, he stood on the no side. The data he collected indicated that it had been of slight or no value in adding to Canada's population. Immigration had been effective, he contended, only at the expense of the native-born. Any population growth in Canada that had resulted from natural increase had been virtually nullified by emigration; fearing economic competition from immigrants, the native-born also 'used preventive checks on reproduction' in order to maintain their standard of living or to ensure that their children moved higher up the occupational scale. In response to the argument that without immigration western settlement would have been slower, Berry retorted – like Dawson before him – that careful encouragement of native immigration would have seen more easterners settle on the land with a greater degree of success and would have prevented the exodus to the United States. It was also his view that the mixing of races was not altogether valuable, that the experience of the United States and Canada with 'the mosaic of population' was not promising. In addition to everything else, the extreme mobility caused by mass immigration made for increasing difficulty in the development of an effective social structure. He recommended in conclusion that during the Depression, unless there was a shortage of labour to develop the country's resources, Canada should not accept additional population. When economic conditions improved, he thought, a policy of selected immigration should be implemented – it would produce, he said, more stable population elements and offset whatever emigration was inevitable.[15]

II

There were a number of reasons why immigration became the most important – and thorniest – of issues with which Dawson and his students had to deal. By 1931 the proportion of Montreal's residents who were neither of British nor French extraction had risen to 13.5 per cent of the population (or 135,262 souls) from a percentage of 4.5 (or 16,233 souls) in 1901.[16] Despite the change in Montreal's racial composition, very few studies of how immigrants had adapted to life in the city existed, though numerous tales were told of their crime, dependency, and deliquency, and fears were frequently expressed about foreigners overrunning the country.[17] Dawson was eager to use the Rockefeller funds to study immigrant groups and their assimilation into the mainstream of Canadian life, following approximately the same lines as Park's program at Chicago. The studies had another, more controversial purpose. In August 1930 an order-in-council limited immigration to Canada to British subjects entering the country via Great Britain, North Ireland, the Irish Free State, Newfoundland, the United States, New Zealand, and South Africa, and to American citizens entering it from the United States, provided that they had sufficient means to sustain themselves until they secured employment. Wives and unmarried children (under eighteen years of age) of any persons legally admitted to and residing in Canada (and capable of supporting their dependents) were also admitted, as were agriculturalists with sufficient means to farm in Canada. The restriction succeeded in reducing the number of immigrants drastically: from an average of about 140,000 a year entering the country during the period 1926 to 1930, the number dropped to 27,530 in the fiscal year 1931–2.[18] While Dawson was not entirely opposed to the restrictive legislation, he questioned the wisdom of its being imposed without any kind of prior scientific research, and he particularly disagreed with its liberality towards British subjects. He believed that immigration policies ought to be based not upon patriotic and nativistic sentiments but upon assessments of a country's population requirements and resources, and of how well different groups had adapted socially and occupationally to the new land.

In the late 1920s the fears of cultural disunity being voiced in Canada disturbed Dawson. The claims of many alarmists that the west in particular was turning into a hotbed of racial conflict reminded him of the atmosphere that existed in the United States during the First World War, when measures of propaganda and repression were used to convert the immigrant to Americanism, and names of everything that sounded faintly Teutonic were changed.[19] He could well have pointed to similar incidents in Canada, but did not. He could also have pointed a finger at someone like Hubert R. Kemp, an economist at the University of Toronto, who decried what the old immigration policy had done to the country by admitting so many illiterate, unassimilable groups who gravitated towards their own kind on the prairies and in the larger eastern cities. It was Kemp's contention that if these groups had continued to be admitted into Canada at the same rate as in the pre-war years, their descendents would have reproduced 'something like the mixture of unassimilated racial groups which eventually brought about the disruption of Austria-Hungary.'[20] As Dawson explained it, the United States had implemented its restrictive immigration policy in the 1920s with the intention of ensuring that only the most assimilable elements were admitted into the country; for similar reasons Canada tended to encourage and assist immigration from English-speaking nations, countries whose cultural heritages were supposedly so similar to Canada's. While he saw nothing wrong in trying to ensure a stable social structure by limiting immigration, Dawson had little patience for the 'ultra-Britisher,' as he called them, who throughout the 1930s (and particularly towards the end of the Depression) called for increased British immigration into Canada.[21]

Throughout the 1920s and 30s there had been considerable support both in Britain and Canada for the assisted immigration and settlement of Britons, especially for subsidized agricultural immigration. British advocates saw it as a way of alleviating their country's surplus population, and Canadian supporters argued that it would aid in developing the country's unsettled areas; obviously their desire to balance the presence of European groups was a major factor as well. Surprisingly, the numbers of British immigrants who came to Canada in the years between 1919 and 1929 had not been that high, averaging little more than 50,000 per year. There were a number of reasons for this, among them the fact that the adoption of social and unemployment insurance in Britain helped many families through the hard economic times. Then, too, many of those who were willing to emigrate did not have sufficient funds. A free-passage scheme for ex-servicemen was adopted and brought 26,650 men to Canada between 1919 and 1922, but the British government otherwise initially refused to go along with a policy of assisted immigration throughout parts of the empire as a solution. The Empire Settlement Act was passed in 1922, giving the British government the right to spend £1.5 million annually for fifteen years to settle people in the dominions. Since it did not wish to carry the full financial burden, however, the British government tried to work out co-operative agreements with the dominions. In most cases the receiving countries agreed to provide for immigrants after their arrival; in some cases they furnished starting farm capital, but the act was never fully implemented because of the dominions' reluctance to receive such a large number of immigrants. Under the plan Canada accepted intended agriculturalists and domestic servants. The demand for the latter was brisk, but not many of the British unemployed fell into the former category, and as a result 127,654 assisted British immigrants came to Canada between 1922 and 1931, only two-fifths as many as the number who came unassisted.[22]

Despite the Empire Settlement Act's lack of apparent success, calls for the subsidized agricultural immigration of Britons continued unabated in Canada. It was partly in response to this, to the immigration policy that favoured the British, and in order to shatter the myth of how well they adapted to life in Canada that Dawson began his immigrant-study program at McGill by looking at the British immigrant. Three students investigated the areas in which British immigrants had settled in Montreal and the social influences bearing on their employment. All of the data was incorporated into one study, Lloyd Reynolds' *The British Immigrant* (1935). One of the first publications of the McGill Social Science Research Project, it was a remarkably controversial book that brought both Dawson and Reynolds under severe criticism.

In his introduction to *The British Immigrant* Dawson alluded to the belief still held in some circles within Canada that a large number of British immigrants should be settled on the land. In the past many had done so successfully, he conceded, but such was not the case in more recent years. In the first place, British wage-earners could not succeed as Canadian agriculturalists, he argued, because they lacked the proper background and were not likely to gain it through the training schemes 'advertised on both sides of the Atlantic.' Moreover, he thought it was unwise to encourage British immigrants, with or without money, to settle on the land because the agricultural market did not warrant expansion beyond what could be taken care of by the Canadian population. Under current conditions, not even Canada's surplus rural population could find satisfactory opportunities in agriculture. In the aftermath of the First World War, with most countries favouring closed national economies and a balanced industrial and agricultural development, Canada, a country that specialized in agriculture and other primary products, had been compelled to follow the trend towards self-sufficiency. As a result the agricultural export market declined, while protected manufacturing, catering to the home market, steadily expanded until 1929. In any event, coming from a country in an advanced industrial state, the British had done well not in agriculture but in artisanal and clerical work. However, these were fields, Dawson predicted, in which they would find fewer opportunities in the future, owing to the ever-increasing numbers of Canadians entering them. Indeed, during the boom years between 1926 and 1929, as 'boatload after boatload of immigrants' was brought into the country, the demand for additional labour supply was met by the young men and women drifting from rural areas into the city. Accordingly, Dawson recommended further restrictions in Canadian immigration policy – in particular, that the door be closed to British unskilled workers and farm labourers (who ultimately ended up, he claimed, in the unskilled bracket). Unable to compete with Canadians and immigrants from other countries, they placed a heavy burden upon relief agencies, he charged. To those concerned about the loss of Canada's British identity, he argued that in the future, imperial unity would have to depend upon 'a regional division of labour and a community of interest' on the part of the nationalities that constituted the empire. Dawson's typical ecological language did not do much to conceal his belief – if indeed he was trying to hide it – that the age of imperialism was over, as was the need for Canada to retain its British character.[23]

In the text of *The British Immigrant* Lloyd Reynolds echoed his supervisor's beliefs about the considerations that should shape immigration policy. The flow, he said, 'should neither be so small as to restrict economic activity, nor so large as to add to unemployment and depress wages.' More particularly, he believed that all immigrants accepted into the country should possess the skills that would enable them to fit into those occupations where there was the greatest demand. That no attempt had been made to assess Canada's occupational needs and that government policy in the field 'cater[ed] to the wishes of individuals and corporations who had an interest in sponsoring or opposing immigration' enraged Reynolds, and he spoke out against it more strongly than Dawson had ever done. 'Railway and steamship companies,' he argued, 'obviously have much to gain by extensive immigration and usually maintain an active propaganda to encourage it. Industrialists, too, will usually lend their support to the immigration movement, in their desire to be assured of an abundant supply of labour. Organized associations of manufacturers sometimes maintain immigration offices abroad; in prosperous periods agents may be sent far afield in search of workmen, who are then assisted to emigrate.' As Reynolds saw it, the government's tolerance of such activities created problems for native-born Canadians: the willingness of immigrants to take jobs at low rates depressed wages and weakened trade-union organization.[24]

In obvious scorn of those who considered the maintenance of Canada's British identity important, Reynolds decided to investigate the social and occupational adjustment of British immigrants to Canada in much the same way as other members of the project examined European immigrant groups. Moreover, he insisted that the experience of the British immigrants differed only in degree from that of other immigrant groups in Canada. Even though they entered the country with certain advantages – they spoke the same language and had the same culture, roughly similar institutions, and public opinion in their favour – all of which made the process of adjustment smoother, the British still experienced the same problems of unemployment, home-making, and cultural transference as any other group.[25]

Despite all the discussions that focused on British rural settlement, Reynolds found that two-thirds of all British immigrants in Canada were urban-dwellers and that they were concentrated in the eastern cities. Some of them had drifted to urban areas from rural regions, but Reynolds was certain that since 1900 not more than a quarter of all British immigrants to Canada had actually settled on farms. To him, the British experience in Montreal illustrated that British immigration to Canada was a decidedly urban phenomenon. He estimated that between 1850 and 1900 some twenty thousand British immigrants became permanent settlers in Montreal, and another seventy thousand settled in the city between 1900 and 1935. There they followed trends of industrial development both in their choice of occupations and in their places of residence. Unlike most European groups they did not enter at the city's centre but settled in those parts of the city – Griffintown, Hochelaga, Rosemount, and Verdun – where industry was expanding. They avoided jobs requiring a knowledge of French, choosing to work instead in large enterprises managed by English Canadians, particularly in the skilled trades and clerical work, iron and steel, the printing trades, and service fields – areas in which they had the most experience. They shunned boot and shoe manufacturing, cotton-spinning, and garment-making, industries in which they could only compete by lowering their standard of living. Reynolds also found that since the war the number of British immigrants in the chemical, mineral, and non-ferrous metal industries (consisting predominantly of the manufacturing of electrical equipment) had risen markedly and that one-fifth of the bricklayers, masons, plumbers, and electricians in Montreal were of British origin. Among these groups, clerical workers and domestic servants seemed to have adapted most satisfactorily; manual workers had the most difficulty, Reynolds assumed, because of their own lack of experience and the state of the unskilled-labour market in Montreal – the stiff competition with European and French Canadian groups, the existence of a floating labour supply, and the heavy seasonality of most labour work. One of the most remarkable revelations of Reynolds's book, and the factor that his recommendations suggesting a need for further restrictions in Canadian immigration policy hinged upon, was the discovery that the rate of unemployment among British immigrants in Montreal during the years following 1929 was higher than that of other English-Canadian workers. The British unemployed tended to be recent arrivals who had experienced difficulty in finding jobs, low-skilled seasonal and casual workers (among them, agricultural workers insufficiently paid to weather the crisis), and chronic cases – those who were either too old or had personality problems that made them unemployable. Perhaps more damaging was Reynolds' finding that an especially high number of boys and youths who had come to Canada to work as farm labourers under the Empire Settlement Act had drifted to the cities, where, as he put it, they 'constituted a drain on public relief moneys.' Montreal, a seaport city, which offered the possibility of a return to Britain, seemed to be their favoured destination. As if that were not enough, Reynolds contended that the extent of the problem was indeterminable because the immigration departments of the two railway companies, whom he suspected had the most accurate information on the subject, consistently refused to release it to the public. Nevertheless, the number of British labourers he had encountered at the Vitre Street Refuge and the Andrews Home in Montreal led Reynolds to suspect that the problem was widespread.[26]

In light of his discoveries Reynolds charged that in the twentieth century a loose policy of 'indiscriminate encouragement' of immigration (which included bonuses to steamship and travel agencies for each immigrant engaged for one year as a farmer, farm labourer, gardener, carter, stableman, railway surfaceman, navvy, and miner – all unskilled occupations) had brought to Canada thousands of low-skilled men for whose services there was no demand. Some of them were deported; the rest were a burden upon public funds. This led him to recommend that the restrictions on the immigration of manual workers should not only be retained but should become a permanent part of Canadian immigration policy. As far as the admittance of clerks and domestic servants was concerned, he thought it should be allowed to continue as long as research showed there was a demand for such individuals; he also suggested that advertising designed to attract immigrants to Canada be strictly regulated. Finally, he strongly advised that the British unemployed, the farm labourers and families with little capital who were anxious to migrate to Canada, not be permitted to enter. Reynolds felt that if some truly effective method of placing settlers on the land were found, and indeed if it were determined to be desirable to stop the urban-rural drift, the thousands of potential settlers among Canada's urban unemployed deserved first consideration. He knew that his recommendations suggested the implementation of a more restrictive and selective immigration policy than had ever existed in Canadian history, one that would welcome domestic servants, high-grade clerks, professional workers, artisans from selected trades, and others – if research revealed the necessity. He insisted that the policy would only reduce, not eliminate, British immigration to Canada.[27]

The reception of *The British Immigrant* was quite negative in some quarters. In general, astonishment was expressed over Dawson's proclamation that the era of high immigration was over. A writer in the Winnipeg *Free Press* could not believe that with the varied resources of a new and expansive country there were no opportunities for the surplus population of other nations, and he branded Dawson and Reynolds 'exclusivists.' A.F.W. Plumptre criticized the book, together with W.A. Mackintosh's contribution to the Frontiers of Settlement series, *The Economic Problems of the Prairie Provinces* (1934), as an overly pessimistic view of Canadian settlement. He thought that Robert England's *The Colonization of Western Canada* presented a more balanced approach. A reviewer from the University of Saskatchewan argued that although *The British Immigrant* was brilliantly conceived, it rested on too narrow a basis (in its concentration on urban conditions) to draw such broad conclusions on policy. He too believed that England's findings were preferable and that all that was required to ensure successful rural settlement was a more careful analysis of the land and a better selection of settlers and methods of financing them.[28]

One of the most hostile reactions to *The British Immigrant* came from P.C. Armstrong, an economic adviser on the staff of the CPR who had worked as an engineer in the north of England and was involved in both engineering and agricultural enterprises in Canada. Asked by J.N. Macalister, chief commissioner of Immigration and Colonization, to review the work,[29] Armstrong charged that although it pretended to be scientific, *The*

British Immigrant was far from that. Not only did Dawson's introduction immediately expose its anti-immigration bias, but it was illogical and unscientific in its methods and conclusions. That did not surprise Armstrong, considering that it was a sociological study – subject, as far as he was concerned, that fell into the category of 'pseudo-science': 'The pseudo-science of sociology differs from ordinary man's every day thought concerning public affairs and the conditions of our society only in that it employs a highly technical terminology,' he explained. Moreover, he considered the book to be so marked by 'the illogical sentiment of sociology' that it could not be regarded as a contribution to a discussion of public affairs 'reflect[ing] credit upon the great institution which fostered its production.'[30]

Armstrong found, as others had before him, that too many generalizations about British immigrants in Canada had been based upon their experience in Montreal. What he condemned as even more unacceptable was the section of the book dealing with rural settlement. As he saw it, the arguments contained therein were based upon the erroneous assumption that the world was facing the end of agricultural expansion and that no purpose could be served in encouraging agricultural immigrants to settle in Canada. As far as he understood, the evidence contradicting Reynolds's view was overwhelming, and even if it were not, unemployed Europeans were still better off migrating to Canada than remaining where they were. 'People will not starve to death while Canada remains undeveloped,' he proclaimed. He also warned that if Canadians continued to adhere to the kind of exclusivist attitudes expressed by Dawson and Reynolds, they had better build up a military defence.

Armstrong found Reynolds' arguments about urban unemployment as flawed as the rest of the book. To counter it, he claimed that the only reason there was such a surplus of urban unemployed was that the artificial prosperity of the period between 1925 and 1929 had created high standards of living and comfort in the city. All those who had flocked to the cities during those years, together with the immigrants who had settled there, should have returned to the land en masse when the boom collapsed, Armstrong argued. They did not because there was 'a deliberate and planned attempt in [Canada] to prevent the incidence of economic law by all sorts of measures intended to protect the unemployed from seeking the only means of subsistence available.' As for the argument that the mechanization darkened future prospects for successful rural settlement, Armstrong contended that that was just another red herring. He believed that the exodus to the country would have abolished any tendencies to mechanization and that the real exploitation of agriculture came from 'a swollen civil service and a lazy urban proletariat.'[31]

The professors involved in McGill's Social Science Research Project were irate about Armstrong's critique. The same P.C. Armstrong had criticized the League for Social Reconstruction's *Social Planning for Canada* (1934) when it was published, and copies of that review were distributed to all Canadian universities. After reading his opinions of *The British Immigrant*, some members of the project claimed that Armstrong was 'a CPR propagandist working in anonymity.'[32] This was a charge that Sir Edward Beatty, chancellor of McGill and president of the CPR, vigorously refuted as untrue and unfair, claiming that Armstrong was a serious student who worked on his own without any instructions from his supervisors as to the nature of his comments. Beatty wanted to dispel the impression in fairness to the university, to himself, and to Armstrong, he said, that 'the President of the CPR retain[ed] someone for the purpose of criticizing unfavourably books published by the staff of the university of which he [was] Chancellor.' No employee of the CPR, he explained, was permitted to engage in public controversy with members of the university staff regarding publications as long as he was chancellor, with the exception of cases 'where the company's interests [were] attacked or misrepresented.' Beatty had decided to let Armstrong express his views on this occasion because of his expertise and because the CPR had had greater experience in the field of immigration than any other corporation in Canada.[33]

If McGill faculty suspected Beatty's involvement in the criticism of *The British Immigrant*, there was reason enough. He was a strong advocate of increased immigration, believing that Canada would be in a more balanced economic condition if it had a larger population, and he argued that the only way to determine whether or not a country was underpopulated was to leave men and women free to decide whether they would like to move into it or out. He once told Escott Reid that claims that the Canadian railways and other interests had attempted, by too glowing accounts of prospects in Canada, 'to stimulate immigration into the country beyond the limits of economic justification' was nothing but propaganda. He could argue 'from a lifetime of knowledge' on the subject that nothing of the kind had occurred. 'In the great days of immigration,' he proclaimed, 'people came to Canada – it was unnecessary to bring them here. The efforts of those who solicited business in this direction were concentrated on getting the immigrant away from the steamship company.'[34]

Whether or not Beatty was directly involved in its writing, Armstrong's critique found its way to the desk of A.E. Morgan, then the principal of

McGill. After reading Armstrong's criticisms of *The British Immigrant* – but not the book itself – Morgan informed Beatty that he agreed with him that McGill needed to hire a more eminent economist, a man 'with a quality of mind and personality who [would] be the pivot of all this work.' He wondered how the appointment could be financed but concurred with Beatty that in the interim, the social-research publications should be examined.[35] Once Morgan read *The British Immigrant*, his opinion changed: he expressed sympathy with Reynolds' point of view and support for sociology as a legitimate subject, telling Beatty that it could not be expected to have the same exactness of expression and interpretation as economics. Moreover, Morgan spoke to Reynolds about the work and accepted his arguments that the trends that he had examined could not be accounted for merely in terms of economics, a treatment that would have 'ignored psychological and emotional human qualities.' He was convinced, he informed Beatty, that Reynolds had handled his theme objectively and dispassionately.[36]

In May 1935 Lloyd Reynolds, then enrolled in a PH D program at Harvard, where he had been given a graduate fellowship in economics, wrote a long response to Armstrong's critique. He conceded that although the book had many weak points, including its use of sociological jargon, which he himself disliked, it was wrong to denounce all of sociology as unscientific; such an attitude displayed nothing but ignorance of the development of social science for the past half-century. Moreover, he contended that Armstrong, with a supercilious attitude that was neither scholarly nor courteous, had no appreciation for the solid contribution that the book made to an understanding of the labour-market and that most of his detailed criticisms were nothing but mere 'pin-pricking.' Reynolds recognized that the issue of agricultural settlement was a hotly disputed one, but after a year's study in agriculture and agricultural economics at Harvard had discovered that the views presented in *The British Immigrant* accorded with those of some of the greatest authorities on the subject in Britain and the United States. Therefore, he was not afraid to put his opinions against those of Armstrong, who cited no authority. As for the public-policy recommendations contained in the book, Reynolds confessed to an interest in social welfare, or, as he put it, 'to the economist's bias towards the promotion of the economic welfare of the whole population.' In this instance, he did not think that a resumption of agricultural settlement would make for a higher standard of living for the Canadian people. Armstrong criticized the sentimentalism of the work, Reynolds concluded, but his review, especially the military-defence argument, was itself laden with 'emotionality' and non-academic thinking.[37]

The fight was not yet over. Beatty sent a copy of Reynolds' retort to Armstrong, who wrote another rebuttal, but Beatty decided that since 'both contestants [had] had innings,' enough was enough. Nevertheless, he could not restrain himself from telling Morgan that there were a number of things in the book on which neither he nor the greatest authority on immigration in Canada, J.N.K. Macalister, and the experts in England and other countries – Lord Blediscoe, Christopher Turnor, and André Siegfried – could agree.[38]

Morgan's handling of the controversy surrounding *The British Immigrant* probably did little to help prolong his tenure at McGill. Reynolds fared better despite the fact that McGill authorities were irritated by his book and by his involvement in left-wing activities. (Stirred to political activism by what he witnessed in Montreal during the Depression years, Reynolds became president of the McGill Labour Club and editor of what he called 'the faintly subversive' student magazine *The Alarm Clock*, which was banned from sale on the university campus after it published an editorial supporting the CCF.)[39] *The British Immigrant* was accepted as his doctoral dissertation at Harvard; he worked for a while as a member of the staff for the American Social Research Council, and then became a member of the faculty of Yale University.[40]

III

Although he believed that in the interests of those already living in Canada, immigration during the Depression years should be limited to individuals having occupational skills that the country required, Dawson was not an exclusionist. He and some of his students recognized that all the clamour for British rural migration was not merely intended for the purpose of liberalizing the existing policy; on the contrary, they charged, those individuals who were proposing schemes for settling British immigrants on outpost agricultural lands were more caught up with what they perceived as threats to Canada's national character than concern for the economic welfare of the populace. As one of Dawson's students noted, such people advocated British immigration in order 'to maintain the cultural integrity of our country and loyalty to the Motherland.'[41] For such objectives Dawson and his students had little sympathy. Not only did the proposals ignore their labours – research that revealed that the majority of British immigrants to Canada were urban-dwellers and that life on the fringes of settlement could not provide families with decent standards of living – but they saw them as expressions of the sort of ardent nationalism that they could not countenance. Rooted in Chicago sociological theory was the idea that a community, rather than being a political entity, was composed of people who were dependent on one another for their economic survival. That community might have territorial and geographical boundaries but it was linked, symbiotically, to a larger network of communities covering a region, a continent, or the entire world. Social institutions and culture – including nationalistic sentiment – grew out of that interrelationship and tied all the communities together. By the interwar years it had become a fact of life that Canada was composed of many different ethnic and cultural groups, and it was Dawson's belief that all of them would meld – but their differences not entirely disappear – into the mainstream of Canadian life to form a new community of interests and, inevitably, a nationalism quite different from the one that had been tied to the British heritage. That conviction created a spirit of tolerance in McGill's Sociology Department towards immigrants and Canadians of all classes and walks of life. It was an attitude that informed the immigrant studies and one that did not pervade most other parts of the university.

When he served on the Arts survey committee, Stephen Leacock, an ardent admirer of all things British, hypothesized that one of the major reasons why the Faculty of Arts had relatively lower standards and less of a reputation than did McGill's scientific faculties was that it drew its students from the local community, from families with impoverished cultural backgrounds. As was only natural in a manufacturing metropolis, he elaborated, that part of the community that was not French belonged to 'the less fortunate ranks of mankind, people close to the poverty line and with scarcely any of the home traditions of books and education which, in other lands, like Scotland, have redeemed and illuminated poverty.' Many of these people represented the refugee population of Europe, he continued, 'shrewd perhaps in mentality but without the characteristic culture and aptitudes and ideals which, for good or ill, make up the British ideal of an educated man.' In order to find students with English and Scottish heritages stretching back generations, Leacock suggested that the university look outside, particularly to Ontario, for material.[42] Other methods had already been implemented for dealing with the problem. In the interwar years Jewish immigrants constituted the largest ethnic group in Montreal, and during the 1920s their children enrolled in McGill in ever-increasing numbers; 25 per cent of the students in the Faculty of Arts, 15 per cent in Medicine, and 40 per cent in Law were Jewish. As the official historian of McGill has noted, the university, 'liberal as its traditions might be, was not ready for such a change in its constituency and measures were taken towards the end of the 1920s and 1930s to control the influx of Jewish students.' A quota system was employed in Medicine, while in the Arts Jewish students required a higher matriculation standard than others. By 1939 these restrictions (which were dropped during the Second World War) had succeeded in reducing the number of Jewish students to 12.1 per cent in the Arts, 12.8 per cent in Medicine, and 15 per cent in Law.[43] Even at that, questions were raised as to the wisdom and efficacy of the policy. Charles Hendel, another member of the Arts survey committee, noted that the system 'by which only the top-notchers among the Jewish students were admitted gave these students an unfair advantage over the average Gentile students.' It was suggested that McGill write to Harvard and perhaps follow its policy.[44]

McGill, like many other Canadian universities, also turned a deaf ear to pleas from German and Italian refugee scholars to find places for them on the faculty. It consistently responded to them (and to the organizations representing their interests) that it had no vacancies. The attitude of such individuals as the dean of Arts, Ira Mackay, illustrates that there were other considerations. Mackay once counselled Currie that it might be wise not to respond to the letters at all, for if 'the unsentimental, impartial truth' were told, it would be quoted in public and in the press, and accusations would be levelled that McGill was anti-Semitic. But, as he saw it, in light of dozens of reports in the English-language newspapers that Canada was importing too many non-British people, it did not make sense for McGill to import Jews, especially professors, school teachers, and judges for the courts. 'The simple obvious truth,' he said, was that Jews were 'of no use to Canada.' Almost all of them went into merchandising, money-lending, medicine, and law, professions which were already overcrowded. Moreover, Mackay did not feel that Jews as a race 'fit in with a high civilisation in a very new country.' He thought that what Canada needed was men who would 'explore and work and make the very best of our natural resources for the welfare of ourselves and other peoples.'[45] (One McGill official who did try to do something about the situation was L.W. Douglas. Deluged with appeals from refugee scholars after he became principal, he wrote to T.A. Crerar, minister of Mines and Resources, asking if the government could not relax its regulations in favour of 'these pitiful cases of German Jews' – especially professors, he said, who would make better Canadian citizens than other applicants. Crerar told Douglas that he received thousands of such letters from various countries and that the government was trying to help with the refugee problem, but there were 'difficulties in opening Canada's doors.' He promised to look into a specific case that Douglas had mentioned, but in the end granted no special consideration.)[46]

A student of Dawson's in the 1930s recalled that although there were stratifications on the McGill campus between students who came from middle-class and professional families and those who did not and between Jews and gentiles, divisions that reflected larger ones in the city, none of these was apparent in the Sociology Department. There, distinctions were not important to staff or students; everyone felt at home, and they all shared an excitement, a feeling of being at the frontier, on the edge of something new.[47] Reflecting that atmosphere, the immigrant studies that Dawson's students undertook in connection with the social-research project would have been published, had there been sufficient funds, in a volume entitled *New Canadians*. Dawson's certainty that Canada's many ethnic groups could be absorbed into a new nationality was evident even before those studies began. In the first edition of their sociology textbook he and Warner Gettys referred to the work of Franz Boas and other anthropologists illustrating that there was no correlation between race and culture but that one people borrowed culture traits from another. The observations of immigrant groups made by sociologists in the United States, they also insisted, indicated that races with divergent cultures could be incorporated into the Canadian body politic. They conceded that the fact of colour and feature could serve as impediments to assimilation, but equally responsible were the attitudes of the native-born. Immigrants came to the new land, Dawson and Gettys explained, with hopeful and expectant attitudes, but when rebuffed by its native-born citizens they became disillusioned and cynical, and those feelings caused them to turn in upon themselves and slow down the assimilation process.[48]

The ideas about assimilation that Dawson taught his students to apply to their studies of ethnic groups in Montreal were all adopted from Robert Park. The Chicago sociologist was responsible for formulating a theory of intergroup relations that endured in his discipline for many years. It was not as widely influential as the work of Franz Boas, but it also represented a departure from the tendency to ascribe differences in racial character to inheritance and stressed instead the cultural and environmental factors affecting group relations.[49]

Like all other aspects of Chicago sociology, Park's theory of group relations emphasized social process. What he called 'the natural history of the interaction cycle' classified group relations into four stages, each dependent on the degree of conscious or 'symbiotic' communication that took place among members of a group and the rest of society. (Although the theory was most commonly employed in the Chicago ethnic studies, Park stressed that it was applicable everywhere where diverse groups came into contact.) Competition was the first stage – this was the contact made between individuals, whether they were conscious of it or not, because of the exigencies of the marketplace. When these relations became hostile (because the participating groups sensed differences between themselves), the second phase – conflict – was reached. (Conflict in its most extreme phase was war.) When the parties grew tired of the struggle and agreed to get along, accommodation – the third phase of the cycle – was achieved. The gradual mingling of the groups and blending of their traits finalized the cycle – this was assimilation. Assimilation was not a conscious decision to coexist, because that was more in the way of accommodation, but it signalled that the diverse groups had melded into a new community, though not an entirely uniform one.[50]

In addition to departing from biological explanations for differences in race and culture, Park's theory suggested that uniformity among its culturally distinct groups was not necessary for the social cohesion of a nation. This in turn implied that immigrants need not completely reject their pasts in order to become part of the new community of interests; they need only learn enough of the language and social rituals to fit into the mainstream. After all, Europe provided the best illustration that the modern state was but a collection of smaller groups with only superficial uniformity; the city was a similarly complex structure wherein conformity was unnecessary. What was perhaps most significant about Park's theory, as Fred Matthews has pointed out, was that it injected an element of optimism into views of race relations in the United States during the 1920s, at a time when the nation had just gone through a period of strident nativism. It envisioned not a solidly gelled culture but more of a mosaic – this to accord with Park's conviction that the United States had a 'civilization' but not a culture that all of its inhabitants shared.[51]

Although Park considered the United States a 'melting pot' that blended its immigrants into one civilization, he was not as strict an assimilationist or environmentalist as some other social thinkers and for that reason could conceive of America in terms of a mosaic. That metaphor, however, has been more commonly applied to Canada, whose civilization, in part because of the existence of two founding races, has always been regarded as somewhat more pluralistic. In his article 'Metaphor and Nationality in North America' Allan Smith has explained the nuances of the two terms. The United States was described as a melting pot because, although it did not require its immigrants to repudiate their pasts, there was only one national type – the Anglo-American – towards which they had to assimilate. The same was not true of Canada: the presence of English,

Irish, Scottish, and more particularly French elements had made it a pluralistic nation from the start; the massive immigration of the Laurier years made it even more complex. In the nationalistic atmosphere of the 1920s English-speaking Canadians had to confront the fact that the nation was composed of people who did not have the same backgrounds or a common language and that there was no single type towards which they could assimilate. It was that set of circumstances that caused them to uphold the idea of the mosaic.[52]

The manner in which Canadians struggled during the interwar years to come to terms with the national character is evident in the work of Dawson's students. Although they paid lip-service to the mosaic metaphor (their bibliographies usually included K.A. Foster's *Our Canadian Mosaic* [1926]), it was not uncommon for them to use it interchangeably with the idea of a melting pot. One of Dawson's students remarked, for instance, that 'the pattern of distribution of racial groups in Canada resembled a patch-work quilt rather than a neatly uniform and symmetrical picture. Here the mosaic of Middle Europe appears to be superimposed on the French and Anglo-Saxon background, for here many of the same stocks are segregated.' He proceeded to note that the resemblance to Europe was extremely close in western Canada and that this complicated Canadian cultural unity. 'For better or worse,' he concluded, 'Canada is to-day a melting pot in a way she never was before.'[53] It is likely that their tendency to follow Park's theories almost unquestioningly also explains the propensity of Dawson's students to use both concepts. Their inability to distinguish between them may also have stemmed from the fact that no immigrant group in Canada – particularly not in those parts of the west and Montreal where Dawson's students focused their attention – was as completely assimilated into the mainstream of Canadian life as was true of such groups in the United States. The students accordingly were compelled to deal with the earlier phases of the interaction cycle and with such subjects as segregation rather than assimilation.

A measure of the proportionate weight that Dawson gave to the early phases of the interaction cycle is evident in his extensive treatment of segregation. In his textbook he explained that segregation was a necessary phase of immigrant life that helped the individual move from one culture to another: the immigrant found in his own nationality the reference points that made him comfortable until he got a foothold in the new land. The emergence of agencies and mutual-aid societies organized by the more settled predecessors of his nationality provided him with lodging, board, and services like banking and help in securing employment. It was not unusual for these societies to expand into local or nation-wide nationalistic organizations designed to keep the immigrant's sentiments about his native land alive. The most powerful of these societies were the Sons of Italy in the United States and, with the rise of Fascism under Mussolini, the fascist organizations that proliferated in England, the United States, Hungary, and Austria. The Société de St Jean Baptiste l'Amérique among the French Canadians and the Zionist organizations of the Jews were similar examples of such associations in both North American nations. Like Park, Dawson cautioned the native-born not to be alarmed by the emergence of such societies. He understood how they might seem puzzling to patriotic citizens, seemingly a threat to the institutions that the native-born held dear, but he explained that they were 'schools for citizenship' and taught immigrants how to perform in public life.[41]

One of the greatest laboratories for examining the natural history of group interaction was the Canadian west. The decision of government authorities to allocate blocs of land to such groups as the Doukhobors and Mennonites, thereby enabling them to maintain their language and institutions, furnished investigators with perhaps the clearest example of immigrant segregation that existed in North America. At bottom Dawson's *Group Settlement* (1936), another of his contributions to the Frontiers of Settlement series, was an examination of this phenomenon; it was, as the introduction made clear, a study of 'culture islands' not 'foreigners.'[55]

By tracing the factors that brought the Doukhobors, Mennonites, Mormons, Germans, and French Canadians west, and by describing the areas in which they settled and the lives they led, Dawson showed that the tendency of immigrant groups to segregate themselves did not solely arise from their natural desire to settle beside neighbours of the same culture and language. In the case of the Doukhobors and Mennonites it was a product of the repression they suffered in other countries and deliberate government policy. Among the Mormons, Germans, and French Canadians it was fostered by the colonization activities of land-settlement societies and nationalistic organizations. Although Dawson believed – and illustrated – that the period of cultural isolation would inevitably end, precipitated by the approach of the railway, which brought in settlers and a process of anglicization, he was not negative about the worth of group settlement. In fact, in contrast to the bleak picture he presented of individual homesteading in the Peace River region, he argued that group settlement made for greater residential stability. He and his investigators – among them Glenn Craig and Lloyd Reynolds – found that with the exception of chronic fringe areas the number of settlers able or willing to remain on their farms was very high. Moreover, the pooling of resources within the Doukhobor, Mennonite, and Mormon communities in the early years of settlement had contributed to a high degree of productive efficiency.[56]

Dawson emphasized numerous times in *Group Settlement* that it was natural forces that would break down the barriers separating homogeneous groups from their neighbours. The arrival of the railway was only one harbinger of change; participation in the labour-market, the invasion of commercial towns and their secular institutions, and the construction – with some resistance – of public schools were all ways in which this process would be set in motion. If school and other governmental regulations were wisely administered, he contended, they would ease the assimilation of ethnic minorities. Attempts to hasten assimilation by 'ill-chosen' methods, he warned, would only retard it 'by arousing the self-consciousness and recalling the receding solidarity of these colonies.'[57] The best example of policies backfiring in such a manner was the government's handling of the Doukhobors. Dawson insisted that the seeds of secularization had been planted in the Saskatchewan colony from the beginning: for financial reasons it had been necessary for its young men to seek outside work on the railway. But the government's attempts to dispose of the Doukhobors' reserves because they were located on highly desirable land simply aroused their sectarian zeal. Refusing to take the oath of allegiance, which was a prerequisite for gaining a homestead, they moved on to more isolated regions, and eventually to British Columbia. The Independents who remained behind eventually assimilated into the mainstream of Canadian life, but the group who moved on to British Columbia managed to have such limited contact with Canadians that their traditional ways of life were only slightly modified. At the other extreme were German Catholics; their regional and social isolation did not persist for very long because there were no topographical barriers to prevent the approach of other settlers and because they were more tolerant of Canadian ways, as illustrated by their willingness to have their children learn English.[58]

Dawson's strongest message in *Group Settlement* was that antagonistic attitudes on the part of native-born Canadians only served to reinforce a sense of separateness among immigrants. In the west the existence of those sentiments had made it difficult for government representatives to extend their activities into immigrant colonies, with the result that attempts to incorporate them into the social and economic structure of the prairie region placed a heavy burden upon all its inhabitants. It was better, he concluded, to let things take their natural course.[59]

The studies of the Germans, Italians, Ukrainians, Finns, Slavs, and Jews undertaken in connection with McGill's Social Science Research Project reiterated the point that the atmosphere of 'a Canada for Canadians' was one of the greatest inhibiting factors in the assimilation process. It had caused each body of immigrants to turn in on itself and to settle in a segregated area. 'They have established in every city of size,' one of Dawson's students commented, 'a little Italy, Germany, Ukraine, Poland, etc., located in areas commensurate with their economic status.'[60] The other serious impediment to which all the studies alluded (and which called into question the validity of Park's theory in anything but a relatively stable period) was the economic depression of the 1930s. Almost all of Dawson's students commented that with Depression conditions causing such a high degree of unemployment and mobility, it was difficult to assess such things as social and occupational adjustment and stability. The student assigned to investigate the Ukrainians, for instance, found that unskilled Slavic immigrants predominated in Montreal's municipal relief shelters and were being demoralized through instability and prolonged unemployment.[61] The student concerned with the Finns remarked that the group had unfortunately been in Canada only a short period before employment conditions deteriorated. They had initially settled in northern Ontario, an area similar to Finland, and worked in the extractive industries. Forced to the cities in search of employment, they were unable to hold jobs for more than one year. Where Finns should have been at the accommodation stage, the student estimated, the Depression had thrown them into slum living.[62]

To further reinforce the argument that employment stability was a necessary prerequisite for assimilation, an examination of the means and modes of living of several immigrant groups in Montreal revealed that in terms of income the British, Poles, and Italians had adjusted with the greatest degree of success to life in the new land.[63] A more intensive study of the Italians and Ukrainians revealed that a large majority of the Italians had settled in Montreal between 1900 and 1910, at a time when there was remunerative work in unskilled labour. They were not upset by periodic casual unemployment, the student insisted, because they knew that the docks would open in the spring, that construction would begin again, and that factories would produce for the busy season. Up to 1929 most Italian families in Montreal could anticipate sustenance over a year-long period; some even had enough to purchase consumer articles, but all that changed after the economic collapse. Since that time Montreal's Italians had suffered from unemployment stemming from the cessation of construction and curtailment of general maintenance rather than seasonal inactivity.[64]

In terms of cultural assimilation it was the Ukrainians and Italians in

Montreal who had moved beyond the protective-society stage and were in the second phase of development. This was manifested in the fact that both groups had become highly conscious of their national origins and had established institutions to do more than just knit families together into the community social structure. The student who investigated the group argued somewhat naïvely that the Italians had reached a new position in Montreal with the increasing prominence of Fascism and Mussolini: the movement, he said, acted as a cohesive force, leading to the establishment of Fascio organizations. He contended, further, that although a number of Italians disliked the idea of their urban compatriots supporting an ideology contrary to the democratic notions of Canadian society, most of the immigrants had little understanding of national changes overseas and merely desired to be members of a mass movement, with all its attendant excitement, glamour, and social satisfaction. Another factor that had helped the Italians adapt to life in Montreal was their tendency to associate with French Canadians, not just in industry but in their decision to learn French first and English second and to send their children to French Catholic schools.[65]

Adhering to Parkian orthodoxy, one of the immigrant studies argued that the Jews of Montreal offered a picture different from all the other racial and ethnic communities in the city. What began as a small, compact nucleus in the nineteenth century expanded and developed in the twentieth into a large, heterogeneous and widely scattered yet solidly integrated, self-conscious community. Because they were set apart by race and religion, Montreal's Jews had established a more complete and self-sufficient community: assimilation was achieved by few, if any members, but the completely unassimilated were likewise practically non-existent. Beyond these and a few other obvious conclusions, the student investigator could not venture. She had circulated a questionnaire among 512 schoolchildren in an attempt to ascertain their families' religious practices, but these were greeted with suspicion and resentment, particularly among the most economically stable Jews. The problem, she surmised, was that the questionnaire was distributed in February and March of 1938, at the same time as a number of 'unhappy events' had been occurring in Europe.[66]

What were Dawson and his students prepared to conclude from their immigrant studies? Perhaps the clearest insight was contained in Charles Bayley's study of the Italians and Ukrainians. Bayley argued that in light of Canada's experience with immigrants, the following prognostication could be made: in spite of urban traits that tended to eradicate external cultural differences, immigrants would continue to come to Canada with deeply ingrained characteristics and attitudes that would set them apart from Canadian society. Moreover, if they continued to come in sufficient numbers, they would seek the fellowship of their own kind. Finding themselves set apart socially and separated geographically, he continued, they would also preserve the traits they brought with them and maintain the sort of isolation to keep Canada 'a congeries of nationalities.' By the same token, he also argued, despite the haphazard fashion in which the Italians and Ukrainians had come to Montreal, with no planning or guidance, they had moved towards each other and had adjusted as groups; they had developed a social life that was 'amazingly and highly satisfying' and had found a place for themselves in Canadian society. Such factors, he concluded, could not be overlooked in considerations of the consequences of immigration.[67]

IV

Any project devoted to examining Montreal's social and industrial structure could not fail to include research on the French Canadians. The participants in McGill's Social Science Research Project were aware of this and from the start attempted to find a French Canadian student who could study dependency problems and relief organizations for the indigent and unemployed among Montreal's francophone population. They searched a number of years for a candidate with the requisite background to do graduate work in social science, but after coming up empty-handed, solicited Edouard Montpetit's assistance, and even considered asking the premier, Louis-Alexandre Taschereau, to suggest candidates. Finally realizing that no francophone institution of higher learning in Quebec furnished students with the sort of training they considered necessary for social research, they decided to choose a student of French Canadian extraction from a New England college.[68] The student, William Roy, was assigned to study the French-English division of labour in the province of Quebec. That study was followed a few years later by a more intensive examination of the division of labour among French and English Canadians in Montreal, and then, on a somewhat different tangent, an analysis of the urbanization of the French Canadian parish.[69] (The students involved in the latter two projects were not French Canadians: so difficult had the search for francophone students been that it was decided to put the best students available – and one of them was Stuart Jamieson – to work on the later studies.) All this work was envisaged as part of a larger study on the evolution of French Canadian society from one of a rural to that of an urban, indutrial character. The project was never completed, but much of the McGill students' work and the themes upon which they touched were incorporated into *French Canada in Transition*, published in 1943. The first sociological analysis of the changes affecting twentieth-century Quebec,[70] the book was written by the American academic who had been responsible for supervising the French Canadian studies at McGill – Everett C. Hughes.

Everett Hughes came to McGill in 1927 as an assistant professor of sociology. Like so many early twentieth-century sociologists, he too was a minister's son. Born in Beaver, Ohio, he did his undergraduate work at Ohio Wesleyan, a small Methodist college north of Columbus. Upon receiving his BA he worked for a few years in the steel and lumber industry, where, through the auspices of the Chicago YMCA, he gave night-school classes to immigrants. After a short stint of supervising recreational activities in a Chicago community park he enrolled in the graduate sociology program at the University of Chicago.[71] There Hughes and the woman he married before going to Montreal, Helen MacGill, a native Canadian, became Park's favourite students. In addition to enjoying a close friendship with Park that lasted for many years after they left Chicago, they extended Park's influence through their work perhaps to a greater degree than any of his students. Park, whose first career had been in journalism and who continued to be interested in the subject of public opinion, persuaded MacGill to do her doctoral work on the human-interest aspects of news. (Her thesis, entitled 'News and the Human Interest Story,' was completed in 1937 and published by the University of Chicago Press three years later.) Everett Hughes, meanwhile, inherited and continued his supervisor's interest in race relations.[72]

It was at a meeting of the American Sociological Society in St Louis, Missouri, in 1927 that Park, who was soliciting for the Chicago department, arranged for Carl Dawson to meet Hughes, who he thought would be a good candidate for the position that Warner Gettys had vacated. Then and there Dawson invited Hughes to join the McGill department, and Hughes accepted. When Hughes arrived at McGill, he and Dawson immediately decided upon a division of labour that would enable them to study relatively untouched aspects of Canada's social development from perspectives with which they were familiar. Because of his interest in rural sociology Dawson chose the west, and Hughes, French Canada. The focus upon Canada's two 'frontiers,' as Dawson called them, led Dawson to look at regional development and the adaptation and adjustment of settlers, and Hughes to investigate race relations and the effects of industrial change. As Hughes saw it, the relations of the French and English in Canada were of theoretical importance as part of the field of race relations, and of practical significance in that, having been a constant and central problem in Canadian history, they had taken a new turn during the twentieth century as a result of the tremendous industrial development of the period and the movement to the cities on the part of vast numbers of formerly rural French Canadians. At the time Hughes began teaching at McGill, much rhetoric had been expended on the subject, but no university had studied it in anything but a historical way.[73]

There were a number of reasons why Hughes as an American was more comfortable with studying French Canada than was his Canadian-born colleague. Although Dawson was always friendly and helpful towards French Canadians – every year he succeeded in attracting francophone students to do work in the department at an undergraduate level – he never made an effort to learn French.[74] Hughes was more cosmopolitan. For his Chicago seminars he read Pareto's *Treatise on General Sociology* in French and much of the work of Durkheim, Simmel, Weber, and Mause in their original languages.[75] It was through Hughes's lectures, moreover, which they found more stimulating and exciting than Dawson's, that McGill sociology students gained an understanding of European social thinkers.[76] In addition to being proficient in French, Hughes and his wife liked to live in the thick of things – indeed, that was what Park had found so attractive about them[77] – and when they moved to Montreal, they chose to live in a flat in the city's 'area of transition,' where they could watch the activities on the street. Perhaps the more important reason for Hughes's decision to study French Canada, however, was his interest in social organization and collective behaviour, the field in which he had done his doctoral work at Chicago.

Though on the surface it seemed vastly removed from the work he would do at McGill, Hughes's dissertation on the Chicago Real Estate Board contained the themes that helped him to understand – and misunderstand – French Canada.[78] The story of the Chicago Real Estate Board as Hughes told it was one of how a 'boom' business of unprecedented magnitude – the sale of land and the maze of transactions stemming from it in the phenomenally growing Chicago of the early twentieth century – had been reduced to order and stability. Hughes demonstrated that the men who dealt in land, the real-estate agents, had initially set out to solve problems 'as simple as the price of eggs' on a day-by-day basis but ultimately built up a standard set of solutions that succeeding generations followed involuntarily. In so doing they created an institution, and that institution, in addition to controlling the commodity with which they dealt, also controlled their behaviour, determining, for instance, the prices they could set and the way in which they presented themselves to the public.[79] Therefore, where Park had argued that an institution embodied and reflected community interests to the degree that it developed out of the determination of a group to act jointly for some end,[80] Hughes demonstrated that once well established, the institution acquired a life apart from its members and, rather than reflecting public opinion, controlled it.[81]

There were two ways in which this argument influenced Hughes's perception of the French Canadians in twentieth-century Quebec. He believed that their adaptation to urbanization and industrialization was proving to be difficult because their culture was deeply rooted in the institutions of the parish and the family. The problem was exacerbated by the fact that the distribution of French and English Canadians in certain occupations within the small industrializing towns and the great metropolis was becoming so entrenched along racial lines that it was making mobility – at least for the French Canadians – impossible.

In undertaking his study of French Canada, Hughes was fortunate to have at his disposal not only the Rockefeller student research assistant-ships but additional funding from the American Social Science Research Council. The council's grant enabled Hughes and his wife to do their own research on an industrializing Quebec town and also funded an anthropologist – Horace Miner – to do work on a rural village under Hughes's supervision.[82] Together with the work of the McGill students, these studies were intended to depict the evolution of French Canada from a simple village society to a complex industrial structure.[83] Although there were plans to study other Quebec industrial towns, they were never implemented, partly because Hughes left McGill in 1938 for a position at the University of Chicago. Thus, *French Canada in Transition*, the story of an unnamed town, presented the arguments and conclusions that the entire projected study would likely have illustrated in more abundant detail.

French Canada in Transition was only superficially an analysis of a single town. Although the Hugheses undertook an intensive study of the community following Chicago lines, living in the town for one summer, observing the activities of its residents, and mapping land-use,[84] they viewed the changes it was undergoing as representative of what an entire society based upon a rural or folk culture experienced with the advance of industrialism. Hughes never really concealed the fact that they were presenting a more general analysis[85] – that, after all, was the purpose of sociology done in a natural-history framework. Indeed, in order to broaden his perspective he spent a year in Germany, funded by the Social Science

Research Council, investigating the Rhineland, where in the nineteenth century Protestant entrepreneurs had initiated industrialization in an area that was predominantly Catholic.[86] Hughes's objective was to formulate a theoretical model of a society's adaptation to industrialization somewhat along the same lines as Chicago anthropologist Robert Redfield's work on Mexico.[87] As he noted, Quebec, like so many other places in the world, was being invaded by people with superior technical knowledge and capital; not only was the invasion causing a social and industrial revolution among the inhabitants, who were used to simpler ways of living, but a consciousness of cultural differences was being sharpened because the agents of change were strangers.[88]

Much of *French Canada in Transition* and the subsidiary studies were necessarily devoted to discussions of the rural parish as the dominant institution shaping the French Canadian mentality. For these arguments Hughes leaned on the work of the pioneering French Canadian sociologist Léon Gérin. He explained how, unlike a midwestern township, the parish was not merely a place but an institution, whose values permeated every aspect of French Canadian life. In her study of the changing nature of the parish Pearl Lieff demonstrated that first because of the French government's lack of interest towards New France and then because of the Conquest, it was the parish, the dominant institution of the French Canadian peasant, that ensured the cultural survival of the *canadien*. Before industrialization, it was the safeguard of the French language and religion; initially concerned only with matters within its traditional confines, as society grew it integrated the family, religious, and secular matters into a wider network, with colleges, hospitals, monasteries, convents, and seminaries. It also, however, created a mentality that was carried over into the towns and cities.[89]

The case of 'Cantonville' was intended to show how difficult it was for the French Canadians' dominant institution to safeguard their interests in the changed conditions of the twentieth century. Cantonville was a town, as Hughes described it, whose character was midway between the rural parish of St Denis and the metropolis of Montreal. Located in the centre of what was a well-settled farming district, it had become a major centre of textile manufacturing. It was composed of people who had moved directly from farms to work in the large new industries, and also townspeople long accustomed to commercial and professional pursuits. The town's leadership had come from this second group: the French Canadian business and professional men occupied leading positions in parish and civic institutions; most of the lawyers were involved in politics – one was even a national figure; a French Canadian lawyer had established the *chambre de commerce*. But the town and its traditional institutions were then faced with a crisis and forced to respond to means and mores with which they had no experience – extreme individualism and capitalism. As Hughes explained it, Cantonville had recently been invaded by a number of new industries all initiated and managed by English-speaking people. The English held all the positions of authority in these enterprises and performed all the functions requiring technical training (in part because French Canadian institutions of higher learning had failed to provide education in engineering and applied science). The English were in the majority in the middle and minor executive positions, numerous among clerical workers and mechanics but less commonplace among skilled operators and virtually non-existent in the ranks of the semi-skilled and unskilled. More to the point, only a minority of them were employees; it was the French who constituted the labour force and were to be found in fewer and fewer numbers as one moved up the occupational scale.[90]

The situation in Cantonville was only the tip of the iceberg. Hughes referred to the investigations that had been done on employment in Montreal, repeating Jamieson's findings that among the directorates of the eighty-three largest corporations whose headquarters were in Montreal, 768 were held by English people and only 93 by French. The results of Roy's investigation of fourteen major types of industry showed that in firms engaged in heavy industry, requiring a large capital outlay and extensive use of modern engineering, the overwhelming majority of high-ranked managers and executives were English. In such industries the French were employed at the rank below foreman – in some cases they were numerous among skilled workmen. It was only in a few traditional industries with smaller plants and artisanal operations that French Canadians were in management and ownership positions.[91] Roy contended that this was a situation likely to be perpetuated because English owners preferred to hire English managers. He also faulted the church for the economic position that French Canadians found themselves in: his interviews with English managers led him to the conclusion that they liked to hire the French because they were good, obedient workers, more easily controlled and docile, less subject to strikes and labour troubles than any other group.[92]

For all the attention Hughes intended to pay to social organization and collective behaviour in his study of French Canada and despite his objective to present a new theoretical model for explaining a rural society's adaptation to industrialism, *French Canada in Transition* was written in the great Chicago tradition of metropolitan dominance. In fact it could be argued that Hughes's theory was little more than a sophisticated twist on the theme. Metropolitan dominance began to figure in Hughes's arguments in his discussion of Cantonville as a town midway between the old and the new Quebec. 'The contrast between the rustic and the urban, the agricultural and the industrial, strikes the eye more sharply [here] than in most parts of North America,' he said. 'The physical change from town and country seems abrupt and complete. A town does not cast its shadow as far as the American or English expects it to. City newspapers and city ways do not penetrate deeply into this country. Yet it would be absurd to suppose that the new industrial communities and the old agricultural parishes of Quebec are merely contrasting tiles in a mosaic. *There are organic ties between the two.*'[93] By that Hughes obviously meant that Cantonville was tied into an interconnected web dominated by Montreal and that the changes it was experiencing were being wrought by that metropolis. This was the natural order of things, but it created problems in Quebec because the metropolitan element was of a different culture and mentality. The English, Hughes explained, directed the great economic institutions that operated throughout Canada and beyond her borders. They controlled industry and finance, most of the institutions and cultural amenities. Since English Montreal's hinterland was half a continent, he explained, the French could only enter her institutions in minor and less specialized roles. French Canadians fortunate enough to have dominant positions were concentrated in institutions that had 'for their hinterland, not the continent but merely the province.' More importantly, he argued, the presence of so many French Canadians in minor economic roles enabled the English group to become more specialized and more devoted to attaining power than they could have been if Montreal were entirely English.[94]

Hughes's arguments about the division of labour in Quebec illustrate that the idea of metropolitan dominance was so strongly entrenched in Chicago sociology that graduates of that school failed to seek other explanations for phenomena they were examining. Once again it is evident that the city loomed so large in their eyes that they conceived of it as the mechanism that sifted and sorted people into classes and occupations. Ironically, the McGill students involved in Hughes's project did not feel bound by the metropolitan interpretation and ventured other hypotheses to explain the subordinate position of French Canadians in the Quebec economy. William Roy, for instance, presented something of a 'conquest hypothesis' argument. The whole problem of the racial division of labour in Quebec dated from 1760, he contended. Amherst's capture of Montreal broke down the political barriers established by the French Empire and opened the St Lawrence frontier to the expanding commercial communities of the Atlantic seaboard colonies. 'The clash which followed between the profit-seeking Yankee and the British trader, eager for new fields to exploit, and the French Canadian habitant, resulted in social and economic complications which have been written deeply into French Canadian history.' The formation of the Northwest Fur Trading Company, the coalition of Montreal fur-trading interests with the Hudson's Bay Company, the development of the lumber industry, the promotion of railway construction, the expansion of ocean shipping at the port of Montreal based upon trade with an expanding agricultural hinterland, and the establishment of manufacturing enterprises facilitated by the development of hydroelectric power 'have but served to make more secure the supremacy of the English-speaking entrepreneur in the Quebec economy.'[95]

Stuart Jamieson spoke of a double conquest, and were it not for a closing reference to metropolitan dominance, his arguments might have sounded like a Marxist interpretation of colonial exploitation. 'The Province of Quebec has been twice conquered by the English,' he said, 'once by military force, and again by economic invasion. The first was followed by a constitutional arrangement ... The second conquest has resulted, at least temporarily, in a *de facto* difference in economic position between the French and English elements in the Province.[96] He concluded by saying that the economic exploitation of Quebec had assumed 'the quasi-imperialistic pattern characteristic of other bi-cultural regions' but also argued that as the process of industrialization moved from the metropolis to the frontier, it transcended political and cultural boundaries and brought enormous changes into the lives of people who came into its orbit.[97]

V

One of the advantages of an interdisciplinary project such as McGill's was that the information it unearthed could be employed for different ends. Dawson and Hughes used the Rockefeller student research assistantships to pursue subjects that they considered to be of central importance in understanding twentieth-century Canada. But the primary objective of McGill's Social Science Research Project was to gather information on employment and unemployment in Montreal and, to whatever extent was possible, in the rest of Canada. In *Canadians In and Out of Work* Leonard Marsh incorporated all the material collected from the project to present a picture of the Canadian working force.

In fitting together the studies done in connection with the McGill project,

Marsh concluded that Canada was a vertical and horizontal mosaic. As he himself noted, by 1940, the year in which *Canadians In and Out of Work* was published, the latter part of that argument would have surprised few people. Canada was a large country covering the northern part of an entire continent. It was populated by French and English and a variety of other ethnic groups; a growing body of literature on those groups and on its geographical regions attested to its diversity. He was also aware none the less, that the first part of his argument was not likely to be readily accepted. Canadians were unwilling to believe that their country had a class structure, Marsh said; they preferred instead to attribute its economic stratifications to its newness, to the fact that it was still evolving from a frontier to an urban society or from an agricultural to an industrial base. Marsh contended that such arguments belied the fact that Canada was growing from a substantially industrialized stage to an even more intensive one and that its urban class structure could easily be compared to that of many American and English cities, to the degree that the population was just as likely 'to be immobilized in the rigid moulds of an occupational hierarchy.'[98] Class divisions were not uniform over the whole of the country: in some spots they derived from local conditions; in others they were the product of national conditions. Nevertheless, inequalities of wealth, opportunity, and social recognition cut across geographical barriers and engendered as many problems as in a nation that was smaller and less diverse – this was a fact, Marsh insisted, that was only obscured by the country's vastness.[99]

The purpose of Marsh's account was to present as complete a picture of the Canadian socio-economic strata as possible and in so doing to provide a foundation upon which a national welfare policy could be built.[100] It was just this sort of objective that drew criticism from members of McGill's administration and led, along with a number of other factors, to the Social Science Research Project's demise.

Conclusion

In the development of sociology at McGill University during the interwar years an example can be seen of the way in which an institution shapes the character of a discipline. By virtue of the measures it enforced as well as the strength of its traditions, McGill imposed constraints upon what its professors could research and write. Supported financially by the business elite of English Montreal and with a private status in which it took pride, McGill stood first among Canadian universities in its scientific achievements. It claimed that this was attributable to its freedom from government control, a freedom that fostered an atmosphere conducive to research. In fact, it was partly because of this that the Rockefeller Foundation decided to support a program in social research at McGill, with the expectation that it would stimulate an interest in the social sciences across Canada. In the end, ironically, the university's Board of Governors interfered as much with research as any government would have, and by various means obstructed the work of the social scientists and the development of their disciplines.

In the aftermath of the First World War the work of McGill's Sociology Department was regarded as indispensable to the needs of the community that the university served; by the end of the 1930s it was perceived as needlessly provocative. The Sociology Department had been born out of a compromise: recognizing the need to have some sort of program to train social workers but not willing to fund its operation, university administrators accepted a proposal to set up a course in scientific sociology in the Arts faculty. In the context of the nationalist ethos of the 1920s the department's program of research into immigration, rural life, western settlement, regional development, and urbanization was regarded as valuable. But those academics like Ira Mackay who had been trained in the moral-philosophy tradition did not care for its intrusion into so many diverse fields. Its eclecticism – not to mention its popularity – made it seem as though sociology was displacing philosophy or political economy as the major integrative discipline. In the depression conditions of the 1930s these academic concerns turned into ones of a political nature, and what had initially been a great boon to the department – its involvement in the Social Science Research Project – became the source of its misfortune. The provision of funds from the Rockefeller Foundation provided McGill's sociologists with the resources to undertake research that might otherwise have been impossible. But when the university's Board of Governors decided in the late 1930s to take action against political radicalism within the institution, the social-research project and many of the individuals connected with it became a major target.

McGill University officials fought many battles in the 1930s: they watched carefully the activities of LSR members; were alarmed at the attachment of Christianity to socialist – or what some perceived as Marxist – principles; eased King Gordon out of the United Theological College; and redefined tenure and promotion policies so as to rid the university of individuals like Eugene Forsey. But, as the official historian of McGill has recently noted, 'none of these teachers and movements were as much of an embarrassment to the board of governors as was the Social Science Research Project, for this was an activity conceived and sponsored by the university itself.' He also implies that their reaction might have been a little extreme. 'With titles like *Employment Research*, 1934, *Industrial Diagnosis*, 1935, *The Railway Workers* [sic], 1936, and *The British Immigrant*, 1936, the studies gave the appearance of being more socialistic than they were, especially (since each of them ran to several hundred pages) to those who were contented to know them only by the title.'[1]

If they had examined the situation a little more closely, the Board of Governors would have seen that the participants in the social-research project were not all united for some political end. By 1935, at McGill as elsewhere, the enthusiasm for interdisciplinary work had diminished, and the academics involved in the project were more interested in using the grants to strengthen their own disciplines. Marsh's attempts to create a more integrated project by turning the Social Science Research Department into a degree-granting program and having students participate in an interdisciplinary seminar were rejected.[2] Members of the Department of Economics and Political Science, Leacock, Hemmeon, and John Culliton, wished instead to see a greater separation between the disciplines involved in the program, particularly sociology and economics. Initially, they claimed that this was because the attempt at co-operation beyond a certain point weakened a study. Later, in a private meeting with A.E. Morgan, they revealed what was perhaps of greater concern to them – that under the program's existing structure good economics students were being diverted from their particular line of work in order to conform to 'the sociological scope' of the committee's work, and to that extent, the economic studies suffered. Leacock added that although sociology was an open and interesting field for 'speculation and culture,' it was not the sort of disciplined, academic subject that belonged in a university curriculum.[3]

A.E. Morgan became the first victim in the university's attempts to deal with the social sciences. When Morgan first came to McGill, he told the university's graduates that he supported academic freedom. But only a few months later, when Beatty inveighed against the radical doctrines of young professors, many McGill faculty members feared that they were actually going to be prevented from teaching certain theories to their classes. A deputation of fifty of them went to see Morgan and asked him to clarify his position. He assured them that he would employ the same strategy he had used in Britain when complaints about faculty were raised – which was to side-track the issue.[4] One tactic was to avoid attending the Social Science Research Project's council meetings; another was suggested by his response to Beatty's explanation of why he, the chancellor, felt it was necessary to do something about the situation at McGill. 'We will have no business-university co-operation,' Beatty insisted, 'unless confidence in the mental honesty of the professors is established.' Perhaps referring to the work of the social-research project, he elaborated: 'No responsible executive will turn over his data to an economist if he feels it is to be used for political propaganda purposes at any time, and unfortunately, some of our most vocal professors have become political propagandists.' What McGill needed, he told Morgan, was to build up in its own Economics Department men of 'the calibre, ability, and appreciation of business affairs which is so essential.' To this Morgan responded that he agreed with Beatty on the necessity of building up the Economics Department.[5]

Incidents such as a letter Frank Scott wrote to the *Canadian Unionist* in February 1936, urging trade unions to become more politically active because 'capitalism [would] never produce plenty,'[6] only strengthened Beatty's opinion of McGill's problem. As he told Morgan, he believed that McGill professors were not only preaching socialism constantly but were actively trying to induce others to accept their doctrine, 'more so than any other class of propagandist in this country.'[7] In a little more than a year Morgan was gone. Although it was a financial matter that precipitated his resignation – disagreement over who should control the university's budget[8] – on his departure newspaper headlines screamed: 'Resignation Laid to Failure to Curb Pinks,' 'Free Speech Fight Sweeps Campuses: Head of M'Gill Quits in Fight for Liberalism,' 'Morgan Gives up Post Rather than Gag His Faculty as Ordered by School Governors: Attempt at "Capitalist" Rule Charged as Beatty, Railway President Suggests Bennett for Next Principal.'[9] The stories had it that Morgan had been ordered to silence both liberal and radical elements within the faculty and that when he refused to do so, the university tried to replace him with the ex-prime minister, a millionaire, whose views would accord with that of 'the reactionary, capitalistic view of the governors, better than that of Mr. Morgan, who is as great a democrat as he is a scholar and administrator.' Even Currie had run into trouble with the governors, one report argued, because of his refusal 'to crack down on the unorthodox utterances of some of the faculty.' Currie compromised, ruling that when professors discussed economic or political matters in public, they had to explain that their opinions were not necessarily those of the university. Morgan, by contrast, was said to have assured faculty that as long as he was principal, they would have full liberty to discuss controversial subjects.[10]

Whether or not the McGill Board of Governors ever intended to hire R.B. Bennett as principal, they found in L.W. Douglas qualities they were seeking. A critic of the New Deal, he came to McGill directly from the presidency of the American Cyanimid Company; he was also a trustee of the Rockefeller Foundation,[11] something the university hoped would prove useful in fund-raising drives. It may have been useful in another respect, too. The Rockefeller Foundation's policy towards the social sciences began to change in 1933, and by 1935, in the throes of the Depression, it had abandoned the principle of assisting the social sciences in general in favour of concentrating on such specific areas as banking, unemployment, national planning, and taxation.[12] Consequently, the McGill project had had difficulty in getting its grant renewed in 1935, but since Morgan argued that the project fell under the heading of 'economic stability' and that its findings would be applicable to the American scene, the grant was extended but on a gradually decreasing scale – declining from twenty thousand dollars the first year to five thousand in the fourth, and then ceasing.[13] In 1938 Douglas told Marsh that it was his understanding that the Rockefeller grant would terminate on 1 June 1940 and that all the project's work should be completed by then. He wanted everyone connected with the project to be warned of that, and made it clear that the university would not provide funds for its continuance; he doubted whether another extension would be granted by the foundation and insisted that the university would not sanction the application in any event.[14]

Douglas's next step in dealing with the problem of political radicalism was to strengthen the Economics Department. In pursuit of that goal he tried two different strategies, both of which involved and angered members of the Sociology Department. In the spring of 1938 Everett Hughes was offered a position at the University of Chicago for a much higher salary than he was paid at McGill. Before he left, he and Dawson engaged in a battle with the university administration over his replacement. It had been suggested to him that instead of appointing a first-class scholar, he and Dawson should consider hiring one of their own MA students. Dawson believed the recommendation had been made because, as he explained to Harold Innis, 'Budgeteer Douglas is not anxious to allow the social sciences (sociology in particular) to develop in a natural way. They are developing too fast to suit him ... Perhaps too the type we have here is none too "safe."' He also related to Innis how the university had turned into a battleground over the issue and that for six weeks there had been an intense struggle, 'kept within the family' but which some McGill faculty had been prepared to publicize widely if necessary.[15] Douglas had questioned whether the growth of sociology had been necessary and referred to what members of the Arts survey committee had said about it in 1931. He observed that their recommendations had not been followed; in fact the department had grown – the Social Science Research Project threw a great burden upon it, but since that was about to end, he wondered whether the department could be reduced by hiring a lesser man; in that way the money saved from Hughes's salary could be put towards the appointment that he and Beatty had been wanting to make in economics. Perhaps in an attempt to justify the tactic, he remarked that it would conform to the Arts committee's recommendations. He also had another objective, and that was to encourage a different integration of subjects. As Douglas saw it, the social sciences represented cognate subjects that had been 'hived off the main stem.' He believed that the Department of Philosophy should be made the main department and that it should take both psychology and sociology under its wing. Such action, he stated, would prevent 'starting and growing all these projects which should be studied as a whole and not in these minute subdivisions each one jealous of the other and feeling that they are doing an important job.' Sociology in particular 'should never have been allowed to branch out.'[16]

Whether Dawson and Hughes knew about Douglas's ulterior motives is unclear: he wrote them out in a memorandum to himself. Nevertheless, Hughes was enraged enough about the suggestion that his replacement should be an MA student that he wrote a long memorandum to Douglas that catalogued all of the Sociology Department's accomplishments. In it he argued that the department was nationally known and within McGill easily had the best record of achievement in teaching and in the investigation of Canadian problems; enrolment in some classes reached almost two hundred (remarkable in a university of three thousand men and women); and it had 'by stubborn effort' gathered an enormous amount of Canadian data. Hughes also pointed to Dawson's involvement in the pioneer-belts project, proclaiming that no other department within McGill had taken an active interest in it though it dealt with one of the most vital problems of the country; he also explained that through the project a social-research laboratory had been set up in the university and that it was taken over by the social-research project when the Rockefeller grant was made. Under that fund, he informed Douglas, thirteen sociology students had received MA degrees and some of their work had been published. None of the studies done by the sociologists connected with the project, he argued, would have been undertaken by anyone else. All that had been learned from the research was put back into the teaching, and it was the vitality and reality of the sociology courses, he insisted, that attracted students to the department in such vast numbers.[17]

In the end Douglas acquiesced to the Sociology Department's demands for an experienced scholar,[18] though neither he nor the dean of Arts, Charles Hendel, liked the idea of hiring another Chicago graduate and made inquiries elsewhere. But Dawson won out on that score, too, and another student of Robert Park's, Robert Faris, then teaching at Brown University and a specialist in the field of mental disorders in primitive and urban cultures, was appointed.[19]

After the fight with the Sociology Department Douglas turned his attention to dealing with tenure policy and the plan to hire visiting professors in economics. He noted to Beatty with some satisfaction that the guest lecturers seemed to be giving the collectivists on staff 'quite a good shock.' He hoped this would encourage them to question the premises of their own theories, 'with which,' he said, 'they have been indoctrinated by their high priest, Harold Laski.'[20] But guest lecturers were not enough, and in February 1939 Douglas took steps to accomplish his objectives more directly: he offered a visiting professorship to a distinguished English economist and monetary expert, T.E. Gregory, for a three-year term, with plans to make a similar appointment in the natural sciences. Before he could go any further, however, more trouble erupted.

Douglas had acted without consulting J.C. Hemmeon, head of the Department of Economics and Political Science. The lapse was understandable, given that Douglas wanted Gregory to come to McGill because he had 'had enough,' as he put it, 'of the romantic theorists, unrealistic splitting of hairs, and indifference to observable facts.' Although Douglas apologized to Hemmeon, the executive committee of the Board of Governors had already approved of the offer, and so Hemmeon accepted it as a *fait accompli.* A little later, however, arguing that he had not realized that it was for a three-year term, Hemmeon asked Douglas to withdraw the offer, especially since Gregory's qualifications did not accord with the needs of his department. A number of professors joined in the demand – Dawson and E.R. Adair of the Department of History among them – but Douglas refused to accede to the request and took the matter to the senate; the senate endorsed the policy of establishing visiting professorships and argued that since the offer to Gregory had already been made, it could not be withdrawn. Douglas, for his part, was sure that the opposition expressed by the Political Science Department had nothing to do with the procedure but stemmed from their personal opposition to Gregory: he was a monetary expert, an area in which the department was already well staffed, and he was also a highly nervous person who had had trouble getting along with his colleagues at LSE.[21]

On 20 March 1939 the heads of all the departments in the Faculty of Arts met to discuss the affair. In the hall after the meeting Dawson stopped Douglas and told him that the whole policy of visiting professorships had to be reviewed. The conversation made enough of an impact on Douglas that when he returned to his office, he dictated it to his secretary. 'He inferred,' Douglas noted about Dawson's remark, 'that it was not a good policy, at any rate he expressly said "We," (I presume he meant sociology), "have a deep interest in this."' The principal told Dawson he would consider the matter.[22] In later years Douglas recalled that the opposition grew to such violent proportions that he feared it would have far-reaching consequences throughout the university, and since no commitment had been made to Gregory, the offer of an appointment was withdrawn.[23]

Despite the difficulties they endured at McGill, the work of Carl Dawson, Everett Hughes, and Leonard Marsh was not without long-term effect. Even though Cyril James saw to it that the rest of his predecessor's three-point plan to neutralize the socialist element within McGill was implemeted by redefining tenure and requiring both Leonard Marsh and Eugene Forsey to leave the university, he later took a step that ensured that the work done in connection with the Social Science Research Project left an indelible impact upon Canadian politics and society. Three months after the outbreak of the Second World War the federal government began to consider what to do about the problem of returning veterans, and towards that end set up the Cabinet Committee on Demobilization and Re-establishment. Inevitably, the discussions of this group turned to the whole matter of post-war planning, and to deal with that larger problem, a Committee on Reconstruction was established in 1941. Composed of economists and scholars, authorities on industry, agriculture, and labour, the committee's task was to recommend to the government policies it should implement in the transition from wartime to peace. Cyril James was appointed to head the committee, and he asked Leonard Marsh, because of his long experience in such work, to serve as research director. [24]

With its broad objective to ensure that a post-war depression was averted, the Committee on Reconstruction recommended a large measure of government planning, with means to achieve full employment, maintain consumer spending, and guarantee economic security for the average individual. For reasons too complicated to be elaborated here, the federal bureaucracy grew somewhat jealous of the committee and its activities and took steps to reduce its importance. Members lost their direct access to the Cabinet and were ordered to report to the interdepartmental Economic Advisory Council. Made redundant, the work of James's committee diminished, and it dissolved at the end of 1943. [23] It nevertheless fostered work of significant influence, most notably Leonard Marsh's *Report on Social Security for Canada* (1943). The report forwarded the idea of 'a social minimum,' to be secured through social insurance, social assistance, and children's allowances. Although it received some negative reactions, the work proved to be fundamental in Canadian welfare and planning policies. In the second edition of the report, published in 1975, Marsh admitted that although the work was prepared in haste, as his critics had argued, he had been employed for ten years in a similar project at McGill, wherein he had surveyed such issues as employment, housing, education, social welfare, and social services and had made contacts with administrators and welfare specialists throughout Canada. Moreover, he specifically stated that it was through his report that a decade of social studies on the McGill campus had come to fruition and made a national impact. [26]

The long-range influence of Carl Dawson and Everett Hughes remained within the realm of academia, finding its strength not at McGill but in different institutions and disciplines. When Hughes left Montreal for the United States, where he went on to become one of that country's most eminent sociologists, many McGill students followed him in order to do their doctorates under his supervision at the University of Chicago. Although he built up quite a coterie of English Canadian students – among them Oswald Hall, Aileen Ross, Leo Zakuta, and David Solomon[27] – it was the links he established with French Canadian scholars that proved, in Canada, to be more intellectually significant. In addition to writing *French Canada in Transition* and numerous articles on French-English relations in Canada, Hughes had become acquainted with Father Georges-Henri Lévesque. A Dominican priest who had trained at the Université de Lille, Lévesque built up l'Ecole des Sciences Sociales, Politiques et Economiques at Laval and in the academic session of 1942–3 invited Hughes to teach for a semester at the university.[28] During that period the two of them began to work out a program of research and teaching in sociology that was published a year later in a pamphlet entitled *Programme de recherches sociales pour le Québec*. Its suggestions, that research, using the parish as the focus, deal with ecological studies of rural and urban communities as well as investigations of the family,[29] were followed for many years at Laval under the direction of Jean-Charles Falardeau after 1943. Falardeau, who had received his degree from Laval but also studied with Hughes at Chicago, was the first full-time professional sociologist in French Canada. He was to have an enormous influence upon the development of the discipline in francophone Quebec, serving as chairman during the early years of the department, which until the 1960s was the leader in French Canadian sociology.[30]

Personal contacts alone do not explain the acceptance of Hughes's ideas at Laval. Chicago sociology and incipient French Canadian social science shared some of the same influences: in their desire to pursue rural themes, French Canadian sociologists followed the models of Léon Gérin and the French human geographers and demographers,[31] and as we have seen, Chicago sociology adopted many of its precepts from the latter group. Another influence forged even tighter links: between 1885 and 1886 Gérin had studied social science in Paris with LePlay and adopted his emphasis on the family approach, which, as S.D. Clark has explained, found expression in Hughes's work through LePlay's influence on Robert Park.[32]

If Chicago sociology flourished in the intellectual culture of French Canada, the legacy it left in English Canada is more difficult to weigh. For another few years Dawson's students at McGill continued to employ the ecological approach in their studies, but in general the theory of human ecology ceased to hold a prominent place in sociology. By the late 1930s the influence of the Chicago school was on the decline. With Robert Park's retirement in 1934 the Chicago Sociology Department lacked the stimulus from the sort of intellectual integration he had emphasized. Moreover, Chicago's dominance was resented by other sociology departments, and this resulted in the severance of the connection between the American Sociological Society and the Chicago-based *American Journal of Sociology* in 1935–6.[33] With the onset of the Second World War, finally, the underlying assumption of Chicago sociology, that progress was inherent in the social structure if only the processes could be observed and investigated, seemed somewhat naïve. Similarly, the faith that sociologists had placed in the collection of 'facts,' as well as their understanding of what constituted facts and how simple it was to ascertain them, led in the late 1950s and 60s to attacks on the myths of objectivity and value-free analysis.

With the exception of Hughes's studies on French Canada, the work of the McGill Sociology Department tended to be forgotten by later generations of Canadian sociologists, and more particularly by historians. When John Porter set out to write *The Vertical Mosaic: An Analysis of Class and Power in Canada* (1965), he was not aware of the existence of Leonard Marsh's *Canadians In and Out of Work*,[34] which had already shown that vast discrepancies in wealth and income existed among Canadians and which employed the same metaphor in making the point. Although Dawson's books did not enjoy longevity, his labours were not fruitless. He collected an enormous amount of data on Canadian society, succeeded in establishing a strong research emphasis in one facet of Canadian social science, and through his involvement in the founding of the Canadian Social Science Research Council strove to ensure that all social scientists had the resources and conditions necessary to pursue their research interests. He also indirectly, and in a way that has not been sufficiently recognized, introduced into Canadian intellectual life a concept that had an important influence upon English Canadian historical writing. The role that N.S.B. Gras and the Chicago school of urban sociologists played in the development of the metropolitan-hinterland theory has been acknowledged, but the specific contribution made by R.D. McKenzie has not. McKenzie found at Chicago, in the city itself as well as within the university's influential science and social-science departments, ideas that accorded with what he had witnessed growing up in Winnipeg in the early twentieth century, and these led him to formulate a systematic theory of metropolitan dominance. In effect, when Dawson applied the theory of metropolitanism to his study of western settlement in the 1930s, he was taking it back to the milieu from which it had emerged.

Most studies of metropolitanism in Canadian historiography begin by citing Harold Innis. By contrast, the lack of recognition accorded to

Dawson and McKenzie as founders of the theory of metropolitanism is one of the most perplexing oversights in Canadian historical writing, and the reasons for it complex. With few exceptions Canadian historians tend not to see Innis as a product of the University of Chicago of the 1920s. Yet the similarities in his work and that of McKenzie, Dawson, and Park are so strong that they are impossible to deny. While Innis never studied directly with Robert Park, he was influenced by the Chicago Economics Department, particularly C.S. Duncan's lectures on marketing. Duncan's ideas on marketing – that the physical characteristics of a commodity influence its marketing structure and in turn the cultural community built in relation to it – all stemmed from Park's ecological theories and penetrated into Innis's books. The Chicago connection may also have been overlooked, as one student of metropolitanism has argued, because Canadian historians did not understand the theoretical implications of Innis's work, preferring as they did in the 1950s and early 1960s to steer clear of overt theorizing. One result was that Donald Creighton could call Innis and Dawson 'environmentalists' without recognizing that the ecological bases of their studies involved an examination of both 'biotic' and 'cultural' aspects of society.[35] The problems the McGill sociologists faced in the 1930s, both with the university administration and with academics of the more traditional disciplines, who looked askance at the new upstart, may also have played a role in this oversight. Then too, despite all the rhetoric in the 1930s about the need to reintegrate knowledge, academics then and in later years continued to guard what they saw as their separate preserves. Despite his admiration for Innis, for example, Donald Creighton considered it important to keep history a distinct and autonomous discipline. As he observed at the Canadian Historical Association meetings in 1957, 'In the 1930s, when the influence of Harold Innis was at its height and everybody was writing and talking about staple production, it began to seem possible that history would degenerate into a sub-department of Political Economy.'[36]

Such concerns contributed to the popularity of biography in Canadian historical writing in the 1950s because it so clearly differentiated history from other kinds of social science. It was not until the 1960s that attention was once again paid to the contributions that social science could make to the discipline. Thus it was that Canadian historians could contrast their understanding of how Canadian society developed – through the influence of metropolitan centres and institutions – with the American historians' use of the metaphor of the frontier, without recognizing that in American sociology, particularly that of the Chicago school, it was the theory of metropolitanism that held sway.

Regarded as ancillary to the major developments in English Canadian intellectual life, the story of C.A. Dawson's development as a professional sociologist touches upon the main themes in the emergence of sociology as an independent discipline in the early twentieth century. As scientific sociology emerged out of theology and social work in the aftermath of the First World War, so Dawson started out in the ministry and then rejected the religious calling at some point during the Great War to become a scientific sociologist. The path he travelled at that point – to Chicago's influential Divinity School – had already been taken by many other Canadians, some of whom played a significant role in the school's emergence as a centre of liberal protestantism. His doctoral thesis, dealing with the social nature of knowledge, reflected all the ideas he was exposed to there – the social philosophy of Dewey and Mead, modernism, Robert Park's notions about institutions and communities. He spent a couple of years at Chicago, helping to build the research program on local studies for which that institution would become famous, and then departed for McGill, where he would attempt, with some encouragement and many more difficulties, to implement a program devoted to the same objectives he had learned at Chicago, but adapted to Canadian conditions.

Notes

CHAPTER ONE: MCGILL AND THE TRADITION OF UTILITY

1 See Stanley Brice Frost, *McGill University: For the Advancement of Learning*, vol. 1, *1809–1895* (Montreal: McGill-Queen's University Press 1980), chaps. 2–5; Cyrus Macmillan, *McGill and Its Story, 1821–1921* (Toronto: Oxford University Press 1921).

2 Robin S. Harris, *A History of Higher Education in Canada, 1663–1960* (Toronto: University of Toronto Press 1976), 43, 53–4; Frost, *McGill University*, vol. 1, 268–79, 282; Edgar Andrew Collard, 'Dawson's Principalship, 1855–1893,' in *McGill: The Story of a University*, ed. Hugh MacLennan (London: George Allen and Unwin Ltd; Toronto: Nelson and Sons 1960), 60–1

3 Frost, *McGill University*, vol. 1, 185; Collard, 'Dawson's Principalship,' 56, 65

4 John George Bourinot, 'Our Intellectual Strength and Weakness: A Short Review of Literautre, Education and Art in Canada,' *Transactions and Proceedings of the Royal Society of Canada* (1893): 3–36

5 Laurence Veysey, *The Emergence of the American University* (Chicago: University of Chicago Press 1965), 3

6 Frost, *McGill University*, vol. 1, 214–19, 243; Report of the Principal, in *Annual Report of the Corporation of McGill University* (1931–2), 8

7 *Annual Report of the Governors, Principals, and Fellows of McGill University* (1904–5), 22; *Annual Report ...* (1910–11), 12; A.W. Currie, *Six Years at McGill: A Review* (Montreal: The University 1926), 45

8 A.B. McKillop, *A Disciplined Intelligence: Critical Inquiry and Canadian Thought in the Victorian Era* (Montreal: McGill-Queen's University Press 1980), 28–33, 58, 95–9; Veysey, *Emergence of the American University*,

23–31, 60; Collard, 'Dawson's Principalship,' 66–7; R.A. Falconer, 'Scottish Influence on the Higher Education in Canada,' *Transactions and Proceedings of the Royal Society of Canada* 21 (May 1927): 7–20

9 See S.F. Cannon, 'Humboldtian Science,' in *Science and Culture: The Early Victorian Period* (New York: Dawson and Science History Publications 1978), 73–4.

10 Veysey, *Emergence of the American University*, 180–98

11 Ibid., chap. on 'Liberal Culture,' passim

12 McKillop, *Disciplined Intelligence*, 95

13 Edgar Andrew Collard, 'Sir William Peterson's Principalship,' in MacLennan, ed., *McGill*, 84

14 David Thompson, 'McGill Between the Wars,' in MacLennan, ed., *McGill*, 105–6; Report of the Principal [A.W. Currie], in *Annual Report of the Corporation of McGill University* (1930–1), 13

15 McGill University, *Annual Report* (1937–7), 26

16 Ira Mackay, 'Some Internal Economies,' in *Annual Report of the Corporation of McGill University* (1923–4), 126

17 Stephen Leacock, 'Literacy and Education,' in *The Social Criticism of Stephen Leacock*, ed. Alan Bowker (Toronto: University of Toronto Press 1975), 19; See also R.C. Wallace, 'The Higher Learning,' *Queen's Quarterly* 44 (Spring 1937): 5; W.D. Woodhead, 'The Decline in the Study of Classics and Its Consequence,' National Council of Canadian Colleges and Universities, Eleventh National Conference, *Proceedings* 8 (1927): 97–103.

18 'Address of the Principal and Vice-Chancellor [A.E. Morgan]: Upon the Occasion of His Installation into Office on 5 October 1935,' in *McGill University Annual Report* (1935–6), 95

19 Veysey, *Emergence of the American University*; see espec. chap. 6, 'The Tendency to Blend and Reconcile,' 342–60, and 221–33.

20 McKillop, *A Disciplined Intelligence*, 229–30

21 McGill University Archives [MUA], acc. 83, box 208, memo of Ira A. Mackay, 'Some Reflections on the Place of Commercial Studies in the University,' 6 Feb. 1932

22 Veysey, *Emergence of the American University*, 210; Alexander Meiklejohn, 'What the Liberal College is Not,' address delivered at the founding of Allegheny College, 23 June 1915, in A. Meiklejohn, *The Liberal College* (Boston: Marshall Jones Co. 1920; repr. edn, New York: Arno Press and the New York Times 1969), 20–6

23 Alexander Meiklejohn, 'What the Liberal College Is,' inaugural address delivered at Amherst College, 16 October 1912, in Meiklejohn, *The Liberal College*, 29–50

24 John Higham, 'The Matrix of Specialization,' in *The Organization of Knowledge in Modern America, 1860–1920*, ed. Alexandra Oleson and John Voss (Baltimore and London: Johns Hopkins University Press 1979), 9

25 Gladys Bryson, 'The Emergence of the Social Sciences from Moral Philosophy,' *International Journal of Ethics* 42 (Apr. 1932): 304–23

26 At the University of Toronto, for example, the social sciences remained under the jurisdiction of the Department of Political Economy until 1960. See Alan Franklin Bowker, 'Truly Useful Men: Maurice Hutton, George Wrong, James Mavor and the University of Toronto, 1880–1927,' PH D diss., University of Toronto 1975, 325.

27 Barry Karl, *Charles Merriam and the Study of Politics* (Chicago and London: University of Chicago Press 1974), 123

28 Cyril F. James, Principal's Address, 'The Installation of F. Cyril James as Principal and Vice-Chancellor,' 12 Jan. 1940, in *McGill University Annual Report* (1939–40), 110–13

29 Ibid., 112

30 Ibid.

31 *The State in Society: A Series of Public Lectures Delivered under the Auspices of McGill University*, foreword by L.W. Douglas (Toronto: Oxford University Press 1940), iii

32 MUA, acc. 16, box 64, 'Summary of Social Science Research,' by 'D.M.' [the principal's secretary, Dorothy McMurray], 'Confidential to the Principal,' nd

33 S.B. Frost, 'Lewis Williams Douglas: The Right Man at the Right Time,' *McGilliana* (9 (Mar.-Sept. 1980): 7

34 L.W. Douglas, 'A Host of Golden Recollections: Principal Douglas' Memories of McGill,' in Collard, ed., *The McGill You Knew*, 242; Principal's Address, *The Installation of Lewis Williams Douglas as the Principal and Vice-Chancellor of McGill*, Jan. 1938 (Montreal: The University 1938), 18. 'Since that memorable day more than seven hundred years ago, when the mother of universities, the University of Paris, came into being ... it has been the primary purpose of the university to cultivate that variety of mind, which specialized as it might be, sees its own specialty in relation to the whole field of thought and knowledge and experience.'

35 Douglas, 'Memories of McGill,' 247–8

36 See for example, S.B. Frost's comments in 'The Right Man at the Right Time': 'The thrust of social science research at McGill was dissipated and has never again achieved the sense of unified purpose' (10).

37 Lewis Williams Douglas, *The Liberal Tradition: A Free People and a Free Economy*, the Godkin Lectures, delivered at Harvard University 6–10 May 1935 (New York: D. Van Nostrand Co., Inc. 1935), 101–2

38 Douglas, *The State in Society*, iii; for a similar view, see 'Closing Address of His Excellency the Governor-General,' in *The State in Society*, 139–40.

39 MUA, acc. 641, box 279, L.W. Douglas to Edward Beatty, 23 Nov. 1939, on James's appointment as principal: 'As you know, he has recently been elected Principal, and I have no doubt that under his direction, qualified as he is, a change will become evident.'

40 Veysey, chap. 5, 'The Pattern of the New University,' *Emergence of the American University*, 302–17; Thorstein Veblen, *The Higher Learning in America: A Memorandum on the Conduct of Universities by Businessmen* (New York: B.W. Huebsch 1918); Richard Hofstadter and Walter Metzger, *The Development of Academic Freedom in the United States* (New York: Alfred Knopf 1955), 452–3

41 MUA, acc. 557, box 8, Faculty of Law, P.E. Corbett, Social Science Research transfer file, 'Governors of McGill,' nd

42 Mackay, 'Some Internal Economies,' 126–7; Leacock, 'Literacy and Education,' 25

43 The administrative structure of Canadian universities more closely resembled the American model, in which the principal (or president) was responsible to the board of governors, than it did the English, in which he was considered to be a spokesman for a community of scholars. See Stewart Reid, 'Origins and Portents,' in *A Place of Liberty: Essays on the Government of Canadian Universities*, ed. George Whalley (Toronto and Vancouver: Clarke, Irwin and Co. Ltd 1964), 13–20

44 'New Statutes and Senate,' *McGill University Annual Report* (1934–5), 12–13; MUA, Board of Governors Minutes, Statutes 1935, 30 Jan. 1935, 749, and Governors Minutes, 28 Nov. 1939, 1069; Frost, 'The Right Man at the Right Time,' 10; Dorothy McMurray, *Four Principals of McGill* (Montreal: Graduates' Society of McGill University 1974), 44–5

45 Frost, 'The Right Man at the Right Time,' 10

46 MUA, Board of Governors Minutes, 28 Nov. 1939, 1069; MUA, Senate Minutes, 17 Jan. 1940, Resolution of the Faculty of Arts and Science, 246; MUA, Faculty of Arts Minutes, Address by Principal James, 29 Jan. 1940, 342; McMurray, *Four Principals*, 44–5

47 MUA, Faculty of Arts Minutes, 12 Jan. 1940, 331–2

48 Ibid.; and MUA, Faculty of Arts Minutes, Address by Principal James, 29 Jan. 1940, 338–41

49 Ibid., 341, 345–7

50 MUA, acc. 16, box 54, Charles Hendel to Cyril James, 11 Mar. 1941

51 MUA, Governors Minutes, Report of the Executive and Finance Committee to the Board of Governors: Tenure of Appointment, 14 Nov. 1939, 1053–5;

Report of the Principal, *McGill University Annual Report* (1938–9), 8; Frost, 'The Right Man at the Right Time,' 8

52 MUA, acc. 641, box 279, L.W. Douglas to Chancellor Beatty, 3 Feb. 1939
53 MUA, acc. 16, box 59, 'The Record Regarding Mr. Eugene Forsey,' extracts of correspondence to and from various people regarding Forsey, 1932–41. Cited here: A.W. Currie to Premier Taschereau, 21 Oct. 1939; see also A.W. Currie to Principal W.L. Grant, Upper Canada College, 16 Oct. 1933; A.W. Currie to A.J. Nesbit, Thomson Co., 22 Nov. 1932.
54 In the 1930s E.W. Beatty delivered a number of addresses on the subject. See E.W. Beatty, 'Freedom and the Universities,' *Queen's Quarterly* 44 (Winter 1937): 463, 469.
55 Ibid., 467
56 'Visitor's Address,' in *The Installation of Lewis Williams Douglas*, 20–2
57 MUA, Faculty of Arts Minutes, Address by Principal James, 29 Jan. 1940, 343–4
58 J.B. Brebner, *Scholarship for Canada: The Function of Graduate Studies* (Ottawa: Canadian Social Science Research Council 1945), 32
59 See, for example, B.S. Kierstead and S.D. Clark, 'Social Sciences,' in *Royal Commission Studies: A Selection of Essays Prepared for the Royal Commission on National Development in the Arts, Letters, and Sciences* (Ottawa: Edmond Cloutier 1951), 179–84. The development of sociology and political science could not keep pace with economics: 'Economics has been thought of as "practical" and has secured a greater measure of support from the community than has political science or sociology ... In general this has meant that sociology and political science have had to depend for support on such financial crumbs as have been left over after the needs of economics – or in some cases history – have been taken care of' (179).

CHAPTER TWO: SOCIAL SERVICE AND THE ORIGINS OF SOCIOLOGY

1 Fred H. Matthews, *Quest for an American Sociology: Robert E. Park and the Chicago School* (Montreal: McGill-Queen's University Press 1977), 1–2, 90–2
2 Walter I. Trattner, *From Poor Law to Welfare State: A History of Social Welfare in America*, 2nd edn (New York: The Free Press 1979), 194–5
3 Report of the Chancellor, in *McGill University Annual Report of the Corporation for the Year* (1933–4), 9–13. Enrolment figures do not include students in extension courses or in the School for Teachers since these did not come under the juridiction of the corporation.
4 *McGill Annual Report* (1917–18), 30; *McGill Annual Report* (1918–19), 12, 24; Col. William Wood, *The Storied Province of Quebec*, vol. 2 (Toronto: Dominion Publishing 1931), 760

5 *McGill Annual Report* (1918–19), 11, 12; Harris, *History of Higher Education*, 231

6 Macmillan, *McGill and Its Story*, 262–3

7 *McGill Annual Report* (1914–15), 6, 8

8 J.A. Nicholson, *McGill's War Record*, Centennial Endowment booklet (Montreal: The University 1920), 12: *McGill Annual Report* (1914–15), 6–8

9 *McGill Annual Report* (1917–18), 21

10 Macmillan, *McGill and Its Story*, 263

11 Ibid., 265–6; A.W. Currie, *Six Years at McGill*, McGill University pamphlet, 1–2; Report of the Chancellor, in *McGill Annual Report* (1933–4), 9–13. The remarks concerning the role of an army general were Currie's; see 'Prospects,' in *McGill Annual Report* (1923–4), 39.

12 A.W. Currie, in *McGill Annual Report* (1919–20), 19–20

13 Currie, 'Prospects,' 40

14 Report of the Principal, in *McGill Annual Report* (1924–5), 49–50

15 J.M. Bliss, 'The Methodist Church and World War I,' 54, 590, in C. Berger, ed., *Conscription 1917*, CHR readings no 8 (Toronto: University of Toronto Press, nd; repr. from CHR 49 [Sept. 1968])

16 See, for example, Cecil Fairfield Lavell, *Reconstruction and National Life* (New York: Macmillan 1919), v–vi; G.T.W. Patrick, *The Psychology of Social Reconstruction* (Boston and New York: Houghton Mifflin 1920), 8, 12; G.E. Partridge, *The Psychology of Nations* (New York: Macmillan 1919), 290, 325.

17 Rt Hon. Lord Sydenham, preface to Henry Chellew, *Human and Industrial Efficiency* (London: University of London Press 1919), x

18 Ibid., 41, 68, 136

19 'Changes in the Academic Side of the University,' in *McGill Annual Report* (1919–20), 4

20 Sir Arthur Currie, 'The Universities and Technological Education,' in *Report of the Proceedings of the Second Congress of the Universities of the Empire* (1921), 193; Frank Dawson Adams, *McGill and Science*, McGill Centennial Endowment booklet (Montreal: The University 1920), 9–10

21 Report of the Principal for the Session, 1923–1924: Our System and Its Results: 1 / The University and the Undergraduate, *McGill Annual Report* (1923–4), 2

22 Currie, 'The Universities and Technological Education,' 189, 193–4

23 Edouard Montpetit, 'The Universities and the Teaching of Civics, Politics, and Social Economics,' Second Congress of the Universities of the Empire *Report*, 73–4

24 Sir William Beveridge, 'The Universities and the Teaching of Civics, Politics,

and Social Economics,' Second Congress of the Universities of the Empire *Report*, 66; Lynda Grier, 'The Universities and the Teaching of Civics, Politics, and Social Economics,' Second Congress of the Universities of the Empire *Report*, 54–63

25 Montpetit, 'The Teaching of Civics,' 72, 76
26 Ibid., 87; William Caldwell's argument was made in his piece 'A New Birth for Education,' *Hibbert Journal* 18 (Oct. 1919–July 1920): 60.
27 'William Caldwell,' *Who's Who in Canada 1927* (Toronto: International Press 1927), 42
28 William Caldwell, 'Philosophy and the Newer Sociology,' *Contemporary Review* 74 (Sept. 1898): 420–1
29 William Caldwell's discussion of the speeches presented at the session, 'The Universities and the Teaching of Civics,' Second Congress of the Universities of the Empire *Report*, 90
30 William Caldwell's discussion of the session, 'The Universities and Adult Education,' Second Congress of the Universities of the Empire *Report*, 174
31 William Caldwell, *Pragmatism and Idealism* (London: Adam and Charles Black 1913), 54, 71, 178; Caldwell, 'A New Birth for Education,' 53–9
32 Leslie Armour and Elizabeth Trott, *The Faces of Reason: An Essay on Philosophy and Culture in English Canada 1850–1950* (Waterloo: Wilfrid Laurier University Press 1981), 300
33 Terry Copp, *Anatomy of Poverty: The Condition of the Working Class in Montreal* (Toronto: McClelland and Stewart 1974), 30
34 Wood, *The Storied Province of Quebec*, vol. 2, 751–2
35 Copp, *Anatomy*, 34; Marcus L. Hansen and J.B. Brebner, *Mingling of the Canadian and American Peoples* (New Haven and Toronto: Yale University Press 1940), 252
36 Copp, *Anatomy*, 34. See also 'Family Welfare in Montreal,' *Social Welfare* 4 (1 July 1922): 219–20, which reported on the unemployment situation during 1921 as one of great distress; thousands of wage-earners were out of work over a long period of time.
37 Wood, *The Storied Province of Quebec*, vol. 2, 764
38 Wood was secretary of the arbitration board that was established to settle the strike.
39 A.P.S. Glassco and W. Vaughan, *A Greater McGill*, McGill Centennial Endowment booklet (Montreal: The University 1920), 14–16, 18; *McGill Annual Report* (1918–19), 12–13; *McGill Annual Report* (1919–20), 14
40 Glassco and Vaughan, *A Greater McGill*, 16
41 Ibid., 7–8
42 Report of the Chancellor, in *McGill Annual Report* (1933–4), 9–13

43 Glassco and Vaughan, *A Greater McGill*, 38; Stephen Leacock, *The Need for Dormitories at McGill*, McGill Centennial Endowment booklet (Montreal: The University 1920), 6
44 On the role of college residential life in shaping the behaviour and mores of American youth in the 1920s, see Paula S. Fass, *The Damned and the Beautiful: American Youth in the 1920s* (Oxford, New York, and Toronto: Oxford University Press 1977).
45 The Peterson Memorial Address, appendix to Macmillan, *McGill and Its Story*, 298
46 Edgar Andrew Collard, 'Sir William Peterson's Principalship,' in MacLennan, ed., *McGill*, 90
47 The information in this paragraph is largely derived from Philip Seed, *The Expansion of Social Work in Britain* (London and Boston: Routledge and Kegan Paul 1973), 5–9, 13–27, 49; the discussion of 'indiscriminate giving' is taken from Gareth Stedman Jones, *Outcast London: A Study in the Relationship Between Classes in Victorian Society* (London: Peregrine / Penguin 1976), chap. 13, 'The Deformation of the Gift,' 241–61.
48 James Leiby, *Social Welfare and Social Work in the United States* (New York: Columbia University Press 1978), 113–14; Roy Lubove, *The Professional Altruist: The Emergence of Social Work as a Career* (Cambridge, Mass.: Harvard University Press 1965), 158; *Encyclopedia of the Social Sciences*, ed. E.R.A. Seligman, sv 'Charity Organization'
49 Charles Loch Mowat, *The Charity Organisation Society: 1869–1913* (London: Methuen 1961), 105–13, 171 n 1
50 Leiby, *Social Welfare and Social Work*, 113–14
51 Trattner, *Poor Law to Welfare State*, 196
52 William Shepherd, 'Genesis of the Montreal Council of Social Agencies,' MSW thesis, McGill University 1957, 36; Public Archives of Canada [PAC], MG 28 I, 164, vol. 7, file 2; Montreal Council of Women Papers, 'The Origin of the Charity Organization Society of Montreal,' by Carrie M. Derrick
53 Lubove, *Professional Altruist*, 22–3, 49 n 66, 220
54 *Report of a Committee of the Montreal Council of Social Agencies: Being the Findings of a Social and Financial Survey of Protestant and Non-Sectarian Social Agencies of an Undenominational Character in the City of Montreal, 1919*, 18
55 PAC, MG 28, 164, vol. 12. Montreal Council of Women Papers, *Montreal Charity Organization Society Annual Report 1915*, np
56 *MCOS Annual Report* (1916–17), 6, 12
57 Ibid., 27
58 *MCOS Annual Report* (1915–16), 14, 22

59 Ibid., 37; and in same source, 'Confidential Exchange: March 15 to Sept. 30, 1916,' 34–6

60 Barbara M. Finlayson, 'Professor Dale,' *Social Welfare* 9 (Dec. 1926): 324–5; McGill University Calendar (1922–3), 407; Margaret Gillett, *We Walked Very Warily: A History of Women at McGill* (Montreal: Eden Press Women's Publication 1981), 360

61 Leiby, *Social Welfare and Social Work*, 127–32; Seed, *The Expansion of Social Work*, 32; Olive Checkland, *Philanthropy in Victorian Scotland: Social Welfare and the Voluntary Principle* (Edinburgh: John Donald 1980), 303–4

62 *McGill Annual Report* (1910–11), 13

63 Information on the McGill University Settlement is derived from the following sources: *McGill Annual Report* (1910–11), 13; Robert A. Percy, 'Dufferin District: An Area in Transition,' MA thesis, McGill University 1928, 82–4; 86–7; 'Alumnae Work' *McGill Fortnightly* 1 (7 Oct. 1892): 119; Gillett, *We Walked Very Warily*, 374.

64 *McGill Annual Report* (1917–18), 12–13; McGill University Calendar (1918–19), Department of Social Study and Training, 147

65 Harris, *History of Higher Education*, 294–5

66 University of Toronto Calendar (1915–16), Department of Social Service: Historical, 36–7; University of Toronto Calendar (1920–1), Department of Social Service, 368; 'Social Service Department Forms Links with the Masses,' *University of Toronto Monthly*, Nov. 1922, 71–2

67 McGill University Calendar (1922–3), Department of Social Science: History of the Department, 407; *McGill Annual Report* (1917–18), 12–13

68 *McGill Annual Report* (1917–18), 12–13; McGill University Calendar (1922–3), Department of Social Science: History of the Department, 407; Keith Markell, *The Faculty of Religious Studies, McGill University* (Montreal: Faculty of Religious Studies, McGill University 1979), 9

69 Calendar of the Montreal Theological Colleges Affiliated with McGill, 'Plan of Cooperation and Announcement of Common Courses: First Session, 1912–1913,' 13; Wesleyan College Calendar (1915–16), 47; Wesleyan College Calendar, 47–57; Calendar of the Montreal Theological Colleges (6th session, 1917–18), 28

70 McGill University Calendar (1922–3), Department of Social Science, 407

71 McGill University Calendar (1918–19), Department of Social Study and Training, 147; McGill University Calendar (1922–3), 407

72 Esther Kerry, Prospectus, McGill School of Social Work, 1918–1931 (Montreal, Nov. 1968, mimeographed)

73 Though he moved from place to place, Falk was involved in setting up

social-welfare councils in many cities and towns; these included the central social-planning body of the Vancouver Council of Social Agencies, the Vancouver Welfare Federation, and the School of Social Work at the University of British Columbia. In 1936 he returned to Christadora House in New York, staying there as head worker until 1937, when he was appointed executive director of the Community Chest and the Council of Social Agencies in Charlotte, North Carolina; eighteen months later he became secretary of the Community Chest and Council of Elizabeth, New York. During the Second World War he was acting director of field operations for the United Seaman's Service in the United States. In 1946 he went back to work for the Community War Chest and the Social Planning Council in Yonkers, New York. Leaving that position in 1946, he served as campaign director for the United Chinese Relief of New York, a position he was compelled to resign from because of ill health. He thereupon went to Amherst College, Massachusetts, with the intention of taking life easier; he worked there as a research assistant until a few months before he died in April 1950. Biographical information on J.H.T. Falk is based upon the following sources: Charlotte Whitton, 'Falk is Dead,' *Canadian Welfare* 26 (15 Apr. 1950): 17–18; F. Ivor Jackson, 'Howard Falk,' *Canadian Welfare* 41 (Nov.-Dec. 1965): 266–73; William F. Shepherd, 'Genesis of the MCSA,' 47–51; Esther Kerry, Prospectus, McGill University Calendar (1918–19), Department of Social Study and Training, 147; PAC, MG 27 III c7, J.S. Woodsworth Papers, 575–9

74 Jackson, 'Howard Falk,' 266; Shepherd, 'Genesis of the MCSA,' 51
75 *MCSA Report* (1919), 21
76 J.H.T. Falk, 'The Future of Social Work in Canada,' *Dalhousie Review* 1 (July 1921): 183; McGill University Calendar (1919–20), Department of Social Service (written by Howard Falk), 140
77 Falk, 'The Future of Social Work in Canada,' 183; Falk, *MCSA Report* (1919), 17; William Lyon Mackenzie King, *Industry and Humanity: A Study in the Principles Underlying Industrial Reconstruction* (1918; repr. Toronto: University of Toronto Press 1973), 76, 174–5, 178; King's conviction reflected a general North American belief in the power of economic growth as a means to avoid class conflict. See for example Reginald Whitaker, 'The Liberal Corporatist Ideas of Mackenzie King,' *Labour / Le Travailleur* 2 (1977): 137–69.
78 Falk, *MCSA Report* (1919), 17; Falk, 'The Future of Social Work in Canada,' 184–5. In *The New Christianity*, Salem Bland praised the labour movement for demanding that every man and woman make a just contribution to the welfare of the social organism. 'There shall be no place in society for

idlers and exploiters. It is the deadly enemy of parasitism in all its forms.'
Salem Bland, *The New Christianity* (1920; repr. Toronto: University of
Toronto Press 1973), 53

79 Falk, 'The Future of Social Work in Canada,' 185. See similarly J.H.T. Falk,
'The Federation of Social Agencies,' in *MCSA Report* (1919), 42, reprint of an
article written for the *Montreal Star*, nd: 'Social agencies are dealing with
incapacitated, broken down pieces of machinery; machinery used or going
to be used in adult life in the operation of industry and industry itself, should
not only in the interests of suffering humanity but also from the standpoint
of the material prosperity of the nation, require that the social agencies for
which it has to provide the entire financial support should ascertain,
reveal, and remove by social legislation or other action the causes of their
incapacitation.'

80 Falk, 'The Future of Social Work in Canada,' 185

81 Ibid., 185; Falk, *MCSA Report* (1919), 21.

82 Falk, *MCSA Report* (1919), 17, 43; Falk, 'The Future of Social Work,' 182

83 The Alumni Book: McGill University School of Social Work, 50th anniversary
project, compiled by Esther Kerry (Montreal 1975)

84 MUA, acc. 641, box 290, A Memorandum from Director Falk to Members of the
Board of Cooperating Theological Colleges, nd; Calendar of the Montreal
Theological Colleges (eighth session, 1919–20), 29–30; Wesleyan College
Calendar (1919–20), General Conference Requirements, 47

85 MUA, acc. 641, box 290, Department of Social Service, McGill University no 1,
Confirmation of a Conference between Professor J.A. Dale and the Director Mr. Falk, Thurs. 15 Aug. 1918; Falk also explained to Currie that he saw
the department as one that would connect the university with the city at
large. MUA, acc. 641, box 290, J. Howard Falk to Sir Arthur Currie, 16 Sept.
1920

86 Richard Allen, *The Social Passion: Religion and Social Reform in Canada,
1914–1928* (Toronto: University of Toronto Press 1973), 19, 66–7

87 *MCSA Report* (1919), 6; Shepherd, 'Genesis of the MCSA,' 70

88 'The Montreal Council of Social Agencies,' *Social Welfare* 3 (1 Jan. 1921): 98;
MCSA Report (1919), 24–5, 35

89 'The Montreal Council of Social Agencies,' 98

90 *MCSA Report* (1919), 17, 20

91 Ibid., 18–19; Falk, 'The Future of Social Work in Canada,' 185

92 MUA, acc. 641, box 290, Howard Falk to Sir Arthur Currie, 1 Dec. 1921

93 MUA, acc. 641, box 290, Sir Arthur Currie to Lord Byng of Vimy, 2 Dec. 1921

94 'Lord Byng of Vimy Calls for Service,' *Social Welfare* 4, no 7 (1922): 143

95 MUA, acc. 1563/1, Board of Governors Minutes, 30 Sept. 1920, 128; 'Social Agencies Engage J.H.T. Falk,' *Montreal Gazette*, 1 Oct. 1920, 5

96 MUA, acc. 1563/1, Board of Governors Minutes, 30 Sept. 1920, 128

97 'The Montreal Council of Social Agencies,' 93, 95, 98

98 James Smyth, *Report of the 8th Annual Meeting of the Jt. Board of the Theological Colleges Affiliated with McGill, 1920–21*, 6

99 MUA, acc. 641, box 290, Department of Social Service, memo on Staff Conferences held Feb. 14 and 28th, nd; *Report of the Ninth Annual Meeting of the Jt. Theological Board* (1921), 14

100 MUA, acc. 641, box 290, Sir Arthur Currie to Reverend James Smyth, principal, Wesleyan College, 28 Mar. 1921

101 MUA, acc. 1563/1, Board of Governors Minutes, 30 Sept. 1920, 128

102 MUA, acc. 83 (Faculty of Arts), box 214, Statement from the Principal on the Closing of the School of Social Workers at McGill University, 4 Aug. 1931; J.H.T. Falk, in *McGill Annual Report* (1920–1), 114–15; Report of the Principal, *McGill Annual Report* (1931–2), 8

103 Allen, *Social Passion*, 67

104 MUA, acc. 641, box 290, Report of a Committee Appointed to Make Recommendations Regarding Sociology and Social Service, nd

105 See for example, MUA, acc. 641, box 290, Sir Arthur Currie to Mrs George MacDonald, 13 Feb. 1922.

106 *Report of the Ninth Annual Meeting of the Joint Theological Board*, 14; MUA, acc. 641, box 290, Report of a Committee to Make Recommendations; MUA, acc. 641, box 290, Director of the Department [J.H.T. Falk] to A.P.S. Glassco, 9 Feb. 1922

107 MUA, acc. 641, box 290, J. Falk to Sir Arthur Currie, 13 Feb. 1922

108 MUA, acc. 641, box 290, A Memorandum on a Department of Sociology and Social Service, by Stephen Leacock

109 MUA, acc. 641, box 290, Memo from Helen Reid to Committee of Management of Social Service Department, 15 Apr. 1922.

110 MUA, acc. 641, box 290, C.A. Dawson to Sir Arthur Currie, 24 Feb. 1921 (possibly misdated); MUA, acc. 641, box 290, Academic Record of Carl Addington Dawson.

111 MUA, Corporation Minutes, vol. 8, 8 May 1922, 312

112 MUA, acc. 83, box 214, Correspondence between Ernest M. Best and Gordon Laing, 26 July 1922

113 See for example Harry H. Hiller, 'Paradigmatic Shifts, Indigenization, and the Development of Sociology in Canada,' *Journal of the History of the Behavioural Sciences* 16 (July 1980): 266.

CHAPTER THREE: CARL DAWSON AND THE CHICAGO SCHOOL

1 C.A. Dawson's speech to the Alumni Conference of the Presbyterian College, Montreal, Oct. 1922, on 'The Church and Social Service,' reported in the United Church Archives [UCA], 'Synod of Montreal and Ottawa,' *Presbyterian Witness*, 26 Oct. 1922, 2

2 Carl Dawson, 'Research and Social Action,' *Social Welfare* 5 (Feb. 1923): 93–5

3 Ibid., 95; C.A. Dawson, 'The Rural Sociologist, His Point of View and Fields of Interest,' *Canadian Society of Technical Agriculturalists Review* 12 (Mar. 1937): 168. Paper read before the Canadian Society of Agricultural Economics at the University of New Brunswick, Fredericton, NB, 15 July 1936

4 C.A. Dawson, 'Social Research in Canada,' *Social Welfare* 9 (July 1927): 470

5 Such literature as exists on the development of social science in Canada tends to focus on the issue of academic involvement in (and opposition to) the formulation of public policy during the Depression years. See for example, Barry Ferguson and Doug Owram, 'Social Scientists and Public Policy, 1920–1945,' *Journal of Canadian Studies* 15 (Winter 1980–1): 3–17; Carl Berger, 'Harold Innis: The Search for Limits,' in *The Writing of Canadian History* (Toronto: Oxford University Press, 1976), 85–111; Michiel Horn, 'Academics in the Depression and the War Years,' *Journal of Canadian Studies* 13 (Winter 1978–9): 3–10.

6 'C.A. Dawson,' *Acadia Record*, nd, 110; Helen (Dawson) Strachan to D.W. Magill, 21 March 1979; Helen Strachan to M. Shore, 1 Feb. 1981

7 The Citation for Professor Dawson, read at convocation when Dawson received an honorary DCL from Acadia University, 14 Aug. 1956

8 C.A. Dawson's BA transcript, Acadia University

9 William S. Learned and Kenneth C.M. Sills, *Education in the Maritime Provinces of Canada* (New York: The Carnegie Foundation for the Advancement of Teaching 1922), 22

10 'Dawson,' *Acadia Record*, 110; Strachan to Shore, 1 Feb. 1981

11 Matthews, *Quest for an American Sociology*, 38

12 'Dawson,' *Acadia Record*, 110; MUA, acc. 641, box 290, Academic Record of Carl Addington Dawson; Strachan to Shore, 1 Feb. 1981; John Dawson to D.W. Magill, 5 June 1979

13 University of Chicago, Divinity School Announcements (1921), 81–3; Daniel Meyer, archives research specialist, Special Collections, Joseph Regenstein Library, University of Chicago, to M. Shore, 28 Oct. 1982

14 The Citation for Professor Dawson; Meyer to Shore, 28 Oct. 1982

15 MUA, acc. 641, box 290, Academic Record of Carl Addington Dawson; 'Dawson,' *Acadia Record*, 110
16 Strachan to Shore, 1 Feb. 1981
17 Duncan MacFarlane to D.W. Magill, 10 Feb. 1979
18 Ross, 'Development of the Social Sciences,' 115, 128; Ellis W. Hawley, *The Great War and the Search for a Modern Order: A History of the American People and Their Institutions, 1917–1933* (New York: St Martin's Press 1979), 150; Jean B. Quandt, *From the Small Town to the Great Community: The Social Thought of Progressive Intellectuals* (New Brunswick, NJ: Rutgers University Press 1970), 1–3, passim
19 Strachan to Shore, 1 Feb. 1981
20 Oswald Hall to D.W. Magill, 27 Feb. 1979, 5; Charles Young to D.W. Magill, 15 Feb. 1979
21 S.D. Clark, 'Sociology in Canada: an historical overview,' *Canadian Journal of Sociology* 1 (Summer 1975): 227
22 Richard J. Storr, *Harper's University. The Beginnings* (Chicago: University of Chicago Press 1966), 9–10, 41–2
23 Robert T. Handy, 'The Influence of Canadians on Baptist Theological Education in the United States,' *Foundations: A Baptist Journal of History and Theology* 23 (Jan.-Mar. 1980): 43, 54
24 Withrop S. Hudson, 'The Interrelationship of Baptists in Canada and the United States,' *Foundations* 23 (Jan.-Mar. 1980): 27–8
25 George Edward Levy, *The Baptists of the Maritime Provinces 1753–1946* (Saint John: Barnes-Hopkins 1946), 103–5
26 Sills and Learned, *Education in the Maritime Provinces*, 21–2. The authors also comment that 'the educational institutions of the Maritime provinces cannot be understood apart from the denominational religious life which created them and still definitely fosters them' (14).
27 Robert A. Falconer, 'American Influence on the Higher Education of Canada,' *Transactions and Proceedings of the Royal Society of Canada* 24 (1930): 26
28 Sills and Learned, *Education in the Maritime Provinces*, 21, 26; Falconer, 'American Influence,' 26. On the beginnings and objectives involved in the opening of a Baptist institution, see Barry Moody, 'The Maritime Baptists and Higher Education in the Nineteenth Century,' in Moody, ed., *Repent and Believe: The Baptist Experience in Maritime Canada* (Hantsport, NS 1980), 82–102; see also D.C. Masters, *Protestant Church Colleges in Canada* (Toronto: University of Toronto Press 1966), 12–13, 130, 153
29 Hudson, 'Interrelationship of Baptists,' 29
30 Acadia College Calendar 1898–9, 23

31 Masters, *Protestant Church Colleges*, 130–1; Acadia College Calendar (1900–1), 21
32 Acadia College Calendar (1910–11), 53–4; Calendar (1911–12), 61
33 V.A. Tomovic, 'Sociology in Canada: An Analysis of its Growth in English Language Universities, 1908–1972,' PHD thesis, University of Waterloo 1975, 85, 89
34 Hamilton Cravens, *The Triumph of Evolution: American Scientists and the Heredity-Environment Controversy, 1900–1940* (Philadelphia: University of Pennsylvania Press 1978), 123–4, 135; Graham Morgan, 'The Development of Sociology and the Social Gospel in America,' *Sociological Analysis: A Journal in the Sociology of Religion* 30 (Spring 1969): 48
35 Morgan, 'Sociology and the Social Gospel,' 43, 45, 51; Cravens, *Triumph of Evolution*, 123–4, 127
36 See for example the discussion in E.R. Forbes, 'Prohibition and the Social Gospel in Nova Scotia,' *Acadiensis* 1 (Autumn 1971): 13.
37 Morgan, 'Sociology and the Social Gospel,' 43, 52
38 McKillop, *A Disciplined Intelligence*, 217–22, 226
39 See for example Hudson's comments in 'Interrelationships between Baptists,' 38. Relative to their numbers, he argued, the Baptists played a major role in the social gospel. The Methodists were more prominent as leaders because they were more numerous, but in proportion to their numbers the Baptists do not seem to have lagged behind.
40 John S. Moir, '*The Canadian Baptist* and the Social Gospel Movement, 1879–1914,' in Jarold K. Zeman, ed., *Baptists in Canada: A Search for Identity Amidst Diversity* (Burlington: G.R. Welsh 1980), 147, 149, 155
41 Forbes, 'Prohibition in Nova Scotia,' 11, 14, 16
42 Quoted in ibid., 17, from Maritime Baptist Convention Year Book (1903), 22
43 Various pieces of evidence attest to the American influence on the Maritime Baptists. See for example Hudson, 'Interrelationship between Baptists,' 32–3. In the early months of 1903 the *Canadian Baptist* was full of stories about the University of Chicago, including a front-page editorial on the university; in April of the same year the principal speaker at McMaster commencement was William Rainey Harper, president of the University of Chicago. See also Levy, *Baptists of the Maritime Provinces*, 298–9, and Tumovic, 'Sociology in Canada,' 89.
44 Darnell Rucker, *The Chicago Pragmatists* (Minneapolis: University of Minnesota Press 1969), 107, 113–14, 130; William R. Hutchison, *The Modernist Impulse in American Protestantism* (Cambridge and London: Harvard University Press 1976), 114–15
45 Handy, 'The Influence of Canadians on Baptist Theological Education,' 43–4

46 Matthews, *Quest for An American Sociology*, 88–9; Rucker, *Chicago Pragmatists*, 158; Stephen J. Diner, *A City and Its Universities: Public Policy in Chicago, 1892–1919* (Chapel Hill: University of North Carolina Press 1980), 9; Martin Bulmer, *The Chicago School of Sociology: Institutionalization, Diversity, and the Rise of Sociological Research* (Chicago and London: University of Chicago Press 1984), 8

47 Storr, *Harper's University*, 304; Diner, *A City and Its Universities*, 21, 32–3, 122; Bulmer, *The Chicago School of Sociology*, 15, 16

48 Gerald Birney Smith, 'Practical Theology: A Neglected Field of Theological Education,' in *The Decennial Publications of the University of Chicago*, 1st ser. (1903), edited by a committee appointed by the Senate, 86

49 Hutchison, *Modernist Impulse*, 4–6

50 Rucker, *Chicago Pragmatists*, 138, 159; Hutchison, *Modernist Impulse*, 227–8. In 1924 Shailer Mathews published his *Faith of Modernism*, in which he argued that modernism was the determination to use scientific, historical, and social methods to understand and apply evangelical Christianity to the needs of human beings; see Rucker, *Chicago Pragmatists*, 131.

51 University of Toronto Archives (UTA), acc. A-66-003, Office of the President (Robert Falconer Papers), J. Davidson Ketchum, Journal and Impressions of a Visit to Chicago, Oct. 1927, 14

52 Rucker, *Chicago Pragmatists*, 4–5, 28; see also the discussion on 'the revolt against formalism' in Eric Goldman, *Rendezvous with Destiny* (New York: Vintage Books 1955), 120, and Cravens, *Triumph of Evolution*, 7

53 John Dewey, *The Influence of Darwinism on Philosophy and Other Essays in Contemporary Thought* (New York: Henry Holt 1910), 1–11

54 Rucker, *Chicago Pragmatists*, 28

55 Goldman, *Rendezvous with Destiny*, 122–3

56 Dewey, *Influence of Darwinism*, 11–12, 17

57 Quoted in Rucker, *Chicago Pragmatists*, 44; see also in ibid., 29, 43–4.

58 Ibid., 50–1; Hutchison, *Modernist Impulse*, 107–9, 111. Hutchison points out that another Chicago philosopher, Frederick G. Henke, explained in his *The Psychology of Ritualism* that the functional view of religion attempted to relate it to the total life-process. It represented the way in which human beings adapted themselves to their environment (110).

59 Ellsworth Faris, quoted in Rucker, *Chicago Pragmatists*, 137–8; Bulmer, *The Chicago School of Sociology*, 31, 38

60 Dewey, *Influence of Darwinism*, 17

61 Ross, 'Development of the Social Sciences,' 114

62 Hawley, *Search for a Modern Order*, 6, 156–8, 226, 229

63 Matthews, *Quest for An American Sociology*, 101–4, and in greater detail in chap. 5, 'The City as Symbol'; Cravens, *The Triumph of Evolution*, 123–4

64 Robert E.L. Faris, *Chicago Sociology 1920–32* (San Francisco: Chandler 1967), 32, 80
65 MUA, acc. 641, box 290, Gordon Laing to Sir Arthur Currie, 10 July 1922
66 C.A. Dawson, 'The Social Nature of Knowledge,' PH D diss., University of Chicago 1922, 1–2
67 C.A. Dawson and W.E. Gettys, *Introduction to Sociology* (New York: Ronald Press 1929), 696
68 Hutchison, *Modernist Impulse*, 104
69 Dawson, 'Social Nature of Knowledge,' 65
70 Ibid., 62–3
71 Ibid., 57–9, 64; Dawson and Gettys, *Introduction to Sociology* (1929 edn), 774
72 Dawson, 'Social Nature of Knowledge,' 60
73 Dawson and Gettys, *Introduction to Sociology* (1929 edn), 328–329, 341
74 Matthews, *Quest for an American Sociology*, 50–6
75 Ibid., 7–12, 56, 83–8, 94
76 Ibid., 168
77 Ibid., 19. Dawson extracted the analogy of the buffalo herd from Robert E. Park and Ernest W. Burgess, *Introduction to the Science of Sociology* (1921; repr. Chicago and London: University of Chicago Press 1969). They, in turn, adopted it from D.L. Sharp, 'The Spirit of the Herd,' *Atlantic* 113 (Mar. 1914): 338ff
78 Dawson, 'Social Nature of Knowledge,' 16. For much of his discussion on man's vocal mechanism, Dawson cited the influence of George Herbert Mead's lectures and articles; he did not give specific citations. On the development of symbols and common meaning he was influenced by John Dewey's *Human Nature and Conduct: An Introduction to Social Psychology* (London: George Allen and Unwin 1922), 60, and Emile Durkheim, as quoted by Park and Burgess in *Science of Sociology*, 39; the quotation is from Ghelke's translation, 'Emile Durkheim's Contribution to Sociological Theory,' *Studies in History, Economics, and Public Law* 63, p 30.
79 Dawson, 'Social Nature of Knowledge,' 156–7, 170, 178
80 Ibid., 31–3. Once again, Dawson cited the influence of Park's *Masse und Publikum*, np; Dewey, *Human Nature and Conduct*.
81 Dawson, 'Social Nature of Knowledge,' 165–8
82 Ibid., 185
83 Ibid., 96
84 Dawson, 'Research and Social Action,' 94
85 Matthews, *Quest for An American Sociology*, 38. See also Anselm Strauss, in Strauss, ed., *George Herbert Mead in Social Psychology, Selected Papers* (rev. edn, Chicago and London: University of Chicago Press 1969), xix: 'As species disappear and evolve, so do institutions and societies. In man

292 Notes to pages 93–6

evolution can be directed through intelligent action, itself made possible by the purely human capacity for symbolization. "Science is the finest instance of intelligence at work and represents the hope of mankind for the solution of social problems."'

86 Raymond Aron, *Main Currents in Sociological Thought II*, trans. Richard Howard and Helen Weaver (New York: Doubleday 1970), 26

87 Dawson, 'Research and Social Action,' 95–6

88 Learned and Sills, *Education in the Maritime Provinces*, 14. See also Masters, *Protestant Church Colleges*, 207; Samuel J. Mikolaski, 'Identity and Mission,' in Zeman, ed., *Baptists in Canada*, 1–20. On the competency of the individual in the Baptist faith and the role accordingly played by laypersons in establishing and spreading the faith in the Maritime region, see Esther Clark Wright, 'Without Intervention of Prophet, Priest or King,' in Moody, ed., *Repent and Believe*, 66–74.

89 H.A. Innis, preface to *Letters of William Davies, Toronto: 1854–1861*, ed. William Sherwood Fox (Toronto: University of Toronto Press 1945), vii–viii

90 G.A. Rawlyk, *Ravished by the Spirit: Religious Revivals, Baptists, and Henry Alline*, Hayward Lectures (Kingston and Montreal: McGill-Queen's University Press 1984), 80, 103–4.

91 Matthews, *Quest for An American Sociology*, 139–40; Amos Hawley, intro. to R.D. McKenzie, *On Human Ecology: Selected Writings* (Chicago and London: University of Chicago Press 1968), xi

92 James A. Quinn, 'The Development of Human Ecology,' in *Contemporary Social Theory*, ed. Harry Elmer Barnes and Howard Becker (New York and London: Appleton Century 1940), 212 n 1; Emma Llewelyn and Audrey Hawthorn, 'Human Ecology,' in *Twentieth Century Sociology*, ed. George Gurvitch and Wilbur Moore (New York: Philosophic Library 1945), 492

93 C.A. Dawson, 'Human Ecology,' in *The Fields and Methods of Sociology*, ed. L.L. Bernard (New York: Ray Lang and Richard Smith 1934), 286–302. The chapter was cited frequently by Milla Aïssa Alihan in her *Social Ecology: A Critical Analysis* (New York: Columbia University Press 1938).

94 Hamilton Cravens and John C. Burnham, 'Psychology and Evolutionary Naturalism in American Thought, 1890–1940,' *American Quarterly* 23 (Dec 1971): 635. Cravens' *Triumph of Evolution* is a more general discussion of the same theme; see also Rosalind Rosenberg, *Beyond Separate Spheres: Intellectual Roots of Modern Feminism* (New Haven and London: Yale University Press 1982). Rosenberg demonstrates the important contribution that academics at Chicago and Columbia made to feminist theories by breaking away from mechanistic philosophies of human behaviour to stress environmental conditioning.

95 Sharon Kingsland, *Modeling Nature: Population Ecology and Evolution in the Twentieth Century* (Chicago: University of Chicago Press 1985), chap. 2, 'The Entangled Bank.'
96 Robert P. McIntosh, 'Ecology Since 1900,' in *Issues and Ideas in America*, ed. Benjamin J. Taylor and Thurman J. White (Norman: University of Oklahoma Press 1967), 353; Alihan, *Social Ecology*, 242–3; Dawson and Gettys, *Introduction to Sociology* (1929 edn), 213
97 While Dawson noted that studies of plant ecology had been conspicuous since the beginning of the nineteenth century, he did not trace them back any farther than that. See Dawson, 'Human Ecology,' 288.
98 Ibid., 144, 149–50
99 See Dov Ospovat, *The Development of Darwin's Theory: Natural History, Natural Theology, and Natural Selection, 1838–1859* (Cambridge, London, New York: Cambridge University Press 1981), who shows in detail how the idea of 'relative adaptation' resulted from Darwin's emphasis upon biotic relations: see espec. chap. 8, 'The Principle of Divergence and the Transformation of Darwin's Theory,' 191–209.
100 Frank W. Egerton, 'Ecological Studies and Observations before 1900,' in *Issues and Ideas in America*, 341; Matthews, *Quest for An American Sociology*, 137
101 McIntosh, 'Ecology since 1900,' 353
102 Dawson, 'Human Ecology,' 288; Dawson and Gettys cited Warming in *Introduction to Sociology* (1929 edn), 213; Robert Park, 'The Concept of Position in Sociology,' in *The City*, Publications of the American Sociological Society 20, pp. 1–14. In what was his presidential address to the American Sociological Society, Park also argued that Warming called attention to the fact that different species of plants tended to form permanent groups, which he called 'communities.'
103 McIntosh, 'Ecology since 1900,' 353; Worster, *Nature's Economy*, 206
104 Worster, *Nature's Economy*, 206
105 Ibid., 209
106 McIntosh, 'Ecology since 1900,' 354; Worster, *Nature's Economy*, 206–8
107 Matthews, *Quest for An American Sociology*, 138
108 Frederic Clements, *Plant Succession: An Analysis of the Growth of Vegetation* (Washington: Carnegie Institution 1916), 75–6, 124–5
109 Worster, *Nature's Economy*, 212
110 In the decades after Darwin most of the ecological work on competition and succession was conducted in a neo-Larmarckian framework, stressing the inheritance of acquired characters. This was because by the 1890s, when self-professed ecologists did emerge, the idea of natural selection as an all-pervasive force in evolution was on the wane and there was a tendency to

use a hybrid picked up from Darwin, Lamarck, and Spencer (who was a Lamarckian). F.E. Clements, for instance, was a neo-Lamarckian in his belief that it was possible to create new species by changing the location. (I would like to thank Sharon Kingsland for explaining the complexities of ecological theory to me and for referring me to Peter J. Bowler's work, *The Eclipse of Darwinism.*)

111 Robert Park, 'Human Ecology,' *American Journal of Sociology* 42 (July 1936): 6
112 Dawson, 'Human Ecology,' 286, 288
113 Park, 'Human Ecology,' 3
114 James A. Quinn, 'The Development of Human Ecology in Sociology,' 212. For other definitions of human ecology, see R.D. McKenzie, 'The Ecological Approach to the Study of the Human Community,' *American Journal of Sociology* 30 (Nov. 1924): 287; R.D. McKenzie, 'Human Ecology,' *Encyclopedia of the Social Sciences* (1936), 314; Alihan, *Social Ecology: A Critical Analysis*; Llewelyn and Hawthorn, 'Human Ecology,' chap. 16, in Gurvitch and Moore, eds. *Twentieth Century Sociology*, 492–5.
115 Dawson and Gettys, *An Introduction to Sociology* (1929 edn), 220
116 Park, 'Human Ecology,' 1–3
117 Alihan, *Social Ecology*, 29–42
118 Park, 'Concept of Position,' 1; Alihan, *Social Ecology*, 1; Llewelyn and Hawthorn, 'Human Ecology,' 492
119 Worster, *Nature's Economy*, viii, 37–8
120 Ibid., 158
121 Ibid., 286–90
122 Ibid., 286
123 Dawson and Gettys, *An Introduction to Sociology* (1929 edn), 826–7
124 The link between natural history and ecology has been noted by Paul Sears, 'Some Notes on the Ecology of Ecologists,' *Scientific Monthly* 83 (July 1956): 23, and Carl Berger, *Science, God, and Nature in Victorian Canada* (Toronto: University of Toronto Press 1983), 33; the integrative nature of ecology as a discipline that ranged over plants, insects, aquatic organisms, and terrestrial vertebrates and employed elements of physiology, morphology, natural history, taxonomy, and geography has been noted by McIntosh, 'Ecology Since 1900,' 355–6, and Kingsland, 'The Entangled Bank,' in *Modeling Nature.*
125 Dawson, 'Human Ecology,' 287; Ellen Churchill Semple's discussion of Ratzel's *Anthropogéographie* in her *Influences of the Geographic Environment: On the Basis of Ratzel's System of Anthropo-geography* (1911; New York: Holt, Rinehart, and Winston 1968), vii, 51, 71

126 Paul Vidal de la Blache, *Principles of Human Geography*, ed. Emmanuel de Martonne, trans. Millicent Todd Bingham (New York: Henry Holt 1926), 10, 165–6
127 J. Nicholas Entrikin, 'Robert Park's Human Ecology and Human Geography,' *Annals of the Association of American Geographers* 70 (Mar. 1980): 44–5, 54–5; Park, 'Concept of Position in Sociology,' 2
128 Dawson, 'Human Ecology,' 288. In the 1930s McKenzie elaborated upon the differences between human ecology and other closely related fields. He noted that human ecology differed from human geography in that the main object of its attention was 'neither the population aggregate nor the physical-cultural habitat but rather the relations of man to man.' The human ecologist concerned himself with 'the nexus of sustenance and place relations of individuals and institutions which [gave] the community its characteristic form and organization.' McKenzie, 'Demography, Human Geography, and Human Ecology,' 33–48, in R.D. McKenzie, *On Human Ecology*, repr. from L.L. Bernard, ed., *The Fields and Methods of Sociology*.
129 Alihan, *Social Ecology*, 3
130 R.D. McKenzie, 'The Ecological Approach to the Study of the Human Community,' *Journal of American Sociology* 30 (July 1926): 141–54; Hawley, intro. to McKenzie, *On Human Ecology*, vii–ix
131 R.D. McKenzie, 'The Concept of Dominance and World-Organization,' *Journal of American Sociology* 33 (July 1927): 28–41
132 See Carl Berger, *The Writing of Canadian History*, 123, 176–8, 243: the idea that the metropolis was the organizing centre of business, politics, and culture and that it exerted control over a hinterland grew out of the economic history of N.S.B. Gras, the Innis staples approach, and the Chicago school of sociology.
133 Hawley, intro. to McKenzie, *On Human Ecology*, viii–ix; Edward Shils, 'Tradition, Ecology, and the Institution in the History of Sociology,' *Daedalus* 9 (Fall 1970): 797
134 McKenzie's definition of plant ecology in 'The Ecological Approach to the Study of the Human Community,' 287, is taken from *Encyclopedia Americana* (New York 1923), 555; the comment on mobility as the distinctive factor in human society is derived from McKenzie, 'The Ecological Approach to the Study of the Human Community,' 288–9.
135 Dawson, 'Human Ecology,' 294; Dawson and Gettys, *Introduction to Sociology* (1929 edn), 5, 9, 10. See also E.W. Burgess and D.J. Bogue, 'Research in Human Society: A Long View,' cited in Burgess and Bogue, eds., *Contributions to Urban Sociology* (Chicago: University of Chicago Press, Phoenix edn, 1964), 1–5; Alihan, *Social Ecology*, 42

136 Charles C. Galpin, 'The Social Anatomy of an Agricultural Community,' *Research Bulletin* 34 (University of Wisconsin 1915)

137 Dawson, 'Human Ecology,' 290–1

138 McKenzie, 'The Ecological Approach to the Study of the Human Community,' 298; Dawson and Gettys, *An Introduction to Sociology* (1929 edn), 217–19

139 Alihan, *Social Ecology*, 43–4

140 Llewelyn and Hawthorn, 'Human Ecology,' 492

141 Dawson, 'Human Ecology,' 294–5; Dawson's argument was noted and reiterated by Alihan, *Social Ecology*, 114–15; see also McKenzie, 'The Ecological Approach to the Study of the Human Community,' 289–90.

142 C.M. Child, *Physiological Foundations of Human Behaviour* (New York: Henry Holt 1920)

143 Dawson and Gettys, *An Introduction to Sociology* (1929 edn), 159

144 Alihan, *Social Ecology*, 108–9; McKenzie, 'The Concept of Dominance,' 28. (McKenzie's article began with a very lengthy discussion of Child's *Physiological Foundations of Human Behaviour*.)

145 McKenzie, 'The Concept of Dominance,' 29–32; Alihan, *Social Ecology*, 112–13

146 See Matthews, chap. 5, 'The City as Symbol,' *Quest for An American Sociology*.

147 McKenzie, 'The Concept of Dominance,' 32

148 See, for example, Berger, *The Writing of Canadian History*, 142, and the more general discussion of Canadian academics in the United States during the interwar years in chap. 6, 'A North American Nation,' in ibid.

149 Henrika Kuklick, 'A "Scientific Revolution": Sociological Theory in the United States,' *Sociological Inquiry* 43 (1): 10

150 Cravens, *The Triumph of Evolution*, 15–16, 18; Faris, *Chicago Sociology*, 15–16

151 Much of this paragraph is based upon Cravens and Burnham, 'Psychology and Evolutionary Naturalism,' 636–8; see also George W. Stocking Jr, 'Lamarckianism in American Social Science, 1890–1915,' *Journal of the History of Ideas* 23 (1962): 239–56.

152 Cravens and Burnham, 'Evolutionary Naturalism,' 642, 648–9, 655

153 'Society for Social Research,' *Social Research Bulletin* no 2 (Aug. 26), in Dawson and Gettys, *An Introduction to Sociology* (1929 edn), 586, 590, 591

154 Cravens and Burnham, 'Evolutionary Naturalism,' 656 n 51; the development of this new 'interactionist paradigm' is the subject of much of Cravens, *Triumph of Evolution*; see espec. 89.

155 Cravens, citing L.L. Bernard, in *Triumph of Evolution*, 121

156 McKenzie, 'Human Ecology,' *Encyclopedia of the Social Sciences*, 314–15
157 Park, 'Human Ecology,' 12, 14
158 Matthews, *Quest for an American Sociology*, 132
159 Ibid., 137–40; Alihan, *Social Ecology*, 94–5
160 Dawson and Gettys, *An Introduction to Sociology* (1929 edn), 3, 586, 605; Alihan, *Social Ecology*, 97
161 Cravens, *Triumph of Evolution*, xx, 8–10, 89–90, 219
162 Melville J. Herkovitz, *Franz Boas: The Science of Man in the Making* (New York and London: Charles Scribner's Sons 1953)
163 Cravens, *Triumph of Evolution*, 1–8, 121
164 Park and Burgess, *Science of Sociology*, cited in Dawson and Gettys, *Introduction to Sociology* (1929 edn), 116
165 Dawson and Gettys, *Introduction to Sociology* (1929 edn), 76–8. Much of Dawson and Gettys's ideas about language came from Edward Sapir's work. They quoted a lengthy section of his *Language* (New York: Harcourt and Brace 1921), 7. When that work was published, Sapir believed that language had an entirely physiological basis. Dawson added, however, that on its physical side, language was a function of the individual organism, while on the social side it was a product of social interaction. See Dawson and Gettys, *Introduction to Sociology* (1929 edn), 228, 234.
166 Alihan, *Social Ecology*, 12
167 Dawson and Gettys, *Introduction to Sociology*, 3–5, 76–8, 568
168 Ibid., 564–5. Adapted from Cooley, *Social Process*
169 Dawson and Gettys, *Introduction to Sociology* (1929 edn), 566, 568
170 Ibid., 277

CHAPTER FOUR: METROPOLIS AND HINTERLAND

1 Dawson, 'Research and Social Action,' 95
2 Matthews, *Quest for An American Sociology*, 28
3 Dawson, 'Research and Social Action,' 95–6
4 Kerry, Prospectus, 2–3; *McGill Annual Report* (1923), School for Social Workers: Foreword and History, 468; *McGill Calendar* (1922–3), 412–14; Laing to Currie, 10 July 1922
5 *McGill Annual Report* (1923), School for Social Workers, 463
6 C.A. Dawson, 'Social Workers in the Making,' *Social Welfare* 13 (Nov. 1930): 27
7 *McGill Annual Report* (1923), School for Social Workers, 463
8 Dawson and Gettys, *Introduction to Sociology* (1929 edn), 823

9 MUA, acc. 641, box 290, Memorandum Concerning Sociology, Everett Hughes to L.W. Douglas, 8 Apr. 1938, 4–5, 8

10 C.A. Dawson, 'The City as an Organism. With Special Reference to Montreal,' in *McGill University Publications* (ser. 13, no 10 (1926): 3–4; repr. from *Town Planning* (Ottawa, Aug. 1926)

11 Ibid., 9–10. The article on the city, initially published in a town-planning publication and then reprinted in a McGill architectural volume, received fairly wide attention. In 1927 it was reprinted in *La Revue municipale* 5, (Dec 1927): 11–12; in 1943 it appeared in *Montréal économique*, a collection of articles published by Esdras Minville and the Ecole d'Hautes Etudes Commerciales. In the latter the theory of concentric circles was accepted as valid for all cities, and Dawson's explanation of how they varied in Montreal was regarded as equally true.

12 Dawson, 'The City,' 9

13 Ibid., 10

14 Dawson and Gettys, *Introduction to Sociology* (1929 edn), 826. The argument about the usefulness of city research for reformers also appeared in one of Dawson's students' theses – see Wilfrid Emmerson Israel, 'The Montreal Negro Community,' MA thesis, McGill 1928, 242; Dawson, 'The City,' 10.

15 Paul Rutherford, ed., *Saving the Canadian City: The First Phase 1880–1920* (Toronto: University of Toronto Press 1974), ix–xii, xvii, xxi

16 Matthews, *Quest for An American Sociology*, 121; Park, 'The City,' *American Journal of Sociology* 20 (Mar. 1915); Claude S. Fischer, 'The Study of Urban Community and Personality,' *Annual Review of Sociology* 1 (1975): 67

17 Mary Harper, 'Chicago Revisited,' *Harper's*, April 1931, 541–7, cited in Matthews, *Quest for An American Sociology*, 126

18 Fischer, 'Urban Community and Personality,' 67–8; Matthews, *Quest for An American Sociology*, 130

19 Louis Wirth, 'The Urban Society and Civilization,' *in Eleven Twenty-Six: A Decade of Social Science Research*, ed. Louis Wirth (Chicago: University of Chicago Press 1940), 63; that a distinct urban sociology had emerged from the Chicago school in the 1930s was evident with the publication of Louis Wirth's 'Urbanism as a Way of Life,' *American Journal of Sociology* 44 (July 1938): 3–24, reprinted in *Community Life and Social Policy*, ed. Elizabeth Wirth Marvick and Albert J. Reiss, Jr (Chicago: University of Chicago Press 1956).

20 Wirth, 'The Urban Society,' 63

21 Muriel Bernice McCall, 'A Study of Family Disorganization in Canada,' MA thesis, McGill 1928, 66

22 Matthews, *Quest for An American Sociology*, 141–2

23 Percy, 'Dufferin District,' 109–10; Matthews, *Quest for an American Sociology*, 104
24 Frederick Austin Ogg, *Research in the Humanistic and Social Sciences: Report of a Survey Conducted for the American Council of Learned Societies* (New York and London: Century 1928), 63
25 Matthews, *Quest for an American Sociology*, 128
26 Dawson, 'Human Ecology,' 294
27 Ibid., 294; Ketchum, 'Impressions,' 2–3, 13
28 Dawson, 'Human Ecology,' 292–3
29 Burgess and Bogue, 'Research in Urban Society,' 1–5; Faris, *Chicago Sociology*, 55; Matthews, *Quest for An American Sociology*, 141
30 R.D. McKenzie, *The Neighborhood: A Study of Local Life in the City of Columbus, Ohio* (Chicago; University of Chicago Press 1923); Richard M. Hurd, *Principles of City Land Values* (1903; repr. New York: The Record and Guide 1924). See also Dawson, 'Human Ecology,' 291; Dawson and Gettys, *Introduction to Sociology*, 9.
31 E.W. Burgess, 'The Growth of the City,' *Publications of the American Sociological Society* 18 (1924): 85–97; Dawson, 'Human Ecology,' 292–4
32 Dawson, 'Human Ecology,' 292–3
33 Dawson and Gettys, *Introduction to Sociology* (1929 edn), 212
34 Matthews, *Quest for An American Sociology*, 126, 141
35 Alihan, *Social Ecology*, 54–5. See, for instance, Robert Park, 'The Concept of Position,' 1. Park explained that local transportation and geography divided the city into areas that acquired definite occupational and population groups.
36 Park, 'Concept of Position,' 1
37 McKenzie, 'Ecological Approach to the Study of the Human Community,' 298–300
38 Robert Park, 'The City as a Social Laboratory,' in *Chicago: An Experiment in Social Science Research*, ed. T.V. Smith and Leonard D. White (Chicago: University of Chicago Press 1929), cited in Matthews, *Quest for An American Sociology*, 10
39 Matthews, *Quest for An American Sociology*, 132, 143–4; Park, 'Concept of Position,' 3. On the centrality of the idea of mobility to human ecology in general and the city in particular, see Alihan, *Social Ecology*, 59, 101.
40 Dawson, 'Human Ecology,' 299–300; Nels Anderson, *The Hobo: The Sociology of the Homeless Man* (Chicago: University of Chicago Press 1923); Frederic Thrasher, *The Gang* (Chicago; University of Chicago Press 1927); C.R. Shaw, *Delinquency Areas* (Chicago: University of Chicago Press 1929), and *The Jackroller* (Chicago: University of Chicago Press 1930)

41 Matthews, *Quest for an American Sociology*, 142; Faris, *Chicago Sociology*, 56–7
42 Dawson and Gettys, *Introduction to Sociology* (1929 edn), 30, 128, 223
43 Ibid., 223. Dawson cited as support Charles Cooley's article 'Personal Competition,' in American Economic Association, *Economic Studies* vol. 4, no 2 (New York: Macmillan 1899).
44 C.A. Dawson, 'Population Areas and Physiographic Regions in Canada,' *American Journal of Sociology* 33 (July 1927): 50
45 Wood, *The Storied Province of Quebec*, vol. 2, 775–81; Dawson, 'Physiographic Regions,' 51. Dawson also admitted that Canada had two centres of dominance – Montreal and Toronto. Paul-André Linteau, René Durocher, Jean-Claude Robert, *Quebec: A History 1867–1929*, trans. Robert Chodos (Toronto: Lorimer 1983), 344–5, 352, 361
46 Dawson, 'Physiographic Areas,' 51
47 Wood, *The Storied Province of Quebec*, vol. 2, 776
48 Linteau, Durocher, et al., *Quebec*, 322, 331, 360, 513; Susan Mann Trofimenkoff, *The Dream of Nation* (Toronto: Gage 1983), 225–6; Albert Faucher and Maurice Lamontagne, 'History of Industrial Development,' *French Canadian Society* ed. Marcel Rioux and Yves Martin (Toronto: McClelland & Stewart 1964), vol. 1, 266–8
49 Linteau, Durocher, et al., *Quebec*, 356–7, 362; Trofimenkoff, *Dream of Nation*, 74, 223
50 Dawson, 'The City,' 3–7
51 Dawson and Gettys, *Introduction to Sociology* (1929 edn), 69, citing Harvey W. Zorbaugh's *Gold Coast and Slum* (Chicago: University of Chicago Press 1929)
52 See, for instance, Wilfrid Emmerson Israel, 'The Montreal Negro Community,' MA thesis, McGill 1928, preface, np.
53 Ruth Rutnam, 'Mobility and Boy Behaviour,' MA thesis, McGill 1927, 6
54 Sidney Garland, 'The Church in the Changing City,' MA thesis, McGill 1929, 1–3; Israel, 'The Negro Community,' 10
55 Israel, 'The Negro Community,' 10, 16
56 Richard E.G. Davis, 'The Montreal Young Men's Christian Association as a Religious and Social Institution,' MA thesis, McGill 1927, 6–7; Israel, 'The Montreal Negro Community,' 9, 16–17
57 Ibid., 1, 6, 2–26, 44–5
58 In 'A Sociological Study of the Dependent Child' (MA thesis, McGill 1931), Margaret Millicent Wade argued that in the centre of Montreal, a modern city in the new world, there were conditions that could rival those existing in any European slums, 'conditions which many would not believe existed in the twentieth century' (18). This was the famous 'City below the Hill.'

59 Percy, 'Dufferin District,' 110
60 Ibid., iv
61 Ibid., 6, 15
62 Ibid., 3
63 Ibid., 12–17, 20, 31
64 Ibid., 6, 89–93
65 Ibid., 8–9
66 Ibid., 103–5
67 Ibid., 17, 103–5
68 Rutnam, 'Mobility and Boy Behaviour,' 3, 72
69 Wade, 'The Dependent Child,' 17–22
70 Garland, 'The Church in the Changing City,' i–ii
71 Ibid., 25–40, 124–5
72 Davis, 'The Montreal YMCA,' 6
73 Ibid., 6, 10–12, 18
74 The statistics were derived from the Montreal YMCA's report of 1879, cited in Davis, 'The Montreal YMCA,' 44.
75 Ibid., 44, 48–59
76 Ibid., 62–7
77 Dawson and Gettys, *Introduction to Sociology* (1929 edn), 147, 150, 157–8; McKenzie, 'Concept of Dominance,' 159; Hughes, 'Memorandum Concerning Sociology,' 5–6
78 J.W. Jeudwine, *Studies in Empire and Trade* (New York and Toronto: Longman's, Green 1923), cited in McKenzie, 'Concept of Dominance,' 32–4; Dawson and Gettys, *Introduction to Sociology* (1929 edn), 159–60
79 N.S.B. Gras, *An Introduction to Economic History* (New York and London: Harper and Brothers 1922), 183–269
80 Dawson and Gettys, *Introduction to Sociology*, 171–2
81 Ibid., 127, 178, 220; McKenzie, 'Concept of Dominance,' 39
82 Dawson, 'Physiographic Regions,' 45, 48; see a similar discussion in A. Moellman, 'The Germans in Canada: Occupational and Social Adjustment of German Immigrants in Canada,' MA thesis, McGill 1934, 1–2
83 Dawson, 'Physiographic Regions,' 47
84 S.D. Clark, 'The Role of Metropolitan Institutions in the Formation of a Canadian National Consciousness – with Special Reference to the United States,' MA thesis, McGill 1935. Clark came to McGill in the 1930s, when the Sociology Department had funds, granted by the American Social Science Research Council, to take on graduate students as research assistants. For background on the Carnegie series and how it grew from the increasing

interest in the late 1920s in Canadian-American connections and in a continental approach to North American history, see Carl Berger, 'Internationalism, Continentalism, and the Writing of History: Comments on the Carnegie Series on the Relations of Canada and the United States,' in *The Influence of the United States on Canadian Development: Eleven Case Studies*, ed. Richard A. Preston (Durham, North Carolina: Duke University Press 1972), 35–6; Berger, *The Writing of Canadian History*, chap. 6, 'A North American Nation,' 145–59.

85 While he was still a student at McGill, Clark met with Harold Innis and later wrote to him about his dissatisfaction with the McGill Sociology Department. While he felt that he had got a great deal out of studying sociology – it had given him a theoretical background, and he had a pleasant relationship with Dawson and Everett Hughes – most of the research dealt with immigration, and he had taken on something quite different. University of Toronto Archives, Department of Political Economy Papers, acc. A76-025, S.D. Clark to H.A. Innis, 24 May 1935

86 Clark, 'Metropolitan Institutions,' i–iii

87 Ibid., 49–50, 178

88 Ibid., 3–4

89 Ibid., 19, 29–32

90 Ibid., 21–2

91 Ibid., 24

92 Ibid., 87, 106

93 Ibid., 86

94 Ibid., 64–76, 91–3

95 In some respects Clark's PH D study on the Canadian Manufacturers' Association grew out of his McGill masters thesis. In the latter Clark examined metropolitan interest groups, the CMA among them, and the role they played in the formation of Canadian nationalism; the objective of his later study, *The Canadian Manufacturers' Association: A Study of Collective Bargaining and Political Pressure* (Toronto: University of Toronto Press 1939), was to analyse the history of an association that reflected the difficulties of organizing markets, manufacturing industrial products, and securing a common aim in a transcontinental country. While Clark acknowledged his indebtedness to Dawson and Hughes for first arousing his interest in the study, he said that the quality of the finished product owed much to the direction of Harold Innis and Alexander Brady (see vii, xiii). Clark had explained to Innis that he did not want to get 'bogged down' in Canadian social history and thought that a study of economic pressure groups would enable him 'to delve further into the social theory of organized groups and the theory of the

state' (UTA, Political Economy Papers, acc. A76-025, box 9, S.D. Clark to H.A. Innis, 15 Mar. 1938). Ironically, that objective seems to have been closer to the basis of his McGill study, particularly his conclusions regarding the motive force in nationalism.

96 Dawson and Gettys, *Introduction to Sociology* (1929 edn), 173; see also McKenzie, 'The Scope of Human Ecology,' 146–7.

97 Dawson and Gettys, *Introduction to Sociology*, rev. edn (1935), 156; Dawson, 'Rural Sociology,' 170; see also the extended discussion of regional sociology in Jean Hunter, 'The French Invasion of the Eastern Townships,' MA thesis, McGill 1939, xiv–xv. Other prominent members of the Chicago Sociology Department did further research on the subject of regional sociology, advancing the notion that a region was tied together by a main city; they showed that in the United States the matrix in which settlement, institutions, and customs grew conformed to the area of trade relations and that political and social institutions followed. Of course, they believed that the area of trade relations was determined by the influence of the area of dominance. See, for instance, Robert Park, 'Urbanization as Measured by Newspaper Circulation,' *American Journal of Sociology* 35 (July 1929): 60–79; and R.D. McKenzie, *The Metropolitan Community* (New York and London: McGraw-Hill 1933), which illustrated that a pattern of city regionalism was evident in the United States by 1900 – the railway had laid the foundation for it by creating a network of large gateway cities that served to integrate surrounding territories and draw the nation together into a single economic unity; motor transportation was more influential because it reduced the scale of social distance and extended the horizon of the community while not fundamentally changing the main outlines of the railway pattern of settlement.

98 Dawson, 'Physiographic Areas,' 43–4; Dawson and Gettys, *Introduction to Sociology*, rev. edn (1935), 157

99 Ibid., 43, 51–2

100 Ibid., 49–51, 54

101 Ibid., 44, 54–5

102 Ibid., 56

103 Ibid., 54–5

104 Dawson, 'Rural Sociology,' 169

105 Dawson and Gettys, *Introduction to Sociology* (1929 edn), 173

106 Ibid., 296–7

107 Roderick Peattie, 'The Isolation of the Lower St. Lawrence Valley,' *The Geographical Review* 5 (1918): 102–18. Cited in Dawson and Gettys, *Introduction to Sociology* (1929 edn), 286–95

CHAPTER FIVE: FRONTIERS OF SETTLEMENT

1 Dorothy Swaine Thomas, 'Research Memorandum on Migration Differentials,' Social Science Research Council bulletin no 43 (New York: Social Science Research Council 1938); Cravens, *The Triumph of Evolution*, 180–2

2 Cravens, *The Triumph of Evolution*, 180–2. Cravens argues that the hallmark of the sociologists' studies on immigration was the attention they paid to biological as well as to cultural influences and that the work they published during the 1920s and 30s signalled the importance of the cultural aspects of human existence while implying that it was the domain of the social sciences.

3 Robert M. Yerkes, 'The Work of [the] Committee on Scientific Problems of Human Migration, National Research Council,' *The Journal of Personnel Research* 3 (1924–5): 189–96

4 Cravens, *Triumph of Evolution*, 181–3; Social Science Research Council, *Report on Scientific Aspects of Human Migration*, 18 Dec. 1926, 34. The Social Science Research Council was formally organized in 1923, though in 1922 the research committee of the American Political Science Association, through its chairman, Charles Merriam of the University of Chicago, submitted a report urging close co-operation between students of politics and other kinds of social scientists and among biologists, engineers, economists, and historians. He envisaged the creation of a clearing-house for projects of investigation and hoped to encourage institutes to work in social fields. The ssrc began as a joint enterprise of political scientists, economists, sociologists, and statisticians, but in 1925 historians, anthropologists, and psychologists also voted to participate. See Ogg, *Research in the Humanistic and Social Sciences*, 21; Elbridge Sibley, *Social Science Research Council: The First Fifty Years* (New York: Social Science Research Council 1974), 90.

5 'Report of [the] Committee on the Scientific Aspects of Migration,' 1–2; Cravens, *Triumph of Evolution*, 183

6 Ibid., 184

7 Ibid., 184; 'Report of [the] Committee on the Scientific Aspects of Migration,' 2

8 Frederic Ogg, 'The Immigration Laws of Canada and Their Administration,' in 'Report of [the] Committee on the Scientific Aspects of Migration,' 21–5

9 Isaiah Bowman, *The Pioneer Fringe*, ed. G.M. Wrigley, American Geographical Society, Special Publication no 13 (New York: American Geographical Society 1931), vii; Gladys M. Wrigley, 'Isaiah Bowman,' *The Geographical Review* 41 (Jan. 1951): 31

10 W.A. Mackintosh, *Prairie Settlement: The Geographic Setting*, vol. 1, Canadian Frontiers of Settlement, ed. W.A. Mackintosh and W.L.G. Joerg

(Toronto: Macmillan 1934), viii; Wrigley, 'Isaiah Bowman,' 30: Bowman was born in Waterloo, Ontario, in 1878 and grew up in Michigan. He claimed that he was inspired by the theme of the pioneer fringe from his travels in Canada.

11 Isaiah Bowman, 'The Scientific Study of Settlement,' *Geographical Review* 16 (Oct. 1926): 652

12 Bowman, *Pioneer Fringe*, v, 14, 85–6; Isaiah Bowman, 'The Pioneer Fringe,' *Foreign Affairs* 6 (1927–8): 49–50

13 Bowman, 'The Pioneer Fringe,' 50–1; Bowman, 'Scientific Study of Settlement,' 647; Bowman, *Pioneer Fringe*, 1–3

14 Bowman, 'Scientific Study of Settlement,' 647–8; Bowman, *Pioneer Fringe*, 8

15 Bowman, preface to *Pioneer Fringe*, v; Bowman, 'The Canadian Fringe of Settlement,' in *Pioneer Fringe*, 148–9. Bowman cited as support A.R.M. Lower's article 'The Assault on the Laurentian Barrier, 1850–1870,' in *Canadian Historical Review* 10 (1929): 294–307

16 Bowman, *Pioneer Fringe*, v; Bowman, 'The Scientific Study of Settlement,' 647–8. See also Eva Younge, 'Social Organization on the Pioneer Fringe with Special Reference to the Peace River Area,' MA thesis, McGill 1933, i, which outlines the broad purposes of the project.

17 Bowman, *Pioneer Fringe*, 76

18 Ibid., 1, 76

19 Ibid., 46–7

20 Bowman, 'The Scientific Study of Settlement,' 652–3

21 Bowman, *Pioneer Fringe*, v; Isaiah Bowman, 'Planning in Pioneer Settlement,' presidential address delivered before the Association of American Geographers, Ypsilanti, Mich., Dec. 1931, *Annals of the Association of American Geographers* 22 (June 1932): 105–6

22 *The Social Science Research Council Decennial Report* (1923–33), 59

23 Bowman, *Pioneer Fringe*, vii; Mackintosh, *Prairie Settlement*, vii; Younge, 'Social Organization on the Pioneer Fringe,' i

24 Isaiah Bowman in Mackintosh, *Prairie Settlement*, ix–x; H.A. Innis, 'Canadian Frontiers of Settlement: A Review,' *The Geographical Review* 25 (Jan. 1935): 92; W.A. Mackintosh, 'The Pioneer Problems of the Prairie Provinces of Canada,' in W.L.G. Joerg, ed., *Pioneer Settlement: Co-operative Studies by Twenty-Six Authors* (New York: American Geographical Society 1932), 7 n 10; SSRC *Decennial Report* (1923–33), 59

25 Bowman, *Pioneer Fringe*, vii; Wrigley, 'Isaiah Bowman,' 32. W.L.G. Joerg, ed., *Pioneer Settlement*, was a product of that joint effort.

26 Bowman in Mackintosh, *Prairie Settlement*, ix–x. Although no mention about a struggle is made in the printed literature, evidence that there was one

can be gleaned from a draft of a letter that Harold Innis wrote to James Shotwell. Innis was unhappy that an American was overseeing the Canadian-American–relations series sponsored by the Carnegie Endowment for International Peace. He constantly emphasized the importance of Canadians being given full responsibility for the work they were expected to undertake, threatening to resign unless the principle was granted in the Canadian-American–relations project. 'The principle was fully conceded in the Pioneer Belt project,' he added, 'a principle which had been gained at considerable cost.' UTA, Department of Political Economy Papers, acc. A76, Innis (draft of letter) to James Shotwell, nd

27 Dawson, 'Social Research in Canada,' 470–4
28 For similar concerns expressed by other academics, see UTA, Department of Political Economy Papers, acc. 65–0005, ser. 4, box 1, Memorandum on Research into Economic Problems Presented to the Ontario Research Foundation by the Departments of Political Economy in Queen's, Western Ontario, and McMaster University, First Tentative Draft, 1928, 1–2. Gilbert E. Jackson and H. Michell, professors at the University of Toronto, discussed the possibility of applying for a grant to support studies in economics that would imply co-operation among Ontario universities. The memo pointed to the growth of foundations supporting such research in the United States but noted that with the exception of a co-operative arrangement carried out between McMaster and Queen's through the summer of 1928, nothing of a co-ordinated character had been attempted in Canada because of the lack of funds. They expressed alarm that Canadian students were being attracted by the inducements offered by American graduate schools and believed that if a scheme of fellowships were inaugurated in economic research in Canada, Canadian students would turn out work of the highest value. See also UTA, Political Economy Papers, acc. A56 A9 007, box 3, H. Michell to E.J. Urwick, 1929.
29 Chester Martin, 'Early History and Land Settlement of the Prairie Provinces of Canada,' in Joerg, ed., *Pioneer Settlement*, 20–1
30 W.A. Mackintosh, 'The Pioneer Problems of the Prairie Provinces of Canada,' in Joerg, ed., *Pioneer Settlement*, 6–7; D.A. McArthur, 'Immigration and Colonization in Canada, 1900–1930,' in Joerg, ed., *Pioneer Settlement*, 30
31 McArthur, 'Immigration and Colonization in Canada,' 22
32 Bowman, 'The Canadian Fringe of Settlement,' in *Pioneer Fringe*, 143, 146
33 Mackintosh, 'The Pioneer Problems of the Prairie Provinces of Canada,' 6
34 Bowman, 'The Canadian Fringe of Settlement,' in *Pioneer Fringe*, 143
35 Mackintosh, 'The Pioneer Problems of the Prairie Provinces of Canada,' 6

36 C.A. Dawson, 'The Social Structure of a Pioneer Area as Illustrated by the Peace River District,' in Joerg, ed., *Prairie Settlement*, 42, 49
37 Bowman, 'The Canadian Fringe of Settlement,' 145
38 McArthur, 'Immigration and Colonization in Canada,' 26–8
39 R.W. Murchie, 'Agricultural Land Utilization in Western Canada,' in Joerg, ed., *Prairie Settlement*, 17
40 See outline in Mackintosh, 'The Pioneer Problems of the Prairie Provinces of Canada,' 11.
41 Mackintosh, *Prairie Settlement*, viii
42 This was Bowman's estimate. See Bowman, *Pioneer Fringe*, 163.
43 Murchie, 'Agricultural Land Utilization,' 16; Bowman, *Pioneer Fringe*, 163; Innis, 'Canadian Frontiers of Settlement,' 103
44 W.A. Mackintosh, foreword to C.A. Dawson, *The Settlement of the Peace River Country: A Study of a Pioneer Area* (Toronto: Macmillan 1934), x–ix
45 Dawson, *Peace River*, xi, 253–6
46 The assistant was Glenn Craig, who did his MA work in sociology at McGill but was a specialist in agricultural economics. He went on to pursue a PH D at Harvard in economics, after which he worked for the American government in a variety of capacities, including going on a mission to Afghanistan.
47 Dawson, *Peace River*, xi; Younge, 'Social Organization on the Pioneer Fringe,' i–ii; Glenn H. Craig, 'The Means and Modes of living on the Pioneer Fringe of Land Settlement with Special Reference to the Peace River Area,' MA thesis, McGill 1933), iii
48 Mackintosh, foreword to *Peace River*, ix; Dawson in *Peace River*, xi; Dawson, 'Human Ecology,' 296; Eva Younge, interview with D. Magill, 1974
49 S.D. Clark, review of C.A. Dawson and E.R. Younge, *Pioneering in the Prairie Provinces* (Toronto: Macmillan 1940), in *Canadian Historical Review* 21 (Sept. 1940): 336–7
50 Mackintosh, foreword to *Peace River*, ix; F.H. Kitto, *Peace River County*, Ottawa: Department of the Interior 1916; 1927–8
51 Dawson, *Peace River*, 1
52 Dawson, 'The Social Structure of a Pioneer Area,' 36–7
53 Ibid., 38
54 James N. Lewis, 'The Human Ecology of the St. John River Valley,' MA thesis, McGill 1939, 11
55 In his review of the Canadian Frontiers of Settlement series, H.A. Innis noted that in the first chapter of the Peace River volume, 'The Life Cycle of the Region,' Dawson traced the growth of the region from its pioneer to its mature stages. Innis thought the chapter included a number of important generalizations but argued that Dawson did not warn his readers sufficiently

of their limitations. Innis, 'Canadian Frontiers of Settlement: A Review,' 103

56 Dawson, *Peace River*, 3–13. An abridged description of the stages in the regional life-cycle can be found in Dawson and Gettys' *Introduction to Sociology*, rev. edn (1935), 159–62.

57 Dawson, *Peace River*, 2–8

58 Ibid., 9

59 Ibid., 13

60 Younge, 'Social Organization on the Pioneer Fringe,' 31, 125

61 Dawson, *Peace River*, 225; Dawson, 'Social Structure of a Pioneer Area,' 48–9. See also W.A. Mackintosh: 'Assuming successful settlement, it is the social lacks of the frontier that constitute the most significant item in the costs of settlement. Only as those social institutions are filled does the successful settlement pass out of the pioneer into the mature stages' ('The Pioneer Problems of the Prairie Provinces,' 10).

62 Much of the work on social institutions in the Peace River volume was derived from Eva Younge's study 'Social Organization on the Pioneer Fringe.'

63 Craig, 'Means and Modes of Living on the Pioneer Fringe.' Another of Dawson's graduate students examined the evolution of religious organizations in Peace River country; see Henry G. Tuttle, 'Frontier Religious Organizations in the Peace River Area,' MA thesis, McGill 1931.

64 Younge, 'Social Organization on the Pioneer Fringe,' 140–1, 143–4

65 Craig, 'Means and Modes of Living on the Pioneer Fringe,' ii

66 Dawson, *Peace River*, 113–14, 128–30

67 Dawson, 'The Structure of a Pioneer Area,' 49; Dawson, *Peace River*, 254–5; Craig, 'Means and Modes of Living on the Pioneer Fringe,' ii

68 Dawson, *Peace River*, 254–5; Innis, review of Canadian Frontiers of Settlement, 105

69 Dawson, *Peace River*, 254–5

70 Ibid., 253

71 Ibid., 254–5

72 In addition to the fact that it dealt with all the prairie provinces rather than just one area, the field work for *Pioneering in the Prairie Provinces* was much more extensive. It involved some fifteen individuals who collected data from two thousand farm families, government officials, school inspectors, clergymen, and businessmen over the summers of 1930 and 1931. Among the assistants were Glenn Craig, Lloyd Reynolds, and Leonard Marsh. See Dawson and Younge, *Pioneering in the Prairie Provinces*, xi.

73 Ibid., 2–4

74 S.D. Clark, 'Sociology in Canada: An Historical Overview,' *Canadian Journal of Sociology* 1 (Summer 1975): 228

75 Dawson and Younge, *Pioneering in the Prairie Provinces*, 11–14

76 S.D. Clark, review of Dawson and Younge, *Pioneering in the Prairie Provinces*, in *Canadian Historical Review* (1940): 337–8

77 Dawson and Younge, *Pioneering in the Prairie Provinces*, 39–40

78 Ibid., 40

79 Gladys L.H. Smith, 'The Regional Basis of News Distribution in the Prairie Provinces of Canada: A Study of Regions Defined by Newspaper Circulation,' MA thesis, McGill 1930, 64–8

80 Dawson and Younge, *Pioneering in the Prairie Provinces*, 41–3

81 Nathan L. Whetten, 'The Social and Economic Structure of the Trade Centres in the Prairie Provinces with Special Reference to Its Changes, 1910–1930,' PHD thesis, Harvard 1932. See Dawson's comments on Zimmerman's work on regional centralization in 'Human Ecology,' 296.

82 See Robert Park, 'Urbanization as Measured by Newspaper Circulation,' *American Journal of Sociology* 35 (July 1929): 60–79; and Dawson's comments on Park's work in *Pioneering in the Prairie Provinces*, 44.

83 Smith, 'News Distribution in the Prairie Provinces,' 2, 22, 70

84 Ibid., 34–6, 53

85 Dawson and Younge, *Pioneering in the Prairie Provinces*, 250–1

86 Ibid., 286

87 Ibid., 286

88 Ibid., 130. Innis, in his review of the Canadian Frontiers of Settlement series, 98, alludes to *Economic Problems of the Prairie Provinces* by W.A. Mackintosh, assisted by A.B. Clark, G.A. Elliot, W.W. Swanson (Toronto: Macmillan 1935) – specifically, to their evidence that a catastrophic drop in wheat prices between 1929 and 1933 created an economic crisis of first magnitude in the prairie provinces.

89 Dawson, 'The Rural Sociologist,' 170

90 Ibid., 171–2

CHAPTER SIX: THE SOCIAL SCIENCE RESEARCH PROJECT

1 Letter of Sir Arthur Currie, 26 Nov. 1930, reprinted in Survey, report by Sir Arthur Currie, *Annual Report of the Corporation of McGill University* (1930–1), 5–7

2 Ibid., 7

3 MUA, acc. 641, box 285, McGill College or the Faculty of Arts, Pure Science,

and Commerce, Notes by the Dean, Dec. 1929, Dean of Arts [Ira Mackay]
to Sir Arthur Currie, 19 Dec. 1929, 1–2

4 Currie, Survey, 7

5 MUA, acc. 641, box 284, Arts Survey Committee, 6 Mar. 1931, 27 Mar. 1931

6 Wesley C. Mitchell, 'Research in the Social Sciences,' in *The New Social
Science*, ed. Leonard D. White (Chicago: University of Chicago Press
1930), 12; Ogg, *Research in the Humanistic and Social Sciences*, 1–2; 354–5;
Karl, *Charles Merriam*, 123–4

7 Karl, *Charles Merriam*, ix, 124, 129

8 Matthews, *Quest for an American Sociology*, 110; Merle Curti and Roderick
Nash, *Philanthropy in the Shaping of American Higher Education* (New
Brunswick, NJ: Rutgers University Press 1965), 214, 222–3

9 Karl, *Charles Merriam*, 120–7, passim

10 Ibid., 132–4

11 Ogg, *Humanistic and Social Sciences*, 164–5

12 Beardsley Ruml, 'Trends in Social Science,' in White, ed., *The New Social
Science*, 110; Ruml, 'Social Science Research in Retrospect and Prospect,'
in *Eleven Twenty-Six: A Decade of Social Science Research*, ed. Louis Wirth
(Chicago: University of Chicago Press 1940), 23–6

13 Karl, *Charles Merriam*, 135; Ruml, 'Social Science Research,' 23–6

14 Karl, *Charles Merriam*, 136

15 MUA, acc. 641, box 289, file 1927–1933, Social Science Research Council,
Minutes and Pamphlets; Social Science Research Council, *Decennial Report* (1923–33), 48

16 See Social Science Research Council, *Decennial Report* (1923–33), 24, and in
the same source, Advisory Committee on Personality and Culture, 1930,
57.

17 UTA, newspaper clippings, acc. A73-00261, 151 (78), Hincks, Clarence Meredith; 'Hincks, Clarence Meredith,' in *Canadian Who's Who* ed. Charles
G.D. Roberts and Arthur Leonard Tunnell, vol. 2 (1936–7), 511–12

18 Robert Reade in the Toronto *Star Weekly* nd, np, quoted in 'Hincks, Clarence
Meredith,' *Canadian Who's Who*, 512

19 C.M. Hincks, 'How Can We Promote Social Welfare in Canada?' *Proceedings
of the Canadian Conference on Social Welfare*, *2nd Conference* (1930),
8–10

20 MUA, acc. 641, box 290, Summary of Social Science Research, Confidential to
the Principal; Social Science Research Project, nd (document appears to be
a summary based upon McMurray's memorandum)

21 MUA, acc. 641, box 289, Sir Arthur Currie to Sir Josiah Stamp, 13 May 1930;
box 290, Sir Arthur Currie to Stephen Leacock, 10 Aug. 1930

22 MUA, acc. 641, box 289, Sir Arthur Currie to Dr James B. Angell, 30 Dec. 1929
23 MUA, acc. 641, box 289, copy of circular from Yale University, 'The Human Welfare Group at New Haven: A Series of Informal Discussions of a New Educational Project,' np; memo by Professor Elliott Smith, Institute of Human Relations: Industrial Investigation, Apr. 1931
24 MUA, acc. 641, box 289, L.C. Marsh, Memorandum on Social Research at Chicago University, Feb. 1931
25 Mitchell, 'Research in the Social Sciences,' 10–13
26 Harold G. Moultin, 'Co-operation in Social Science Research,' in White, ed., *The New Social Science*, 55; 'The Human Welfare Group at New Haven,' np
27 Celestin Bouglé, 'The Present Tendency of the Socal Sciences in France,' in White, ed., *The New Social Science*, 70; Social Science Research Council, *Report of the Director for 1931*, 10; Ogg, *Research in the Humanistic and Social Sciences*, 342–3
28 Karl, *Charles Merriam*, 123
29 MUA, acc. 641, box 289, copy of pamphlet, 'Yale's Institute of Human Relations,' by President James B. Angell
30 Ogg, *Humanistic and Social Sciences*, 19
31 Sir William Beveridge, 'International Cooperation in Social Science,' in White, ed., *The New Social Science*, 54
32 Robert M. Hutchins, Address of Dedication, in White, ed., *The New Social Science*, 1
33 MUA, acc. 641, box 289, C.M. Hincks (writing in his capacity as medical director of the Canadian National Committee for Mental Hygiene) to Sir Arthur Currie, 4 Mar. 1930
34 Ibid.
35 MUA, acc. 641, box 289, Sir Arthur Currie to Dr Day, 29 July 1930; Ira Mackay to Sir Arthur Currie, 8 Mar. 1930 (Some Notes on a Proposed Course of Social Studies at McGill), and Mackay to Currie, 10 Mar. 1930; Scheme for the Establishment of an Institute for Research on Problems of Human Relations at McGill University, nd (no author is cited but it likely was John Beattie, professor of Anatomy at McGill); C.E. Kellogg to Sir Arthur Currie, Tentative Suggestions for Investigation re Unemployment to be Undertaken by an Institute of Human Relations; Institute of Human Relations, nd, no author cited; J.W. Bridges, research director of the Canadian National Committee for Mental Hygiene, Research Division, to Sir Arthur Currie, 8 Mar. 1930
36 MUA, acc. 641, box 289, Memorandum Regarding Human Relations Research, nd, no author cited

37 MUA, acc. 641, box 289, Beattie to Currie

38 MUA, acc. 641, box 285, Ira A. Mackay to Sir Arthur Currie, 19 Dec. 1929

39 MUA, acc. 641, box 289, Mackay to Currie, 10 Mar. 1930

40 Ibid.

41 MUA, acc. 641, box 289, memo, 27, 28 Aug. 1930 (Currie's notes on his visit to Hanover to consult with Drs Day and Ruml of the Rockefeller Foundation)

42 MUA, acc. 641, box 289, Stephen Leacock to Arthur Mathewson, 5 Feb. 1930

43 MUA, acc. 641, box 289, Arthur Mathewson to Stephen Leacock, 7 Mar. 1930

44 MUA, acc. 641, box 289, Kellogg to Currie, Tentative Suggestions

45 MUA, acc. 641, box 289; see, for example, Mackay to Currie, 8 May 1930

46 L.C. Marsh, *Employment Research: An Introduction to the McGill Programme of Research in the Social Sciences* (Toronto: Oxford University Press 1935), 45–6

47 Oswald Hall, 'The Size and Composition of the Canadian Family with special reference to sample areas of the Metropolitan Regions in Central Canada,' MA thesis, McGill 1937, vii

48 MUA, acc. 641, box 290, Sir Arthur Currie to Josiah Stamp, 13 May 1930 and 6 June 1930; Stamp to Currie, 9 June 1930; copy of telegram from Leonard Marsh to Dean C.F. Martin, 31 May 1930; Sir Arthur Currie to Stephen Leacock, 20 Aug. 1930; Governors Minutes, vol. 7, 575; Rockefeller Foundation Archives [RFA], record group 1.1, ser. 427s, 'McGill University Fluid Research,' Correspondence 1930–2, Sir Arthur Currie to Dr Edmund E. Day, 29 July 1930

49 Interview with L.C. Marsh, Vancouver, BC, 10 June 1980; L.C. Marsh scrapbook, newspaper clipping, no source cited; MUA, acc. 641, box 289, news clipping; UTA, Political Economy Papers, acc. A56, A69-0007, box 4, correspondence between E.J. Urwick and Leonard Marsh, 11 Feb. 1930 to 17 June 1930; Sir William Beveridge, 'International Cooperation in Social Science,' 51

50 Interview with Marsh, 10 June 1980

51 RFA, 'McGill University Fluid Research,' Correspondence 1930–2, Sir Arthur Currie to Dr Edmund E. Day, 29 July 1930; MUA, acc. 641, box 289, Currie memo of 27, 28, Aug.

52 MUA, acc. 641, box 290, Social Science Research, 10 Oct. 1930 (Dorothy McMurray's notes on meetings held at Currie's house); Summary of Social Science Research ('D.M.')

53 MUA, acc. 641, box 290, Summary of Social Science Research ('D.M.')

54 MUA, acc. 641, box 289, draft of appeal to the Rockefeller Foundation, nd, and Sir Edward Beatty's additions, see correspondence, Sir Edward Beatty to Sir Arthur Currie, 22 Oct. 1930.

55 Ibid.

56 Ibid.
57 MUA, acc. 641, box 289, Sir Arthur Currie to Dr E.E. Day, 23 Oct 1930
58 MUA, acc. 641, box 289, Edmund E. Day to Sir Arthur Currie, 27 Oct. 1930; Currie to Day, 1 Nov. 1930
59 MUA, acc. 641, box 289, Currie to Day, 1 Nov. 1930
60 RFA, 'McGill University Fluid Research,' Correspondence 1930–2, Edmund E. Day to Sir Arthur Currie, 1 Dec. 1930; MUA, acc. 641, box 289, Day to Currie, 5 Dec. 1930
61 MUA, acc. 641, box 289, Norma S. Thompson, secretary, Rockefeller Foundation, to Sir Arthur Currie, 10 Dec. 1930
62 MUA, acc. 557, box 8, P.E. Corbett, Social Research Transfer File; 'McGill Granted Hundred Thousand Dollars by Rockefeller Foundation,' *McGill Daily*, 11 Dec. 1930
63 MUA, acc. 641, box 289, E.A. Bott to C.F. Martin, 24 Dec. 1930
64 Ibid.
65 MUA, acc. 641, box 289, George S. Brett to Carleton Stanley, 24 Jan. 1931
66 MUA, acc. 641, box 289, copy of L.C. Marsh's address 'Unemployment. An International and Community Problem,' delivered at the Montreal Forum 25 Jan. 1931
67 *Annual Report of the Corporation of McGill University* (1931–2), The Survey: Report of the Principal, 5, 9–11, 44; MUA, acc. 641, box 289, Report of the Principal and Vice-Chancellor of McGill University to the Board of Governors, 21 Dec. 1931; Thompson, 'McGill between the Wars,' 101; J.W. Berry to Dennis Magill, 18 Feb. 1979
68 MUA, acc. 641, box 289, File: Social Science Research Executive Committee Minutes. Unemployment and Related Problems: General Plan of Research; Social Science Research Council: Unemployment Research (1931): The Programme and Its Rationale, submitted to the executive committee 1/12/31; Report to the Rockefeller Foundation on the Social Science Research Project for Session 1932–1933, pp. 1–3; RFA, record group 1.1, ser. 427s, Report 1932–41, 'Report to the Rockefeller Foundation, 1931–32, on Social Science Research Project for Session 1931–32,' 25 Oct. 1932; Marsh, *Employment Research*, 34
69 MUA, acc. 641, box 289, L.C. Marsh memos: McGill University: Social Research Development and Unemployment Problems Survey, and Syllabus of Basic Material for Social Research in Montreal (submitted to executive committee, 19 Dec. 1930, and to the council, 9 Jan. 1931); Marsh, *Employment Research*, xiii; L.C. Marsh scrapbook, newspaper clippings, 'Industrial Survey of Montreal Arranged'
70 MUA, acc. 641, box 289, Marsh, Syllabus of Basic Material for Social Research.

71 MUA, acc. 641, box 289, Marsh, Research Projects, memo submitted to executive committee, 21 May 1931 (written 19 May 1931)
72 MUA, acc. 641, box 289, Minutes of the Executive Committee meeting of 21 May 1931; Marsh memo, Minutes of Social Research Council meeting, 21 May 1931: Departmental Research Projects; Corporation Minutes, vol. 9, 21 Oct. 1931, 241
73 MUA, acc. 641, box 290, Memorandum from Dr Leacock; box 289, Social Research Council: Minutes, 8 Dec. 1931; Minutes of the Executive Committee of the Social Research Council, 2 Feb. 1932; RFA, Reports 1932–41, Report on Social Science Research Project, 1931–2.
74 Interview with Marsh, 10 Jan. 1980; Dawson, 'Social Research in Canada,' 95–6
75 *McGill University Annual Report* (1937–8), 42; MUA, acc. 641, box 289, Minutes of the Executive Committee, 5 May 1932
76 *McGill University Annual Report* (1934–5), Post Graduate Awards, 99; RFA, Reports 1932–41, Report on the Social Science Research Project, 1935–6, 7; Dennis Magill's correspondence with Oswald Hall, 27 Feb. 1979, 1; with Stuart Jamieson, 11 June 1979, and with Lloyd Reynolds, 9 Mar. 1979
77 MUA, acc. 641, box 289, report to the Rockefeller Foundation on the Social Science Research Project for the session 1932–3, 1–2; RFA, Reports 1932–41, Reports to the Rockefeller Foundation on the Social Science Research Project for the session 1935–6.
78 RFA, Reports 1932–41, Report of the director [for the] session 1935–6, 1–6; MUA, acc. 641, box 290, Minutes of Social Research Council Meeting, 25 Apr. 1935; Memorandum to the principal, Social Science Research (Rockefeller grant), 30 Sept. 1935; acc. 557, Faculty of Law, L.C. Marsh to F.R. Scott, 20 Dec. 1937

CHAPTER SEVEN: UNEMPLOYMENT, IMMIGRATION, AND ASSIMILATION

1 MUA, acc. 641, box 290, Social Science Research memo by 'D.M.'
2 MUA, acc. 641, box 289, newspaper clipping, nd, 'Marsh Emphasizes Aspects of Unemployment'
3 Marsh, 'Unemployment, A Community Problem,' 5, 8
4 Ibid., 9–13
5 Ibid., 5, 7, 17–23
6 See Michiel Horn, *The League for Social Reconstruction: Intellectual Origins of the Democratic Left in Canada, 1930–1942* (Toronto: University of Toronto Press 1980), espec. chap. 10, 'Professors in the Public Eye.'

7 Phyllis Heaton, 'Standard of Living Studies and Their Significance, Including a Special Study in Montreal,' MA thesis, McGill 1932, 1–7, 11–12

8 Ibid., 52–5, 68–73

9 Ibid., 114, 156–60

10 Quoted in ibid., 160

11 Hall, 'Size and Composition of the Canadian Family,' 3–20, 67–70

12 Ibid., ix–xv, 34–9, 45–52, 64–5

13 Mary Aikman, 'The Nature of Women's Employment in Montreal,' MA thesis, McGill 1937, 4–9, 19, 27, 81–91

14 John Berry, 'The Peopling of Canada: A Statistical Analysis of Population Growth in Canada,' MA thesis, McGill 1933, 52

15 Ibid., 184–8

16 Linteau, Durocher, Robert, *Quebec: A History*, 366

17 Dawson and Gettys, *Introduction to Sociology* (1929 edn), 498–9; see also Albert Moellman, 'The Germans in Canada: Occupational and Social Adjustment of German Immigrants in Canada,' MA thesis, McGill 1934, i.

18 University of Toronto Rare Books Department, Hubert R. Kemp Papers, memo, Canadian Immigration Policy, 2

19 Dawson and Gettys, *Introduction to Sociology* (1929 edn), 552–3; Moellman, 'The Germans in Canada,' 4

20 University of Toronto Rare Books Department, Kemp Papers, Canadian Immigration Policy, 2–3

21 Dawson and Gettys, *Introduction to Sociology*, (1929 edn), 552–3

22 Lloyd Reynolds, *The British Immigrant* (Toronto: Oxford University Press 1935), 56–8

23 Dawson's introduction to *The British Immigrant*, xvi–xx, and Reynolds, 49–50

24 Ibid., 1, 2, 8

25 Ibid., 4

26 Ibid., 84–104, 110, 130, 189, 261–79

27 Ibid., 280–9

28 From L.C. Marsh scrapbook, copies of the following reviews: 'Opposed to Immigration,' Winnipeg *Free Press*, 20 Mar. 1936 (by 'H.P.G.,' np); A.F.W. Plumptre on W.A. Mackintosh, *Economic Problems of the Prairie Provinces*, Robert England, *The Colonization of Western Canada*, and Lloyd Reynolds, *The British Immigrant*, in *Economic Journal* (Mar. 1937); review by W.W. Swanson of *The British Immigrant*, in *American Economic Review* (June 1936)

29 MUA, acc. 641, box 279, Beatty's correspondence with A.E. Morgan, 21 Feb. 1936

30 MUA, acc. 641, box 279, copy of letter that P.C. Armstrong sent to J.N.K. Macalister, 30 Dec. 1935, 1,5; Armstrong to Beatty, 23 Mar. 1936
31 Ibid., 4, 5, Armstrong to Beatty
32 Interview with Marsh; MUA, acc. 641, box 279, Beatty to Morgan, 21 Feb. 1936
33 MUA, acc. 641, box 279, Beatty to Morgan (on CPR letterhead), 23 Mar. 1939
34 University of Toronto Rare Books Department, copy of letter, Beatty to Escott Reid, national secretary of the Canadian Institute of International Affairs, 3 Mar. 1937
35 MUA, acc. 641, box 279, correspondence between Beatty and Morgan, 19, 20 Feb. 1936
36 MUA, acc. 641, box 279, Morgan to Beatty, 16 Mar. 1936
37 MUA, acc. 641, box 279, Reynolds' response to Armstrong, 15 May 1936, 1–3
38 MUA, acc. 641, box 279, Beatty to Morgan, 23 May 1936
39 Reynolds to Magill, 7 Mar. 1979, 2; MUA, copy, *The Alarm Clock* (Feb. 1933), vol. 1, no 2: 'Outside the Gates,' 4, and vol. 1, no 3, Mar. 1933, 8; UTA, Cody Papers, Box 1, Sir Arthur Currie to Rev. H.J. Cody, 15 Feb. 1933. A number of other participants in the Social Science Research Project also contributed to the issue, and this was pointed out to Beatty.
40 Sibley, *The Social Science Research Council*, 128
41 Charles M. Bayley, 'The Social Structure of the Italian and Ukrainian Immigrant Communities in Montreal, 1935–1937,' MA thesis, McGill 1939
42 MUA, acc. 641, box 284, Stephen Leacock, Remarks and Suggestions for the Principal's [Survey] Committee, 18 Feb. 1931
43 Frost, *McGill University: For the Advancement of Learning*, vol. 2, 128; MUA, acc. 641, box 272, Sir Arthur Currie to E.W. Beatty, 23 Aug. 1929; Sir Arthur Currie to A.R. McMaster, 7 Oct. 1929; Sir A. Currie to W.M. Birks, 18 Sept. 1935
44 MUA, acc. 641, box 284, Arts Survey, 23 Mar. 1931. On Harvard's policy, see Marcia Graham Synott, *The Half-Opened Door: Discrimination and Admissions at Harvard, Yale, and Princeton* (Westport, Conn.: Greenwood Press 1979), 79–88, 106–12
45 MUA, acc. 641, box 272, Dean Ira A. Mackay to Arthur Currie, 21 July 1931
46 MUA, acc. 641, box 272, L.W. Douglas to T.A. Crerar, 29 Nov. 1938; Crerar to Douglas, 16 Dec. 1938, and follow-up letter from Crerar's private secretary to Douglas, 3 July 1939. For other correspondence on this issue, see MUA, acc. 641, box 272 (file: Jews, Matriculation); acc. 641, box 284, file no 1 on the Carnegie Foundation and placement of German Jewish refugees; see also Lawrence D. Stokes, 'Canada and an Academic Refugee from Nazi Germany: The Case of Gerhard Herzberg,' *Canadian Historical Review* 57 (June 1976): 150–70; Irving Abella and Harold Troper, *None Is Too Many:*

Canada and the Jews of Europe (Toronto: Lester and Orpen Dennys 1982).

47 David Solomon, 'My Life as a Student and Teacher at McGill: 1935–1974,' unpublished paper, Aug. 1974, 1–2

48 Dawson and Gettys, *Introduction to Sociology* (1929 edn), 541, 551

49 Matthews, *Quest for an American Sociology*, 157

50 The explanation is derived from Matthews's discussion in *Quest for an American Sociology*, 160–3.

51 Ibid., 164–9; Faris, *Chicago Sociology*, 35–6

52 Allan Smith, 'Metaphor and Nationality in North America,' *Canadian Historical Review* 51 (Sept. 1970): 248–9, 250, 254–5

53 Moellman, 'The Germans in Canada,' 4

54 Dawson, *Introduction to Sociology* (1929 edn), 541, 543, 550–2

55 C.A. Dawson, *Group Settlement: Ethnic Communities in Western Canada* (Toronto: Macmillan 1936); see espec. Mackintosh's introduction, ix.

56 Dawson, *Group Settlement*, xv, 377

57 Ibid., 380

58 Ibid., 21, 24, 36, 291

59 Ibid., 379–80

60 Bayley, 'Italian and Ukrainian Immigrant Communities,' 4, 6

61 Stephen W. Mamchur, 'The Economic and Social Maladjustment of Slavic Immigrants: with Special Reference to the Ukrainians in Montreal,' MA thesis, McGill 1934, 51

62 Harold A. Gibbard, 'The Means and Modes of Living of European Immigrants in Montreal,' MA thesis, McGill 1934, 200, 272, 273, 277

63 Ibid., 288–90

64 Bayley, 'Italian and Ukrainian Immigrants,' 251–2

65 Ibid., 110–11, 119–21, 194–5

66 Judith Seidel, 'The Development and Social Adjustment of the Jewish Community in Montreal,' MA thesis, McGill 1939, i, 1, 55, 67

67 Bayley, 'Italian and Ukrainian Immigrants,' 7, 236–8

68 MUA, acc. 641, box 289, Minutes of the Executive Committee Meeting, 11 Oct. 1932, 22 Nov. 1932; Departmental Research Projects (1932–3): Graduate Research Assistantships, 2

69 See William J. Roy, 'The French-English Division of Labour in the Province of Quebec,' MA thesis, McGill 1935; Stuart M. Jamieson, 'French and English in the Institutional Structure of Montreal: A Study of the Social and Economic Division of Labour,' MA thesis, McGill 1938; Pearl Jacobs Lieff, 'The Urbanization of the French Canadian Parish,' MA thesis, McGill 1940.

70 Everett C. Hughes, *French Canada in Transition* (Chicago: University of

Chicago Press 1943; repr. Chicago and London: University of Chicago Press, Phoenix edn, 1963)
71 See Everett C. Hughes, *Programme de recherches sociales pour le Québec*, Cahiers de l'Ecole des Sciences Sociales, Politiques et Economiques de Laval, vol. 2, no 4 (Quebec: Presses Universitaires Laval 1943).
72 Faris, *Chicago Sociology*, 109–10
73 M. Shore, taped correspondence with E.C. Hughes, 18 Jan. 1981; Hughes, Memorandum Concerning Sociology, 6
74 Correspondence with Hughes, 18 Jan. 1981
75 Faris, *Chicago Sociology*, 34
76 For example, Mary Aikman to Dennis Magill, 1 Apr. 1979
77 Winnifred Raushenbush, *Robert E. Park: Biography of a Sociologist* (Durham, NC: Duke University Press 1979), 103
78 Everett C. Hughes, 'A Study of a Secular Institution: The Chicago Real Estate Board,' PH D thesis, University of Chicago 1928, published as *The Growth of an Institution: The Chicago Real Estate Board*, The Society for Social Research of the University of Chicago, ser. 2, monograph 1 (Chicago: University of Chicago Press 1931); Hughes, epilogue to Raushenbush, *Robert Park*, 188
79 Hughes, *The Growth of an Institution*, preface, np, 5, 16, 20, 33, 40
80 See explanation of institutions in Dawson and Gettys, *Introduction to Sociology* (1929 edn), 31.
81 Hughes, *The Growth of an Institution*, preface, np, 114
82 Hughes, memorandum Concerning Sociology, 6
83 S.D. Clark, 'Sociology in Canada: An Historical Overview,' *Canadian Journal of Sociology* 2 (Summer 1975): 227–8
84 Helen MacGill Hughes, 'Wasp / Woman / Sociologist,' *Society*, *Transactions* (July-Aug. 1977): 76
85 See, for instance, preface to *French Canada in Transition*, x, and preface to Phoenix edn, xv.
86 Correspondence with Hughes, 18 Jan. 1981
87 Clark, 'Sociology in Canada,' 227–8
88 Hughes, *French Canada in Transition*, 2, 3
89 Ibid., 4, 9, 10, 11; Lieff, 'Urbanization of the French Canadian Parish,' 3, 13, 14, 37, 45, 48–50
90 Ibid., 28, 33–4, 47, 61
91 Ibid., 202–5
92 Roy, 'The French-English Division of Labour,' 149
93 Hughes, *French Canada in Transition*, 1
94 Ibid., 202, 207–8

95 Roy, 'The French-English Division of Labour,' 1
96 Jamieson, 'French and English in the Institutional Structure of Montreal,'
   50–1
97 Ibid., 215
98 Leonard C. Marsh, *Canadians In and Out of Work: A Survey of Economic
   Classes and Their Relation to the Labour Market* (Toronto: Oxford University Press 1940), xvii, 55
99 Ibid., 403–4
100 Ibid., xvii

CONCLUSION

1 Frost, *McGill University*, vol. 2, 195
2 MUA, acc. 641, box 290, Memorandum to the Principal on Social Sciences
   Research and Social Research Project, 18 Sept. 1935; General Considerations and Recommendations for the Future, from Social Sciences Research
   Programme: Report of an Executive Committee, Oct. 1935
3 MUA, acc. 641, box 290, Memo [to A.E. Morgan] from Professor Leacock on
   Social Research, 30 Sept. 1935; The Principal's Confidential Memo of Interview with Professors Leacock, Hemmeon, and Culliton on 4 October 1935, at
   4 pm; Stephen Leacock to Principal Morgan, 10 Oct. 1935
4 UTA, registrar's newspaper clippings, box 1, 'Resignation Is Laid to Failure to
   Curb Pinks,' Toronto *Star*, 29 April 1937
5 MUA, acc. 641, box 279, confidential letter, Beatty to A.E. Morgan, 18 Feb.
   1936; Morgan to Beatty, 19 Feb. 1936
6 F.R. Scott, *Canadian Unionist*, Feb. 1936, cited in Frost, *McGill University*,
   vol. 2, 193
7 MUA, acc. 641, box 279, Beatty to Morgan, 28 Feb. 1936
8 Frost, *McGill University*, vol. 2, 196
9 UTA, registrar's newspaper clippings, box 1, 'McGill Staff Want Voice in Selection of Principal,' Toronto *Star*, 1 May 1937; 29 April 1937
10 Ibid. See also MUA, acc. 191, box 8, Senate Minutes, 1935–7: Private and
   Confidential to Members of Senate, 17–19.
11 UTA, registrar's clippings, Toronto *Telegram*, 4 October 1937; MUA, Governors' Minutes, 4 Oct. 1937, 991
12 SSRC, *Decennial Report* (1923–1933), 17; Beardsley Ruml, 'Social Science Research in Retrospect and Prospect,' in Wirth, ed., *Eleven Twenty-Six*, 26
13 MUA, acc. 641, box 274, The Principal's Memorandum of His Interview with
   Dr E.E. Day, Dec. 17, at the Rockefeller Foundation Offices, NY City, 18
   Dec. 1935

14 MUA, acc. 641, box 290, L.W. Douglas to Professor Hemmeon, chairman, Social Sciences Research Council (memo of conversation); see also Hemmeon to H.A. Innis, in UTA, Pol. Ec. Papers, A76-025, 13 June 1939.
15 UTA, Innis Papers, B72-025, box 21, C.A. Dawson to H.A. Innis, 16 May 1938
16 MUA, acc. 641, box 290, memo from the principal and vice-chancellor to principal, 5 Apr. 1938
17 Hughes, Memorandum Concerning Sociology, 1–10
18 UTA, Innis Papers, B72-025, box 21, C.A. Dawson to H.A. Innis, 18 May 1938
19 MUA, acc. 641, box 290, L.W. Douglas to Robt E. Lee Faris, 19 Sept. 1938; C.W. Hendel to L.W. Douglas, 22 June 1938; acc. 16, 19 Apr. 1940, 23 Apr. 1940
20 MUA, acc. 641, box 279, L.W. Douglas to Sir Edward Beatty, 1 Feb. 1939. Laski taught at McGill from 1914 to 1916 but did not get along with Principal Peterson and proved to be too radical for the university. See MUA, acc. 16, box 24, 'Curious Type This Laski'
21 MUA, Senate Minutes, Visiting Professorship in Economics, 15 Mar. 1939; acc. 641, box 286, Minutes of Meeting of Heads of Departments of Faculty of Arts and Science, 20 Mar. 1939; box 290, Douglas to T.E. Gregory, 29 Mar. 1939
22 MUA, acc. 641, box 290, principal's private memo for the file (dictated by L.W.D. to D.M.), 21 Mar. 1939
23 Douglas, 'Principal Douglas' Memories of McGill,' 245
24 Frost, McGill University, vol. 2, 229–30; Leonard Marsh scrapbook, Public Lectures, etc ..., and newspaper clippings: 'Canada Now Giving Deep Consideration to Reconstruction When Conflict Ends,' 29 Nov. 1941; 'Economist Will Plan Reconstruction,' July 1941
25 Frost, McGill University, vol. 2, 230; Marsh scrapbook, 'Canada Now Giving Deep Consideration to Reconstruction'
26 Leonard Marsh, Social Security for Canada, report prepared for the Committee on Postwar Reconstruction and presented to the Special Committee on Social Security, House of Commons, Apr. 1943 (Ottawa: King's Printer 1943; repr. Toronto: University of Toronto Press, Social History Series, 1975); see Marsh's introduction, xx.
27 Correspondence with E.C. Hughes, 18 Jan. 1981
28 Ibid.
29 Everett C. Hughes, Programme de recherches sociales pour le Québec, Cahiers de l'Ecole des Sciences Sociales, Politiques et Economiques de Laval, vol. 2, no 4 (Laval: Presses Universitaires Laval 1943)
30 David Nock, 'History and Evolution of French Canadian Sociology,' Insurgent Sociologist 4 (Summer 1974): 21

31 Ibid.; see also pt 1, 'The Sociology of French Canada in Historical Perspective,' in Rioux and Martin, *French Canadian Society.*
32 Clark, 'Sociology in Canada: An Historical Overview,' 229
33 Bulmer, *Chicago Sociology*, 205–6
34 Interview with Marsh, 10 June 1980
35 Elizabeth Moore Walsh McGahan, 'The Port in the City: Saint John, N.B. (1867–1911) and the Process of Integration,' PH D thesis, University of New Brunswick 1979, 23, 24, 37, 40; Donald Creighton, 'Towards the Discovery of Canada,' *University of Toronto Quarterly* 25 (Apr. 1956): 277–81
36 McGahan, 'The Port in the City,' 30–1; D.G. Creighton, Presidential Address, Canadian Historical Association *Annual Report* (1957), p 3

Note on Sources

Since all the sources used in this study are indicated in the notes and a complete bibliography may be found in my doctoral dissertation for the University of Toronto, 'The Science of Society: The Development of Sociology at McGill University, 1918-1939' (1985), I have included here only a compressed list of the most important works consulted. The major primary sources used in this study consisted of university administrative and departmental papers. Containing material dealing with official matters as well as correspondence between professors and their colleagues, they were a rich source for both institutional and intellectual history. Published books and articles of the McGill academics with which this work was concerned, the unpublished theses of their students, and the work of their teachers and associates at other institutions composed the other major source of primary material. The most important secondary sources included intellectual histories covering the period between 1890 and 1940 and studies of the development of the social sciences in the United States and Britain.

MANUSCRIPT COLLECTIONS

McGill University Archives (MUA): Principal's Files (Cyril F. James), acc. 16; Principals' Files, 1920-1939 (Sir Arthur Currie, A.E. Morgan, Lewis Williams Douglas), record groups 2c, 2M, and 2D, acc. 641; Faculty of Arts and Science Papers, acc. 83, box 214 (Sociology and Social Science); Faculty of Arts Minutes, 1919-1940; Governors' Minute Book, 24 July 1919 to 7 June 1935; McGill University Governors' Minutes, Aug. 1935 to Dec. 1944; Minutes of the Corporation, vols. 8 & 9

Rockefeller Foundation Archives (RFA; North Tarrytown, NY): record group 1.1, ser. 427s: Correspondence 1930-1932; Reports; 'McGill University Fluid Research,' 1932-41

University of Toronto Archives (UTA): Office of the President (Falconer Papers), acc. A-66-003; Office of the President (Cody Papers), acc. A68-006; boxes 1–23; Department of Political Economy Records: acc. A-65-0005, ser. 4, boxes 1–3 & acc. A56 A69-0007, 1928–30, & acc. A76-025, boxes 1, 2, 6, 7, 8, 9, 10, 11, 13, 14; Innis Papers, acc. B72-025; Innis [Family] Papers, acc. B72-003, boxes 1, 2, 23, biographical

Other important institutional material included annual reports and calendars of McGill University for the entire period under consideration here, as well as selected issues of calendars and annual reports for Acadia University, the University of Chicago, and the University of Toronto.

JOURNALS

American Journal of Sociology
Social Welfare

INTERVIEWS

With Leonard C. Marsh, 10 June 1980, Vancouver, British Columbia. Leonard Marsh was also kind enough to lend me, from his private files, scrapbooks from his years at McGill: McGill University: Research Program and Allied Educational Work, 1930–1937; Public Lectures, Conferences, Adult Education Activities, 1935–1941; Book Reviews of the Publications of the McGill Social Research Series

Taped correspondence with Everett C. Hughes, 19 Jan. 1981

HISTORIES OF THE SOCIAL SCIENCES

Hamilton Cravens, *The Triumph of Evolution: American Scientists and the Heredity-Environment Controversy, 1900–1940*. Philadelphia: University of Pennsylvania Press 1978
Robert E.L. Faris, *Chicago Sociology, 1920–1932*. San Francisco: Chandler Publishing 1967
Thomas L. Haskell, *The Emergence of Professional Social Science: The American Social Science Association and the Nineteenth Century Crisis of Authority*. Chicago and Urbana: University of Illinois Press 1977
Barry D. Karl, *Charles E. Merriam and the Study of Politics*. Chicago and London: University of Chicago Press 1974
Bruce Kuklick, *Rise of American Philosophy: Cambridge, Massachusetts, 1860–1930*. New Haven and London: Yale University Press 1977

James Leiby, *A History of Social Welfare and Social Work in the United States.* New York: Columbia University Press 1978

Roy Lubove, *The Professional Altruist: The Emergence of Social Work as a Career.* Cambridge, Mass.: Harvard University Press 1965

Fred Matthews, *Quest for an American Sociology: Robert E. Park and the Chicago School.* Montreal and London: McGill-Queen's University Press 1977

Jean B. Quandt, *From the Small Town to the Great Community: The Social Thought of Progressive Intellectuals.* New Brunswick, NJ: Rutgers University Press 1970

Darnell Rucker, *The Chicago Pragmatists.* Minneapolis: University of Minnesota Press 1969

Laurence R. Veysey, *The Emergence of the American University.* Chicago and London: University of Chicago Press 1965

Index

Weismann, August 113
Whetten, Nathan L. 190
White, David 166
white slavery 142
Winnipeg xiv, 144, 189–90
Winnipeg Associated Charities 53
Winnipeg *Free Press* 239
Winnipeg General Strike 92
Winnipeg Grain Exchange 53, 189
Wirth, Louis 86, 95, 128, 298 n 19
Wissler, Clark 117, 163
Wolman, Leo 15
women, in higher education 7–8, 26
Women's Canadian Club of
    Montreal 61
Women's University Settlement (South-
    wark, London) 42
Women's University Settlement of
    Montreal 43, 48; *see also* Univer-
    sity settlement, McGill
Wood, Robert A. 128

Wood, Col. William 36
Woodsworth, J.S. 53
Workers' Educational Association
    (Britain) 35, 47

Yale University 38, 74, 198, 205
Yerkes, Robert M. 163–4, 165
Young, Erle Fiske 86
Young, Kimball 169
Young Men's Christian Association
    (Chicago) 66, 67; college 71
Young Men's Christian Association
    (Montreal) 145–7
Younge, Eva 183, 186, 188, 190, 192

Zakuta, Leo 270
Zimmerman, C.C. 178, 190
Znaniecki, Florian 165
zones: in ecological theory 97, 100; in
    the city, in Chicago sociology
    125–8, 130–2
Zorbaugh, Harvey 128